Defiance in Taxation and Governance

Defiance in Taxation and Governance

Resisting and Dismissing Authority in a Democracy

Valerie Braithwaite

Australian National University

Edward Elgar

Cheltenham, UK • Northampton, MA, USA

Published by
Edward Elgar Publishing Limited
The Lypiatts
15 Lansdown Road
Cheltenham
Glos GL50 2JA
UK

Edward Elgar Publishing, Inc.
William Pratt House
9 Dewey Court
Northampton
Massachusetts 01060
USA

A catalogue record for this book
is available from the British Library

Library of Congress Control Number: 2009925911

PEFC
PEFC/16-33-111
CATG-PEFC-052
www.pefc.org

ISBN 978 1 84720 003 7

Printed and bound by MPG Books Group, UK

Contents

Preface vii

1 Defiance to resist or dismiss institutional constraint 1

2 Defiance and responsive regulatory relationships 26

3 The expression and management of motivational postures 60

4 Measuring motivational postures and defiance 101

5 Approaching defiance through threat and coping 137

6 Approaching defiance through integrity and trust 175

7 Approaching defiance through social modelling 214

8 Integrative models of defiance 248

9 Reasoning with defiance 292

Appendices 314
References 318
Index 353

Preface

Many of us in the social sciences long to transfer knowledge across disciplinary boundaries in a way that is true to our discipline yet useful to other disciplines. One way to satisfy this longing is to seize articles that address similar issues from different disciplines and piece them together to forge new intellectual coherence that can push forward the frontiers of knowledge. This seems to be the way in which new fields of study take root. While I applaud this style of scholarship and its development, this book attempts to do something a little different.

Over the past two decades, I have been fortunate in being immersed in a research culture that knew little of my home discipline, psychology, but knew a great deal about institutional design, governance and regulation. I was also privileged in being able to work closely with government, not only with senior bureaucrats, but also with the rank and file who do the hard yards in actioning regulatory frameworks. As a foreigner in each of these landscapes, I was struck both by what I knew and what I didn't know. They were perfect environments for learning a great deal more about how things work.

The approach I have taken is to bring together great swathes of quite traditional psychological research and ask how this knowledge might inform scholars, policy makers, regulators and concerned citizens who look to authorities to better coordinate the activities of the society. While acknowledging that occasional pieces of psychological work already make their presence felt in regulatory research, the more broadly based psychological principles and controversies that underpin the cited works can be lost in translation. What I have tried to do in this monograph is bring these principles to the fore, articulate and empirically test as rigorously as I could the relevance of the principles, and then reach out to the field of regulation and governance – in a bid to show that its theories and practices might be enriched through exposure to such knowledge. Needless to say, I can make no claim to have represented the whole of psychology. This is a personal translation of psychological knowledge to a broader field of enquiry concerned with how we regulate and govern with fairness, effectiveness and commitment to our own humanity.

The research is highly quantitative, drawing on numerous statistical analyses and large data sets. A statistical appendix appears in the book but is supplemented by further details in the supplementary statistical appendix on the web. Reliance on a quantitative methodology meant that the building blocks for this research had to be well grounded in measurable concepts and a concrete regulatory context. That context was taxation, a domain of social activity that, in spite of being private and confidential is widely and openly contested by the public. Good and bad, powerful and powerless, competent and incompetent, fair and foul, coercive and voluntary are labels that have been openly linked with taxation through the centuries, ensuring that tax defiance is steeped in both nobility and bastardry.

The research would not have been possible without funding and support from a number of institutions to whom I am deeply indebted: the Australian Taxation Office, the Australian National University and the Australian Research Council (Discovery Grant DP0666337). Opportunity to develop the ideas was provided by Geoffrey Brennan and Ian McAllister from the Research School of Social Sciences; to them my sincere thanks. To my new RegNet colleagues, and to my old colleagues from the Centre for Tax System Integrity (CTSI), too many to name, my heartfelt thanks for making the journey of this book challenging, enjoyable and always surprising. In particular, my thanks to our doctoral students, past and present, who sometimes seemed to have more faith in this work than I did myself. Eliza, Nathan, Helene, Carla, Jenny, Anna, Sarah and Sophie – your interest turned the ideas into chapters. As important as inspiration is help in doing the hard yards of collecting, analysing and organizing research data and materials. To my data soul-mate, Monika Reinhart, whose obsession over detail equals my own, my deepest gratitude. I could wish for no one better. Not once did Monika blanch at the many requests for one more analysis, and she left no stone unturned in her determination to understand what the data were telling us. To Malcolm Mearns from Datacol, for administering our surveys and providing advice and assistance, our thanks. Appreciation also extends to those who provided research assistance over the course of the project – Vika Waradi, Beth Lyons, Tony Hodges and Pete Maguire. My thanks also to the labours of love provided by Sari Braithwaite in the archives and over microfiche to broaden my perspectives on history and the arts. To Paulina Piira and Sally Thompson, who tolerated a distracted head of department for so long and kept RegNet running smoothly while the manuscript was in its final stages, my thanks.

By far the most fun in doing the research came through my engagement with staff of the Australian Taxation Office. Their eyes lit up when talking tax and they were wonderfully generous in allowing me to enter their world and catch a glimpse of what it was like to be a tax official. To

Andrew Stout, Jenny Job, Neil Mann and Phil Dwyer, for their interest in the big picture, for their appreciation of academic scholarship and for their guidance, thank you. Thanks also to the many staff who shared their thoughts and experiences with me over the years. Also I am indebted to Commissioners of the Australian Taxation Office, initially Michael Carmody and later Michael D'Ascenzo, and of Internal Revenue of New Zealand, David Butler, for the interest that they have shown in our responsive regulatory ideas – contesting some aspects, improving on others, while always engaging helpfully and constructively with the RegNet enterprise.

Whenever I start out on a major piece of work, I promise myself to keep it within limits and definitely spare the family any signs of my angst and obsession. As on previous occasions, I have failed miserably. I can offer only a shame-faced apology and my gratitude for their tolerance and support. To Brian, who is left to manage all my technological melt-downs, I promise to be better in the future. To my children, Ben and Sari, who left home in the course of writing this book, but returned to enquire about its progress, offer encouragement and listen patiently, you were right – it is satisfying to have the project finished, and even better to have you home again. To dear John, who followed the children's lead and also left home for lengthy periods of jungle fieldwork, I understand; and am deeply grateful for the helpful comments on earlier drafts, the lists of things I should read and know about, and the inspirational notes pinned next to the bed to get me out of my place of refuge. The writing retreats at the beach were definitely a highpoint. Last but not least, while the family looked longingly for escape as I struggled to get the manuscript ready for the publisher, my 86-year-old mother arrived for a visit. Her assessment was that the book had taken over my life and she'd burn it if I didn't finish it before she went home – love you, Mum! In celebration of defiance, the dispatch of the manuscript was negotiated to coincide with her departure.

Valerie Braithwaite
Canberra
2008

1. Defiance to resist or dismiss institutional constraint

Dying is not difficult, yielding is impossible.

Jane Grey Swisshelm, from an editorial written after a vigilante attack on her newspaper office, St Cloud, Minnesota in 1858 (Larsen 1934: 10)

Defiance can be of two kinds, dismissive or resistant. An individual can experience both, moving from one to the other. This is the crux of the findings from the multivariate quantitative analyses in this book. The theory derived inductively from a number of data sets collected over five years has wide ramifications for democratic governance. Defiance is dismissive when individuals assert their freedom against an authority. A defiant posture need not be so much about the specifics of what one is *against*, but rather what one is *for* – namely one's own liberty. Dismissive defiance often has a highly individualistic element. It can be passive, completely ignoring efforts by others to take control, or it can be active, issuing a challenge to authority and wresting back control. We engage in these behaviours when we believe that authority has no right to interfere with our freedom (Brehm and Brehm 1981[1]). The goal in such cases is not to modify the obstacles in our way, but to take issue with those who think they have a right to put them there. Dismissive defiance is a grab for autonomy. The message to authority is: 'You have no right to expect subservience of me.'

A different form of defiance is resistance. Resistant defiance involves standing up against an authority's rules, or ways of administering them. The objective is to change the mindset or practices of an authority so that a different course of action will be pursued. Whereas dismissive defiance signifies freedom from constraint, resistant defiance signals dissatisfaction with the form the constraints are taking. When we talk about resistant defiance, we might point to citizen revolts against tax decisions, or protests against government policy. Or we may even be referring to the resistant defiance of leaders of state who refuse to sign international protocols or follow international law (e.g. Australia's refusal for a decade to ratify the Kyoto Protocol and set targets to reduce greenhouse gas emissions, Japan's refusal to curb its whale kills in the Pacific, China's rejection of human rights law, the USA's resistance to the UN General Assembly consensus against invading Iraq). Resistant defiance is not about jettisoning rules or constraints more generally. The hope is not to do away with an authority altogether but rather to change the way an authority operates or thinks about things. The message to authority is: 'If you were reasonable and fair in the way you exercised your authority, I would not resist you.'

It is important that we find ways of differentiating dismissive and resistant defiance. All societies are challenged by both, but lack of understanding of the distinction means that defiant actions are likely to be misinterpreted. This book teases apart dismissive and resistant defiance to understand how each is justified and how each changes in response to institutional pressures. Ultimately the goal is to show how authorities can live symbiotically with defiance. Resistant defiance requires a response that offers voice and participation, so that outcomes can be deliberated in a socially inclusive and respectful way. Dissatisfaction with outcomes may still prevail, but satisfaction with process will do much to meet the expectations of those engaging in resistant defiance.

Dismissive defiance, however, is different. Dismissive defiance gives rise to conflict between an individual and institutions of governance, the point of resolution coming with demarcation of the freedoms that must be relinquished by the individual or respected by the institution in order for a truce to be drawn. Dismissive defiance is about the legitimacy of the institution that seeks to curtail the activities of the individual. The problem is less with how power is used, and more with the fact that power sits in the hands of another.

Disentangling dismissive and resistant defiance is easier in theory than in practice. Discussions about terrorism and Islamist struggle illustrate how intertwined these types of defiance are in the discourses of the defiant as well as of the authorities charged with its management. Public unease about authority's confusion over the two types of defiance is apparent in stories about anti-terror laws being used inappropriately to monitor and detain peace protesters in the USA (*New York Times*, 23 November 2003) and environmentalists and Maori social justice activists in New Zealand (*BBC News*, 1 November 2007). More generally, authorities are stifling legitimate social and political protest around the world because they cannot differentiate resistant and dismissive defiance (Article 19, 2006).

At one level the confusion on the part of authorities is understandable. The mindsets of resistance and dismissiveness are not poles apart. A glimpse at a more detailed case study from Australia shows just how easily individuals can slip from one type of defiance to the other. The purpose in telling this story is not to justify authorities assuming the worst and resorting to their newest and heaviest legal 'artillery' to contain any form of protest. Rather the story is a means of introducing the burning question driving this research: what are the distinctive features of resistance and dismissiveness, and what are the common features that allow individuals to switch from one to the other with relative ease?

A CASE OF ESCALATION FROM RESISTANCE TO DISMISSIVENESS

Post 11 September 2001, Australia followed the USA, the UK and many other countries in introducing anti-terror legislation. Counter-terrorism laws passed in 2002 raised public concern about infringement of civil liberties (*The Age*, 15 October 2002), but the intrusiveness of these measures paled when compared with the measures taken by the Australian government after the London bombings in 2005. In December of that year, Australia's Anti-Terrorism Bill came into effect, giving the state greatly increased powers to arrest and detain anyone suspected of planning, supporting or engaging in terrorism. In the lead-up to this event and just days after amending legislation to strengthen the state's prosecutorial powers, pre-dawn raids were carried out on more than 20 homes. Arrested were alleged Muslim extremists suspected of planning a terrorist attack in Australia. As Australians were plunged into fear over their personal safety, concerns persisted about the abandonment of longstanding traditions of due process and civil liberties. Australia's anti-terror laws acquired a taint of injustice (*The Age*, 7 December 2005; Chong 2006).

One of those arrested in the pre-dawn raids was an Australian Islamic leader, Abu Bakr, who two months earlier had been recorded on radio adopting what could be called a dismissive posture. In an interview aired by the Australian Broadcasting Commission, Abu Bakr expressed difficulties in reconciling Australian and Islamic law: 'This is a big problem. There are two laws. There is an Australian law. There is an Islamic law . . . The only one law which needs to spread, it can be here or anywhere else, has to be Islam' (ABC Radio National, 8 November 2005). This has the hallmark of dismissive defiance because Australian law is being put to one side as a regulatory institution to which Australians should defer.

A Muslim cleric, Sheikh Mohammed Omran, became involved in the debate over the anti-terrorist laws on Australian national television, but adopted a more resistant posture – at least initially. He expressed shock and disapproval over the reports of a planned terrorist attack, but questioned the government's way of dealing with the problem through pre-dawn raids and arrests: 'put[ting] so much fear in the people's mind' and later, '[this is] not how we tackle these problems' that are 'supposed to be dealt with in a delicate way' (ABC Television, 10 November 2005). When presented with the possibility that he too could be 'in trouble' for things he'd said in the past under the new anti-terrorist laws, the sheikh strongly affirmed Australian law: 'I never break any of the Australian laws. And I hope I will not break any of these laws.'

At this point in the television interview, tension increased and the sheikh's position became more defiant. Suddenly, an appeal was made to shared Australian values: 'usually the [law] goes from the date they implement it . . . if they go . . . back, I might yes, yes I might be in trouble. And I don't regret that, anyhow. I give my views and I feel I am in a free country . . .' This was still resistant defiance because the abuse of civil liberties under the anti-terrorist legislation remained the target of the comment. Yet the absence of regret suggested some wavering on the trustworthiness of Australian institutions.

As the interview continued, the sheikh's unease escalated. Later in the exchange, he was asked: 'If there is enough anger out there to bring some young men to the brink of making terrorist attacks on Australia, what . . . could possibly motivate them?' The sheikh replied: 'Nothing more than the injustice. And this is the worst sickness could come to any society and destroy it.' The sheikh was presumably not speaking of his own view, but rather that of others. Yet the interviewer pushed him, as a leader within the Islamic community, to declare a sentiment found among the dismissively defiant: destruction of systems of governance can be justified when injustice prevails.

The interviews provide insight into a common element in the social construction of dissidence. At one level, feelings of injustice and hopes for justice become the base for resistance, which in this case took the form of speaking out against the anti-terror laws. At another level, the same feelings turn into despair among disaffected people, becoming an excuse for dismissing Australian authorities and their laws more generally. In the course of the television interview with Sheikh Mohammed Omran, the problem changed from the state making an incorrect decision in response to terrorism to Australia being at risk of becoming a 'sick society'. Defiance moved from the injustice of a particular law to the injustice of the system of governance as the root cause of the problem.

UNDERSTANDING INDIVIDUAL EXPRESSIONS OF DEFIANCE

There are good reasons why dismissive and resistant defiance are so intertwined in the narratives people use to explain their actions to themselves and others. All narratives of defiance are social. We experience defiance when someone is using some kind of power, arbitrary or non-arbitrary, perceived as legitimate or illegitimate, to block our preferred course of action. To justify our defiance, we compose our narratives so that we are not villains. We all have a basic need to feel good about ourselves and we have a range of cognitive 'tricks' to deal with anxiety or doubt that we may not be living up to expectations (Paulhus and John 1998; Maruna and Copes 2004; Maruna and Mann 2006).

Sykes and Matza (1957) coined the term 'techniques of neutralization' to describe a set of ways in which we mentally counter social criticism of our position. These include denying responsibility for causing any harm, brushing aside the significance of the harm, condemning the condemners, blaming the victim, or justifying the harm through appeal to higher loyalties. A similar typology was offered by Bandura and colleagues who used the term 'moral disengagement' to refer to techniques for avoiding self-sanctioning: providing moral justification for harm done, denying responsibility, discounting injurious effects of the harm, and blaming the victim (Bandura et al. 1996). Bandura (1999) went further to situate moral disengagement within a broader and more complex social, cognitive and emotional system of moral agency. Institutional, environmental and personal factors can make it easy for us to morally disengage from unpleasant truths about ourselves, but given the right circumstances, we can face up to the moral complexity of our actions and our responsibility in initiating them (Braithwaite, J. 1989; Ahmed et al. 2001).

Bandura's (1989) notion of moral agency is proactive and self-reflective, allowing us to think about and express our moral standards in ways that are meaningful and fulfilling to us. Moral reasoning is turned into moral actions through a self-regulatory system of beliefs, emotions, values and perceived social norms that tells us whether possible courses of action will be satisfying and will build our sense of worth or whether they will cause us grief. If we are to fully appreciate defiance as a social phenomenon, it is necessary to link defiance to an individual's purposeful construction of self-worth, and not simply to deflection of negative feedback.

When we practise defiance publicly we are inventing an identity that is attractive to ourselves and to others (Maruna 2001); our defiance needs to be couched as strength of character or competent insight: for example, standing up for a principle or having the ability to foresee a disaster. In the process of self-legitimation, we draw on shared norms and values to make our defiance understandable to others; we want 'public acceptability' (Cohen 2001: 59), we 'want to look right' (Zelditch Jr 2001: 49). A fight against injustice is not an uncommon theme among those wishing to excuse or justify defiance and enrol sympathy for their cause (Matza 1964; Turk 1982; Sherman 1993; Bandura 1999; Miller 2001; see also Sheikh Mohammed Omran's story above). In the public domain and on a larger scale, social justice and environmental movements are 'legitimate' institutions of defiance, dedicated to speaking out against discrimination, abuse of rights and ecologically unsustainable practices.

While defiant individuals work to establish their credibility in their own and others' eyes, authorities work to strip those who are defiant of any justification for their action. We see this daily: when we watch a DVD, warnings against infringing intellectual property rights are communicated through imagery of 'piracy' and 'stealing'. On the world stage, leaders of developing countries who challenge more powerful global players run the risk of being discredited, if not publicly demonized and vilified, along with their cause. Despots and tyrants from 'rogue states', or more dramatically still, from 'an axis of evil',[2] struggle to have their voice heard. Bandura describes how 'nations cast their enemies in the most de-humanized, demonic, and bestial images' (1999: 200), making it virtually impossible for anyone to feel empathy or connection with them. Authorities recognize that it is in their interests to drive out the resistant narrative and expose the dismissive narrative as a threat to the social fabric of society: not to do so risks popular support for the resistant narrative, should it prove credible (Turk 1982).

Defiance may smoulder, unnoticed or discounted for a long time. Once visible on a grand social scale, defiance is accompanied by unpredictable, non-transparent and volatile events, involving the attack on institutions and the suppression of dissidents (Turk 1982). Defiance can therefore be difficult to study as a social phenomenon in real time. People tend to harbour their defiance, either because they believe themselves to be alone, or because they fear the consequences of exposure.

There are some institutions, however, that almost everyone 'loves to hate'. Defiance can then come out of the closet, in some contexts even assuming heroic proportions. Such institutions have learnt to live with defiance in their communities of influence. Defiance becomes a voice in the 'regulatory culture' (Meidinger 1987a), and as such, always has the potential for 'influencing the flow of events' (Parker and Braithwaite 2003: 199).

Such an institution is taxation. Taxation has precipitated countless revolts (e.g. English 'poll tax' Peasants' Revolt 1381 and German Peasants' Revolt of 1525), led to the formation of new nations (American Revolution of 1775–81), fuelled disaffection to topple monarchs (French Revolution of 1789), and incited citizen humiliation and national aggression on the world stage (Germany's harsh tax regime demanded by the Treaty of Versailles after World War I, subsequently fuelling resentful German nationalism). There is good reason to have an ear to the ground to listen for the rumbles of taxation defiance.

Established public discourses promote and defend taxation defiance of both the dismissive and resistant kinds. Dismissive defiance is practised openly by professionals who set themselves up as an alternative authority, offering ways of avoiding or getting around tax law, while being indifferent to the powers of the authority and contemptuous of its *raison d'être*. Resistant defiance is displayed when taxpayers organize a protest against a tax that they regard as unfairly high or unfairly levied, with the expectation that the government will heed their concerns and be responsive to their discontent. In short, resistant defiance in the context of taxation is a cry for attention from government. Dismissive defiance, on the other hand, is a call for the state to look the other way, and accept the individual's right to use ingenuity to circumvent tax law.

The aim of this book is to provide a deeper understanding of defiance of individuals beyond taxation and beyond Australia, but the story is assembled through a set of empirical building blocks that have a tax and Australian focus. The first building blocks comprise analyses of responses to national panel surveys administered in 2000, 2002 and 2005 (Braithwaite, V. et al. 2001; Braithwaite, V. and Reinhart 2005a, 2005b). Detailed statistical analyses of the micro posturing of Australians to the tax system and tax authority are used to make generalizations about Australians' defiance of taxation and their propensity to defy government more broadly. Through analyses of these data, the dimensions of resistant and dismissive defiance empirically take shape.

The empirical building blocks are assembled to test three theoretical approaches to understanding defiance and differentiating dismissiveness from resistance. These approaches examine taxpaying first, as a threat to self; second, as an institution of variable integrity in the public's view; and third, as an exercise in social modelling. Finally, integrated models of resistant and dismissive defiance are developed. Poor governance plays a significant role in creating defiance that, if allowed to 'dig in', weakens democracy.

The research approach to understanding defiance takes place at the micro level, but macro forces are not lost from view. The spotlight is on how individuals see their world, but these perceptual accounts are not divorced from the broader social context in which they occur. What we perceive to be happening is inevitably a complex interplay of who we are, where we are located and have been located in the social system, and how the social system is impinging on our lives. Kurt Lewin (1951) introduced the idea that what we do and who we are at any point in time cannot be understood by focusing on the individual alone; we must also examine that person's 'life space'. Life space is psychological in that it captures all the forces that impinge upon a person in a particular situation, that are 'sensed' and processed by that person, and that have the potential for shaping thoughts, feelings and actions.

OBJECTIVE VERSUS SUBJECTIVE CONSTRAINTS ON DEFIANCE

It should be acknowledged at the outset that the constraints on individual defiance occur at both the objective and subjective levels. In this context, objective refers to what is happening in the environment, while subjective refers to an individual's perception of these events (Zelditch Jr 2001 adopts similar usage in theorizing legitimacy). Life space is understood as subjective experience that shapes thoughts, feelings and actions. The life space approach drives this research. But interest in the subjective does not deny the importance of the objective. Indeed, the subjective interpretations that individuals make of authority only assume importance because, objectively, societies are so effective in putting in place structures that tie down the human spirit.

In responding to defiance, powerful elites look to objective constraints as the first port of call for controlling the actions and thoughts of those who are less powerful. Jeremy Bentham's panopticon for housing those who need to be 'under inspection' (1995: 29–95), and Michel Foucault's (1977) analysis of the power differentials perpetuated through architecture provide classic illustrations of how objective living arrangements assert dominance over others without likelihood of being challenged. Prisons that are designed as panopticons allow authority to view each prisoner from a central surveillance point. The rooms radiating out from the central surveillance point are occupied by prisoners who can be monitored by the authority, but have no prospect of seeing or communicating with anyone else. Embedded within this 'objective' design is control of any outward expression of defiance among those detained in the prison. Likewise, our nursing home research team observed the control exercised by the panoptic design of these institutions of care (Braithwaite, J. et al. 2007: ch. 3). It was in the nursing home setting, where the objective conditions of the home placed major constraints on the ability of directors of nursing to meet regulatory standards, that our inductive discovery of a theory of defiance began (Braithwaite, V. et al. 1994).

Objective constraints can be subtle, indeed invisible to the uninitiated. When they are, they cannot cause offence. Shearing and Stenning (1984) point to the highly regulated space that is Disney World – architectural regulation, technological surveillance, cartoon characters 'on the beat', all invisible to visitors, at least until some hapless child tests the architectural constraint. Other technological 'fixes' are accepted knowingly as part and parcel of everyday life, without complaint, at times with gratitude; for example, childproof caps on bottles, tamper-proof seals on medicines and foodstuffs, turnstiles for crowd control, automated payment schedules from bank accounts, security alarms, CCTV security cameras, even the gates to our homes that separate our dogs from passers-by.

Objective constraints may not be material but rather social and personal. The exchanges we have with each other do not occur in a social vacuum. They are constrained by social norms, rules and expectations (DiMaggio and Powell 1983; Scott 2001). We spend our lives sharing ideas and sensibilities for understanding our world; we learn and teach each other scripts for social engagement (Geertz 1973; Weick 1979). Attached to these shared scripts and sensibilities are institutions, stable and complex sets of rules and ways of doing things that guide our actions, and the responses of others to those actions (Goodin 1996; Scott 2001). Institutions of family, education, caring, work, leisure, religion and politics may be constituted in different ways in different societies, but within a society they restrict options and imaginings as if no other way were possible (Scott 2001). They put blinkers on our hopes and promote development along particular pathways. Yet we rarely question the social rules for how and why these things are done, instead taking them for granted. In most cases, we are oblivious to their constraints, even their existence. Institutions are both deceptive and powerful; they are not innocuous (Turk 1982).

INSTITUTIONS AS HARBINGERS OF AUTHORITY AND OPPRESSION

Institutions are not changed easily (Douglas 1986), even when a system of interconnected rules, norms, practices and law clearly no longer works to further the interests of most members of the society. Those who acquire status, prestige and authority through the system become champions of the institution, working to defend its established ways of doing things from outside criticism (Turk 1982). Any social change is made difficult by institutionally prescribed procedures for challenging authority; and the gatekeepers to these procedures are often those holding institutional power. Rarely is there provision for unconstrained criticism. To open the institution to such unregulated assault would place the fabric of social order at risk, and jeopardize our collective sense of security. At some level, we all recognize and accept the coordinating function of our institutions (Milgram 1974; McAdams and Nadler 2005). Should we have doubts about the legitimacy of our institutions, we are wary about expressing resentment for fear of being ostracized and judged unlikeable or incompetent (Major and Schmader 2001; Olson and Hafer 2001); or worse, we may fear punishment or torture (Turk 1982). Our institutional heritage, therefore, is to deal with authority respectfully, tenderly, humorously, irreverently, wittily, surreptitiously and, only as a last resort, confrontationally.

When authority is ridiculed, it is most often done in fanciful or entertaining settings. American political satirist Will Durst goes so far as to claim: 'Comedy is defiance. It's a snort of contempt in the face of fear and anxiety. And it's the laughter that allows hope to creep back on the inhale' (*Los Angeles Times*, 12 May 2002). The arts traditionally provide safe institutional space for appreciating how stultifying and artificial rules can be. Baz Luhrmann's 1992 romantic comedy about a young Australian ballroom dancer trying to express his talent within an ambitious well-connected dancing family touches the soul of every filmgoer who knows what it is to have a creative inkling. *Strictly Ballroom* exposes a dancing authority that is creatively and morally bankrupt as it rigidly 'regulates' the steps that are allowed in competitions and, more fundamentally, places limits on what constitutes excellence in the ballroom dancing championships. By engaging the audience in questioning the steps that comply with the rules, the film mocks authority and makes heroes of the young dancers who have the spirit of confident defiance, creative flair and self-discipline to triumph over it.

The film is a comfortable exposé of institutional constraint that denies individual expression. It is comfortable because we laugh at the foolish antics of the establishment, purportedly defending the institution of ballroom dancing, as they hide skeletons in the institutional closet and preserve the private perks of their status. At the same time, we identify with the integrity and courage of the young artists. Belittled by the dancing community, with little in the way of resources but with the support of a marginalized, close-knit immigrant family, they set their hearts on having their talent and ideas win through. We share their pain and triumph. Through empathizing and sharing their emotions, however, we engage in an exercise of self-deception. We forget that, in real life, we rarely play the role of the defiant. We more often accept the constraints and are among the conventional, albeit well-meaning souls defending the institution, pushing to the margins those who want change or who challenge the fact that 'this is the way it is' (Goffman 1956, 1983; Jost and Hunyady 2002).

DEFYING SOCIAL CONSTRAINTS THROUGH NODES OF INFLUENCE

How people perceive institutions and what people do or don't do to neutralize unwelcome constraints is a study in adaptation and influence at macro, meso and micro levels. We are routinely reminded of how the macro influences the micro as national tax, welfare and security policies steer how we live our lives. The evidence suggests that while we adapt to policy changes, we do not always adapt in the ways expected by authorities (Grabosky 1995a). Sometimes unexpected consequences stem from accidental regulatory oversight, sometimes from system complexity. They can also stem from individuals choosing to defy authority. Australian university students are required to pay their tuition fees only after their income reaches a threshold level. For salaried employees, higher education contribution fees are withheld by the employer under instruction from the tax office. Research has shown that those who are having their fee payment withheld compensate for this loss by cheating the tax system (Ahmed and Braithwaite 2005). When forced to pay one kind of government charge, we are sufficiently resourceful to see opportunities for balancing the financial ledger without attracting government attention (Yaniv 1992).

Of most interest is the way in which individuals make sense of policy that constrains them in unwanted ways: they share stories, absorb the narratives of others, and develop a discourse, often about the injustice and likely ineffectiveness of the policy, that eventually spreads to other players in the regulatory community. Crush (1985) provides a fascinating account of how the imposition of a coercive colonial tax system in Swaziland at the beginning of the twentieth century was at first superficially accepted by the Swazi chiefs, but came to be resisted by Swazi peasants in overt and covert ways. The British authorities were intent on capital accumulation and forcing the Swazi into wage labour. The Swazi could not see the benefits, the system offended their sense of justice, and they became resistant. As a result they chose tax evasion, with devastating results for the British authority:

> The police were spread too thin on the ground, defaulters invariably elected to serve prison sentences rather than pay fines, . . . additional revenue was not collected, . . . the new element of naked force led to still greater dissatisfaction in the country, and the assault largely failed . . . [to move] labour migrants out of the country. (Crush 1985: 186)

In another time and place, Morales (1998) reported that immigrant street vendors in Chicago believed that paying taxes was a good thing in so far as it provided public infrastructure such as quality schooling. At the same time these immigrants did not believe that their relatively poor neighbourhoods would be the beneficiaries of the tax dollars. They therefore opted for looking after their families first, and evading tax so that they could save the money to move out of the neighbourhood, or privately pay for the education that their children needed to have a better life.

The action plans that develop alongside such discourses can seriously undermine government's blueprint for how their policies should work. Governments often are ill prepared for such events. Crashing planes into the World Trade Center seemed to many Westerners an incomprehensibly remote response to the crushing of the Islamic caliphate through the crusades and twentieth-century Western imperialism in the Middle East. Action plans may not be restricted to or constrained by particular contexts of injustice. Nadler (2005) has produced evidence of injustice in one policy area souring cooperation in others. She uses the term 'flouting of law' to describe the leakage of defiance to different domains of government control. Where unexpected action plans and flouting of law occur on a grand enough scale, institutions ultimately feel the pinch and adapt in response to individuals.

But what makes the scale 'grand enough' for authorities to notice that all is not as it should be in the community and that adjustments to their operations are required? We see examples in dramatic events such as terrorist attacks in New York, Bali, Madrid or London that have radically changed national security policy and policing activities across the world. But there are other more mundane, regular and less visible ways in which the micro influences the macro. Webs of influence connect individuals with 'nodes', defined as entities where knowledge and resources give some individuals and groups the power to shape the way in which we do things (Johnston and Shearing 2003; Wood and Shearing 2007). It is within nodes that capacity to pursue institutional change lies. Nodes can coordinate change processes, because they have the knowledge, resources and often connections to give the ideas credibility. Influential nodes or nodes that succeed in shaping institutional practices are the points in social systems that are rich in Bourdieu's different kinds of capital – economic, cultural, social and symbolic (Bourdieu 1984, 1986; Bourdieu and Passeron 1990). Which kinds of capital need to coalesce to enable a node to shape the flow of events depends on the context, but presumably the most effective nodes can marshal the kinds of capital required at each point in the process of generating change.

TAX SYSTEMS: BATTLEFIELDS OF CONSTRAINT VERSUS DEFIANCE

In the twenty-first century, the institution of taxation is coming under increasing pressure to change, and nodes of different kinds are applying the pressure. These nodes range from being dismissive and contemptuous of tax authority, resistant to excessive taxation, to resistant to devaluing taxation. Once, it was witty and fashionable to say that nothing was as certain as death and taxes, but these days, such utterances are left for the unsophisticated and unfashionable. Wealth permitting, people can plan their financial affairs to avoid commonly encountered forms of taxation. The tax systems of the democracies of the world appear to be on developmental trajectories that are strikingly similar. As capital becomes increasingly mobile, tax avoidance is big business for wealthy individuals and corporations, and its growth threatens to change institutions of taxation in fundamental ways (Avi-Yonah 2000). How this change will occur, however, is unclear. As smaller, economically precarious states chance their fortunes as offshore financial centres (Picciotto 1999; Rawlings 2004, 2005), and as governments of the developed world tinker with their systems to contain avoidance and maintain competitive advantage (Commissioner of Taxation 2007), the big question of how tax systems should be designed for this century remains a puzzle (Burgess and Stern 1993; Centre for Tax Policy and Administration 2001, 2006; Owens 2006; Burton 2007; Picciotto 2007).

Imagining how tax systems might be reinvented to cope with globalization goes to the heart of the invisible, and indeed deceptive, power of institutions. The institution itself, even with shortcomings apparent, prevents so many of us from seeing or thinking through what exists 'outside the square'. But people do play at least at the perimeters of the square, being in the system but not completely of it (Merton 1968), seeing and taking opportunities to exploit, challenge and change 'the way it is'. Understanding how and why this kind of defiance is practised allows us to remove our institutional blinkers just a little and creates new opportunities for reflecting on the design of tax systems. Defiance therefore can be beneficial for a society. It can give us our first glimpse of the storm clouds ahead and give us time to plan the changes necessary to preserve the integrity of valued institutions.

While nodes and webs of influence carry our destiny as well as that of our institutions, this book does not make these entities the main protagonists. The focus is not on leaders with noble or ignoble agendas. The story is about ordinary people who observe what is happening in their world, choose their own course of action, and deal with authorities in ways that can have substantial effects on how institutions are reshaped in the future. At the most important turning points of history, individual action, be it a private decision not to agree to being conscripted to Vietnam, or participation in an anti-war protest, has a power that institutional authority cannot match. Whether on the streets of Delhi, Birmingham (Alabama), Manila, Moscow, Kiev or Rangoon, the mob can be decisive and cause the most powerful institutions such as the military to defect to it (Rude 1995). Empire is impossible when there is mass defection, and this includes defection from voluntary tax compliance.

The contrast between dismissive and resistant defiance is important for a number of reasons, but in the tax context, one looms particularly large for how the institution of taxation will change. While both types of defiance are capable of having an effect on future developments, resistance is more likely to lead to fine-tuning the system and tinkering at the margins. Being dismissive of tax authority, on the other hand, can strike at the institutional heart, although change is hardly instantaneous. The change process that takes place on the coat-tails of dismissive defiance is a long-term enterprise, often achieved through a well-targeted, well-resourced and tireless assault on the way things are.

Within democratic societies, professional groups are ideally constituted as nodes that can meet demands for reinvention once dismissive defiance has a foothold. They command talent, particularly collectively, as they pool their expertise through professional associations and societies. Their jobs give them status, both social and economic, so that their desire to be heard is recognized and accepted. They occupy nodes of influence not only because of their knowledge, but also because they are hooked into key economic institutions, and linked with influential political bodies that determine future directions. As we see in Pakistan at the time of writing, even when their institutional connections fail, lawyers as a professional group do not lack efficacy and may still 'govern nodally' from the streets of Lahore, Islamabad, Karachi and Peshawar (*Washington Post*, 6 November 2007).

Within the Australian context, the professions of law and accountancy are at the forefront of a movement that is changing the old-style tax system (see Grbich 1976 for an early critical analysis of this change from within the profession). These professions mediate between individual taxpayers and tax authorities, making public pronouncements on the meaning of tax law, advising on the implications of changes in the tax system for taxpayers, and lodging tax returns or contesting decisions for clients. Available evidence suggests that the situation is much the same across the developed world (Hite and McGill 1992; Tan 1999; Karlinsky and Bankman 2002; Hite et al. 2003; Sakurai and Braithwaite 2003).

While acknowledging the competing authorities that interpret, prioritize and implement the rules that comprise the institution of taxation, it is of note that few are sharing their thoughts in the public arena on what a sustainable tax system might look like in the future. For governments not to have such a vision and, more importantly, not to engage their citizens in dialogue about the form that such a vision should take appears short-sighted, if not irresponsible (Picciotto 2007). Perhaps through telling the story of Australians' commitment, acceptance and defiance in relation to the legally constituted authority of the Australian Taxation Office, we shall come to a better understanding of how people are engaging with systems of taxation in this globalized world. By having a clearer view of 'what is', policy makers might aspire to a broader vision of 'what might be'.

FRAMEWORK AND STRUCTURE OF THE BOOK

All legally constituted authorities are regulators: they steer events and influence how we live our lives (Parker and Braithwaite 2003). The research presented in this book is framed by the premise that individuals are aware of the ways in which authority can pressure them to do things that they would not otherwise do. The potential threat to liberty is always there: it may be tacit knowledge, but it is knowledge that we all have and share, acquired through socialization (Turk 1982). Throughout our lives, we soak up information about authorities, we appraise them and develop strategies for coping should they choose to make their presence felt; more generally we develop strategies for dealing with threatening experiences (Lazarus and Folkman 1984). How we cope with the possible threat of authority is part of a cognitive–affective system that brings together values, beliefs, feelings, observations and experiences acquired through a lifetime.

The authority of central interest in this book collects taxes, but there is no reason to assume that individuals have a mental filing system that segregates tax-focused beliefs and attitudes from beliefs and attitudes about democracy, good governance and well-being. All of these ideas are likely to be interconnected in a value–attitude–belief system (Rokeach 1973). The knowledge we have about ourselves, who we are and who we want to be, is likely to be central to the system, with memories of and beliefs about taxation, government and authority organized around this core (Rokeach 1973). The value–attitude–belief system will be organized in ways that help construe and protect a sense of self, and advance the associated needs and motives that give the individual impetus to act. Appraisals of authority's demands and preferred coping styles are conceptualized as an upshot of a value–attitude–belief system working to give individuals' lives direction and purpose (Bandura 1986). Moreover, these appraisals and coping styles buffer us. We have a repertoire of scripts and props at our disposal to shield us from criticism, be it from the self, others, or the tax authority.

Individuals bring this psychological infrastructure with them to the taxpaying context. Tax authorities as regulatory agencies attempt to engage with this infrastructure to maintain compliance or increase the likelihood of compliance. The tax authorities have their toolkit of deterrent, educative and persuasive messages that sometimes successfully steer the flow of events, other times not. When the result is not as expected, the assumption commonly made is that incorrect tools have been applied. An alternative explanation is that the authority does not have the kind of relationship with those they are regulating that allows for predictability as to how the intervention will be received. Regulators, in spite of their formal authority, do not make their moves from a position of absolute control (see Zelditch Jr 2001; Reus-Smit 2007, e.g., on the multifaceted nature of legitimacy). The purpose of this book is to show how individuals who are subject to regulation set up different kinds of relationships with authority that have meaning and coherence from their perspective (Antonovsky 1972), relationships to which authorities are often oblivious. Yet these relationships interact with environmental pressures and behavioural realities to dictate the effectiveness of the authority's interventions (Bandura 1986: 22–46).

Taxation is the initial context for empirically drawing out lessons on how individuals manage their relationship with authority, but the analysis moves on to consider the system of democratic governance in which taxation is embedded. Questions include: (a) how do citizens engage with the authority of a tax office; (b) how do they respond when a tax authority invests heavily in relationship building; and (c) how are these relationships influenced by and impact on the engagement of citizens with their system of governance?

In 2000, the Australian government introduced a goods-and-services tax (GST). The change had major repercussions for tax administration – politically, legislatively and practically. It was the central campaign issue in more than one national election campaign towards the end of the twentieth century (McAllister and Bean 2000). When the conservative Howard government won a mandate for tax reform at the 1998 election, no time was wasted in drafting legislation and developing policy to guide implementation. New systems had to be introduced for monitoring and processing payments. Furthermore, the Australian population had to be educated about how their tax obligations would be affected under Australia's self-assessment system and what the tax authority was expecting of them as far as declarations and lodgements were concerned (Commissioner of Taxation 2006). After almost two years of talking about the implementation of the GST, the Australian population was not entirely on side as the first day of the new tax regime approached (*Asian Economic News*, 3 July 2000).

Needless to say, the Australian Taxation Office (ATO) was looking for cooperation from the public in order to successfully negotiate implementation. A campaign of education and persuasion had been undertaken, with a massive advertising campaign, field officers visiting small businesses and hotlines dealing with public concerns and queries. The ATO invested heavily in trying to build a better relationship with the public, a relationship that spoke to integrity, competence and fairness on the part of citizens and tax officers. The tax authority developed the mantra of service, the objective being to listen to the community and deliver to the Australian public a programme that made taxpaying 'easier, cheaper and more personalised' (Commissioner of Taxation 2002; Australian Taxation Office 2004a).

How the Australian public responded and interpreted ATO efforts to oversee the biggest tax reform in Australia's history goes to the heart of this analysis. While the tax authority invested in improving its integrity in the eyes of the public, how its efforts were received was another issue. To a large extent, it depended on the psychological infrastructure that individuals brought to the tax reform context.

The data for this book inform on Australians' perceptions of their relationship with the tax authority: the personal factors, appraisals and coping styles that shape the social distance individuals place between themselves and the authority, the way in which perceptions of the integrity of the authority can alter such distance, and the signals of subservience or defiance that individuals display to authority. The central planks of the argument are represented diagrammatically in Figure 1.1. The three constructs of value–attitude–belief system, integrity and defiance are used here as umbrella terms for a more elaborate set of measures and concepts that will be discussed in detail in subsequent chapters. Also shown in Figure 1.1 are the different time points used for measuring survey respondents' accounts of how they related to the tax authority. The psychological infrastructure that individuals brought to the 'New Tax System' was measured in the 2000 survey, perceptions of the tax authority's integrity in adhering

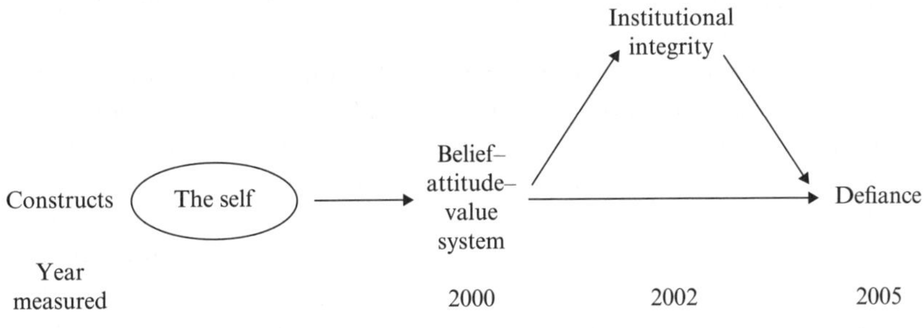

Figure 1.1 A conceptual model linking psychological predispositions in 2000, perceptions of the tax authority's integrity in 2002 and defiance in 2005

to high performance standards was measured in the 2002 survey, and the defiance shown to authority in the aftermath of the reform was measured in the 2005 survey.

The remainder of the chapter outlines the structure of the book and sets out the conceptual and empirical framework for how individuals manage their relationship with authority, its consequences, and why it is so important for authorities to listen to those they regulate and govern.

Chapter 2 argues that understanding what people think of the regulatory activities of government is just as important as eliciting acts of compliance. The desirability of pursuing such knowledge is not self-evident when we consider how authority can use such information to manipulate the mindset of the populace (Turk 1982). There is no doubt that survey findings of the kind presented in this book can become fodder for 'spin', used not only by the state but also by competing nodes of governance to capture the hearts and minds of the public. But survey data are not only used in this way. Survey findings equally can raise the bar for democratic deliberation, bringing to light unrecognized connections and nuances in people's thinking. It is far harder to justify charting a course for the democracy behind closed doors when empirical evidence reveals a population that has agency, both moral and otherwise, and is capable of choosing to cooperate overtly and defy covertly.

Chapter 2 acknowledges that this contribution to regulatory scholarship departs from more traditional approaches because it places so much importance on understanding 'what is in people's heads'. Most regulatory work concerns itself with the actual procedures and processes designed to regulate human activity, and interrogates the effectiveness of such measures. The focus is on what is happening with what results. Here, the emphasis is less on regulation 'as it is done', and more on how it is 'experienced' by those being regulated. The assumption is that through understanding the regulatory experience, there is greater potential for implementing a regulatory system that is not only effective but also respectful of individual liberties. A culture of respect for individuals cannot come about without understanding what is going on 'in people's heads' when they come into contact with a regulatory system, and it is near impossible to cultivate when all an authority cares about is compliant action.

Chapter 2 introduces the central regulatory dynamic that is developed and refined throughout the book. Conflict between authority and members of the community is inevitable and desirable (Turk 1982). Knowing people's expectations and evaluations of authority are frontline data if that authority is to understand defiance and take genuine steps to reconcile points of conflict. Openly and constructively addressing conflict is ultimately in the interests of individuals and authorities. Individuals, even when confronted with the might of the state with an arsenal of law and guns behind it, are not defenceless. China's one-child policy was effective for many years in limiting population growth, but eventually individuals found ways to assert their will by engineering multiple births through a single pregnancy (*China Daily*, 14 February 2006; *BBC News*, 25 May 2007). Human ingenuity knows no bounds. It is no different with taxpaying. Individuals are not powerless. They have many ways of artfully dodging an authority's efforts to control them, sometimes rational, sometimes surprisingly irrational, although almost always satisfying, even if only momentarily.

Where people locate themselves in relation to a system of authority is represented through the concept of motivational postures (Braithwaite, V. et al. 1994; Braithwaite, V. 1995, 2003a; Harris and McCrae 2005; Braithwaite, J. et al. 2007; Braithwaite, V. et al. 2007). People have a range of postures to choose from (commitment, capitulation, resistance, disengagement and game playing) that communicate to an authority how open they are to cooperation with the authority and how open to defiance.

If the authority is listening, motivational postures with their underlying narratives provide the feedback required to build integrity into the system. If individuals see integrity in a regulatory system, they are likely to be more open to requests from that authority and willing to cooperate. When individuals lose hope in the integrity of the system, however, they make their exit – psychologically, if not physically – and the task of regulating becomes extremely difficult. People signal exit by their motivational postures.

Chapter 3 outlines the history of the motivational posture concept. Based on empirical findings in the context of nursing home regulation, motivational posturing theory is proposed to explain how and why such postures come about, and their implications for future behaviour. Of central importance in this chapter is aligning motivational postures with major theoretical frameworks in the social sciences – differential association theories in criminology (Sutherland 1947), modes of adaptation in sociology (Merton 1968), and responsive regulation in law and economics (Ayres and Braithwaite 1992; Selznick 1992). The motivational posture concept is given a theoretical base by drawing on psychological theories of consistency in value–attitude–belief systems (Rokeach 1973), of how social influence occurs (Kelman 1958, 1961), of the importance of procedural justice to social cooperation (Tyler 1990, 1997, 2001; Tyler and Blader 2000), of moral agency and self-regulation (Bandura 1986, 1989; Carver and Scheier 1998; Ahmed et al. 2001), and of the role of social identities in framing thought and action (Tajfel 1978; Turner et al. 1987; Hogg and Abrams 1988).

Motivational postures are defined in Chapter 3 as sets of beliefs and attitudes that sum up how individuals feel about and wish to position themselves in relation to another social entity, in this case a tax authority. They send social signals or messages to the authority about how that authority is regarded. Postures are based on an appraisal of what the authority stands for, what it is demanding of individuals, and how it engages with the needs and aspirations of those it aims to regulate. Postures are subjective – they bind together the cognitive, emotional and behavioural components of attitude. They provide the narrative within which the authority's message is given meaning. They have coherence for the self and are socially acceptable to significant others. In C. Wright Mills's (1940) terms they represent vocabularies of motive: they are presentations of self that feel right and look right; not deep, dark secrets of the human psyche; nor even everyday unconscious needs and motives.

Central to the motivational posturing process is the notion of threat from the authority. Authority threatens everyone, by virtue of its power. Power is a reminder of personal vulnerability. As a tax authority's threat increases, taxpayers use their motivational postures to adjust their social distance and establish a comfort zone for themselves in relation to the authority. Different contexts bring to the fore different postures, and different postures direct individuals to make different responses, some obliging and deferential, others adversarial and dismissive. *Commitment* and *capitulation* are postures that represent willingness to go along with authority either because we want to or because it is too troublesome to refuse. If we are displeased with how the authority is using its power, we might try *resistance*, criticizing and complaining in the hope that it will change its ways. If we consider the authority unworthy of having power, our posturing moves from resistance to dismissiveness. Hope lies not in protesting about how the authority carries out its duties, but in moving the authority to a state of obsolescence. Withdrawal enables us to imagine this has already happened and so we may adopt the posture of *disengagement*. If ignoring the authority is not satisfying, challenge is another option. We adopt the posture of strategic *game playing*.

Chapter 4 sets out the empirical testing ground for the motivational postures concept. Can they be measured reliably and validly, do they represent social distance as presumed, how malleable are they, and to what extent are they shaped by non-tax-related events and experiences? The findings support the basic theoretical underpinnings of motivational postures outlined in Chapter 3, but with some surprises. Postures for taxation are more stable over time than expected, partly reflecting the limited amount of direct interaction that the tax office has with most citizens and taxpayers, partly reflecting their being embedded in the value–attitude–belief system.

Motivational postures displayed to the tax authority are underpinned by an individual's values and hopes for a democratic society. Collective values reflecting concern for others, commitment to equity and social inclusiveness underpin the least socially distant postures. Relatively little interest in such collective values and a preference for national strength, competitive advantage, social and economic status, and less government interference underpin the more socially distant postures.

The second important finding to emerge in Chapter 4 is that social distance can emerge in two different forms, one that corresponds to resistance, the other to dismissiveness. A factor analysis of the motivational postures produced two separate dimensions. The first dimension was defined by cooperation (commitment and capitulation) at one pole, while resistance defined the opposite pole. Cooperation–resistance represented the expected, traditional social distance dimension of evaluation, extending from being positive, open to requests and obliging through showing dislike, criticism and antagonism. The authority is taken for granted. Factor 1 provides the basis for answering the question: how much popular support does the authority have?

The second dimension is more directly concerned with the power relationship between the tax authority and those it regulates. Is the power of the authority something to be taken seriously or something to be discounted as unimportant? Does it have any legitimacy at all? Factor 2 represents dismissiveness, or a refusal to passively accept the domination of the authority. The postures of disengagement and game playing define one pole of the dismissiveness dimension. The opposite pole has no posture to mark it in the empirical analyses. Theoretically, it represents an expectation of control, a state that Mathiesen (2004) describes as being 'silently silenced' by authority. Dismissiveness reflects the inability of authority to be as successful as it would like in holding all the power in its relationship with individuals.

While being dismissive is likely to accompany being resistant – that is, the two defiant postures are positively correlated – this is not always so. When dismissiveness dominates resistance, the result is behaviour much like that displayed in the BBC television series, *Grumpy Old Men*, and later *Grumpy Old Women*. The programmes involve conversations with well-known middle-aged, and some older, men and women about the things that annoy them in modern society – Arthur Smith, Bob Geldof, Bill Nighy, Germaine Greer, Sheila Hancock and Jilly Cooper are among the 'grumpies' that muse on the absurdity of social conventions and the meaninglessness of our 'systems' of regulation. Two popular topics proved to be holidays and the festive season. It is of note that our 'grumpies' are talented and successful, live stylishly and comfortably, with no sign that they have fallen into disrepute by being chronic malcontents. They do go on holidays and celebrate Christmas. In other words, they give in to what society expects of them, if we are to believe them, grudgingly.

In contrast, when resistance dominates dismissiveness the behaviour strikes a more familiar chord. We believe in our obligations to family, work and friends, but can't quite manage all of these systems of social interaction in a way that brings us satisfaction. While wanting to be accepted and do the right thing, we feel irritated, sometimes even outraged, by what is expected of us. The dimensions of resistance and dismissiveness create different problems and demand different solutions. Untangling these two kinds of defiance is the challenge addressed in subsequent chapters.

Chapter 5 demonstrates how perceptions of threat from the tax authority are connected to motivational posturing. Taxation intrudes on the individual at two levels. Like all government authorities, taxation robs individuals of their liberty. Unlike other government authorities, taxation introduces a second layer of intrusion, rubbing salt into the wound by extracting money from us. Taxpayers cope with taxation threat by reframing taxpaying as a moral and legal obligation, or they take on the role of being oppressed by the tax system, or they take control of their taxpaying situation. These coping styles are implicated in motivational posturing. Resistant defiance is strongly associated with feeling oppressed. Dismissive defiance involves not only feeling oppressed but also taking control of one's tax situation. In contrast, cooperation and deference are more likely among those who reframe the threat and think morally about taxation.

Chapter 5 also examines sanctioning. Universally, authorities issue a countervailing threat to the social distancing response, a threat of sanctioning those who do not comply. The threat of deterrence, however, differs from the threat of taxation in that authorities do not initially direct the threat towards the self as such, but rather towards a 'possible' self that may unwisely choose to venture into a space that the authority has defined as 'out of bounds'. Deterrence therefore boosts our conception of what the 'good self' should do.

Chapter 5 shows that most people cope with the taxation threat by opting for the 'good self' pathway and reframing taxation as a responsibility: we all have to live by the rules and obey the law. We internalize an image of ourselves as an honest taxpayer, an ethical identity that brings with it a capacity to self-regulate. We feel guilty and ashamed when we fail to live up to the honest taxpaying self. The honest taxpaying identity creates a 'them and us', the 'them' being those who are punished for doing the wrong thing. While we hold to our honest taxpaying identity, we can take comfort in the knowledge that punishment is not meant for us. We can recognize the threat of deterrence without fearing it personally.

Chapter 6 shifts focus from the self-protective activities of the individual to authorities. A sustainable self-regulatory taxpaying culture depends on authority investing in activities that build integrity in the eyes of the public. The emphasis is on integrity as authenticity – that is, on the public seeing the tax office perform its functions with commitment to community well-being, respect for taxpayers and citizens, fairness and due diligence. Integrity as authenticity incorporates Tyler's (1990) notion of procedural justice. In addition, integrity represents the attainment of the authority's objectives. Survey panel data show that perceived integrity is an important step along the way to building trust in the tax authority. When trust is high, defiance is low, strongly so for resistance, weakly so for dismissiveness. The most important finding, however, is that integrity plays a different role for resistant and dismissive defiance. When individuals perceive the tax authority acting with integrity, their levels of resistant defiance are likely to be lower. This is not the case for dismissive defiance. Perceptions of integrity are irrelevant to dismissiveness.

Chapter 6 demonstrates the importance of the relationship that individuals define themselves as having with authority. When individuals submit to the authority, as they do with resistance, their dissatisfaction is expressed under the assumption that the authority matters and that comfort can be found in knowing that the authority acts with integrity. When individuals regard the authority as an unnecessary intrusion in their lives, however, dissatisfaction is expressed under a different assumption. For the dismissively defiant, the activities of the authority are irrelevant. It does not matter whether or not the authority displays integrity in their world of tax administration. It is not the world of the individual; the authority is trespassing.

The analysis of relationship management and defiance that is presented in these chapters is very much skewed in the direction of deliberation and thoughtfulness. The criticism can rightly be made that people don't think that much about taxation. As is the case with many traditional institutions, responding to tax office expectations is not something we ponder deeply; we just get on with it and do it, or not, as the case may be. If in doubt, we follow the lead of others, identifying with those who share similar goals or think about the state in similar ways. Tax advisers have become important role models for taxpayers, providing knowledge and insight into how the tax system operates and how taxpayers might engage with it. Chapter 7 approaches taxation defiance from a social modelling perspective.

Of central importance in Chapter 7 is the extent to which we put our trust in an aggressive tax adviser or an honest no-risk tax adviser. Those who are defiant, either through dismissiveness or resistance, express a preference for aggressive advisers, and the pathway to these 'alternative authorities' is marked by values favouring economic and social success and a love of winning. The social modelling approach of Chapter 7 proved particularly useful for understanding dismissive defiance. Countering defiance pathways is a moral pathway, rooted in values that prioritize personal growth and inner harmony, and strengthened by a refusal to bend the rules and a preference for an honest tax adviser. The moral pathway is at risk when disillusionment with democracy is high.

In Chapter 8, findings and insights from previous chapters are reviewed and integrated into models of resistance and dismissiveness. The purpose of the chapter is to show how each type of defiance evolves, and its consequences. Dismissiveness links directly to tax non-compliance; resistance does not. Qualitative data reveal that these types of defiance have implications for how individuals engage with government more generally.

Resistant defiance is understood in terms of grievance – being dissatisfied with the democracy, feeling oppressed by taxation and critical of the tax authority's integrity. Dismissive defiance is understood in terms of a competitive pathway – grievance takes a different turn in the presence of wanting social and economic status and being attracted to aggressive tax advisers. Restraining movement down the pathways to both resistance and dismissiveness is a pathway of moral obligation. A credible system of deterrence plays a critical, though complex, role in defiance. Its various influences counteract each other. Deterrence strengthens the moral obligation pathway, while also strengthening the pathways of grievance and competition.

While Chapter 8 integrates, simplifies and resolves the competing stories of previous chapters, it purposefully does not gloss over the many complex relationships that cross over the three major pathways. Coming to terms with these connections substantiates the assertion that intervening at one point is bound to have unexpected repercussions for other parts of the regulatory system. The inference is not that regulatory agencies should never intervene. The inference is that a holistic analysis is necessary to understand the flow-on effects of any proposed change.

Significantly, pathway interconnections are such that the least disruptive starting point for any intervention involves regulatory agencies routinely engaging the community in dialogue. Fundamental to such dialogue is restoring confidence in the democratic process government-wide. The purpose would be to strengthen the moral obligation pathway. When moral obligation is in place, giving a hearing to voices of both grievance and competition will serve the system well in providing feedback on weaknesses and directions for improvement. Without such efforts by authorities, defiance may smoulder.

In the final chapter, the concept that has been the workhorse of the research, motivational postures, is reviewed. Fear means that we fail to engage constructively with defiance. Chapter 9 proposes ways in which we might become better observers and interpreters of defiance through understanding motivational posturing. For resistant defiance, the task of establishing reasoned dialogue has been mapped out. Authority needs to offer respect through listening, explaining, empathizing and problem solving. The task of regulating dismissive defiance, however, goes beyond these standard practices of responsiveness into poorly charted territory. Authorities by their very nature have difficulties with dismissive defiance because here the respect that is denied is respect for authority. Dismissive defiance may be dampened by third parties and nodes of governance aligned with authority, but in the worst-case scenario, dismissiveness demands that authority lose some control while the dismissively defiant gain some. Dismissive defiance tests authority's capacity to balance responsiveness with its legitimacy and responsibility to the rest of the community.

As social beings, we are acutely aware that authority expects things of us and can act against us if we are unable or unwilling to deliver. From the moment of birth, through our school years, marriages and family life, workforce experience, through public service, and our final days in institutions of care, we learn scripts for dealing with authority and protecting ourselves. Scripts of defiance can be critically constructive, nuanced and playful, aggravating and wasteful, or extraordinarily disruptive and harmful. Authority too often responds with a repertoire that is limited – by being defensive, dismissive, bemused, punishing or coercive. For authority not to be able to read motivational postures, to take on board their accompanying scripts and respect their purpose is the stuff of the greatest human tragedies.

NOTES

1. Brehm and Brehm (1981) use the term 'reactant' for what is referred to here as dismissive. The word 'dismissive' expresses rejection, disregard, contempt or indifference. Dismissive better serves current purposes that involve juxtaposing dismissive (or reactant) defiance and resistant defiance.
2. This phrase was used to describe Iran, Iraq and North Korea by US President George W. Bush in his State of the Union Address, 29 January 2002.

2. Defiance and responsive regulatory relationships

> [T]here is a specific Serbian word for the peculiar national characteristic that continues to frustrate NATO. The word is 'inat' . . . which translates very roughly as defiant bloody-mindedness, though the English words are not quite adequate to express what my friend told me are overtones of both nobility and self destructiveness.
>
> Julian Manyon, reporting from war-torn Belgrade, *The Spectator*, 29 May 1999

Defiance is a signal that individuals express attitudinally or behaviourally towards an authority (and, shared with others) that communicates unwillingness to follow the authority's prescribed path without question or protest. Any of us can experience, indeed practise, defiance if the circumstances are right. Delineating the circumstances and understanding how best to respond to defiance is one of the objectives of this book.

Before these bigger issues are addressed, more detail is needed around the defiance concept sketched in Chapter 1. The first section of this chapter differentiates current usage of defiance from other usages and from similar concepts. In the second section, a social conception of defiance within an institutional and regulatory framework is presented. Defiance is reflected in the way an individual controls the social distance between self and authority, developing and sharing narratives to accompany movements of approach, withdrawal, avoidance and challenge. The concept that represents the social distance narratives is motivational postures.

Learning from defiance is a responsibility of authorities in democratic societies. In order for a regulatory community to learn from defiance, there must be an investment in relationship building in which a free and frank exchange of views among members is encouraged and deliberated in the open. Relationship building extends beyond the narrow agenda of what some regulators might construe as defiance management. Section 3 explains why the cultivation of responsive relationships in a regulatory community in a respectful, democratic and inclusive way is essential for effective and decent regulation today.

The fourth section brings the chapter to a close with an analysis of tax authorities and how an understanding of defiance can contribute to their future legitimacy within a well-functioning democratic society. Internationally, taxation illustrates a regulatory regime that has concentrated its resources on more immediate 'battles' of achieving performance outcomes, while turning a blind eye to its relationship 'wars'. A weak link in the operation of tax administrations almost everywhere is their perceived integrity, defined as the degree to which they are seen to show respect, responsiveness and soundness of purpose in their dealings with citizens and taxpayers (Centre for Tax Policy and Administration 2001, 2003; Braithwaite, V. 2003b). By raising their integrity in the eyes of the public, tax administrators can more constructively live with defiance, as well as be in a stronger position to manage risks to the regulatory system.

1. MAPPING THE DEFIANCE CONCEPT

The Boundaries of Defiance

Three aspects of present usage of the term 'defiance' warrant comment. First, defiance describes a particular outlook that may be expressed through words or action. Verbal expressions of defiance are the focus of attention here because the goal is to understand what is in people's heads. There is no implication, however, that action is not also important. In both its verbal and behavioural forms, defiance involves a knowing departure from the conventional, legal or socially desirable pathways. Verbal and behavioural defiance can be mutually reinforcing, as is often the case with political activism. Piller (1991) considered community defiance as both loss of 'technological optimism' over the safe management of environmental threats (e.g. a negative attitude about safe storage of radioactive materials) and political activism (e.g. NIMBY (not in my back yard) protest). By the same token, word and action do not have to coexist for defiance to occur. Verbal defiance can occur without behavioural defiance (e.g. an employee who speaks out against a course of action but behaviourally follows instructions from an employer). Behavioural defiance can occur without verbal defiance (e.g. internet music pirates).

Second, the defiance that is of interest has a deliberative component – individuals can engage in conversation about their defiance and why they think it is defensible. There is no implication that individuals must be able to defend their defiance in highly sophisticated language or reasoning. The point is more that defiance is intentional with some reasoning or feeling behind it that makes it justifiable at the time. Defiance is a means of conveying the message that individuals or groups do not accept unquestioning subservience to rules or authority. In re-analysing film records of Milgram's (1974) famous experiments on obedience to authority, Modigliani and Rochat (1995) tracked the interaction sequence that led 24 of 36 participants to question, object or refuse delivering electric shocks to confederate subjects. Defiance was communicated intentionally to the experimenter as the authority, verbally and behaviourally. Modigliani and Rochat observed tension build up in the encounter between participant and experimenter, with participants actively negotiating how they should proceed. At first, participants acquiesced to the experimenter, trying to be cooperative; but subsequently they began checking that it was safe to increase the shock, notifying the experimenter of the discomfort and distress they were witnessing, arguing with the experimenter and ultimately refusing to obey any more instructions. The earlier in the sequence that participants started questioning and arguing, the more likely they were to progress to behavioural defiance (refusing to continue) rather than capitulate to authority.

Modigliani and Rochat (1995) used their findings to argue that individuals who effectively resist break the momentum of the interaction with the experimenter when the agenda of the authority figure is simple obedience. By asking questions and stating objections, they expose the authority as unwilling to respond in a meaningful and responsible way. Realization of the experimenter's insistence that orders be followed without explanation exacerbates participants' misgivings and provides grounds for defiance. Considering defiance as the outcome of an unsatisfactory interaction sequence with authority fits well with the theme of this book – that tax authorities and their governments invite defiance in circumstances where they expect subservience automatically and refrain from providing adequate or convincing explanation of their actions.

The third aspect of defiance that is distinctive in this research context is that it does not refer to an abnormal or pathological state, although defiance is often used in this way in the literature (Schachar et al. 1986; Crockenberg and Litman 1990; Satterfield et al. 1994). Studies of defiance as behavioural problems, disobedience, or aggressive and antisocial behaviour in children are not irrelevant to the present research context. Hagan (1997), for example, was able to link rebellious school behaviour and delinquency to enduring limitations on life choices: youthful defiance led to poor educational prospects, employment problems and feelings of hopelessness and despair in mid-life. It may be the case that certain individuals are defiant because of personal dispositions such as poor emotional self-regulation or because of adverse life experiences, but this book does not concentrate on this conception of defiance. We start from the premise that defiance can be a rational and healthy response that any individual is capable of making to the demands of institutions. The importance of non-conformity and counter-conformity to group norms is recognized as sometimes being the courageous and morally appropriate course of action (Kelman and Hamilton 1989; Hornsey et al. 2003). When institutions cease to serve citizens well or dominate their lives to the point where they cause distress and destruction, defiance is necessary for forging a path to institutional change.

Related Concepts

Defiance describes the way in which individuals posture to authority. In other research contexts, the term has a broader meaning (see, e.g. Turk 1982), overlapping or used interchangeably with dissent, dissidence, resistance, disobedience, evasion and non-compliance. Narrowing the meaning of the defiance concept has implications for how this work sits alongside other research.

Dissent and *dissidence* refer to expressions of resentment over one's political fate (Turk 1982: 100–103). This kind of broad-based resentment, triggered by discrimination, failure to respect human rights, or failure to honour codes of conduct or principles of governance, may shape the signals that individuals give to authority. Such resentment, however, does not necessarily result in defiance as used here. In other words, dissent and dissidence need not necessarily find expression in the way an individual postures to authority; privately dissenting individuals may publicly praise authority.

Disobedience and *evasion* describe a person's response to an order or command from authority. Defiance may be present when an individual disobeys a command (as in the Milgram study described earlier in the chapter) or when an individual evades a command (as in tax evasion), but defiance has a broader reach. Defiance is a response to authority against a backdrop of requests, expectations and demands, and it is a response that the authority is meant to take on board in relation to how it should behave in the future. Defiance sits between dissent and disobedience, sharing with dissent feelings of hostility and sharing with disobedience intent to question authority.

Defiance is part of what regulatory scholars refer to as a *compliance process*. Moving from non-compliance towards compliance describes a process that is overarching and inclusive of many other concepts. Compliance represents a process of meeting regulatory objectives, often incrementally, taking on board the bigger policy ambitions, and not just abiding by the rules that give the policy objectives legal form (Hawkins 1984; Edelman et al. 1991; Hutter 1997; Morgan and Yeung 2007). The process of compliance may lead a company to surpass the legally prescribed standards: doing more than is required by law to provide a safe workplace (Gunningham 2007); to minimize the environmental footprint (Gunningham and Sinclair 2002); or to promote equal opportunity and human rights in the community (Edelman et al. 1991; Braithwaite, V. 1992). Pursuing regulatory objectives, as opposed to being minimalist and doing only what the law requires, has been referred to as substantive compliance (Edelman et al. 1991; Braithwaite, V. 1992; Yeung 2004). For situations where compliance exceeds the expectations of regulators and points the way to new and higher regulatory standards for the regulatory agency, the term 'beyond compliance' has come into use (Gunningham and Grabosky 1998).

Compliance as process means that the compliance term often encompasses the willingness or cooperativeness of regulatees:

> A recognition of the legitimacy of the demands of an enforcement agent expressed in a willingness to conform in the future will be taken as a display of compliance in itself. Here it is possible for a polluter to be thought of as 'compliant' even though he may continue to break the rules about the discharge of polluting effluent. (Hawkins 1984: 127)

Compliance as process incorporates a range of interconnected, measurable regulatory concepts including knowledge, capacity, willingness, motivations – and motivational postures.

As part of understanding the process of compliance, a number of typologies have been proposed that integrate constituent parts (Kagan and Scholz 1984; Mitchell 1994; Gunningham et al. 2003; Morgan and Yeung 2007). The integration is defended by referring to each type as an ideal or an archetype; in practice it is understood that attitudes, knowledge, capacity and performance may pull in different directions. When considering impediments to compliance progress, Kagan and Scholz identify: (a) doubts about the soundness of the regulatory enterprise (political citizen); (b) refusal to absorb costs associated with being in compliance (amoral calculator); or (c) lack of competence to effect the necessary changes (incompetent manager). Gunningham et al. (2003: 99–102) offer an extended compliance typology that incorporates commitment to going beyond accepted compliance standards. Viewing compliance as a process of excelling in environmental management, Gunningham et al. identify five company prototypes: (a) environmental laggards; (b) reluctant compliers; (c) committed compliers; (d) environmental strategists; and (e) true believers. Each type encompasses a range of information relevant to the compliance process, for example, knowledge, capacity, plans of action and achievements, as well as observations on how cooperatively industry engages with regulators, community and environmental lobby groups.

These models provide a holistic compliance picture. They link values, interests, motives, management practices and performance outcomes with the understanding that outcomes matter. Improving the quality of outcomes for the community is after all how regulatory intervention is justified.

Defiance, however, is not about poor performance outcomes, nor failing to go beyond compliance, nor disobeying specific rules, nor airing a dissenting voice. Defiance is directed to authority and it communicates that we are not on board with that authority. We may concede that it has legitimacy and power in our community, we may even believe that we must obey its directives; but we show defiance because we don't like how the authority is operating or because we object to the reach of its power. Dissidence and dissent may underpin our defiance, disobedience and evasion may be an upshot of it, but none of these terms is synonymous with defiance as used here – as a signal to authority that we don't like or wish to defer to what it is doing.

Given this state of affairs, why should defiance be singled out for investigation? In particular, why should defiance be considered as more important than performance outcomes, which normally count most for regulators, the regulated, and scholars of regulation? In an important sense, defiance is secondary to performance outcomes. Actions speak louder than words in many regulatory contexts. It matters that an engineer in a nuclear facility follows correct safety procedures. It matters that hospital staff abide by standards of best health care practice in infection control. It matters that a factory's chemical analysts are diligent in testing waste materials to ensure they don't pollute the environment. By a failure to achieve performance outcomes as part of the compliance process, individuals' lives and the well-being of communities are placed at risk: there is no shortage of examples of how environmental and human well-being has been compromised through implementing regulatory systems inadequately (Perrow 1984).

Actions that show achievement of performance outcomes also assume greater significance because they are observable, verifiable and more tangible than what people say. Regulators are like attitude theorists (La Piere 1934; Fishbein and Ajzen 1975; Ajzen 1985) in being all too familiar with the fact that defiant words can be quickly transformed into words of deference in a bid to appease authorities about to use the full force of the law. Little wonder that some regulators believe that actions alone are what counts. Because words are little more than smokescreens to conceal the truth of actions from them, regulators need to 'kick the tyres'. From the perspective of such regulators, the only serious indicator of success is progress along the compliance pathway and improvements from one year to the next.

The problem, however, is that compliance progress is a bottom-line indicator of the 'health' of a regulatory system here and now: compliance progress does not provide sufficient data for planning a healthy regulatory system in the future. Visible, measurable compliance with rules in the Soviet Union was awesome, right up to the moment when it utterly collapsed. Beneath outward compliance was seething defiance that made its presence felt when the moment was ripe for tearing down the Berlin Wall. Observable compliance is rarely a sound basis on which to judge the future stability of a regulatory system. Compliance performance tends to be structured around the contingencies of the day. We will find monitoring levels of community defiance to be a better way of planning for a sustainable regulatory system in the future.

If authorities are to monitor defiance in a constructive way, in a way that leads to deliberation over its causes and pathways to reconciliation, then the concept used for measuring defiance should respectfully and honestly capture the signals that communities wish to send to authorities. The concept proposed in this book is one that emerged from listening to the regulated community as new systems of regulation were implemented and bedded down; the concept is motivational postures (Braithwaite, V. et al. 1994; Braithwaite, V. 1995, 2003a). In the next section, motivational postures are contextualized as an individual's response to a regulatory institution that is perceived as purposefully constraining their actions.

2. DEFIANCE AS MOTIVATIONAL POSTURING BY INDIVIDUALS

The Self as Regulator and Liberator

Wherever we are located in the social system, the forces of our life space are in part defined for us and in part constructed by us. The regulation of human conduct involves a complex interplay of the environmental, the biological, the psychological, the social and the economic. What we do and can be is limited by physical characteristics, including our physiological needs, lifespan, health, strength and beauty. Our psychological make-up places further limits on our capacities for adaptation to our circumstances – that is, how we rank among our peers on such attributes as problem-solving capacity, emotional stability, impulsivity, curiosity and sociability. Ultimately, cultures envelop us in a social fabric that shapes the knowledge we have, whom we associate with, how we relate to others, how we define our life stages, and why we believe the things we do. Our understanding of our life space makes some things possible, others not. As we review our lives, some choices may seem sensible, obvious, appropriate and totally justifiable to us; others may seem less wise; still other courses of action are readily dismissed as never having been feasible; and some remain inconceivable – and therefore unconsidered. Together, our humanness and our society constitute, contain and restrain us. Talents, needs, knowledge, values, norms, laws and culture regulate hopes and expectations, determine access to resources and constrain behavioural possibilities (Judd 1926). In these ways, our physical, psychological and social infrastructures temper our ability to exercise freedom.

And yet, as individuals, we never lose sight of freedom or the desire to find opportunities to escape constraint (Skinner 1971). Whether or not such desire guides action depends on our knowing of other possibilities and being motivated or feeling able to transcend the infrastructure that frames and limits us (White 1959; Brehm and Brehm 1981). Where escape is possible, the time horizon can be limited. In spite of our varying degrees of risk taking, we know that actions considered harmful for self and/or others are likely to be reined in. If, on the other hand, the actions are judged by others to be valuable, they will be followed and eventually mainstreamed. Innovations that have the explicit purpose of enabling us to deviate from well-trodden paths can quickly be 'owned' by influential actors as their 'success' is noticed. In time, they are emulated by the majority and become orthodoxy (Moscovici 1976; Turk 1982). History provides many examples of reformations and revolutions of a religious, artistic, educational or political kind in which yesterday's expressions of freedom become tomorrow's straitjacket.

Thus we all have a propensity to play with unorthodoxy. When constraints in the form of values, norms and rules are universal and in place for some time, we tend not to notice how they are regulating our lives (Douglas 1986). Invisibility becomes the ally of durability and tradition. Gramsci (1973) identified culture – institutions, beliefs, values and practices – as the means by which power becomes hegemonic, capturing the thought processes of the masses. For Clegg (1975), rule becomes domination. The consequence is that we simply fail to imagine or hope for other ways of doing things. Perceptiveness and imagination increase in leaps and bounds, however, when constraints apply selectively or change. The process of comparison, 'them' with 'us', 'now' with 'then', stimulates our thinking, generates discussion, and provides insight into both ways in which we are regulated and ways of defying that regulation (Turk 1982). Instability and uncertainty create opportunities (Beck 1999). Some will seize upon these opportunities and others will turn away from them, depending upon how they are framed by their life situation.

Defiance within Regulatory Culture

Defiance always has a following, even when the chances of success are slim and the costs of failure high. Expressions of defiance are wide-ranging and constantly in creation, most obvious in overt oppositional actions to discredit or undermine regulatory authority and practice. Contexts of defiant expression extend from war, protest, mutiny, strike and social movements at the collective level to acts of criminality, deviance, genius, eccentricity and mischief-making at the individual level. Defiance is envisaged as an attitude that an individual has to authority, but it is more sustainable and threatening to social order when it is supported by like-minded others and socially organized (Walzer 1970; Zald and Useem 1987).

Defiance more often than not is associated with discernible conflict, in that the clash of goals or modes of action surrounding the contest between individual and authority is openly acknowledged (Braithwaite, V. 1995). But defiance can be missed when accompanied by feigned cooperation – a not uncommon response, and one that is not particularly effective in advancing regulatory objectives or the acceptability of the authority. A far more effective form of defiance occurs when the discourse of the dominant group is captured and used to change the system (Sawer 1990; Braithwaite, V. 1993, 1998a; Eisenstein 1996). Those who rebel take on the language, aspirations and modes of behaving of those with power. In short, they infiltrate the system and creatively use their newly acquired discourse to turn the regulatory direction towards their subaltern agenda. The game is one of subtle, gradual, invisible guerrilla warfare. The effects can be far-reaching, primarily because the rebellion is silent, while the change that it brings comes to be seen as increasingly normal.

The data collected for this study examine the ways individuals express defiance and acceptance in the face of formal, regulatory constraints, specifically from the Australian Taxation Office. 'Formal' signifies that the legislature has delegated responsibility for implementation of the regulatory code to an agency, and that this bureaucracy has the authority to direct regulatees to act in accordance with the code. While the code may be debated and challenged, and there may be any number of resource-rich nodes shaping the meaning of the code and how it is practised (Shearing and Wood 2003; Wood and Shearing 2007), final decisions and responsibility reside with the delegated authority. Such an authority more often than not 'carries the can' in the public view. This authority therefore is most likely to bear the brunt of publicly expressed defiance.

At this point, it is worth asking if the public is aware of the complexity of the networks that shape decision making and of how nodes of knowledge and resources make their voices heard. It is tempting to conclude that individuals have a naïve understanding of these processes, and that is why they direct their defiance to the authority that 'signs the paper'. This seems hardly likely. The community has been bombarded with messages that communicate the significance of webs of influence. First, governments have launched programmes with great fanfare as they have stepped back from direct service delivery, promoting the image of how their role now is to 'steer' while non-government and private organizations do the 'rowing'. Second, the media has grasped the newsworthiness of networked governance, possibly looking for opportunities to uncover sensational stories of conspiracy, corruption or misconduct. Whatever the motives, the public has become better informed as a consequence. To take taxation as an example, the media diligently reports decisions by the courts on tax matters, challenges to tax authority by professional groups, government expectations of the tax office, ombudsman inquiries into taxpayer complaints, audits of the tax authority, to say nothing of parliamentary inquiries into taxpayer 'revolts'. Individual citizens may not know the ins and outs of how influence is exercised, but they most certainly are aware that there are powerful nodes that shape the flow of events, sometimes for the better, sometimes not.

In Chapter 7, Australians make it very clear that they don't believe that their views are listened to by their elected government: they are fully aware and critical of powerful cliques that push policies in certain directions. In considering whether the government represents their interests, Australians maintain that government *should* be acting with this responsibility at the forefront of their minds (Braithwaite, V. et al. 2006). In expressing defiance towards government authorities, it is likely that individuals operate within the frame of a psychological contract (Scholz 2003; Feld and Frey 2007). Individuals hold firmly to a model of governance in which they meet their obligations of citizenship, including taxpaying, while government meets its responsibility to engage with the community honestly and respectfully, and serve the public interest.

While this research focuses on how individuals and a regulatory authority engage with each other, the activities of influential nodes are not irrelevant to how individuals think about their taxpaying (see Chapter 7). The concepts of regulatory institution and regulatory culture are therefore important for mapping the setting in which the dance between the individual and the regulatory authority takes place.

The regulatory code, those with responsibility for enforcing the code, those with responsibility for assisting implementation, and those with the responsibility for living the code are all part of a regulatory institution. A regulatory institution can be defined as an enduring and organized set of rules, norms and roles that socially prescribe the behaviour expected of occupants of the roles (Goodin 1996). Regulatory institutions, with their historical roots, constrain the actions and choices of actors, and endow power differentially and strategically to ensure that certain social practices are 'stable, valued, and recurring' (ibid.: 21).

Even so, individuals need not be perfectly programmed within these institutions (Wrong 1961). At the same time as being controlled by their environment, individuals bring unique sets of experiences that make them able and willing to intentionally change that environment. Regulatory institutions are superimposed on individuals who are exposed to a range of cultures and subcultures, many of which may nurture contrary world-views and preferences. Thus a regulatory culture of the kind described by Meidinger (1987a) can be conceived as a broader construct than a regulatory institution. In addition to the regulatory institution, regulatory culture encompasses the various subcultures that challenge and defy the dominant norms in unorthodox ways. Moreover, individuals may straddle 'worlds' within the regularly culture. They may play the role of 'institutional protector' in one encounter and 'institutional challenger' in another.

Defiance as Motivational Posturing

The theoretical backdrop to this study is one where there is movement horizontally as people play different roles within the regulatory culture (Goffman 1969) and where there is dynamic interplay between individuals, groups and social structure (Bourdieu 1984, 1986; Giddens 1984). The purpose, however, is not to convey these interactions in all their complexity, but rather to elicit some systematic ordering in individuals' displays to authority, an ordering that entails a degree of durability and consistency across contexts and regulatory communities. The concept to be promoted in this context is motivational postures. Posturing provides a partial explanation of the many events that unfold in regulatory encounters. If postures can educate us about how we may learn from defiance and minimize the social harm it can cause, the concept will have lived up to the ambitions set for it in this book.

In order to measure motivational postures using a survey methodology and examine their theoretical significance by hypothesis testing, the regulatory playing field is truncated. In other words, third parties – be they industry associations, public interest institutions or commercial actors, all of which are important in the field of taxation – are out of view (Grabosky 1995b, 1997). On the playing field we are privy to the actions and perceptions of the regulatee and the regulatee's view of the legally designated authority as regulator. Whether the regulator and regulatee have engaged with each other face to face is not important. The regulatee knows that an encounter is possible and that associated with the encounter is likely to be an evaluation of the regulatee's performance.

The regulatee, therefore, prepares for such an encounter, learning scripts through the stories of others, observing others' interactions where possible, rehearsing options, thinking through comparable regulatory scenarios in which they have had first-hand experience, and attending to the signals that the regulator sends. There is much for regulatees to do if they are to be prepared mentally for possible encounters with regulators. Regulatees are not naïve about the tools at their disposal. Intuitively most of them know that authorities have a self-presentation objective that revolves around reasonableness, while they have a self-presentation objective that revolves around innocence. No one wants to be tagged as 'bad'. The politics of consent literature in which governance is made possible through citizens influencing political authorities and political authorities influencing citizens (Gamson 1968; Walzer 1970) comes close to capturing the give-and-take that regulatees know is in the system and that they ideally would like to capitalize on.

The dance-like quality of the regulator and regulatee relationship has long been recognized in the literature, but mainly from the regulator's perspective. Hawkins (1984) has evocatively captured the dance of regulators with responsibility for pollution control. Exercising autonomy, negotiating outcomes, adapting to the exigencies of particular cases, educating, advising, analysing and only rarely reporting to head office, the pollution control field officer was shown to draw on 'personal qualities' and discretion to 'get the job done'. Hawkins sums up the job of these officers as follows:

> they receive little formal guidance from legal rules or administrative policy. But this is not to suggest that their behaviour is unpatterned. Instead, ways of doing the job are broadly guided by some vaguely interpreted principles about what the organization's legal mandate is supposed to be and organized by the experience they acquire from their membership of an enforcement bureaucracy. Their work is practical; their knowledge concrete and particular. (Hawkins 1984: 56)

Just as regulators have patterned behaviour in exercising their duties, it is proposed that regulatees have patterned behaviour, rehearsed and designed to protect them from unwelcome regulatory intrusion and negative evaluation.

How we react to regulators and their demands has been measured through attitude surveys and the responses factor-analysed to produce five distinct kinds of motivational postures. The postures are displayed in Table 2.1 with a brief description of how they are manifested within the tax context. Table 2.1 also foreshadows the relationship of the postures to resistant and dismissive defiance.

Table 2.1 The empirically derived motivational postures and their contributions to defiance discourse in taxation

Motivational posture	Description (tax-contextualized)	Effect on defiance
Commitment to the regulatory system and its goals	Expressing support for taxation and willingly accepting a personal responsibility to pay	Disables defiance
Capitulation to authority	Recognizing the tax authority's power and endorsing a ritualistic 'keep them happy' philosophy	Disables defiance
Resistance to authority	Opposing tax authority and accusing it of abuse of power	Enables resistant defiance
Disengagement from authority	Dismissing tax authority demands and threats	Enables dismissive defiance
Game playing with law and authority	Enjoying tax-minimizing games with tax officers as competitors	Enables dismissive defiance

The first motivational posture in Table 2.1, *commitment* to the system, represents the degree to which individuals knowingly and willingly embrace the mission of the regulatory institution – in this particular case to collect tax from citizens. Commitment is among the most common responses to regulatory authority in stable democracies. So too is acceptance of regulatory procedures and *capitulation* to the standards imposed by the regulatory authority, without necessarily engaging with the regulatory code or its purpose. Both commitment and capitulation are cooperative postures from the regulator's perspective, but they differ in terms of what they are accepting. With commitment, the purpose of the institution is embraced, and one might expect that any failure on the part of the regulator to live up to that mission will attract criticism. With capitulation, the mission is much more of a blur, but what is important is keeping the authority onside and doing what the authority wants. The difference between commitment and capitulation is the difference between the university student who loves learning and believes in the institution that imparts it, and the student who jumps through the hoops to pass exams.

The remaining three motivational postures in Table 2.1 are the enablers of defiance. Less commonly encountered than commitment and capitulation, but nevertheless visible and influential in tax circles in particular, are postures of resistance, disengagement and game playing. *Resistance* involves outspoken opposition to the way in which an authority uses its powers. Those who resist want to be heard, and they want the system to change for the better. In the field of taxation, they view the authority as vindictive and oppressive.

Other responses to taxation appear to run deeper in their oppositional intention. Individuals who disengage from or 'game' authority appear to be stepping outside or transcending the constraints of the regulatory institution. *Disengagement* entails psychological dissociation from authority. Disengaged individuals develop immunity to the regulatory forces applied to bring them into the fold. Specifically this means that they render themselves mostly immune to punishment.

Game playing represents a more imaginative and bold practice for escaping regulatory constraint by moving around or redefining the rules. This response involves keen engagement with the regulatory code, analysing the system that administers it with disarming acuity and clarity of purpose, and using the code to dismantle or change the meaning of regulations. Interestingly, regulators are seen not as agents of disapproval but as sparring partners in the game.

Motivational Postures and the Concept of Social Distance

The responses described above have a common feature. They convey information about the social distance that individuals wish to place between themselves and the regulatory authority. The idea of social distance has been used previously in the regulatory context, but the focus has been on how this influences the behaviour of the regulator, rather than the behaviour of the regulatee. Black (1976), in his theory of the behaviour of law, postulated that law is less often used to regulate others when the relational distance between regulator and regulatees decreases. Thus, when parties know each other well or are highly interdependent, conflict is likely to be resolved by non-legal means. In contrast, when regulatees have inferior status, the law is more likely to be used. Support for Black's ideas has emerged in the work of Grabosky and Braithwaite (1986) and Hood et al. (1999): regulators were more likely to impose formal sanctions when the relational distance was greater, and punitive sanctions when the regulated were less powerful. This helps account for why, in Galanter's (1974) terms, the legal system is a more manageable institution for citizens who belong to the 'haves' rather than the 'have nots'.

But what goes on in the minds of actors as they come to make sense of their experience as 'a have not', rather than 'a have'? Do they characterize themselves in such terms, or do they build a set of expectations and beliefs that keep them playing their part in the regulatory institution, cooperating at times, contesting regulatory decisions when need be, and sometimes even winning? Proponents of 'just-world theory' (Jost and Hunyady 2002) put forward the idea that those who appear to be 'have nots' learn to accept their inferior status and favour the out-group, thereby legitimating social systems that peddle inequality and discrimination. Assuming that most of us come to terms with our social position through such just-world thinking, it is nevertheless likely to be the case that we hold certain expectations for how we should be dealt with by authority. We don't expect authority to treat us in a manner that pushes us further down the pecking order. Should authorities do this, the micro-interactions of individuals, imagined and real, become a useful means for not only saving face, but also for communicating our displeasure with the authority.

The concept of social distance is used here to describe approaching, withdrawing, confronting and circumventing manoeuvres of the regulated as they manage authority. Social distance is minimal when regulatees want to align with an authority on mission and process, and at its maximum when regulatees perceive little to be admired in the intent of regulatory control or in the manner of its execution.

Following Bogardus's (1928) use of the term, social distance reflects not only the degree to which one is willing to associate with the authority on 'friendly' terms, but also the degree to which one ascribes status to that authority. In the regulatory context, ascription of status paves the way for willingness to cooperate with the authority, even if one is asked to do something one would rather not do. Willingness to cooperate facilitates processes of influence and conflict resolution (Deutsch 1973; Pruitt and Carnevale 1993). It is also part of the legitimization process for that authority (Rai 1995; Tyler 1997).

The application of the social distance concept to the regulator–regulatee relationship has parallels in political theory on citizen discontent with systems of governance. Alienation is the concept that has been most pervasive in shaping our thinking about how citizens respond to a political system that robs them of their sense of being and of a social life that has meaning and worth, and that they cannot change (Durkheim 1952). For the most part, the literature on political discontent envisages a continuum that places the citizen at a location that may range anywhere from engagement (support of the system) to disengagement (alienation from the system) (Gamson 1968).

The way in which social distance is used in relation to posturing, however, is more multidimensional and dynamic. A person can be committed to a regulatory system, yet totally opposed to implementation practices that are regarded as unfair and not in keeping with the spirit of the regulatory code. Simultaneously, an individual can display the postures of commitment and resistance. When poor practice is improved, resistance is likely to recede, but overall commitment to the system will remain stable. The ebb and flow of different postures accompanies routine struggles within regulatory cultures, except perhaps within societies that silence dissent through domination.

A useful schema for making social distance a more dynamic concept is provided by Walzer (1970: 8) with his distinction between a 'total claim' against the state and a 'partial claim'. The idea of being alienated from a political system falls into the category of a total claim. Changing one small part of the practices of government will not solve the problem. For the alienated citizen, discontent is not localized, but rather involves the larger society. A partial claim, on the other hand, involves opposition to a circumscribed aspect of government activity. When citizens have a partial claim, authorities can expect difficulties in relation to the subject under dispute, but can assume cooperation in other areas of governance. Authorities can also expect improved relations if the dispute is settled.

In the regulator–regulatee relationship, partial claims are likely to dominate total claims in both number and intensity. The idea of a regulatory culture in which contestation involves a series of constantly changing partial claims shifts the meaning of social distance in this context quite dramatically. Social distance in the regulator–regulatee relationship involves actors in a dance in which they send social signals of approach, withdrawal, avoidance or challenge to each other at different times, in different places and in relation to different issues. In this way, the motivational posture concept draws on the micro-interactional observations and theories developed by Goffman (1969).

Because the signals of social distance are constantly appearing and disappearing from view, it makes no sense to place individuals in one category rather than another. The signals are not mutually exclusive points on a continuum from 'support for' to 'alienation from' an authority. Sets of signals are likely to be subliminally present in each of us as part of our strategic repertoire for adaptation in a complex society. Any one of us can signal disengagement, game playing, resistance, capitulation or commitment, depending on the circumstances in which we find ourselves being regulated by an authority.

The five signals of social distance under study in this book represent public displays of engagement with the regulatory authority. They are not primarily about covert or unconscious feelings, but rather reflect that part of ourselves that we know and that we want others to know as well. They answer questions about where we are located in relation to this authority. Are we happy to defer to its wishes, are we willing to place ourselves within its path of influence, or do we regard ourselves as safe only when we are outside its reach?

The five motivational postures outlined above are posited as responses to formal regulation that are theoretically and empirically of value for the following reasons. First, they communicate readiness to defy or accept authority. Second, because their purpose is to send social signals, they are accessible and visible, and therefore readily measured. Third, they are amenable to change, rising in visibility and disappearing again in response to encounters with regulatory authority. Authorities that can read them constructively have a vehicle for not only managing defiance but also adapting the regulatory system for its continued relevance and effectiveness.

3. UNDERSTANDING DEFIANCE THROUGH RESPONSIVE RELATIONSHIPS

Motivational postures can be read by authority in a mechanical, poorly informed way or they can be read purposefully, with the intent to get to the bottom of the problem and find a solution. When they are read purposefully, authority will take them on board and consider the damage that might be done to the relationship between the public and the regulator if the more defiant postures are allowed to flourish. Hawkins's observations of the relationship between polluters and pollution control officers illustrate an approach that entails the reading of what have been called here motivational postures and the negotiation that takes place to keep the postures positive, thereby achieving an improved compliance performance:

> Bargaining is central to enforcement in compliance systems . . . Bargaining implies the acquiescence of the regulated, however grudging. And it inevitably suggests some compromise from the rigours of penal enforcement. The essence of a compliance strategy is the exchange relationship, a subtle reminder of . . . mutual dependence . . . The polluter has goodwill, co-operation and, most important, conformity to the law to offer. The enforcement agent may offer in return two important commodities: forbearance and advice. (Hawkins 1984: 122)

Another way of thinking about Hawkins's pollution control officers is that they were managing defiance through their privately tailored form of responsive regulatory practice. The objective of responsive regulation is to use the least intrusive level of intervention to change the flow of events so that the regulator–regulatee dynamic changes and both the regulator and regulatee become more responsive. When regulators are faced with non-compliance, their enforcement strategy not only appreciates the seriousness of the offence and the risk posed to the community, but also credits the efforts of offenders who accept responsibility and take corrective action (Ayres and Braithwaite 1992). In order to regulate responsively, regulators need to have their antennae fine-tuned to pick up signals of remorse, as well as good intentions backed by credible action plans, and agreed follow-up inspections.

Regulators who are responsive in their regulatory encounters have mastered the art of listening (Fromm 2005). They listen to voices of defiance from the non-compliant as well as from the compliant. When an agency cultivates regulatory responsiveness, it opens channels of communication with all those who can articulate the source of their defiance. Their narratives are likely to contain signals of lack of perceived integrity in the regulatory institution. Perhaps the enforcement procedures are unfair. Perhaps they are counterproductive in terms of their purposes. Perhaps the regulatory institution is steeped in disrespect for ordinary people. Listening to the voices of defiance may seem time-consuming and a distraction from standard enforcement action in regulatory quarters. Not to listen can be even more costly.

Regulating responsively does more than ensure that a regulator gets to know what is going on in the regulatory community. Being interested in the public's views and willing to respond constructively to problems and criticism serves to build public confidence (Berman 1997; Bloomfield et al. 2001; Murphy 2004). This aspect of a regulator's role is not to be underestimated in an era when citizens are cynical about government (LaFree 1998) and concerns are expressed about regulatory agencies using excessive powers to elicit compliance (Joint Committee of Public Accounts 1993; National Commission on Restructuring the Internal Revenue Service 1997; Freeman 2002). Public exposure of poorly handled cases can have broader repercussions for regulators. If there are smouldering embers of defiance in the community, a high-profile incident can be stirred up to seriously discredit the authority and undermine its enforcement powers, particularly if the authority has dealt with the matter in an egregious manner.

Even if there is no intent to stir up opposition to regulation by capitalizing on another's misfortune, media exposure transforms high-profile events into a magnet for a litany of complaints about the unfairness and unreasonableness of regulatory authorities. Mass opposition to a regulatory system will eventually threaten the operation of that system in a democratic society (Bernstein 1955). Adverse publicity on taxation in the media heralded a highly critical review of the US Internal Revenue Service (National Commission on Restructuring the Internal Revenue Service 1997). As taxpayer rights legislation was amended and strengthened (IRS Customer Service Task Force 1997), concerns were raised about how such reactions by the US government might provide a foothold for challenges to the authority of the tax office (Greenbaum 1998). Recently, claims have been made that the IRS is no longer able to do its job properly because of the way in which its powers were curtailed in response to public criticism: lower-income groups have become the easy pickings for tax auditors, while the wealthy are spared attention (*San Francisco Chronicle*, 2005). Once credible arguments are aired in the public domain, particularly arguments constructed around appeals to broader themes of justice, citizenship and governance (Walzer 1970; Zald and Useem 1987), the sustainability of the regulatory system can be brought under threat. Cultivating responsive relationships with the community so that discontent does not fester and defiance does not spread becomes important for any authority reliant on community cooperation for implementing its compliance programme.

Responsive Regulation, Postures and Adaptation

Arguably among the most important reasons for regulating responsively and reading motivational postures is to lead regulatory agencies successfully through periods of social change. The role of government and the way it engages with the public has changed (Hood 1991). Government is outsourcing functions to providers, and at the same time is expected to be accountable, transparent and efficient. As managing risk becomes a priority of governments and their agents, compliance with government requests is becoming more complex and less intelligible for the ordinary citizen. The complexity is compounded by demands to comply with a proliferation of non-government authorities – from professional ethics groups to industry self-regulators to hybrid bodies that write international codes.

Moreover, what we need to know in order to comply with regulations changes as our circumstances change. At the individual level, compliance is not a static uncomplicated phenomenon. People move in and out of compliance (Braithwaite, V. 2003a, 2003b), often through ignorance and apathy, rather than calculative design, and the job of regulators is to keep them 'in' more than 'out'. The task becomes easier if regulators maintain mutually respectful relations with the community, so that information and explanations of both compliance and defiance can flow freely, from one to the other.

Cultivating responsive relationships marks a departure from a 'command-and-control' style of operation (see Gunningham 1993 for a discussion of command-and-control regulatory models). Within a command-and-control structure, the regulator calls the shots and exerts power to elicit action, while regulatees do what is expected to avoid punishment. Increasingly, the effectiveness of this regulatory approach has been questioned.

Command-and-control structures often place distance between the regulator and the regulatee by the stringent application of rules and the absence of regulatory discretion. Bardach and Kagan (1982) have argued that by 'going by the book', regulators expose themselves to accusations of regulatory unreasonableness. Such perceptions provide fertile ground for the development of feelings of injustice, resistance, minimal cooperation and mistrust (Kagan 1978; Bardach and Kagan 1982). In contrast, through building positive social relationships with the regulatory community, regulators are in a better position to influence, persuade and ultimately improve compliance in the regulatory context (Bardach and Kagan 1982; Braithwaite, J. 1985; Tyler 1990; Ayres and Braithwaite 1992). They are also likely to learn more about what is going on in the regulatory community (Bardach and Kagan 1982), a particularly important benefit when regulatory codes and practices are being challenged by an ever-changing environment.

Just as compliance goes up and down with people's changing life circumstances, so regulatory institutions are forced to change the rules to adapt to outside forces. We live in a world where change is ongoing, often unplanned and unwanted by regulators and regulatees alike. This is particularly so when changes are triggered by distant events, such as globalization, that push us to the limits of our understanding and management capacities (Giddens 1998; Beck 1999). At such times, regulators need to be able not only to enforce the rules, but also to justify the rules to a sceptical and wary public. Frequently and iteratively, they need to go further, and be able to lead the way in changing the rules. Managing relationships inclusively and through partnerships is a critical element in steering change processes towards improved regulatory systems. Otherwise, institutions will change, not with deliberation and planfulness for the common good, but rather with frenzied reactivity, driven by short-term goals and narrow interests. We see adaptation of this kind when leaders prioritize their own political survival in dealing with national crises. This kind of knee-jerk self-interest can be contained when responsive relationships are in place to counsel towards a broader worldview that makes salient the responsibilities of office.

Responsiveness to Whom?

With the argument of cultivating responsive relationships and listening to multiple voices of supporters and dissidents alike comes the question of whose voice should be listened to. Regulators are prone to capture, that is, to becoming too sympathetic and under the sway of those they regulate (Bernstein 1955). Regulatory conversations are thought to increase the likelihood of capture (Black 1998, 2002). Undoubtedly tussles are likely to ensue over whether regulatees capture the regulator to undermine the integrity of the system or whether the regulator captures the regulatee to bolster commitment to the compliance process. Obviously regulatory agencies work towards achieving the latter, but there is always the risk that the influence will flow in the opposite direction, with the regulator forfeiting the leadership role in the compliance process. Sometimes regulatory failure of this kind arises from corruption, extortion and pecuniary self-interest. Other times, regulators simply feel unable to assume a leadership role by pursuing regulatory objectives in the face of resistance. Consensus is a more comfortable social condition for most of us than conflict.

Standing Apart and Deciding Whom to Heed

Moscovici and Doise (1994) have observed that consensus building is an important institution for social and political life. It is a response to uncertainty caused by losing confidence in authorities to guide us through difficult transitions. Institutions of consensus building are increasingly evident in a range of regulatory contexts (Braithwaite, J. and Drahos 2000). Developing the rules for these institutions is no easy task. At the heart of this challenge is ensuring quality of decision making along with quality of process (Habermas 1996; Stern and Fineberg 1996).

Critics argue that the goal of consensus building is often achieved at considerable cost, namely by excluding voices of difference and defiance from the conversation (Phillips 1991, 1999; Young 1990, 2000). Within the regulatory context, it is not difficult to understand how and why this happens. As regulators move from the traditional command-and-control style of operation, they become acutely aware of a loss of power, and the temptation to compensate by making sure that the voices they hear are not too dissimilar from their own is likely to be high.

As regulators struggle with including others in regulatory decision making, they are confronted with a different assumption about where power resides and where it should reside. Consensus building, despite its shortcomings, challenges the strategic and normative value of working within a framework that treats the power relationship between regulator and regulatee as immutable across the different contexts in which regulator and regulatee meet. There is no question that, within an enforcement context, regulators need to be seen to have power, and to be able to use power, should it be justified, to elicit compliance. But in regulatory communities, particularly in deliberative contexts, 'power can exist virtually everywhere, and can be marshaled by many different actors for many different purposes' (Meidinger 1987b: 40–41). With this realization, regulators have become anxious about their capacity to do their job, and administrators struggle with the fear that consultation will prevent them from keeping the overall integrity of their authority intact (Hobson 2003; Shover et al. 2003; Job et al. 2007; Waller 2007).

It seems a lazy solution, however, for regulators to respond to this scholarly debate in an either/or fashion: that is, either regulators pay heed to different voices and allow their regulatory integrity to fragment, or they silence voices that create uncertainty and doubt in the name of preserving momentum and regulatory coherence. Through thoughtfully designed procedures, it is possible to recognize and deliberate publicly with dissident voices and yet produce an integrated, coherent and purposeful plan of action. Sometimes dissident voices may find their way into the plan of action, sometimes their concerns may be singled out for a watching brief and sometimes they may be dismissed altogether. The point is that they be heard and valued as an important part of the debate, that there be contestation (Pettit 1997). For this to happen, institutional processes need to be established with the express purpose of providing opportunity for the listening phase.

Iris Marion Young (1990, 2000) has made the case for designing space within consultative bodies that promotes difference as opposed to consensus. Giving individuals who are marginalized the right to veto the decisions of the powerful is one way of redressing power imbalances in deliberative contexts (Young 1990). But Young was not content to rein in domination by powerful interests: her quest rather was to enable those so often excluded or ignored to feel comfortable expressing their views and be heard. Young has offered institutional safeguards to ensure that we listen to voices that contradict our own or that represent a different world, thereby allowing us to compensate for our human weaknesses of ignorance, bias and domination. Once hearing these voices, Young was of the view that we would become part of a dynamic process that 'facilitates the transformation of the desires and opinions of citizens from an initial partial, narrow, or self-regarding understanding of issues and problems, to a more comprehensive understanding that takes the needs and interests of others more thoroughly into account' (Young 2000: 112–13).

In order to liberate deliberative fora from the rationalist strictures of debate and argument, Young (2000) proposed institutionalizing greeting, rhetoric and narrative. Greeting can be used to acknowledge the value of others as contributors to the dialogue, to communicate interest in what others have to say, and to welcome views that may be different. Providing a place for rhetoric and narrative, as well as the more conventional style of argument, was seen by Young as a way of expanding avenues for communicating ideas and putting them forward for deliberation. Rhetoric and narrative become powerful vehicles for informing the dominant group of perspectives outside their experience, but that are nevertheless important to segments of the community. The dominant group may be novices in understanding and finding the language and arguments to analyse the problem. But rhetoric and narrative can be effective for capturing the dominant group's attention and resolve to engage with different perspectives. Listening, thinking and working hard at understanding these new perspectives become the responsible thing for authorities to do. The idea is not to replace reason, logic and argument, but rather to supplement these processes by broadening the base of our understanding by taking on board the experiences and communication styles of others.

Once heard, dissident voices need to be subjected to some kind of systematic analysis. Too often, the bounded nature of our thinking, our attachment to our own groups and our stereotypes of others lead us to hear dissident voices but then discard them as not particularly relevant, useful or practical. Here again, procedures can be institutionalized for ensuring that dissident voices are given due consideration. Within the regulatory context, this might mean keeping a record of viewpoints that depart from the mainstream, no matter how different they may seem, and reviewing them periodically with other information to refresh understanding of regulatory issues. It is not uncommon for apparently bizarre complaints from so-called fringe elements to be early warning signs that all is not well in the social order.

The challenges that regulatory institutions face because they do not have strong cultures of social inclusiveness have not gone unnoticed by regulatory scholars. Recent work on deliberative polls, citizen juries and panels, and direct democracy provide models that can be applied to the regulatory context, although change has been slow. The enforcement power of regulators and fears of their possible corruption and capture create wariness of social inclusiveness in regulatory communities (Bernstein 1955). Arguably, there is less risk in finding ways to institutionalize voice within a democratic political system. But politics and regulation cannot be segmented in anything other than an arbitrary way. Habermas (1987), with his notion of communicative democracy, threw his net wide, signalling that modernity created the opportunity to move away from the restricted and constrained dialogue that has been 'institutionalized in bureaucratization, administration, and social control' (Dryzek 1990: 12). According to Dryzek, competent individuals, if allowed to engage in 'uncoerced and undistorted interaction' (ibid.), can reconstruct the way they conceptualize problems and thereby find new solutions. Underlying the approach is the belief that people 'can coordinate their actions through talk rather than unthinking compliance with norms' (ibid.).

Perrow (1984) pursued this line in the rather practical context of analysing why some of the more catastrophic accidents of the twentieth century happened. Perrow used the term 'social rationality' to highlight the benefits of collective problem solving. He argued that by bringing together individuals from different subcultures within the regulatory community, society could transcend the bounded rationality of any one individual and analyse future hazards from a range of perspectives. Each and every one of us 'prejudges the problem and prejudices the answer' (Perrow 1984: 322). We know, for instance, that experts assess risks by examining the probability of certain outcomes based on past events, while lay people are more prone to assess risk in terms of worst-case scenarios. With such different bounded rationalities, collective capacity to manage risk increases: 'our world is immeasurably enriched because our limits are not identical, that is, because we emphasize different skills and cognitions' (ibid.: 323).

Perrow (1984) and deliberative democracy theorists such as Dryzek (1990) oppose privileging the risk assessments of elites over those of ordinary people and insist on inclusive dialogic processes. In so doing, Dryzek has gone further to take on the concerns of those who may be sceptical of the outcomes produced:

> Any such pooling [of ideas] need not produce a (horribly complex) supermodel, but instead sensitizes the individuals involved to the scope and variety of possible effects of interventions in the system at hand. One could see interventions that are robust across different perspectives (Dryzek, 1983b, pp. 360–1). This strategy may be termed 'integrative' of diverse specialties. (Dryzek 1990: 66)

Regulators, as experts, have their own bounded rationality imposed by what Bardach and Kagan (1982) would call the official perspective. Regulatees invariably assess the situation from the civilian perspective. In times when no one is sure of the answers for dealing with newly emerging risks, free and frank exchanges among regulators and regulatees representing diverse skills and experiences must be advantageous.

Managing relationships in such a way as to be able to harness the energies of such potentially divergent interest groups means having a regulatory institution that has legitimacy and healthy levels of trust and respect among regulatory players (Gamson 1968; Tyler and Lind 1992; Tyler 1997). Trust and respect depend on understanding the position of others, recognizing different viewpoints, and knowing how to respond to them in a way that is accepted as just and fair. Such understanding does not come from compliance records or knowing compliance triggers. Regulatory authorities need to understand motivational postures, how individuals regard the institution's goals, evaluate its performance, and make sense of what is happening to them and to others. It is only through regulators and regulatees understanding their different agendas that the foundation will be in place for establishing the working relationships necessary to deal with the pressures on regulatory institutions from rapid, global social change.

Dual Tasks: Compliance and Responsive Relationships

Arguing the case for cultivating responsive regulatory relationships and engaging with motivational postures recognizes two basic tasks. The first is managing routine problems of compliance that are familiar and recurrent: such tasks are rooted in the present. The second is future oriented and involves having the social infrastructure in place to manage the unexpected problems that may require changes to the regulatory institution itself. As regulators are forced to deal with a world where they do not control the specific levers that boost or break compliance outcomes, they require greater sophistication in their capacities to manage unforeseeable change in a timely and effective fashion. Having responsive relationships that are inclusive of a variety of regulatory players gives regulators greater opportunity to plan for a healthy and adaptive regulatory system in the future.

Maintaining a high compliance rate now and planning for a healthy regulatory system in the future means that regulators are required to function simultaneously under two models of governance. Gamson (1968) referred to these as the social control model and the social influence model. The social control model accepts the power of the regulator to make demands and expects the regulated to respond accordingly. In the social influence model, both regulators and regulatees are acknowledged as being influential actors who are able to marshal support within the regulatory community to drive different agendas.

Does this imply that regulators need to function as divided selves? Some regulators are known to struggle with this aspect of responsive regulation (Job and Honaker 2003: 121). If we look past the straitjacket imposed by bureaucracy, however, we see that regulators are like everyone else. They have multiple identities that come to the fore when they are required to play different roles in different contexts (Goffman 1969). The capacities to exercise social control and social influence coexist within the one individual through the creation of a range of institutional spaces that assign different roles to a regulator. Attached to these institutional spaces and roles are different scripts that regulators learn through experience and dialogue. Creating these spaces and arriving at norms for discourse within them are the responsibility of regulatory agencies (Waller 2007). The point to be made is the same one that has been made throughout this section. The task is made more manageable and is likely to lead to more productive outcomes if attention has been given to the building of relationships among critical players within the regulatory community (Bardach and

Kagan 1982; Perrow 1984; Meidinger 1987b; Giddens 1998). Together, regulators and regulatees learn to interact under both conditions of social control and social influence.

4. TAX ADMINISTRATION – DOMINATION, DEFIANCE AND COMPETING NODES

Breaking Command and Control in Taxation

The advantages to be reaped from creating responsive relationships have been linked closely with global technological and social change, and its unpredictable impact on the operations of regulatory systems. Nowhere is this impact more apparent than in the context of tax systems. The choice of the tax system as the object of study in this book is significant for several reasons. One is that if relationship building is centrally important for regulation in the twenty-first century, tax administrations present a challenging case study. They are large, cumbersome, complex bureaucracies that have a poor history of seeing taxpayers in relational terms (James and Alley 1999; Hobson 2003; Job and Honaker 2003; Job et al. 2007; Waller 2007). Moreover, most of us communicate with the tax office by paper or electronic means; few of us have the face-to-face encounters that characterize regulatory inspections in domains such as occupational health and safety or water pollution (see, e.g., Hawkins 1984, 2002). Therefore, if tax authorities can create responsive relationships successfully with the public, any regulatory agency might be able to do the same.

While change is afoot in tax administration practices worldwide (Centre for Tax Policy and Administration 2001, 2003; Hamilton 2003), the social dimensions of regulating taxpaying behaviour have traditionally taken a back seat to predominantly economic approaches (Freiberg 1990; Andreoni et al. 1998). Tax practitioners, administrators and researchers have tended to begin with the same theoretical starting point, that is, a cost–benefit analysis of compliance and non-compliance for the economic well-being of the tax unit, be it an individual or a company (Slemrod 1992; Alm et al. 1995; Shover et al. 2003).

In other regulatory systems, the social forces that build and maintain cooperative compliance and responsive regulation have a longer history of systematic analysis (Freiberg 1990). Tom Tyler's (1990, 1997) work on procedural justice has demonstrated convincingly that citizens are more likely to obey the law when they are treated with respect by law enforcers and lawmakers. Ian Ayres and John Braithwaite (1992) acknowledge the importance of Tyler's work in their conception of a regulatory pyramid in which institutional practices for eliciting compliance proceed according to a series of stages, from persuasion and education, through negative sanctions if persuasion fails, culminating in incapacitation when all other options have been exhausted.

It is of note that proponents of the regulatory pyramid (Ayres and Braithwaite 1992; Gunningham and Grabosky 1998) credit the actual application of negative sanctions (as opposed to availability) with infrequent success for building a cooperative future relationship between the regulatee and the regulator. Sanctions mostly simply force compliance here and now. Building cooperative relationships in the future involves persistent engagement at the bottom of the pyramid, at the level of education, dialogue and, most importantly, persuasion. Persuasion can be mutual on this model. A regulator may persuade a regulatee to obey a law, but the regulatee may persuade the regulator that the law has problems and needs to be changed.

Undoubtedly, one reason the social side of regulation has not been given much attention by tax administrators in the past is that it has been seen as irrelevant, given the historical attachment to a command-and-control style of operation (Freiberg 1988; Job and Honaker 2003; Job et al. 2007). Grabosky and Braithwaite described the Australian Taxation Office as prosecuting on a 'monumental scale' in the early 1980s, making it by far 'the most prosecutorial regulatory agency in Australia' (1986: 162). Recently, Nielsen and Parker compared business views of four national government regulators, including the Australian Taxation Office (2005: 156–9). The tax office was rated lowest in terms of cooperation, fairness, reasonableness and offering assistance, and highest in terms of toughness. Internationally, tax administrations tend to have enormous powers at their disposal to nudge non-compliant taxpayers into paying the money they owe the state. As Al Capone found out, the costs of not submitting to the Internal Revenue Service were high.

Associated with the command-and-control image of tax authorities is a near-universal and timeless distaste for taxation among the populace. Given that taxes historically have been used to assist rulers to build empires and wage war, enduring and widespread disillusionment with taxation among the citizenry is understandable. These days, however, taxation is also linked with the public interest and with having a robust democracy (Brooks 1998). Yet scepticism remains; the most optimistic reading of popular opinion is that taxation has been accepted grudgingly as an inevitable downside of modern life. This view has been echoed from politics to literature, across continents and centuries. As illustrated in Box 2.1, taxation is the quintessence of unchallengeable power enjoyed by sovereign states.

BOX 2.1 PROCLAMATIONS ON TAXATION AS COERCIVE, INEVITABLE AND UNPALATABLE

On the imposition of taxes by the powerful:
'And it came to pass in those days, that there went out a decree from Caesar Augustus, that all the world should be taxed.' (Luke, ch. 2, v. 1)

On the oppression of taxes:
'Taxation without representation is tyranny.' (James Otis 1761)

On the inevitability of taxes:
'Things as certain as death and taxes, can be more firmly believed.' (Daniel Defoe, *History of the Devil*, 1726: bk 2, ch. 6)

On the unpopularity of taxes:
'To tax and to please, no more than to love and to be wise, is not given to men.' (Edmund Burke, *On American Taxation*, 1775: 49)

The endurance of taxpaying institutions in the face of persistent scepticism about their goals and means provides intriguing subject matter for those interested in institutions of regulation. Part of the success of the system lies in the capacity of many governments to withhold tax so that taxpayers, in particular wage and salary earners, have no choice but to comply with the law. Even so, not all tax is collected this way. Many countries rely on a social norm whereby citizens almost voluntarily pay taxes (Schmölders 1970). Countries such as the USA and Australia include a substantial component of self-assessment whereby individuals, companies or their agents declare their income and earnings, calculate their deductions, and lodge a return with their tax authority. How then does one explain what appears to be high behavioural compliance accompanied by high verbal defiance? One might consider the regulatory system fragile given the unpopularity of tax, global pressures for low-taxing governments and fiscal constraints on the enforcement capacities of shrinking tax bureaucracies. Yet tax systems continue to survive. Every year, most citizens of Western democracies comply voluntarily with tax laws most of the time in circumstances where it would be economically rational for them to cheat (Alm et al. 1995; Andreoni et al. 1998). From where do tax authorities draw their legitimacy?

Some might say that force, fear and bluff have been the secret weapons. Others see tax systems as meeting an important need: citizens pay their taxes so that government can provide goods and services to benefit the community as a whole (Feld and Frey 2005, 2007). But will these strategies and arguments sustain tax systems in the twenty-first century? National tax systems are being buffeted by international economic forces (Picciotto 1992; Vann 1996, 1997; Avi-Yonah 2000; Braithwaite, J. and Drahos 2000; Tanzi 2000). Multinational conglomerates are able to hold sovereign states hostage in the area of tax collection by moving profits to non-taxing countries and avoiding tax liabilities in the states in which they operate. Sovereign states signing bilateral and international agreements in a bid to retrieve some of their lost tax dollars may be a partial solution, but ultimately the problem needs to be dealt with on an international level. In the meantime, governments pander to large corporates, going so far as to lower tax rates progressively to hold them in their tax jurisdiction (Maranville 2004; Braithwaite, J. 2005). Governments are in a difficult situation. On the one hand, lowering taxes may mean fewer resources to look after citizens; but on the other hand, losing the corporation to another jurisdiction may mean a loss of jobs and no taxable entity. Already, there is growing discontent that tax systems can be manipulated by the wealthy and powerful, and are oppressive of those with more modest wealth (Braithwaite, V. 2003c; Taylor 2003). US businessman Warren Buffett, among the world's super-rich, has spoken out against failure to redress inequities in the US tax system, complaining that he paid a lower rate of tax than any of his staff:

> The taxation system has tilted towards the rich and away from the middle class in the last 10 years. It's dramatic; I don't think it's appreciated and I think it should be addressed . . . There wasn't anyone in the office, from the receptionist up, who paid as low a tax rate and I have no tax planning; I don't have an accountant or use tax shelters. I just follow what the US Congress tells me to do . . . Hedge fund operators have spent a record amount lobbying in the last few months – they give money to the political campaigns. Who represents the cleaning lady? (*The Guardian*, 31 October 2007)

Concerns about the legitimacy of government instrumentalities are not confined to the tax system. A widely held view is that democratic political systems have been suffering a legitimacy crisis (Inglehart 1997; LaFree 1998; Pharr and Putnam 2000; Putnam 2000). Kettl pinpoints the increasingly common mismatch between governance capacity and the capacities required to manage the most pressing problems, using the USA as an example:

> the nation-state is becoming too small for the big problems of life . . . because there are no effective international mechanisms to deal with such things as capital flows, commodity imbalances, the loss of jobs, and the several demographic tidal waves that will be developing in the next twenty years. It is too big for the small problems because the flow of power to a national political center means that the center becomes increasingly unresponsive to the variety and diversity of local needs. (Kettl 2000: 496)

Given US–EU hegemony on the international stage, Kettl's concerns can be magnified in the case of smaller countries that are more often at the receiving end of US–EU decision making than in the driver's seat. In such a political climate, will tax authorities win citizens over to a new tax system through fear, bluff and contract, or will they need something else?

The Role of Institutional Integrity

The 'something else' that is postulated as central to making an institution adaptable and sustainable is integrity. Institutional integrity refers to the synergy between the various rules and practices that define how individuals and groups go about collecting tax and administering the tax system. Institutional integrity also requires that people understand why tax is being collected, that such collection is backed by democratic deliberation, that the inevitable shortcomings that arise in administering such a complex system are openly addressed, and that change is managed with the vision of an overarching purpose and with responsiveness when things go off track.

As the functions of complex organizations such as tax offices multiply, special difficulties emerge in ensuring that the activities of different groups are coordinated to be meaningful and convey soundness of purpose to citizens (Ahmed and Braithwaite 2004). Tax authorities appear to be struggling with communicating their objectives clearly to the public (Picciotto 2007). But tax authorities have at least made significant strides in appreciating the importance of listening to stakeholders (Conference Board of Canada 1998; Centre for Tax Policy and Administration 2003). Information is shared through international bodies such as the Centre for Tax Policy and Administration in the Organisation for Economic Co-operation and Development (Bentley 2003). National tax offices also have their own suite of nodal connections. The Australian Taxation Office, for example, has consultative groups for business leaders, small business organizations and tax professionals, and has opened the door to more diversified community perspectives with its task forces on the cash economy and aggressive tax planning. In these respects, the Australian Taxation Office has taken significant steps forward in the past decade (see Editorial, *The Australian Financial Review*, 11 November 2005).

The nodes of influence for tax authorities do not stop here. In most tax jurisdictions, the legislature plays an active role in determining how a tax system operates (National Commission on Restructuring the Internal Revenue Service 1997). Most tax authorities are 'overseen' by tax ombudsmen or adjudicators who operate within networks of lawyers interested in the protection of human rights (IRS Customer Service Task Force 1997). This node, with access to the legislature and executive, may be highly influential in how the tax authority does its job. Also significant are high-level international meetings such as those convened by the Organisation for Economic Co-operation and Development (2006, 2007) to discuss coordination of future tax policy.

Ideas travel along and around all these networks, generating policy and setting new directions. As ideas and implementation protocols circulate, support snowballs in the regulatory community. One cannot help but question whose voices are being heard, however. It is reasonable to suppose that some nodes are excluded from the deliberative decision-making process (Bevir 2006). In the case of taxation, notably absent is the public voice of individual taxpayers, particularly those of more modest means (Rawlings and Braithwaite 2003).

Tax authorities have tended to remain aloof from taxpayers, and therefore have lacked knowledge and understanding of taxpayer responsiveness to the tax system (Coleman and Freeman 1997). While it is still the case that most of us never talk to our tax authority, we would be involved in a lot of talking if we were to get into serious trouble and if the authority were responsive. Moreover, because our tax authority talks regularly to leaders of our professions, our business associations and our civil society, it is likely that, should we veer off into some orbit of unreasonable defiance, these leaders might head us off through engaging us in dialogue. Thus, as taxpayers, we are enmeshed in webs that regulate our actions. These webs, in theory, could allow us to feel included in regulatory conversations about taxation – that is, to have a voice. There is little evidence, however, to suggest that Australians feel they are beneficiaries of best practice in this regard (Braithwaite, V. 2003c; Braithwaite, J. 2003: 259–62). This means that, for many taxpayers, the integrity of the tax system is likely to be wanting.

Broadly speaking, institutional integrity describes the interplay of overarching objectives, performance standards and administrative processes in such a way that the pursuit of one enhances rather than compromises the attainment of another. For citizens standing outside the institution of taxation, it is difficult to judge how well some of this is happening. The internal indicators are far from transparent. Internal dynamics, however invisible, eventually play out to have a public face. For citizens looking in, the central questions have less to do with the details of the tax system, and more to do with the big picture: to what extent does the tax system pursue democratically supported goals, act in appropriate ways to achieve these goals, treat citizens reasonably and fairly in the process, respond constructively to criticism, and open up to public scrutiny? It is difficult to imagine citizens affirming the tax authority in these terms without meaningful dialogue taking place over time in many different contexts. Thus, again, the challenge arises of building relationships. Creating responsive relationships is not only a means for managing risks into the future, but also for building and maintaining institutional integrity.

Regulating Taxation: The Research Hypotheses

To summarize the argument so far, tax systems have traditionally relied on command-and-control tactics to extract revenue from citizens. Rapid social change and globalization mean that national regulatory systems are no longer insular and are pushed and prodded by outside forces over which they often have no control. Such forces undermine the effectiveness of the command-and-control approach. Unexpected problems demand flexible routes to resolution (Sparrow 2000). Tax officers may need to have the discretion to cross functional lines, or they may need to be forward thinking in their decision making, forming judgements as to whether the literal interpretation of rules makes sense given existing policy and community perceptions of fairness. A command-and-control model does not lend itself to this kind of responsiveness, being constrained in the case of a large bureaucracy by both functional compartmentalization and the rulebook. Without responsiveness and reasonableness (Bardach and Kagan 1982), authorities are ill equipped to face new challenges on the international stage, and bluff and fear appear to be risky weapons for eliciting compliance. Even the traditional bargain between citizen and sovereign state loses persuasive power as a third force, the global economy, makes its presence felt, causing authorities and citizens to change old practices as both fail to honour old expectations (Avi-Yonah 2000). In these circumstances, defiance is likely to flourish. Tax authorities need the cooperation of citizens as much as citizens need the regulation provided by tax authorities for the well-being of their democracy.

In order to obtain cooperation, tax authorities must understand and manage their relationship with the public. A first point of departure for building relationships is recognizing and understanding the motivational posturing of those being regulated. Taxpayers are not passive recipients in regulatory encounters. They evaluate the system and decide where they wish to locate themselves. As individuals choose the social distance they wish to place between themselves and their tax office, they take on board a host of beliefs and attitudes that justify and explain their position. These views are often willingly shared with others, even tax authorities. Expressing such views serves important functions of self-definition and finding support, along with justification for the position the individual is adopting. Motivational posturing enables individuals to create social space that is supportive and not threatening, peopled by those with similar views or who are at least sensitive to a certain point of view. In these social enclaves, defiance can be nurtured and protected from critical scrutiny.

Having recognized the signals of defiance given by motivational posturing, tax authorities need to improve their relationships with taxpayers by being responsive to their concerns. Associated with certain postures may be feelings of personal loss, goal frustration, political disillusionment, or perceptions of a tax system that lacks integrity. To the extent that perceptions of lack of integrity are shaping the motivational postures of individuals, a solution emerges that focuses on the operation of the tax office and how it engages with the community.

If authorities are to learn to read and use motivational postures as a language of communication adopted by those they regulate, some basic research is required. The following propositions require investigation:

1. Motivational postures are consciously held, coherent sets of beliefs and attitudes that communicate the social distance that individuals wish to place between themselves and the authority wishing to regulate them. Motivational postures are a narrative, plausibly defensible and, as such, openly expressed. They signal location within the regulatory culture.
2. Motivational postures can be understood in terms of the perceived and experienced threat that the authority presents to the individual's conception of him- or herself as a free and worthy person. If the individual perceives the authority as diminishing or threatening to diminish his or her sense of self, the social distance placed between the individual and regulatory authority will be greater.
3. Institutional integrity can provide 'an antidote' to the threat posed by the regulatory authority. Institutional integrity gives meaning to the regulatory system through practices that respect individuals and that are tied to serving the public good. As taxpayers come face to face with a high-integrity authority, some of the publicly accepted justification for keeping the tax authority at a distance is undermined. In this way, institutional integrity has the potential to curb the defiance that individuals feel when government uses its power in a manner that

does not meet with public approval. Perceptions of high institutional integrity can reduce social distance between the individual and the tax authority.

4. As will become apparent in the chapters ahead, opportunity to be free from regulatory constraint beckons individuals who observe role models using new and easier pathways to reap the rewards they desire. Alternative authorities enter the market at this point to shape individual behaviour. Tax authorities need to engage diplomatically with alternative authorities and responsively with the public as they take on a leadership role to nurture open deliberation to redefine a shared tax agenda and reintegrate the regulatory community. Strategies for dealing with those claiming freedom from authority, as opposed to justice, involve negotiation that goes beyond the establishment of institutional integrity (without being contrary to it).

These starting propositions frame the analyses in the chapters that follow.

3. The expression and management of motivational postures

> The desire to stand well with one's fellows, the so-called human instinct of association, easily outweighs the merely individual interest and the logical reasoning upon which so many spurious principles of management are based.
>
> Elton Mayo 1949: 39

Motivational postures were introduced in the previous chapter as markers of a community's defiance against a regulatory regime. Both the acceptability and effectiveness of a regulatory system are expected to improve when authorities read and engage with motivational postures through responsive regulatory practice. Responsive regulatory practice, which includes efforts to make sure that the regulatory system is aligned with the democratic will, is reflected in public perceptions of the institution's integrity.

The value of motivational postures, however, extends beyond informing authorities about quality of governance. These postures serve an important psychological function, helping individuals save face as authorities curtail individual choice and freedom. This chapter sets out the psychological infrastructure for motivational postures with a view to demonstrating that postures are part of the individual's determination to survive and grow in capacity and character. Defiance makes its presence felt when such determination goes off track due to institutional pressures to conform. Defiance is the micro response of individuals to macro-social conditions that are harmful and destructive of the qualities that are important to individuals' self-definition and self-worth.

Oliver (1991) has provided a parallel analysis of how organizations fend off pressure to conform to outside institutional pressures. In circumstances where organizations don't acquiesce, they may (a) compromise through placating, juggling demands or bargaining; (b) avoid through concealing activities, changing their domain of operation or finding a buffer for protection; (c) manipulate by co-opting, persuading or controlling outside forces; or they may (d) practise defiance by dismissing pressures, challenging the rules or attacking authority. Oliver's categories of defiance are similar to the motivational postures of disengagement, game playing and resistance respectively. Both schemas depict responses in the face of threat from outside forces. Their theoretical origins and significance, however, are somewhat different.

Oliver (1991) focuses on tactics and strategies to either acquiesce or fend off interference: they are active choices that organizations make to further their quest for stability and legitimacy. In the case of motivational postures, the driving force is maintaining an individual's self-regard, which means that social infrastructure and socially constructed narratives loom large. Motivational postures are not stand-alone tools in the toolbox that are taken out and used strategically to leverage a desired regulatory outcome. They are mentalities that we share as narratives, with moral overtones concerning the worth of self, others and relationships. Motivational postures are signals that communicate identity and request understanding from authority. They are more than rationally determined strategic moves to achieve certain outcomes.

For this reason, the argument of the previous chapter is only half the story of why it is important for authorities to understand motivational posturing. Authority should engage with motivational postures because it will make for better decision making; but equally important, authorities should engage with motivational postures out of respect for individuals. If authorities are to govern responsibly for the collective, they will say 'no' quite regularly to the outcomes demanded by the defiant. Saying no to outcomes, however, does not mean that authorities should deny defiant individuals a fair hearing. The work of Tyler (1990) and his colleagues demonstrates the harm that can be done when we brush people aside because we anticipate we can do nothing for them. An individual is likely to perceive such treatment at the hands of an authority as disrespectful and unfair. This chapter provides psychological insights into why individuals look to authorities to take the trouble to understand their motivational posturing and why they take offence when authority is dismissive of them.

CHAPTER OUTLINE

The first section of this chapter recognizes the importance of optimal social distance between authorities and citizens in a healthy democracy. Citizens should never become enmeshed in the worldviews of authorities; otherwise critical analysis and accountability become meaningless processes. At the same time, citizens need to be sufficiently close to engage in meaningful dialogue, to understand what authorities are demanding and to provide their feedback constructively. The first section of the chapter recognizes the way in which individuals are active regulators of their social distance from authorities, exercising personal power over the degree to which they succumb to, resist or master directives from authorities. Motivational postures serve to protect the self from authority as discursive elements in a person's value–attitude–belief system.

The second section reviews the development of the motivational posture concept in the context of past research on nursing home regulation. Links are also made between motivational postures and theoretical and empirical work in other regulatory contexts. Motivational postures are driven by the quality of the relationships with the regulator as well as by the degree to which regulatory objectives and goals are viewed as worthy pursuits. This section recognizes tension in the social sciences between theories that propose relational accounts of regulatory cooperation and those seeking explanation in terms of the promise of favourable outcomes and the achievement of goals. Put more simply, will I refuse to obey the tax office because I disagree with what they have asked me to do or because they have asked me in a discourteous and disrespectful manner? The tension between these different perspectives is reconciled by following regulation theorists who advocate a regulatory pyramid approach, addressing relational concerns and opposition to goals simultaneously.

The third section returns to the issue of taxation and the consequences of unbridled defiance among elite professionals. Ambiguity surrounding what it means to comply with tax law, together with social divisions over the morality of taxation, have allowed a new motivational posture to flourish – game playing. This posture is not easily managed by regulators because it focuses on the grey areas of tax law, areas where tax administrators are uncertain and taxpayers see opportunity. Taxpayers who 'game' authorities find clever ways of complying on strictly technical grounds while visibly thumbing their nose at the spirit of the law. In theory, a well-functioning regulatory pyramid would nip the game-playing posture in the bud by providing regulators and regulatees with opportunities for deliberation and clarification about what the law means at the pyramid base. Undoubtedly shared understandings of rules come about in other regulatory domains through such dialogic practices. Taxation, however, does not appear to have been so blessed.

1. WHY AND HOW WE MANAGE AUTHORITY

Challenging Authority through Social Distance

A commonly held position is that people have little choice when authorities make demands upon them. Legitimate authorities have 'the quality of requiredness' (Kelman and Hamilton 1989: 90). People believe that they ought to do what is asked of them, because it seems right to them, or because they believe it is their duty or responsibility to obey the request, or because they fear the consequences if they do not. Whatever the mix of reasons for complying, requests from legitimate authority in a democracy are expected to activate the responsibilities of citizenship. This mechanism, while delivering social order and political stability, also presents risks when authority is abused or used foolishly. Atrocities against others committed in the name of obedience have been the subject of much critical analysis in the social sciences (Arendt 1964; Kelman and Hamilton 1989; Milgram 1963, 1974). War, genocide, racial violence, workplace bullying and psychological experiments are all sites for observing individuals doing the most inhumane things to others at the direction of a leader who is believed to have authority.

The idea that a person has authority to regulate is easily generated and is not readily controlled through legal means. Popular culture shows how self-appointed regulators etch out a role for themselves. In 1994, Warren G, a black American rapper, topped the music charts with 'Regulate'. The song heralded the popularity of gangsta rap. The song has Warren G 'trying to consume some skirts for the eve' when he is mugged. A friend comes to his aid, killing the muggers. The two continue on their way, finding dates for the evening. The song begins by laying claim to the right to regulate: 'Regulators/We regulate any stealing of his property/And we damn good too/But you can't beat any geek off the street/Gotta be handy with the steel/If you know what I mean, earn your keep/Regulators! Mount up!' In the years that followed, Warren G would be continually referred to as the 'Regulator'. 'Regulate' illustrates that authority can be claimed outrageously – but successfully, when values of individualism and security are at stake.

Such developments have been accompanied by more official efforts to improve human security, such as better law enforcement, better-trained and -equipped police forces, and surveillance technologies, to name a few. These steps help, but only until another human security failure invites another self-appointed regulator. For this reason, interest has developed in institutional settings in which regulation is exercised without aggression and confrontation. In particular, psychologists have been interested in uncovering the psychological attributes that require nurturing in these institutional settings. Among the most important are empathy (Hoffman 2000), emotional intelligence (Goleman 1995) and the capacity to manage the integration of complex bodies of knowledge (Suedfeld 1992). Generally speaking, the task of defining the institutional settings in which these qualities would flourish has been left to experts in politics, sociology, law and criminology[1] rather than taken up by psychologists. Among the handful of psychologists who moved from asking why human beings could behave so destructively towards each other to asking how institutions could be structured to reduce the likelihood of this happening were Kelman and Hamilton (1989).

Kelman and Hamilton (1989) outlined a set of conditions that on the basis of their psychological research could free individuals from obeying authority when the requests were inappropriate or morally questionable. Central to their recommendations was reconfiguring the social space surrounding the authority and the citizen so that individuals would have the capacity to critically evaluate the wisdom of commands and their consequences. Citizens were not to be entrapped so that their only view of the situation was that offered by the powers that be. Increasing social distance from the authority was part of gaining an independent perspective, and this perspective would be enriched if citizens were well informed and educated, exposed to multiple perspectives, encouraged to participate in decision making, and empowered to present a dissenting view. Kelman and Hamilton argued for a political state where authority was dispersed and occupancy rotated so that citizens, through their social connections, were exposed regularly to power and knew what it was like to have the responsibilities of office. At the same time, the ethos of dissent needed to be cultivated, by giving citizens responsibility for voicing their concerns and ensuring they had the means for doing so. Kelman and Hamilton's analysis focused on changing the way that individuals regarded and understood authority, less as something to be feared and obeyed, and more as something to be engaged with actively, responsibly and discursively.

Since Kelman and Hamilton (1989) put forward their ideas for a more constructively critical society, social changes have occurred that have meant that power is more dispersed, people are more questioning of authority and more avenues exist for drawing attention to unacceptable decision making by those in high office. While we continue to be at risk of being duped by political spin, if not alienated by exposure to reports of those with power behaving badly, progress has been made in the world's democracies along the lines advocated by Kelman and Hamilton. Supporters of a more deliberative democracy have done much to ferment discussions and raise expectations for consultation that is more inclusive and that values difference, reasonableness and thoughtfulness (Bevir 2006). In fields as diverse as health, law, education, child protection, policing, the environment, and occupational health and safety, there is evidence of task forces, review committees, boards of inquiry and consultative bodies widening the net to allow the community greater input and understanding of decision-making processes. Indeed, the ideal of good governance these days is synonymous with an open exchange of views, along with transparency and accountability in decision making (Braithwaite, V. et al. 2006; Maguire et al. 2007), although, as Bevir (2006) notes, achievement often falls short of aspiration.

Bevir's (2006) call for a more radical democratization process is likely to alarm Hobbesian[2] devotees who would remind us of the downside of designing institutions to be inclusive of the defiant, a particularly salient issue in the context of tax regimes. If we ask, 'can such a deliberative and inclusive system be exploited by knaves?' the answer is unequivocally yes. Powerful interest groups are expert at both making their voices heard above all others and exploiting defiant voices, using them to advance their own agenda at the expense of the interests of the collective (Young 1990; Phillips 1991; Knight and Johnson 1994; Mansbridge 1996; van Mill 1996; Bevir 2006). When an institution puts in place procedures whereby its decisions can be challenged, one cannot assume that the challenge will always come from those with the public interest at heart. Thus the social process that encourages dissent can work for the common good or against it, depending on the motives of those whose dissent captures the public's imagination.

Despite the difficulties it creates for government, and authority in general, the tolerance of dissent is regarded as an important corrective in a democracy. At the same time, it would be naïve, perhaps even irresponsible, at this stage not to acknowledge that dissent can be harmful, not only because it may catapult another collectively damaging point of view into the front line of debate, but also because it can bring things to a grinding halt. Two examples will illustrate this point.

Much of the opening up of government that occurred in the latter half of the twentieth century has been desirable in improving transparency and accountability. A not surprising side effect has been increased scepticism born of knowledge of government shortcomings. In this way, social distance between government and the people has increased in most Western democracies, with reports of declining trust and delegitimizing of authority (Inglehart 1997; LaFree 1998; Putnam 2000). In time, the distancing may cause public alarm and trigger a self-corrective mechanism to reinvigorate democracy. Meanwhile, the danger is that alternative authorities will step into the void and capture the allegiance of citizens who are seeking a new source of hope. Increasing consumerism, accompanied by a blind attachment to brands and company logos (Klein 2000), is one example of how collectively we may inadvertently allow ourselves to be seduced by a process akin to psychological transference. Having succeeded in freeing ourselves from the domination of government, we may be enmeshing ourselves in the constructions laid out for us by corporations. Later we return to this issue, asking whether something comparable has occurred with taxation: have taxpayers transferred their trust and dependence from government to tax professionals, with an assumption that the tax profession constitutes a more benevolent alternative authority?

A second example of how institutionalized dissent may set back best regulatory practice comes from the administration of the tax system, and shows how too much dissent, and therefore too much social distance, creates paralysis in some quarters and disjointed, crisis-driven progress in others. The culture of taxpaying and tax collecting encompasses many of the elements that Kelman and Hamilton (1989) claim foster disobedience. People do keep their distance from tax officialdom, they take on board different perspectives, they challenge tax authorities, public debate ensues, and aggressive lobbying takes place to undermine tax office decisions. In the area of taxation, effort expended to challenge and shape both policy and administrative practices has been substantial (see, e.g., the National Commission on Restructuring the Internal Revenue Service 1997; Smith 1993; Review of Business Taxation 1999), an observation at the national level that is echoed at the international level (see, e.g., Avi-Yonah 2000; Picciotto 1992). It is of significance that negotiating tax policy and tax compliance remains big business, internationally and nationally, with the involvement of both private and public actors. Yet too often it seems that there is no discernible movement towards problem resolution.

One way of thinking about the lack of progress is that while the citizenry have become acclimatized to the inevitability of taxation and recognize its value (Braithwaite, V. et al. 2001), the threat that it poses is never far below the surface. Therefore it may be particularly difficult in some of these deliberative fora for people to make the psychological shift from thinking about what is best for the individual personally to thinking about what is fair and reasonable for the group (Wenzel 2003). Taxpaying practices are well institutionalized, but when discussion turns to changing the system, haunting insecurities may resurface. It would not be surprising for people to take offence at the coerciveness of tax systems, for instance, and this could spawn antipathy and resistance (Brehm and Brehm 1981; Littlewood 2001; Smith 1993). Taxation is also a potential threat to status. Tax threatens personal wealth, one of the most important symbols of status. If one does not succumb to loss of wealth, being caught for not paying tax can bring an additional problem – loss of social standing and reputational status. Individuals who value freedom and status are therefore likely to distance themselves psychologically from taxation and the authority that collects it. They are also likely to lobby governments hard for policy and action that protect their interests. Overall, the problem for the regulatory culture of taxation is not one of having insufficient social distance between government and its citizens, but one of too much distance for the effective operation of the system.

The question then arises of how much social distance is desirable between tax officers and taxpayers. Following Kelman and Hamilton's (1989) line of argument, we may be well advised always to place some distance between citizens and authority. By the same token, Pruitt and Carnevale (1993) caution that the key to resolving conflict is to recognize interests not just from our perspective but from the perspective of others. If we are to see the perspective of the other, such as the moral legitimacy claimed by the tax officer, the social distance should not be too great, certainly not so great as to result in an implosion of the tax system.

In sum, neither a war of all against all nor a jolly consensus is a desirable or practical outcome for the tax system. What regulatory responsiveness and integrity demand is vigorous conflict over tax justice and tax efficiency, while granting the elected authority the ultimate legitimacy to make decisions that are binding on us. Institutional contexts for deliberation and contestation are becoming more common in the world of tax administration and policy development. Motivational postures then become a language for signalling when and how such deliberations should proceed.

The Dynamic Nature of Social Distance from Tax Authorities

As part of our value–attitude–belief system, motivational postures are likely to have both stable and dynamic components. The stability of motivational postures stems from a predisposition to respond to tax authorities in certain ways depending on social values and preferences. Some people will place more importance than others on freedom, wealth and social status, and will regard taxation with a degree of disdain because of the threat it poses to realizing such aspirations. Others will be less adversely affected, preferring the equanimity that comes from accepting society's rules and taking comfort in the contribution that taxes make to building a better society. We would expect individuals to have different baseline levels of posturing, with some being prone to defiant posturing and others prone to cooperative posturing. By the same token, we would expect that experience could disrupt these baseline levels. Our resistance might increase dramatically, for example, if we were subject to a tax audit; our game playing might blossom if we were required to fill out tax forms repeatedly providing the same information; and our disengagement might reach new heights if we were repeatedly bombarded with demands from the tax authority with which we could not comply. Uncertainty over the introduction of a new tax system could also unsettle our posturing baselines in unforeseen ways, depending on the rumours we heard and our imaginings of what might happen.

A useful entry point for theorizing motivational postures and how they are affected by, and in turn affect, authority is provided by classic attitude theory. In a landmark study for the social sciences, Bogardus (1928) dealt explicitly with the concepts of threat and social distance, empirically documenting their interconnections. Bogardus (1928) used social distance to describe reactions of US citizens to immigrants from different countries, and observed the way in which social distance increased among citizens who felt antipathy to the new ethnic groups and saw them as a threat to their status and social standing. In Bogardus's words, social distance brought 'a lack of understanding and fellow feeling' (ibid.: 10).

The emotive aspect of Bogardus's definition sits well with taxation, although more often than not emotions are overlooked in this field.[3] As was the case with immigration, taxation is an issue on which individuals are likely to experience conflict between political interests and self-interest, and such conflict is likely to trigger an emotional response (Goffman 1956; Braithwaite, J. 1989). But there is also a difference. When 'the other' is an immigrant group, the distancing is in response to a socially, politically and economically marginalized group. The tax office may not be popular – but disempowered it is not. The 'other' in the tax context is an authority that has an ongoing brief to intrude upon citizens' lives in order to implement government policy. Given that the authority has recourse to legal action and coercion, the social distance that we maintain from the tax authority is unlikely to be set in stone. We feel the push and pull of authority, and respond in kind. Because of the power that authority wields, we can't afford to be rooted to a particular spot. In this respect we behave like Oliver's (1991) organizations: we engage our postures in a dance with authority to keep ourselves out of harm's way.

Movement in our posturing is likely to occur en masse in response to what the tax authority is doing or not doing and what is happening at the political level. Posturing is also likely to fluctuate at the individual level in response to what is happening closer to home in people's daily lives. For example, when Australia introduced tax reform with a goods-and-services tax (GST) in 2000, the Australian public responded at a number of levels: to the politics surrounding the policy; to the competence with which the policy became law and was implemented; and to the impact that the GST had personally (small business and sole traders were affected by the new system far more directly than wage and salary earners).

Tax events such as the introduction of the GST generate community division and uncertainty about why change has occurred with what consequences (Braithwaite, V. and Reinhart 2005a). Australian tax policy and the writing of tax law generally have not been a product of principle-based rule making (Smith 1993; Burton 2007). Rather, tax laws have tended to come on the scene in a reactive fashion, with more than a degree of opportunism and an unfortunate preoccupation with short-term interests (Smith 1993; Burton 2007). Australia is not the only country that lacks a tradition of coherently developed tax policy that people understand and that can be justified in terms of a set of agreed taxation principles (Picciotto 2007). Measures put in place to collect tax elsewhere also often appear *ad hoc*, designed to curry favour with particular interest groups, avoiding the displeasure of others, paying off debt, and holding on to political power. Too often, changes in tax policy have been administered like medicine, as a cure for a problem that is already out of hand. And like medicine, changes to the tax system can cause irritation, displeasure and even defiance if the benefits are not readily apparent to taxpayers.

Paying tax is a compliance issue that has traditionally been grounded in the discourse of self-interest (Freiberg 1990; Slemrod 1992; Alm et al. 1995; Andreoni et al. 1998). This implies neither stability nor movement in posturing, but it does underestimate the complexity of the issues that shape the dynamic aspect of motivational postures. Much to the surprise of many economists, people transcend narrow economic self-interest and pay tax, in many cases believing in the principle of contributing to the common good and supporting those in need in our society (Lipset and Schneider 1987; Freiberg 1990; Slemrod 1992). Simultaneously, people can embrace principles of redistribution, honesty and fairness over taxation, and perseverate with critical scrutiny and complaint over the details (Dean et al. 1980; Wallschutzky 1985; Lipset and Schneider 1987; Taylor 2001). The important message from empirical tax research is that taxpaying attitudes and actions are multifaceted (Smith and Kinsey 1987; Weigel et al. 1987; Kirchler 2007): they are neither uniformly for nor uniformly against paying tax.

At different times and in different contexts, individuals are likely to give different weights to the economic, the psychological, the social and the political in the way they think about taxation (Lewis 1982; Smith and Kinsey 1987; McGraw and Scholz 1991). The ongoing political influence on taxation and the complexity of attitudes towards it have the effect that the social distance that individuals place between themselves and the tax authority is changeable. Motivational postures, therefore, have a dynamic as well as a stable component. Moreover, motivational postures of commitment, capitulation, resistance, disengagement and game playing may move independently of each other. In the remainder of this section, some principles are proposed to explain when and how movement in motivational postures is likely to occur.

Controlling Social Distance from Authority

Authorities may control the rewards and punishments they administer, but individuals control their willingness to cooperate. Providing individuals have freedom to choose, cooperation is the citizen's gift to authorities, and theirs alone to give (Walzer 1970). This argument rests on the premise that individuals have considerable say over the ideas and opinions they take on board, and the degree to which they expose themselves to the social influence of authorities.

In order to be open to influence, people must 'see' the demand. That is, they must understand what actions are being asked of them, they must believe they are capable of acting and they must see some purpose in acting (Bandura 1977; Kelman and Hamilton 1989; Mitchell 1994; Carver and Scheier 1998). If they do not have confidence or respect for the authority, if others validate such concerns, or if these others organize themselves into a viable 'opposition', they will withdraw from the authority. In such circumstances, the capacity of an authority to influence actions is seriously undermined.

This thesis is supported by criminological theory. Differential association theorists recognize the way in which most communities are organized for criminal and anti-criminal behaviour, with each type of behaviour lodged in different cultures, beliefs, aspirations and codes of conduct. For Sutherland (1937, 1947), crime was shaped by differences in an individual's exposure and immersion in the social organization of these competing influences. In the area of taxation, different kinds of social organization are available to those who would like to avoid paying tax and those who are willing to pay what they are told they owe by the tax authorities. Taxpayers, for instance, pair up with tax practitioners who suit their needs for honesty, smartness or risk taking in their tax dealings (Tan 1999; Sakurai and Braithwaite 2003). Through association with various social groups and their socializing influences, individuals differ in how they 'see' tax office expectations, tax law and themselves as taxpayers.

Criminologists have a long tradition of recognizing the active role that individuals play in attending and responding to some aspects of their environment and not others (Cohen 1966; Glaser 1978). They have identities and roles that they pursue and preserve through social interaction (Mead 1934). They can control social space between themselves and authorities, distancing themselves psychologically from a particular authority that threatens their interests and aligning themselves with those who can provide protection (Cohen 1955, 1965). At the end of the day, individuals can exercise mastery over those with power who try to influence them: '[an authority's] persuasiveness . . . depends on the person's preferences' (Kelman and Hamilton 1989: 87). The individual's battle between exercising mastery and succumbing to an authority's influence is particularly apparent in voluntary taxpaying cultures. In this context, preferences can turn into actions because surveillance in parts of the tax system is low, self-assessment is the preferred means for tax collection, and collective and self-interest both have their proponents among respected authorities.

Psychological Drivers of Social Distancing

In the process of finding a comfortable space in relation to an authority, individuals assign meaning to their actions. Disobeying an authority is not something that people do lightly, even when the authority is as unpopular as a tax office. They need to cope with fear of reprisal, embarrassment in departing from the well-travelled path, and perhaps even shame, guilt and disappointment if their actions are labelled as wrong. Individuals need to devote considerable conscious effort to justifying their desire to maintain some distance from the authority, and they need to do so in a way that protects their identity from self-criticism and preserves their status in the eyes of respected others (Cressey 1953; Sykes and Matza 1957; Thurman et al. 1984).

Protection of the self has long been regarded as a central psychological process. James (1915) used the term 'self-seeking' in a broader way than modern-day economists use 'self-interest'. For James, individuals pursued objects, relationships, beliefs and experiences that would benefit and protect their welfare and self-esteem. Steele (1988) has noted the interest in self-preservation by a number of influential psychologists: Allport's (1943) reference to ego-enhancement; Epstein's (1973) elevation of self-enhancement and self-protection above all other needs; and Greenwald's (1980) colourful depiction of a totalitarian ego, a self that is biased in processing information to affirm its own goodness and stability. Steele and his colleagues have contributed a body of research in support of the thesis that the motive of self-affirmation is fundamental to our understanding of how individuals behave when they perceive a threat to their personal adequacy or integrity (Steele 1988). Steele proposes 'a near infinite variety of interchangeable adaptations – cognitive and behavioral . . . [restricted] only by the requirement that they affirm the self' (ibid.: 282).

Within the context of complying with legal authorities, this work is a reminder of the lengths to which individuals are likely to go to defend themselves, that is, to find self-conceptions and images of being 'adaptively and morally adequate, that is, . . . competent, good, coherent, unitary, stable, capable of free choice, [and] capable of controlling important outcomes' (Steele 1988: 262). Individuals who wish to flout the law must therefore find some way of doing so that is acceptable to themselves and to those with whom they associate. In the area of taxation, the high-profile industry of avoidance, as opposed to the hidden industry of evasion, fits this demand nicely (McBarnet 1992). Individuals do not have to defy the law. Indeed they pay particular attention to the law, in order to manoeuvre legally around the intentions of the legislature (see Forsyth 1981; Grbich 1976).

The importance of like-minded spirits in promulgating defiance of this kind emerges from research that demonstrates how each and every one of us relies on groups to simplify and order our world, to define ourselves in relation to others, and to enhance our self-regard (Tajfel 1978). Those with whom we associate provide us with a social reality that gives us a sense of security and confidence in the world in which we operate. Others help us make sense of our world, assuring us that we are correct in our interpretations of what is happening and why. If someone we respect and trust expresses concerns about our interpretations or our intentions to act in certain ways, we are likely to stop and take note. We may follow their advice, try something altogether different, or stick with our decision. The important point is that on a daily basis we put ourselves in situations that expose us to outside influence that gives us our bearings. Groups act like a compass for individuals navigating their way through life. If others do it, if others think it, and if these people are admired and respected by us, we will more than likely follow in their footsteps. If, on the other hand, we regard others as different, as belonging to an 'out-group', their capacity to influence us is greatly reduced (Turner et al. 1987).

Storing Experience to Guide Actions

While the groups to which we belong and with which we identify lead us down various paths, it's important to return to the observation made in Chapter 1 that sometimes we are aware and think through the path that we should choose, while at other times we are blissfully unaware, pursuing life without much reflection, as if on automatic pilot. There is both a conscious and unconscious component to how we function, even with regard to taxation. The experiences to which we are exposed, the things we remember, the ways in which we put together various observations and beliefs to make sense of our world and to aid our future choices resonate with some people more than others. It is with those people that we often feel most comfortable. We talk and share stories, narratives of explanation and importance develop, and when we find ourselves with a problem to solve, we consciously draw on this knowledge to make the best decision possible. Other knowledge that we have about the world is not part of our consciousness, or at least it is not readily accessible. Sometimes we just do things – we have undoubtedly all had moments when someone has said to us 'what were you thinking when you did that?' On reflection, we weren't thinking anything – but it 'felt' right at the time.

Giddens (1984) used the term 'practical consciousness' to represent that part of our unconscious world that visibly guides our actions, where we clearly have tacit knowledge 'about how to "go on" in the context of social life' (ibid.: xxiii), but where we are not able to explain to others how and why we are doing it. It's possible that at least part of obedience to authority follows this path.

To contrast with practical consciousness, Giddens (1984) introduced discursive consciousness. These are the beliefs, attitudes, feelings and responses that we recognize as our own, that we think about and discuss with others. It seems unlikely that we will ever fully understand how people respond to authority without understanding both practical and discursive consciousness. Furthermore, it is likely that the discursive and practical are interrelated, particularly when the practical is unexpectedly challenged or disrupted in some way. Perhaps we even need to go further and delve into unconscious motives and beliefs if we are to fathom the depths of our obedience to authority.

Such a journey, however, can take place only if individuals cooperate in revealing such 'unknown' aspects of the self. When we broach the subject of taxation, the journey of self-revelation has barely begun. A useful starting point therefore is likely to be the least intrusive. That point is discursive consciousness, where individuals are empowered to present their side of the story of what the tax system means to them, how they think they should deal with it, and how they believe they act when demands are made upon them. Starting here, however, does not mean that the discursive approach cannot be pushed to its limits.

Chapters 4 to 6 are very much in the tradition of research that assumes that individuals are guided by their beliefs and attitudes, showing consistency in their preferences as they choose paths that best satisfy their needs. Chapter 7, on the other hand, recognizes that we all have 'what were you thinking' moments or, at the very least, moments when our perceptions of uncertainty and inadequate knowledge led us to follow our instincts or the crowd. Taxation is a field in which herding responses are not uncommon, particularly with regard to aggressive tax planning (Braithwaite, J. 2005).

That said, the focus here is on discursive consciousness. For present purposes, discursive consciousness can be thought of as part of a value–attitude–belief system of the kind proposed by Rokeach (1968, 1973). The building blocks of this system are a multitude of beliefs, simple propositions capable of being preceded by the phrase 'I believe that . . .'. Beliefs may be of different kinds, descriptive (for example, I have a salary that places me in the top tax bracket), evaluative (for example, I feel good about paying tax), or prescriptive (for example, I ought to pay my tax with good will).

Beliefs can be interconnected, and may cluster around a particular object or event. We might say that we have a number of beliefs that relate to not declaring cash income in an income tax return. Clusters of relevant beliefs that focus on particular objects or events of this kind are called attitudes.

Certain prescriptive beliefs have special status in the belief system as values. They spell out for us the principles that should guide our actions. Values are beliefs that are abstract in that they do not focus on specific objects and situations. Scott (1965) demonstrated empirically that values have a quality of non-negotiability about them. They transcend the specific, representing desirable ends in their own right that we believe we should always follow. Moreover, we believe that the world would be a better place if others shared our view.

According to Rokeach (1973), many values, attitudes and beliefs are interconnected to form cognitively consistent subsystems. When change occurs in one part of the system, other parts are also likely to be affected. In general, long-term attitudinal change will occur only if there are changes in the values that underpin the attitude, and providing the change does not do harm to conceptions of the self. The core of the value–attitude–belief system comprises beliefs about the self. Changes that involve values reach to the heart of the system: values serve 'the enhancement of what McDougall (1926) has aptly called the master of all sentiments, the sentiment of self-regard' (Rokeach 1968: 132).

Motivational postures can be conceptualized as subsystems of attitudes and beliefs within a value–attitude–belief system. These sets of interconnected beliefs and attitudes describe, explain and signal to others how individuals relate to a regulatory authority. Do they see themselves in agreement with the authority, captured by the authority, or in opposition to the authority? A posture communicates degrees of endorsement and status for what the authority does, and liking for those who do it. Individuals have a range of motivational postures to suit different situations. These sets of motivational postures can be thought of as official communiqués composed by individuals to sum up their basic predisposition towards the demands of an authority. They can be used to bargain, to justify compliance as well as non-compliance, to provide an escape route should the authority become too oppressive, and to assure people of their intrinsic worth in spite of what the authority says and does. Motivational postures wax and wane, depending on what the social situation has in store for the individual encountering authority.

2. A THEORETICAL FRAMEWORK FOR MOTIVATIONAL POSTURES

Discovering a Niche for Motivational Postures

The concept of motivational postures emerged from work on the determinants of compliance, conducted as part of the 'Nursing Home Regulation in Action Project' (Braithwaite, V. et al. 1994). At that time, one of our objectives was to test the regulatory model of Kagan and Scholz (1984) described briefly in the previous chapter. In order to move regulatory authorities beyond a 'rule by the book' mentality, Kagan and Scholz proposed what was essentially a motivational model of non-compliance with different regulatory strategies accompanying different motivational types. Our goal was to find out if the Kagan and Scholz archetypes corresponded in any way to the cognitive categories and shared sensibilities that regulators and regulatees used to communicate with each other over compliance problems.

Kagan and Scholz (1984) focused on corporations and identified three basic reasons that lay at the heart of regulators' personal theories for why laws were not being obeyed. The first image they described was of the corporation as an 'amoral calculator', that is, as an agent that assesses the costs of compliance and the risks of being caught for non-compliance, and makes a decision that maximizes the corporation's profits. Where the motivation for non-compliance is economic gain, the appropriate regulatory strategy is postulated as being police-like enforcement and the imposition of penalties to change the balance of costs and benefits in favour of compliance.

The second image put forward by Kagan and Scholz (1984) was of a corporation as a 'political citizen', breaking the law in circumstances where there was principled disagreement with the regulations, most commonly because the rules were unreasonable. Where the fundamental problem lies in charges of regulatory unreasonableness, Kagan and Scholz argued that a police-like strategy is unlikely to work, and the corporation needs to be persuaded of the virtue of implementing the regulation. The regulator must adopt the role of politician, seeking to persuade the corporation, but at the same time be ready to be responsive to 'citizen' complaints through adapting the law to accommodate legitimate business concerns.

The third Kagan and Scholz (1984) image was organizational incompetence. Corporations failed to comply because key players were ignorant of what the law required, or because the organizational reporting or problem-solving mechanisms were not functioning properly. Where organizational failure was at the heart of the problem, Kagan and Scholz proposed that education regarding feasible technologies and management practices would prove most useful in ensuring future compliance. The most responsive regulatory role in these circumstances was that of 'consultant'.

The Kagan and Scholz model stands as a milestone in the regulatory literature for two reasons. First, it drew attention to the fact that regulation was not merely about technology and infrastructure, and that regulatory failure could be overcome only if regulators engaged with how people understood and interpreted what was expected and being asked of them. Second, the model explained why regulating by the book could have only limited success as a corrective mechanism. Regulating by the book, in its basic form, involves the sequence of observing a particular practice, identifying the practice as the equivalent of an infringement listed in the regulator's manual, and subsequently applying a designated sanction. But the sanction, no matter how strongly it expresses disapproval, is unlikely to turn an incompetently run organization into a competent one. Nor is it likely to elicit cooperation from a firm that has principled objections to the regulation. If there are multiple reasons for why people and corporations fail to comply, there have to be multiple strategies in place to nudge them into getting it right (Freiberg 1990; Hite 1997).

In order to find out if regulators and regulatees were thinking and acting in line with the Kagan and Scholz model, questions were incorporated in the 'Nursing Home Regulation in Action Project' questionnaires to measure the three images of non-compliance and the strategies that regulators used to turn them around. The findings of this work were surprising. We found little evidence of regulators thinking in terms of the images proposed by Kagan and Scholz (1984). Rather, their judgements of the nursing home were formed along a single 'bad apple' to 'good apple' dimension. At the 'bad apple' end were judgements about incompetence and profit-seeking behaviour. Regulators did not differentiate between amoral calculators and those who could not get it right through incompetence. They seemed to think that these two motives could not be easily disentangled. At the 'good apple' end were political citizens, those who regulators judged to be well intentioned and conscientious in spite of failing to comply with the standards.

Similarly, when we tried to gauge the dominant strategy used by regulators to improve compliance, the nuances underlying the Kagan and Scholz model were not apparent. Regulators themselves reported responding in terms of a single dimension: was this an organization where regulatory intervention was required to bring about compliance or not? Interventions of an educative, persuasive and deterrent kind were considered options for use with problem organizations, be they amoral calculators or incompetent managers. Political citizens, on the other hand, were considered to require little intervention. In other words, a substantial number of regulators were not going by the book – they made an assessment of whether they were dealing with an organization that was likely to be recalcitrant and needed straightening out, or one that was likely to come around of its own accord, making the necessary changes to meet compliance standards. In such cases, they appreciated the advantages of using discretion to make exceptions and to grant extensions of time. What they were doing was focusing on how much outside intervention was required to achieve the desired outcome: they did not go back to diagnose the problem along the lines outlined by Kagan and Scholz (1984).

The next stage of the work turned the spotlight away from the regulators and on to the attitudes and perceptions of the regulatees. This approach proved interesting in that it provided clues as to how the underlying message of Kagan and Scholz (1984) might be taken forward to better mesh with real-world attitudes, beliefs and practices.

An analysis of the perceptions that regulatees held of the regulatory authority provided support for the notion of different motivational predispositions, but the predispositions we were able to measure were predominantly about social relationships, not about knowledge, competence and profit. We did not interpret this to mean that knowledge, competence and profit were unimportant; but these considerations were clearly not at the forefront of regulatees' minds in the regulatory encounter. Thus it was little wonder that they were not in the minds of the regulators either as they tried to negotiate action plans for compliance. The focus for both regulator and regulatee was on dealing with a negative report card and coping with reactions to being judged non-compliant. It was almost as if relationship management had to take precedence over either exposing systemic reasons for non-compliance or discussing action plans for full compliance. On both sides of the regulatory encounter, criticism and reaction to criticism swamped other considerations.

It was the emotional and social swamping that we observed in these encounters that led to the conclusion that the search for 'true' motives in the regulatory context was unlikely to be productive. Instead we opted for the term 'motivational posturing' to describe the manoeuvres we saw regulatees undertake in order to preserve their dignity in the face of criticism from an authority. There could be little doubt that the motivational postures we had identified were composites of a number of forces that individuals perceived as operating in their life space: they were not 'pure' motive, 'pure' strategy or 'pure' reactance to authority. The concept of motivational postures was a window on the perceptual gestalt that Lewin (1951) had signalled half a century earlier.

Types of Postures

Four postures were discovered through factor analysing the data collected from nursing home directors on their perceptions of the inspection process and their views on what they and the inspectors intended to achieve. The factors represented different kinds of social distancing from authority. Two postures were characterized by high, and two by low social distance.

The most socially distant were resistance and disengagement. Resistance involved an 'us' and 'them' way of viewing the world. Resistance was a defensive and oppositional posture. It involved rejecting the regulators as oppressive, unhelpful and unforgiving. The response of resistance has been described behaviourally in other regulatory contexts (Bardach and Kagan 1982).

While resistance signalled conflict and resentment over the power of the regulator, disengagement was defined by complete dismissal of the regulator and the regulatory system. Disengagement involved a state of not caring, of deliberately denying the regulator the satisfaction of believing that what she did mattered. Those who had disengaged placed themselves outside the reach of the regulator psychologically. In this sense, the posture of disengagement communicated an experience of anomie, the perception that rules and norms were meaningless and not observed (Durkheim 1952). Merton (1968) used the phrase 'in the system, but not of it' to describe a mode of adaptation that he described as retreatism, involving rejection of the normative order in terms of both goals and the preferred means for attaining them. This is similar to disengagement – a state of 'cool' detachment from everything the authority stands for.

Both resistance and disengagement were less common in the regulated population than the motivational postures of commitment and capitulation.[4] Commitment involved endorsement of the regulatory code and its integration into the organization's management plan. There was no suggestion that the regulations should be set to one side to be dealt with when time permitted. Instead, they were mainstreamed and improved upon to deliver better outcomes. This was the posture that was most likely to deliver best practice above and beyond that required by the regulations. Commitment involved internalizing the regulatory code as the right thing to do.

The posture of capitulation was a message to authority that said: 'Tell us what we have to do and we will do it.' The emphasis was on meeting the authority's demands and minimizing fuss. To those who adopted the motivational posture of capitulation, belief in the regulatory code as best practice was peripheral. Regulators had captured regulatees in the sense that regulatees agreed to do what was being asked, driven by willingness to please and a desire to avoid trouble, without stopping to think too much about the ultimate goals. This lack of critical thinking about the intentions of legitimate authority, as Kelman and Hamilton (1989) have warned, can have dire consequences. The essential part of capitulation is jumping through hoops without giving any thought to the objectives or achieving desired outcomes. Merton (1968) described this form of adaptation to authority as ritualism, whereby a person goes through the motions without connecting cognitively or emotionally with the desired end.

Importantly, the empirical findings showed that the postures were not mutually exclusive: holding one posture did not prevent those being regulated from holding another. Resistance could therefore increase in response to an unpleasant encounter with an inspector, but other postures such as commitment and capitulation could stay the same. The factor analysis revealed that the postures did not have to move in unison: indeed, there may be more than one low-to-high social distance dimension defining how regulatees locate themselves in relation to authority. Regulatees seem to have a complex response system to authority, giving them some control over the postures that can be brought into action in the next regulatory encounter.

Linking Motivational Postures with Compliance Outcomes

In theory, motivational postures need not align themselves with compliant outcomes. We are all familiar with the situation in which our attitudes and actions don't tell the same story. We may deeply resent regulations and yet comply because refusing creates too much trouble. Or we might comply because we just happen to believe that it is the right thing to do regardless of regulations. The reverse is also true. We may be highly committed to regulations, but be careless in implementation and fall short on expected compliance standards. Some nursing home directors who are sophisticated and committed to high standards of patient care and safety can have a disaster occur on their watch. Commitment does not always guarantee a happy ending, particularly in complex organizations.

In practice, however, the nursing home data showed that motivational postures were predictive of compliance outcomes (Braithwaite, V. et al. 1994). Moreover, the regulatory strategies chosen by regulators were associated with the motivational posturing of regulatees. And the motivational posturing of regulatees was associated with how they perceived the actions of their team of regulators. The main findings were as follows:

1. The postures of commitment and capitulation were more likely to be associated with compliance, while disengagement and resistance were linked with non-compliance.
2. Regulators were more likely to have made the judgement that intervention was required in organizations where managers displayed disengagement and resistance.
3. Organizational managers who displayed disengagement and resistance were more likely to see the team of regulators who visited them as coercive and intrusive and not as helpful and cooperative.
4. The posture of resistance was associated with an improvement in compliance in circumstances where (a) regulatees saw their regulators

as cooperative rather than coercive and (b) regulators made the judgement that intervention was unnecessary.
5. The posture of disengagement was distinctive in that it was associated with worsening compliance, regardless of regulatory action.

The findings on changing levels of compliance were important in demonstrating that resistance is easier to manage than disengagement. When disengagement sets in, it may be impossible to manage. Resistance is a more democratically useful expression of defiance than disengagement. Resistance communicates resentments about what citizens feel moved to resist. Disengagement involves dropping out, with no communication that betrays the source of the injury, and therefore no basis for responsiveness that can repair the situation.

This difference between resistance and disengagement is one that is recognizable in daily life. Parents of children who drop out into a culture of drug abuse generally have a bigger problem than parents of children who rebel by stealing or fighting. Delinquency fuelled by resistance is likely to be part of growing up. The behaviour and resentments of the resistantly defiant can be confronted. Patience and perseverance from parents and community is likely to win out. Delinquency fuelled by disengagement, more sadly, is likely to have a different trajectory. Confronting the social withdrawal of the dismissively defiant risks greater withdrawal. The dismissively defiant are the more likely to embark on a rite of passage that takes them beyond the reach of family and friends into a world of hopelessness, despair and self-harm. They step outside the social infrastructure that we all need to function effectively in our society, and once they are there, it is difficult to draw them back.

Motivational Postures and their Theoretical Parts

Motivational postures, because they are empirically derived constructs, need to be given theoretical legs by linking them back to bodies of social theory. The nursing home regulation project provided an early opportunity for forming such links.

A persistent tension in the social sciences lies in whether collective action should be understood in terms of the pursuit of mutually desirable outcomes or mutually satisfying social bonds. This tension emerges in the regulatory context in the debate over the degree to which citizens' cooperation with authorities can be explained by procedural as opposed to distributive justice (Tyler 2001).

In the present research context, it was therefore of some importance to know whether the empirically derived motivational postures reflected differences in acceptance of regulatory goals, or differences in perception of the quality of the relationship with the regulator (Braithwaite, V. 1995). The research revealed that in the case of each motivational posture, both components were important. Postures could be attributable to disagreement over regulatory goals and means as well as tension in the social relationship between regulator and regulatee in the following ways:

1. Resistance reflected relational stress. Resistance accompanied perceptions of marginalization from the centre of the regulatory culture, that is, feeling excluded from consultations organized by the regulators and believing that one was regarded as untrustworthy by the regulators. Resistance also reflected tensions around means and goals. Resistance was more likely when regulatees disagreed with the outcome of their inspection and questioned the competence of the regulators. Interestingly, resistance was not associated with disagreement over broader shared objectives of providing care.
2. Disengagement was relational in that the posture was linked with low trust and unwillingness to cooperate. Disagreement over regulatory goals, however, was more profound. Disengagement was associated with the rejection of broader shared objectives involving nursing professionalism as well as the legitimacy of the regulator.
3. Commitment was marked by a relationship with the regulators that was respectful and consultative, and by a commitment to the more abstract objective of professional excellence.
4. Capitulation involved appreciation of a positive relationship with the regulator, but at the same time, a willingness to 'jump ship' if provoked. Goal acceptance was somewhat superficial, resting on confidence in the competence of the regulator. The value of the regulatory system lay in the approval and security it offered regulatees.

The Place of Motivational Postures in Regulatory Theory

This work changed the lens for examining the motivations mapped out by Kagan and Scholz (1984). Theirs was a model that was essentially rational and individualistic. Motivational posturing showed that, in practice, rationality was tempered by emotions and individual judgement was shaped by social relationships. Even so, the basic images put forward by Kagan and Scholz were there, and it seemed they were potentially present in any one regulatee. Regulatees were political citizens when they adopted the commitment posture, and they used this mode to engage and influence the regulatory authority. They were also able to put themselves outside the reach of the norms of the regulatory institution through disengagement and play the role of amoral calculator. Later, they could come back into the regulatory system, wanting to improve on their past regulatory practice through the posture of capitulation, or through lowering their resistance.

The new insight emerging through the motivational posturing research was that regulators' actions interact with postures to affect future compliance outcomes. In other words, posturing is not the last word on how the regulatory encounter will turn out. Most importantly, when regulatee resistance was met with regulator helpfulness, compliance improved. This finding suggests that it is possible to adopt the opposite of a tit-for-tat strategy and draw out a responsible self that will deliver on compliance. The same strategy, however, is unlikely to have the desired effect on those who have disengaged. In order to appreciate this difference, we need to progress the theoretical framework for motivational postures by drawing more links with established regulatory and social theory.

Restorative and Procedural Justice

In a series of companion papers that emerged from the 'Nursing Home Regulation in Action Project', John Braithwaite and Toni Makkai provided a substantial body of empirical support for the idea that the quality of the relationship between regulator and regulatee was important if the objective was to improve compliance. The most significant contribution of this collection of papers was to demonstrate the role that the generation of positive and negative emotions was likely to have in shaping future compliance. Where regulators were able to identify areas of non-compliance, and then look beyond to find something praiseworthy about the establishment, compliance was more likely to improve at the next biennial inspection (Makkai and Braithwaite 1993). Compliance also improved when regulatees felt they were being treated as trustworthy, when they felt the inspectors had confidence in them to put things right, and were willing to put past misdeeds behind them (Braithwaite, J. and Makkai 1994; Makkai and Braithwaite 1994a). On the other hand, deterrence, while effective for regulatees with low emotional involvement, proved counterproductive for those who reported themselves as being highly emotional (Braithwaite, J. and Makkai 1991; Makkai and Braithwaite 1994b). High emotionality shared common ground with personality measures of neuroticism: like neurotics, highly emotional people reported themselves as being hot-tempered, getting mad easily, and taking a long time to calm down (Braithwaite, V. 1987).

These papers pointed to the need to take account of shame emotions in managing poor compliance performance. The pay-off in the event of effectively managing shame was improved compliance. Shame emotions are aroused when our ethical identity is offended (Harris 2007). The underlying dynamic appeared to be taking actions that reduced negativity in the encounter, thereby preventing distancing between regulator and regulatee. Drawing the regulatee into the regulatory community meant dealing with their compliance failures in a reintegrative or restorative fashion without stigmatizing them and driving them away (Braithwaite, J. 1989). In sum, these data illustrated how regulators could take action that neutralized negative emotions in a non-complying regulatee and elicit improved performance in time for the next biennial inspection.

In the above studies, people were asked about what happened when the nursing home was inspected, how they felt, and how they interpreted these events. Reactions to others' evaluations, particularly in a legal context, are invariably accompanied by perceptions of fairness. Tom Tyler has amassed two decades of findings to demonstrate how important it is for authorities to abide by procedural justice principles in their dealings with citizens, in particular to deliver those relational components of procedural justice that recognize individuals as valued members of the group (Lind and Tyler 1988; Tyler 1988, 1989, 1990, 1997, 2001; Tyler and Lind 1992; Tyler and Dawes 1993; Tyler and Blader 2000). While Tyler concedes that the distributive justice concerns of delivering fair outcomes are important to people, his data show that the continued cooperation of citizens is more likely to be a consequence of authorities treating individuals with respect, communicating trustworthiness, and exercising their duties with neutrality. Tyler has shown across a range of contexts that meeting the relational needs of citizens is the primary factor that gives authorities legitimacy and elicits voluntary compliance.

The consistent finding that the relational components of procedural justice outweigh instrumental concerns in explaining legitimacy and compliance has challenged authorities that build their regulatory strategies around self-interest. Because the favourability of a decision to oneself, or even the fairness of a decision, is a less important consideration than judgements about the fairness of the process, efforts to regulate through manipulating rewards and punishments are destined for limited success. According to Lind and Tyler's (1988) group-value model, what people are looking for in their experiences with the process is information about how they are viewed by that authority. The authority, by virtue of its status in the society, has the capacity to communicate to individuals their standing in the community. Standing is inferred from the social relationship, the degree to which one is treated with respect and dignity, without prejudice, and with due concern. Through this treatment, one's position as a full and valued member of the community can be validated.

But what happens if we are not convinced by the sincerity of these efforts or if we object so fundamentally to the decisions made by the authority that we don't identify in any way with the group it represents?

Tyler (1997) reported the results of a series of studies where fairness judgements of an in-group and out-group authority were compared. Out-group authorities were judged more in terms of outcomes than treatment. Goals and objectives do matter, more so in communities that are fragmented, without an overarching and shared conception of who they are and where they are heading (Tyler et al. 1998).

Outcomes and Conflict Inevitability

Earlier in this chapter, lack of consensus over regulatory goals was found to be as important as poor treatment in explaining the more distant motivational postures. Given that many citizens approach tax offices with caution, if not scepticism (Taylor 2001), outcomes need to be considered along with process in constructing a theoretical framework in which to embed the motivational postures concept.

Traditionally, outcomes have had the dominant hand in shaping our understanding of compliance and cooperation. Early social theorists focused attention on the way in which social order constrained individual expectations and ensured that people lived harmoniously alongside each other in spite of obvious inequalities in outcomes. However, the imperfections of the system did not escape attention. A vast body of research has addressed the way in which relative deprivation and social comparison can cause social unrest, inter-group conflict and individual despair. Merton (1968) was among the early social theorists to focus attention on how important it was for individuals to attain socially desirable or legitimate goals. While each individual, in theory, could achieve these goals through legitimate means, some were likely to have their opportunities for advancement blocked. Individuals who were deprived of legitimate means for achievement were likely to resort to illegitimate means. Wanting the outcomes that were held up as symbols of success in society provided the justification for breaking or bending rules in ways that were not deemed acceptable by that society.

How then do such theorists explain compliance when it involves forfeiting outcomes that have high social legitimacy? More particularly, how does a tax administration persuade taxpayers to cooperate with them when the sacrifice they are being asked to make is dear to most of their hearts – their hard-earned money?

The Trap of Enforcing Compliance while Creating Defiance

According to Kelman, an authority relies on three paths to overcome citizen resistance to a demand (Kelman 1958, 1961; Kelman and Hamilton

1989). Sometimes people are impressed by the credibility of the authority. Under such circumstances, they are likely to be persuaded by the power of the argument and internalize the regulatory code so that it becomes their personal standard for decision making and action. When the code is likely to become integrated with their values, attitudes and beliefs, Kelman (1958) describes the path of social influence as internalization.

At other times, people see the authority as attractive, and take on the regulatory code to strengthen their relationship with the authority. When they define themselves in terms of their relationship with the authority, their image of themselves is enhanced. This process, which Kelman calls identification, is most likely to result in cooperation when individuals are in a role where the authority's expectations are salient (Kelman 1958). Outside the role demands of the relationship, cooperation may falter.

The third way in which an authority can exert its influence is through control of rewards and punishments. Kelman reserves the term 'compliance' for this particular path of social influence where individuals engage in the behaviour purely for the purposes of winning favour with the authority or avoiding disapproval and punishment. Where surveillance of responses is no longer possible, cooperation is likely to cease because the desired response has been coerced, not voluntarily offered as a worthwhile activity.

Compliance of this latter kind is consistent with a command-and-control regulatory system but is clearly an unwieldy, expensive and unlikely route to achieving any kind of self-sustaining behavioural change. The processes of identification and internalization are much more cost-effective for a regulatory institution, although identification carries some dangers if the democracy is not robust. As observed earlier in the chapter, leaders can be followed blindly down paths of questionable integrity. At the heart of a vibrant democracy is healthy debate about regulatory codes and alternative options. This can only be achieved through the voices of those who have internalized the regulatory code as well as those who question the justification for doing so. As Kelman and Hamilton note: 'to capitalize on their legitimacy, it would be to the authorities' advantage to activate citizens' commitments to the system and to downplay the penalties for disobedience' (1989: 93).

The analysis of social influence that Kelman and his colleagues offer is a reminder that optimal social distance describes an idealized state – no matter how hard regulators work, many encounters take place where the social distance is too great or too small. In order to maintain social order, authorities can and do short-circuit the persuasion–dialogue route. Sometimes, those in authority pull at the 'identification strings' to elicit 'blind' obedience from followers. An extensive advertising campaign to introduce a goods-and-services tax (GST) in Australia in 2000–2001 had as its centrepiece a song of liberation – no other than Joe Cocker singing 'Unchain my Heart'. The government purchased the rights to use the song as background in an advertisement showing surprised supermarket shoppers with chains literally falling from their arms and legs as they entered the GST shopping era. Rational it was not, but a feel-good message to elicit obedience it was. Not surprisingly, not all were impressed by the 'identification' message, least of all some GST-resistant Joe Cocker fans – and Joe Cocker himself (ABC Local Radio 31 May 2000).

For those who remained sceptical and defiant about the GST, the Australian Taxation Office (ATO) relied on 'a supportive compliance approach' with advisory visits, helplines and detailed statements setting out the circumstances in which people would face penalty. From 2000–2002, however, no penalties were imposed, except in cases where people were deliberately avoiding their tax responsibilities (Commissioner of Taxation 2001). After the transition period, auditing of small business increased (Australian Taxation Office 2002a) and the ATO's annual compliance programmes signalled increases in auditing and prosecution in subsequent years (Australian Taxation Office 2002a, 2003a, 2004b, 2005).

The ATO dealt with the introduction of its 'New Tax System' by investing resources heavily in persuasion, education and help in the first two years, and then turned attention to ratcheting up its auditing activities after the change had been bedded down. But how should resources have been allocated? Should the ATO have kept a schedule of audits and prosecutions going when the GST was introduced rather than giving small business time to adjust, and possibly learn to evade; should punishment have been carried out alongside education and persuasion? Some of the findings shared in later chapters suggest that the ATO might have been seen by some to have gone soft in the education and persuasion years and allowed people to get away with too much. How does one balance the functions of helping and monitoring in the compliance process?

Gamson (1968) asked this question in relation to interest groups and political authorities, and argued that alienation can be the price paid for failing to recognize a readiness in the other to be persuaded by argument. Following Gamson's thesis, inducements and punishments can weaken the relationship between regulator and regulatee when the regulatee trusts the authority and is open to persuasion. When an authority seeks to buy favours from a loyal supporter, the transaction sours because there is an implication that the supporter cannot be trusted to follow through without inducement. Frey (1997) described a similar phenomenon through crowding-out theory. Moral commitment to achieve a certain outcome is weakened by the introduction of coercive measures.

Thus the coercive strategies that some may think are a blanket regulatory strategy for getting everyone to comply can be counterproductive and push some out of compliance. What is more, this situation may be difficult to reverse. When trust relationships with others in the regulatory community are systematically weakened, opportunities are lost for constructive and open exchanges of information that are essential for social influence to occur. Moreover, the resources required to rebuild social capital and engage an alienated community are substantial.

Compliance, Defiance and Regulatory Pyramids

Regulatory failures that occur when regulators drive regulatees beyond the zone of persuasion are costly for the regulatory authority and the community, and have led to the development of the concept of regulatory pyramids (Ayres and Braithwaite 1992). Regulatory pyramids give regulators a series of graduated options for responding to non-compliance. The basic premise of the model is that a regulator will not know beforehand which path of influence is most likely to succeed with any individual or group. The proposed solution, therefore, is to build up intervention and intrusiveness in stages so as to inflict no more pressure than is absolutely necessary to elicit compliance. In this way, the regulator starts with a strategy that is least likely to drive the regulatee beyond the zone of persuasion.

Responses to non-compliance initially rely on dialogue, sharing expertise, listening to counter-arguments, and the powers of persuasion. If cooperation is not forthcoming, authorities must draw on power of other kinds, unless convinced by regulatees that their own law is unreasonable and needs to change. Central to the design of the regulatory pyramid is the feedback that authorities can receive from the community about the acceptability of their regulatory standards. Through initial dialogue, regulator and regulatee can each try to persuade the other of his/her point of view.

If the regulator decides that the path to compliance needs to be pursued, further pressures and different kinds of influences are likely to be introduced. The essential principle is that the regulatory mix involves strategies that are complementary or mutually reinforcing (Gunningham 1993): for it to be otherwise would compromise the integrity attributed by the public to the regulator. Third parties with persuasive powers over the non-compliant regulatee may contribute to ratcheting up the pressure applied by the regulator to elicit compliance (Grabosky 1995b). As enforcement intervention increases, regulatees become aware of the negative consequences of non-compliance for them. Eventually, if cooperation remains elusive, sanctions of either a social or economic kind might be brought into play, their severity increasing as regulator and regulatee proceed up the regulatory pyramid. In the event that all else fails, incapacitation of the regulatee occurs. For instance, the regulatee might lose a licence to practise or operate another business.

At all times, regulatees are treated to the procedural justice that has been highlighted as so important through the work of Tyler and his colleagues (Tyler, 1990, 1997; Tyler and Blader, 2000). Maintaining procedural justice, regardless of the level of disapproval shown or sanctions imposed, provides an avenue for moving non-compliant actors down the regulatory pyramid. By maintaining respect and inclusiveness in their interactions with non-compliers, regulators try to keep the communication lines open so that their persuasive efforts may yield a positive regulatory outcome not only in relation to the violation under review, but also on future occasions. Thus, while the regulatory pyramid functions mainly as a model for eliciting compliance, it has the potential for doubling up as a model for creating responsive relationships, providing regulators have sufficient integrity and resources to respond to concerns at the base of the pyramid through persuasion, education, listening and adaptation.

The ATO introduced a model of compliance that recognized the need to have a repertoire of regulatory strategies of varying levels of intrusiveness that could be brought into play with increasing levels of defiance to regulation. The model also prepared staff for the way in which this defiance was reflected through different motivational postures. Figure 3.1 shows the model that the ATO used for training purposes.[5] The objective was to alert ATO staff to the way in which postures on the left side of the pyramid signalled greater social distance and reduced openness to influence through persuasion and education. The model recommended that regulatory strategies and enforcement action be introduced incrementally so that staff could signal a clear intention to escalate regulatory activities if the regulated party was not prepared to adopt a cooperative posture. The strategies on the right side of the pyramid reflected increasing levels of regulatory intrusiveness up the pyramid in order to focus the regulated party on compliance. Specific enforcement strategies that might accompany increasing regulatory intrusiveness and social distance appear on the centre panel of the model. The model emphasized the importance of abiding by principles of procedural justice at all times. These principles were embodied in the Taxpayers' Charter. The next section explains the theoretical justification for matching postures with strategies characterized by different levels of intrusiveness on the regulatory pyramid.

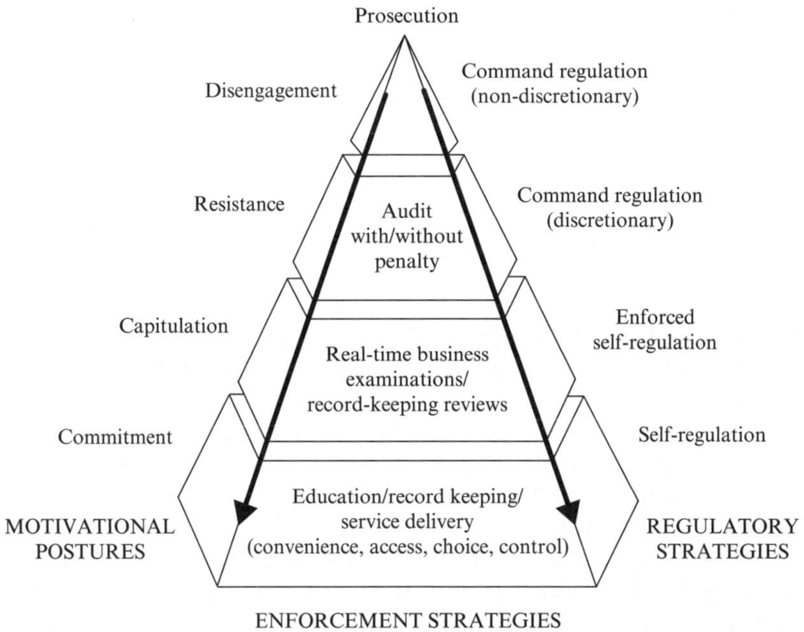

Figure 3.1 The ATO compliance model with distancing motivational postures (left), escalating regulatory intrusiveness (right) and examples of enforcement strategies (centre)

Bringing together Pyramids and Postures

Based on the work of Gamson (1968), Kelman (1958, 1961), Kelman and Hamilton (1989) and Ayres and Braithwaite (1992), motivational postures can be seen as differing not only in their social distance from the authority, but also in the influence processes that are likely to be required to change non-compliant practices. Those who express commitment to the system and who have internalized the regulatory code are looking to persuasive argument and expert knowledge before changing their compliance practices. As such, commitment might be thought of as the motivational posture that, when present, allows regulation to stay at the bottom of the regulatory pyramid and move up a strengths-based pyramid (Braithwaite, J. et al. 2007: ch. 10).

Those who speak in terms of having capitulated to the power of the authority seem to fit Kelman's (1958, 1961) description of being influenced primarily by identification. Status is acquired through meeting the expectations of the regulatory authority. Under conditions of capitulation, regulator and regulatee are part of the one family, each acting out their roles to their mutual benefit. Individuals who have capitulated to the authority believe in and accept the standards, but their compliance is conditional on them being in role.

What can be done, then, if they behave in a non-compliant fashion out of role, and are found out? In these circumstances, the regulator–regulatee relationship will not provide the non-complier with the self-definition that he or she wants. Indeed, the regulatee risks a loss of status because of the breach in the relationship with the regulator. The posture of resistance seems to fit this state of affairs. Persuasion and leadership credibility are not sufficient to elicit compliance. Risks to reputation must be dealt with and ways of restoring reputation through compliant role performance must be found. Compliance options that offer rewards and avoid punishments are likely to work best for those showing resistance. Thus we can conceptualize capitulation and resistance as postures that represent not only increasing distance from the authority, but consecutively higher steps on the regulatory pyramid.

Disengagement represents the most socially distant posture, in Kelman's (1958, 1961) terms providing the regulator with little other option than sanctioning. Those who are disengaged do not believe in the standards enough to be guided by them. Moreover, they are dismissive of what the regulator can do to harm them. But if they are tuned in to their self-interest, they probably will comply if they are closely monitored by authorities and believe that credible sanctioning processes are in place. In practice, however, by maintaining maximum social distance from the authorities, those who are in a disengaging posture can stay out of the view of the regulators and can escape the influence created by fear of sanctions and the likelihood of penalties. Gamson (1968) describes this response as alienation. Of the motivational postures, disengagement has the strongest claim to the highest levels on the regulatory pyramid.

Summary

To sum up, this section has introduced the notion of optimal social distance between an authority and those whom it regulates – optimal from the perspective of the regulatee who wants to influence the authority, and optimal from the perspective of the authority who wishes to guide the actions of the regulatee. Optimal social distance is constantly being negotiated, with chances of success depending on unswerving adherence to principles of procedural justice. Against a background of procedural fairness, dialogue that contests the objectives and rules of the regulatory institution can proceed. Optimal social distance makes possible the persuasion of each party by the other, in a context where each appreciates the interests of self and other. Optimal social distance allows for Iris Marion Young's (2000) quality of reasonableness in dialogic fora.

Optimal social distance, however, is an idealized state. Many individuals will become enmeshed in the authority; others will be too distant to engage constructively in its operations. At the individual level, a regulatory pyramid provides regulators with strategies for dealing with all groups. The goal is to elicit compliance, but also to create understanding of why the request is being made. In this way, everyone has an opportunity to think critically about what is happening to them. Furthermore, by creating space for reflection and dialogue, social distance may be reduced to the point where cooperation is more forthcoming on future occasions.

While individuals will always be found too close or too distant from authority, it is nevertheless possible at the collective level to use such variability to foster the community dialogue necessary for a sustainable and effective regulatory system. Motivational postures can be used to monitor the level of tension in the regulatory community. The hoped-for profile would be one where there was enough discontent to allow critical analysis, but not so much that constructive resolution was not possible. Within a democracy, commitment and capitulation are bound to be high, but one would hope for considerable resistance to periodically foster debate, and one would hope for more resistance than disengagement. Contested governance short of a crisis of governability is the responsive ideal. In such circumstances, more resources are likely to be required at the base of the pyramid to find solutions to people's problems and restore confidence in the system.

3. UNRESOLVED TENSIONS IN TAXATION – A POSTURE OF GAME PLAYING

Posturing with Tax Authorities

To this point, our understanding of defiance and non-compliance has rested on the assumption that there are rules with sanctions for violation, and that these rules and sanctions are generally known to regulatees and administered by regulators. The rules and sanctions may be viewed as unfair or illegitimate, but they are known. This is not the case with tax systems, where legal complexity can befuddle even the most sophisticated players. The law is not only complex, but also unclear. The grey areas of the law create confusion, uncertainty and, for risk takers, opportunity. Exploiting loopholes and avoiding obligations with some claim to legal protection is not captured in the motivational postures discussed above. These relationships lie beyond the bounds imposed by law, authority and expectations of compliance. This new form of defiance that tax authorities are grappling with internationally is reflected in a game-playing posture.

McBarnet, who has analysed game-playing behaviours in a range of contexts, argues that the problem can only be managed through changing attitudes to law (McBarnet 1988, 1991, 1992; McBarnet and Whelan 1999). McBarnet uses the term 'creative compliance' to describe a willingness and capability to manipulate law – 'to work creatively on the fabric of law' (1992: 72). She argues that regulators are complicit with professionals and elites in allowing 'legitimate rackets' to flourish. Economic elites have the resources to 'buy legal creativity' (ibid.: 73) from professionals. They 'buy immunity from law' (ibid.) by capturing regulators who have locked into an enforcement mentality of looking for technical legality. Regulators have caved in to embracing a mindset that values compliance with the letter of the law, while dropping the ball on maintaining standards of compliance with the spirit of the law.

Others have argued that another string to the bow is required to deal with tax avoidance, involving changes to the way the law is written and used (Avery Jones 1996; Freedman 2004; Braithwaite, J. 2005). While avoiding the endless cat-and-mouse games of rule adjustment, there has been considerable support for switching legal mindsets so that tax compliance is interpreted through application of a set of principles that are more secure. Either way, the challenge posed by game playing can only be properly met through acceptance of shared understandings at the bottom of the pyramid.

Management of game playing is bound to be difficult, and at the moment the psychology of game playing lacks the theoretical infrastructure that has been built around the other postures. Yet it is difficult to let the subject go at this point without referring to arguments presented earlier for creating responsive relationships. One argument for inclusive relationship management was the prevention of intractable compliance-related problems. One could argue that if the kind of dialogue advocated in the previous chapter had been taking place, there would be little space in the regulatory culture for what might be called a game-playing posture. But as McBarnet (1992) demonstrated through her fieldwork, a great deal of dialogue does take place over tax avoidance, but the dialogue is contained within particular nodes of influence. As will be illustrated, McBarnet's analysis and insights are applicable to the way in which game playing secured a foothold in the Australian psyche, gaining popularity among exclusive, elite networks while evading scrutiny by the Australian community.

Legitimizing and Sharing a Game-playing Tax Posture

If we are to develop a generalized framework for understanding game playing, it is useful to return to the work of Kelman and Hamilton (1989), who set out conditions for disobeying authority. According to these researchers, if we are to disobey – and game playing is interpreted as a special kind of disobedience with the law's intent – we need an alternative authority, one that has sufficient legitimacy to challenge the dominant authority. In the case of taxation, the alternative authority might be conceptualized as those professionals with expert knowledge of the law. One might argue that this expertise would surely be concentrated in the tax office. Self-assessment, however, has given rise to a market with a professional culture that prides itself on knowing tax law, how to take advantage of it and, most importantly, on meeting customer demands (Erard 1993; Forsyth 1981; Klepper and Nagin 1989; Klepper et al. 1991; Murphy and Sakurai 2001; Braithwaite, J. 2005).

The professional culture that 'sells' tax avoidance is global and is now well enmeshed internationally in legitimate and powerful financial institutions. The social process whereby game playing came to be accepted business practice for individuals, however, has been evolving for some time. The following illustration, based on a debate that took place in Australian legal journals more than 30 years ago, demonstrates the way in which the process of game playing was openly advocated in elite legal circles, was vociferously attacked from within, but ultimately triumphed in reshaping Australia's tax institutions, bringing them into line with those of other Western democracies. The result has been the blossoming of a new kind of defiance that in effect delegitimizes the sovereign state while acting within the law.

In describing the Australian regulatory community's reactions to tax avoidance in 1976, Yuri Grbich, a tax lawyer, singled out his profession as the alternative authority to the tax office:

> Most laymen are only dimly aware of the tax process and any influence they have takes place through the opaque curtain of the tax lawyer's professional language. The lawyer's function is not limited to adjudication. He also participates in teaching of the young, is the expert called into the legislative process, commentator on the media, lobbyist, author of books, a member of reform committees, and often the only politician interested in these uniquely complicated areas. With their half-brothers, the accountants, lawyers hold a practical monopoly of the vital commodity, information, which is the life-blood of the animal they have created. (1976: 231)

Grbich was writing at a time when tax avoidance legislation in Australia was not doing the job expected of it. The legal fraternity, or at least a vocal and active segment of it, was singularly intent on ignoring the legislative objectives of the anti-avoidance provisions, focusing instead on 'an excessively technical reading of the Act' (ibid.: 225) that would undermine the anti-avoidance intent. Grbich conceded weaknesses in the drafting of the provisions, indeed offered a redrafting in his paper, but, most importantly, argued eloquently for the legal profession to turn away from the divisive social role on which it had embarked. Grbich saw the rules created in response to tax avoidance as blatantly unfair, arising from a 'tax paradigm [that] is merely a massive atrophied example of . . . [a] doctrinaire due process emphasis taken to absurdity' (ibid.: 236). At the very least, Grbich's paper called for lawyers to consider the consequences of their actions in promulgating the tax avoidance industry which was to flourish in subsequent years, and to ask the following questions:

> How is it that a profession, which loudly claims that it impartially holds the scales of justice according to law between competing groups in our society, has got to the position where its institutions appear to favour only one part of society? How is it possible for tax institutions to frustrate collective decisions of the democratic process? How has it managed to get so constipated in its own complexity that it produces many norms which are in the interests of none of the participants in the political process and are often contrary to the values of the human beings who operate it? (Ibid.: 225)

Grbich's plea for soul searching among Australia's legal fraternity fell on deaf ears. Possibly the prejudices and beliefs that allowed legal institutions to set themselves up as an oppositional, alternative authority were well entrenched by the last quarter of the twentieth century. Robert Upfold, reviewing the situation in England a century ago, concluded that 'tax avoidance was considered a gentlemen's game and encouraged to a large extent by the judiciary' (1999: 98). Upfold moved through one hundred years and across oceans to note how Australia's Chief Justice Barwick defended tax avoidance measures in the nation's High Court in 1979: 'the citizen has every right to mould the transaction into which he is about to enter into a form which satisfies the requirement of the statute . . . The freedom to choose the form of transaction into which he shall enter is basic to the maintenance of a free society' (1979, 9 ATR 558, cited in Upfold 1999: 98).

Grbich's (1976) hopes that the legal profession would embrace a conception of itself as a leader that gave voice to the excluded players in the Australian community who were the victims of tax avoidance, that checked the power of the shrewd and powerful, that could recognize short-term self-interest, and prioritize the long-term interests of the collective were clearly not shared by the power brokers of the day. At the beginning of the twenty-first century, Grbich's challenge to the legal profession is no closer to being realized. In June 2001, a senior Australian barrister, John Cummins, appeared in court, having not filed an income tax return for 40 years – for most of his professional life. Cummins's reported statement in the *Sydney Morning Herald* (7 June 2001) suggested that social distancing had a part to play in how he protected himself from self-regulation in this matter: 'I kept as far away from the Income Tax Act as possible in my thoughts.' Grbich may have been right in attributing his profession's lack of interest in tax avoidance to 'unexamined intellectual baggage' (1976: 225). It seems equally plausible, however, that social distancing was a strategy used by the legal fraternity to practise defiance of the legislature's intent. At the very least, the emergence of the profession as an alternative tax authority seems to have been boosted by the capacity to keep one's personal legal obligations to pay tax 'blotted' from mind.

While social distancing with its concomitant blind spots is part of the story, ideology constitutes another major component. Ideology provides the rationale and underpins the legitimacy of the competing authorities of the tax office on one side and aggressive tax advisers on the other. By collecting taxes and using the revenue to redistribute resources, democratically elected governments act in the collective interest, 're-ordering the substantive incidents of private property' (Grbich 1976: 227) and overriding individual freedom of choice. While governments differ in how progressive a tax system they support, at the end of the day they all must attend to society's demands. Social goals of democratic societies involve balancing social justice, cooperation and equality (harmony values) against economic prosperity, social order, competition and efficiency (security values) (Braithwaite, V. 1994). Grbich sees engagement in tax avoidance as an expression of security values, as 'the assertion of individual power to undermine collective decisions' (1976: 227).

Blind spots and the philosophical divide are two factors shaping the alternative authorities' story. A third is knowledge dependence. The fact that not too many people understand tax law well enough to make decisions confidently (Kirchler 2007: 31–9) means that people need help to understand what they are supposed to do (Long and Swingen 1988). The evidence is that while they accept the tax office's role as an enforcer of the law, they turn elsewhere for support (Freiberg 1988; Braithwaite, V. et al. 2001). More often than not, they turn to tax agents and advisers (Tan 1999; Sakurai and Braithwaite 2003).

Research suggests that tax advisers and taxpayers in Australia share social space and that most taxpayers look for an honest, no-fuss tax adviser who will keep them out of trouble with the tax authority (Sakurai and Braithwaite 2003). Yet Australian taxpayers also believe that lawyers and tax advisers are among those professional groups who do not pay their fair share of tax (Braithwaite, V. et al. 2001) and are leaders on tax avoidance (Wallschutzky 1985). It appears that while most prefer to identify with honest taxpaying, Australians are only too aware of the possibility of manipulating law 'to legally avoid both control and penalties or stigma associated with outright crime' (McBarnet 1992: 56).

In summary, the capacity to avoid taxpaying responsibilities, preferably without breaking the law, has attracted a following (Coleman and Freeman 1997). Awareness of and attraction to this pathway has spawned the game-playing posture. The posture gains acceptability and sophistication under the auspices of alternative authorities exerting influence within and across sovereign states.

A Game of Mastery Undermining Democratic Governance

Whereas commitment, capitulation and resistance involve acceptance of the authority of the tax office, game playing, like disengagement, does not. Its appeal over disengagement in our individualistic society is not surprising. Game playing differs from disengagement in allowing individuals to transcend feelings of alienation and powerlessness. When individuals are in game-playing mode they are making an assault on the tax system and they expect to win. Game playing involves an appreciation of the intricacy of tax law and delights in finding ways to circumvent its intentions. Thus there is a commitment to law above and beyond that made by most citizens, but the commitment is to the literal reading of the rule, not to the social goals that the law is meant to serve. Game playing involves a rejection of the citizen role in favour of the individualistic role of a defiant winner.

Game playing is not unique to the taxpaying context. As the term implies, it will be found in any situation where playing with the law is rewarding for individuals or groups (McBarnet 2001; McBarnet and Whelan 1999). In the short term, game playing with authorities may yield positive results by educating and sharpening the skills of those charged with the responsibility of drafting legislation. But the costs are considerable. Once an authority has game playing in its backyard, it cannot allow itself to be too distant or aloof from those being regulated. Intelligence becomes vitally important to both sides as they try to outwit each other (Braithwaite, J. 2005).

While game playing may keep an authority on its toes, it is also capable of inflicting enormous social damage, as Grbich (1976) so powerfully reminded us. It is the very fact that the game is in play, not the winning or losing of the game, that threatens the heart of a regulatory authority.

Game playing is endless, bearing less and less relation to the problems that the legislature wants resolved, and focusing more and more on the technical details of the rules as they are created and re-created. Half a century ago, Bernstein (1955) observed these developments in regulatory institutions that were losing public support and legitimacy. The intricacies of the rule-making and rule-avoiding processes shut out generalists with a broader interest in problem resolution. Reversing or stopping the game is difficult because the game is so exclusionary: to understand the play one must have the technical competence to work outside the traditional institutional square.

Pulling these ideas together means that the greatest harm of game playing is to the democracy itself. Game players create a protected and privileged social vacuum for themselves that frees them from responsibility for the broader social consequences. Game playing is morally justified on grounds of individuals asserting their freedom. Passing on the tax burden to those less able to avoid it is tacitly endorsed as an acceptable practice. Exercising freedom in this way and thereby dominating the freedom of others will not sit well as a principle for developing tax policy within the broader regulatory community. There are good reasons why game players segment their activities from those of citizenship. Game playing jars with democratic goals and process. As such, it threatens the sustainability of the tax system at a fundamental level.

4. SUMMARY AND CONCLUSION

Conceptions of authority that assume citizens will adopt a 'your word is my command' response are becoming increasingly outmoded. The public is more aware of individual rights than ever before, is more able to express such rights, and to defend them when necessary. Furthermore, the pursuit of smaller government has lowered community confidence that government authorities will be there in the future to protect the interests of the public. Accompanying the realization that government can no longer provide the security and order it once did is cynicism about the political system and those who operate within it. In an environment where individuals are becoming increasingly liberated from the control of big government, a range of options emerges for dealing with authorities that seek to exert control. An important subset of these options coalesces around individuals giving and withdrawing cooperation in a way that is seen by others and themselves as acceptable and justifiable. These predispositions to cooperate or defy are referred to as motivational postures. Their measurement is described and validated in Chapter 4.

Attitudes to taxpaying are complex. On the one hand, paying tax can be coerced, it threatens one's material well-being, and if one does not comply, one's treatment is, from all accounts, highly punitive. On the other hand, paying tax is a way of acting upon feelings of responsibility for the well-being of the collective and signals that one is paying one's way and is law abiding. What is more, in a progressive tax system, paying tax is a responsibility that comes with acquiring economic stature in the community. If one is fortunate enough to be privileged in this way, one should be prepared to put a little more into the communal pot as a way of acknowledging the material, social and political infrastructure that has enabled one to prosper in the society. Considerations such as these, for and against, are widely discussed and debated. They are part of our shared discourse on tax, with each of us subscribing to these views to differing degrees, depending on circumstance and context.

Public ambivalence over what we think of taxation means that we have the capacity to change our minds as one argument becomes salient while another fades from consciousness. We have the options to commit, resist, capitulate, disengage and game-play. Which takes precedence depends on the signals we receive from tax authorities, from the government in which the authority is embedded, and from our individual interests. At all times, we should be mindful of how we use postures to reduce threat to ourselves.

Motivational posturing provides us with a comfortable social distance from authority. Greater social distance allows individuals and groups in society to unpick the legitimacy of legally constituted authority and create for themselves some space for defiance and non-compliance. Some social distance between citizens and authority is essential for a vibrant democracy. Too much social distance, however, can break down an authority's capacity to influence and persuade, and, in turn, be influenced by dialogue. The greater the distance, the less able we are to see the other's point of view and to find compromises.

Reading and understanding motivational postures can promote constructive dialogue and critical feedback in a compliance management system. An explanatory principle that can be of help in coming to terms with the social distancing actions of regulatees is our shared need to understand our world and find affirmation for ourselves within it. An authority that threatens the self is likely to push the regulatee away, increasing social distance. An authority that affirms the self is likely to draw the regulatee in, reducing social distance.

However, affirmation without censure of non-compliant actions would doom a regulatory system to failure. The imposition of law and its enforcement restricts the freedom of the individual. As a consequence, regulation of all kinds is bound to increase social distance for at least some in the population some of the time.

Regulatory pyramids accommodate motivational posturing by permitting regulators to manage social distance in a way that honours societal expectations for (a) respectful and inclusive treatment by authorities and (b) sound law and its effective enforcement. If set up through dialogue and consensus building, regulatory pyramids enable regulatory authorities to deliver on the firm and fair promise that so many of them make in their mission statements and through their codes of conduct. It also encourages compliance to occur at the level that it ought to occur. In a civilized society, people should base their compliance on soundly argued reasons that unfold into actions that they believe are right.

In cases where reasoning and persuading do not work, and we cannot see eye to eye on the laws that bind us, identification and sanctioning become the strategies waiting in the wings for use by regulators charged with the responsibility of making sure compliance objectives are met. Resorting to these strategies are second best, ideally to be used temporarily with individuals until a more deeply cooperative relationship can be established. At this stage, one regulatory principle stands above all others. Individuals who resist have a good chance of being brought back into the fold by timely action that involves respectful treatment and taking their concerns seriously.

The resources that a regulatory authority allocates to persuasion and education, to bridge building and social networking, or to sanctioning should reflect their reading of the motivational posturing that is occurring in the community as a whole. When a community's commitment is strong and resistance is low to an authority's policies, regulators are in a position to defend their traditional focus on gathering intelligence to help them catch non-compliers. When commitment is weak and resistance is high in the community, however, regulators need to adjust their priorities – dialogue, persuasion, revision of practices, and even changes to the law may be necessary to ensure that the regulatory culture remains supportive of the system.

As these decisions are being made, managing the next compliance crisis should not be allowed to drive out the bigger regulatory picture of responding in a way that will improve and build the authority's reputation for integrity in the community. Game playing may be the price that an authority pays for concentrating on catching the non-compliant, while disregarding consolidation of the law and building respect for the law. Law enforcement without a community-endorsed moral base is likely to promote a game-playing 'catch-me-if-you-can' regulatory culture.

The balance that an authority strikes among the different paths of influence (commitment, identification and sanctioning) has implications in the long term not just for the regulatory authority, but also for society at large. To focus on quick compliance wins, and prioritize identification and rewards and sanctions over commitment, brings its own risks. As we reflect on war crimes emanating from a regulatory philosophy of domination and obedience, such as we have seen in East Timor, Croatia and Serbia, Israel and Palestine, the World Trade Center, and Iraq, we are reminded that to relinquish talk and dissent, sound arguments and reasonableness as the basic building blocks for effective governance is foolishly disrespectful of the lessons of our past.

NOTES

1. To name but a few directly relevant to the central theme of this book: Iris Young (1990, 2000), John Dryzek (1990), Anne Phillips (1991, 1999), Jane Mansbridge (1996) and John Braithwaite and Philip Pettit (1990).
2. Thomas Hobbes in *Leviathan* (1651) points out the disorder and violence that come from having competing powers struggling against each other for supremacy. A Leviathan state forces peaceable settlements of differences, maintains order and offers security to citizens by assuming a position of dominance over the competing powers (Hobbes 1968).
3. This is not unique to taxation. Sherman (2003) has observed the neglect of emotions in policy development and has called for a new paradigm of emotionally intelligent justice.
4. Commitment and capitulation were originally called accommodation and capture respectively. Accommodation took account of innovation in nursing home practices as well as conformity to government standards. Capture acknowledged the way in which some nursing home directors acquiesced to government authority without a deep understanding of purposes and goals. Changing the names of these postures brought them in line with McBarnet's (2003) differentiation of committed and capitulative compliance that she contrasts with creative compliance (McBarnet 2003).
5. The development of this model for the ATO took place within the Cash Economy Task Force (1998) drawing on the responsive regulation work of Ian Ayres and John Braithwaite (1992) and the motivational postures work of Valerie Braithwaite (1995). The idea of bringing together these two bodies of research in a regulatory pyramid was initiated by Jenny Job.

4. Measuring motivational postures and defiance

> [M]any forms of behavior are determined by belief systems consisting of functionally interrelated self-conceptions, . . . values, attitudes, cognitions about behavior, and cognitions about other people's cognitions and behavior.
>
> Milton Rokeach 1973: 338

Motivational postures represent summary statements of how individuals think about their engagement with regulatory authorities. They are also discursive tools. They are relatively coherent, having been rehearsed, shared and fine-tuned through engagement and narration with others in the regulatory culture. In this chapter, motivational postures towards the tax system and tax authority are measured, tracked and linked to non-tax-related cultural markers, specifically social demographic characteristics, values and views on the state of the democracy. One of the important findings of this chapter is that views about taxation are connected with views about how we relate to each other and our democracy, confirming both classic and recent arguments about the cultural dimension of taxation practices (Schmölders 1970; Mumford 2002). The empirical analyses of this chapter also address two central questions that lie at the heart of the motivational postures thesis: (a) do the postures adequately represent social distance from the tax authority as presumed? and (b) are these postures malleable?

MEASURING MOTIVATIONAL POSTURES

Before describing the procedures used to measure motivational postures, a note of explanation is required as to why the departure from scientific parsimony – why the 'invention' of a new concept when so many related concepts (e.g. social identity, interests, social distance, coping strategies and justice perceptions) have a firm foothold in the social science literature.

Because motivational postures chunk together a number of concepts that have traditionally been treated discretely, posturing represents a novel level of conceptual abstraction. The justification for 'chunking' is both theoretical and practical. We need to better understand, predict and manage the ways in which individuals and institutions shape each other. In empirical analyses of this process, we have traditionally called into play myriad discretely theorized and often competing concepts.[1] This body of work continues to grow and provide valuable insights from a scholarly perspective. However, for those who actually bear the responsibility for managing and redesigning regulatory systems, some level of integration of social science wisdom is required. The focus on motivational postures in this work represents one such modest effort. The practical and theoretical usefulness of this initiative begins to be addressed in this book, bearing in mind that replication, generalization and development remain important questions for the future.

If motivational postures are accessible to the individuals who hold them and are shared with others, it makes sense to measure them through a self-report survey methodology. This does not preclude other methodologies. It is highly likely that some individuals will have a wide range of postures, while others have a more restricted repertoire. Qualitative interviews are likely to yield valuable insights into the posturing repertoire (see Harris and McCrae 2005; Cartwright 2009; Braithwaite, J. et al. 2007). This question, however, is not one that is addressed here. Instead, the focus is on measuring and understanding the postures of commitment, capitulation, resistance, disengagement and game playing, and testing their promise as useful analytical devices for both scholars and practitioners. Defiance may involve vocal opposition (resistance), withdrawal (disengagement) or a challenge to authority with a view to winning (game playing). Resistance represents the type of defiance that seeks attention and respect from authority, and change in the way authority uses its power. Disengagement and game playing represent defiance that dismisses, sidesteps and rejects authority.

Motivational postures were measured by asking survey participants how they felt about 29 statements, each representative of one of the postures. Respondents replied using a five-point strongly disagree through strongly agree rating scale. The statements were based on those that had been effective measures in previous studies. Additional statements were derived from open-ended discussions with people about the tax system and the tax office. In particular, the game-playing posture was measured by collecting statements from people about their orientation to the tax system. In these early discussions, it was unclear whether or not gaming the system was a pleasure or a curse for the taxpayers involved. In time, it became apparent that, for game players, voicing discontent with the system was unnecessary. Game playing was the posture of those whose sights were firmly set on winning in their interactions with the tax system. The voice of discontent belonged to those who had lost or feared losing the competition.

The statements that were considered to be satisfactory indicators of each of the postures are listed in Table 4.1. A brief description of the statistical analyses that supported their being compiled in this way will be provided shortly. First, the context for the collection of these data is outlined.

Table 4.1 Statements representing the motivational postures of commitment, capitulation, resistance, disengagement and game playing

Commitment (M = 3.85, SD = 0.54, alpha reliability coefficient = 0.82, homogeneity ratio = 0.43)

Paying tax is the right thing to do.
Paying tax is a responsibility that should be willingly accepted by all Australians.
I feel a moral obligation to pay my tax.
Paying my tax ultimately advantages everyone.
I think of tax paying as helping the government do worthwhile things.
Overall, I pay my tax with good will.
I resent paying tax. (reversed)
I accept responsibility for paying my fair share of tax.

Capitulation (M = 3.40, SD = 0.54, alpha reliability coefficient = 0.63, homogeneity ratio = 0.27)

No matter how cooperative or uncooperative the tax office is, the best policy is to always be cooperative with them.
If you cooperate with the tax office, they are likely to be cooperative with you.
Even if the tax office finds that I am doing something wrong, they will respect me in the long run as long as I admit my mistakes.
The tax office is encouraging to those who have difficulty meeting their obligations through no fault of their own.
The tax system may not be perfect, but it works well enough for most of us.

Resistance (M = 3.18, SD = 0.54, alpha reliability coefficient = 0.68, homogeneity ratio = 0.31)

As a society, we need more people willing to take a stand against the tax office.
It's important not to let the tax office push you around.
The tax office is more interested in catching you for doing the wrong thing, than helping you do the right thing.
It's impossible to satisfy the tax office completely.
Once the tax office has you branded as a non-compliant taxpayer, they will never change their mind.
If you don't cooperate with the tax office, they will get tough with you.

Table 4.1 (continued)

Disengagement (M = 2.31, SD = 0.52, alpha reliability coefficient = 0.64, homogeneity ratio = 0.27)
I don't really know what the tax office expects of me and I'm not about to ask.
I don't care if I am not doing the right thing by the tax office.
If I find out that I am not doing what the tax office wants, I'm not going to lose any sleep over it.
I personally don't think that there is much the tax office can do to me to make me pay tax if I don't want to.
If the tax office gets tough with me, I will become uncooperative with them.
Game playing (M = 2.42, SD = 0.62, alpha reliability coefficient = 0.69, homogeneity ratio = 0.32)
I enjoy talking to friends about loopholes in the tax system.
I like the game of finding the grey area of tax law.
I enjoy the challenge of minimizing the tax I have to pay.
I enjoy spending time working out how changes in the tax system will affect me.
The tax office respects taxpayers who can give them a run for their money.

Note: Respondents were asked to rate each statement on a five-point scale from strongly disagree (1) to strongly agree (5).

THE DATABASE: NATIONAL RANDOM SURVEYS IN 2000, 2002 AND 2005

Between June and December 2000, a national survey was conducted by the Centre for Tax System Integrity at the Australian National University (for details see Braithwaite, V. 2001 and Braithwaite, V. et al. 2001). A stratified random sample of 7754 persons was selected from the publicly available electoral rolls (Australia has compulsory voting). The 'Community Hopes, Fears and Actions Survey' was sent to each randomly selected person, together with a letter explaining the intent of the study and a stamped, addressed envelope for return of the completed questionnaire. Two reminder cards were sent at two- to three-week intervals. After five weeks, a second questionnaire was posted to non-respondents, again followed by two reminder cards (for details of the methodology see Mearns and Braithwaite 2001).

An in-scope sample was compiled by excluding cases no longer living at the address nominated in the electoral roll, and those reporting disability or failing health. Of the in-scope sample, 29 per cent completed and returned the survey, providing 2040 cases for further analysis. While this response rate was lower than that obtained with two companion surveys conducted at approximately the same time (the 'Social Citizenship Survey' produced a 45 per cent response rate (Job 2002), and the 'Graduates' Hopes, Visions and Actions Survey' produced a 33 per cent response rate (Ahmed 2005)), there were reasons for expecting such an outcome. A number of researchers have commented on the way in which questionnaires with a tax focus 'dampen' the enthusiasm of respondents. The general consensus appears to be that a tax questionnaire is likely to yield response rates at the lower end of the spectrum, at best around the 30 per cent mark (Kirchler 1999; Pope et al. 1993; Wallschutzky 1996; Webley et al. 2002).

In spite of the somewhat low response rate, the sample appeared to be surprisingly robust against suspected sources of bias (Mearns and Braithwaite 2001). The biases that were detected pointed to an overrepresentation of people with a post-secondary education, an overrepresentation of people in occupations involving administrative and written tasks – people who were probably more comfortable with a detailed paper-and-pencil questionnaire, and an underrepresentation of younger age groups (18 to 25 years) who traditionally are difficult to recruit for self-completion surveys.

Between November 2001 and February 2002, a follow-up national survey called the 'Australian Tax System: Fair or Not Survey' was conducted. This survey was sent to those who took part in the earlier survey, to a random sample of 2000 people who had not responded to the earlier survey, and to a new random sample of 3000 people drawn from the publicly available electoral rolls. Responses were received from 1161 of the 2040 respondents involved in the earlier survey (a 69 per cent retention rate when respondents who were deceased, who could not take part because of disability or illness, or who had changed address were excluded), from 195 of the 2000 non-respondents from the earlier survey (13 per cent of in-scope respondents), and from 970 of the 3000 new respondents (38 per cent of in-scope respondents). Completed questionnaires were received from 2374 respondents (41 per cent of in-scope respondents).

Between June and September 2005, letters followed by questionnaires were sent to 2740 people who had completed either the 2000 survey or the 2002 survey or both. They were asked to complete a final survey called 'How Fair? How Effective? Collection and Use of Taxation in Australia'. A total of 1146 respondents returned completed questionnaires, yielding an in-scope response rate of 51 per cent. As in 2002, letters and a shortened questionnaire were sent to a random sample of 2943 respondents who had not replied to us in either 2000 or 2002. Completed questionnaires were received from 260 respondents (12 per cent of in-scope respondents).

The strategy of following up non-respondents from 2000 and 2002 and collecting responses from at least some members of this group on the third survey enabled 'least willing' participants to be compared with participants who were 'most willing' in that they took part in surveys in 2000, 2002 and 2005. A sample of 260 least willing respondents replied in 2005 to a shortened questionnaire after having ignored requests in 2000 and 2002 to reply to letters and questionnaires. The most willing were the 511 respondents who constituted the three-wave panel sample for subsequent analyses. A comparison of the responses of the least and most willing provided insight into the kinds of sample biases that would be taken on board when analyses were restricted to the panel sample of 511 respondents. Those in the panel sample were significantly more likely to be older and more educated. In terms of the motivational postures, the panel sample was higher on both commitment and disengagement, and lower on capitulation and resistance. While these differences were statistically significant, they were not substantial. The panel sample provided a satisfactory cross-section of responses for testing causal relations between the central concepts represented in Figure 1.1.[2]

RECOGNIZING MOTIVATIONAL POSTURES

Finding out if individuals recognized themselves in the survey statements representing the motivational postures was the first issue addressed. The assumption made in previous chapters is that individuals can describe themselves in terms of the concepts of commitment, capitulation, resistance, disengagement and game playing. If this is the case, we should be able to identify empirically the statements that articulate each posture, and each set of statements should be relatively independent of the others. This would allow for the presumption that each of us can mix and match the postures in any way that we want.

Translating this into the data-analytic context means establishing that there are high correlations among items measuring the same posture and low correlations with items measuring different postures. For example, the intercorrelations of the commitment items should be higher, on average, than the correlations that the commitment items have with items that represent capitulation, resistance, disengagement and game playing. If this is the case, we can conclude that there is coherence in the way people respond to the items that represent commitment. What is more, knowing scores on commitment does not determine scores on other postures. Other postures need to be measured in their own right, and these postures should similarly satisfy the above criteria of coherence and independence.

Two statistical procedures were used to put these ideas to the test. The first involved calculating alpha reliability coefficients and homogeneity ratios for the hypothesized motivational posture scales. The alpha reliability coefficients ranged from 0.63 to 0.82 (see Table 4.1). The homogeneity ratios (Scott 1968) for the motivational postures were all satisfactory, ranging from 0.27 to 0.43 (see Table 4.1). The intercorrelations among the scales were lower, ranging from 0.13 to 0.38 in absolute value, supporting the idea that the motivational postures are not only coherent but can be empirically differentiated from one another. Of significance, however, is the fact that the correlations between the scales are not negligible, with six of the ten correlations reaching or exceeding 0.30. Some of the postures appear to coexist in a substantial proportion of people.

The second statistical procedure, factor analysis, was used to provide a tougher test of whether the postures could be cleanly separated from one another. A five-factor rotated solution of the 29 items confirmed the existence of postures of commitment, capitulation, resistance, disengagement and game playing.[3] The principal components analysis with a varimax rotation accounted for 46 per cent of variance in the item set. The statements listed under each posture in Table 4.1 were the highest-loading items in the factor analysis.[4] On the basis of this analysis, the five postures can be regarded as relatively distinctive, and we can conclude that people respond to the postures with coherence and consistency.

But what of the overlap among the postures noted previously? Before resolving this issue, let us turn our attention to the question of the validity of the motivational posture scales. Testing their validity could shed light on the question of how much importance should be attached to the interdependence that we have noted.

VALIDITY OF THE MOTIVATIONAL POSTURE SCALES

At face value, the motivational posture scales should resonate with taxpayers and citizens – they should be able to identify with the statements we were placing before them. To gain some insight into whether or not this was the case, the levels of endorsement in the community for each posture were examined. The percentage of the 'Community Hopes, Fears and Actions' sample agreeing that they could see themselves in each of the postures is represented graphically in Figure 4.1.

As expected in a democracy, the dominant postures were those reflecting

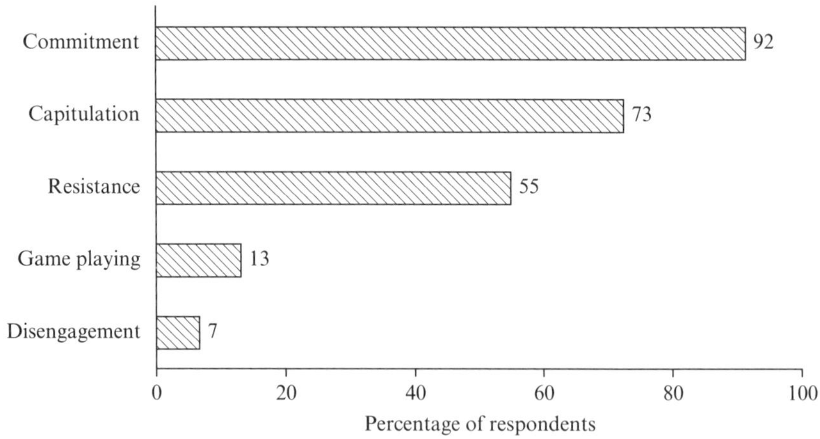

Note: This graph represents the percentage endorsing the posture, that is, the percentage with scale scores greater than the rating scale midpoint of 3.00. Scale scores were calculated by summing responses to the items in the scale and dividing by the number of items.

Figure 4.1 Percentage of respondents displaying the postures of commitment, capitulation, resistance, disengagement and game playing in 2000

a positive orientation to authority, that is, commitment and capitulation. Most taxpayers, either willingly or with resignation, accepted the authority of the tax office and the obligation to respond cooperatively to its requests. Taxpayers generally supported the goals of the tax system and were prepared to go along with the processes involved in collecting tax.

Next most widely endorsed of the postures was resistance, again a sign that the democracy was working as it should. A sizeable proportion of the sample was willing to question the tax office openly and be critical of the way in which it conducted itself. While any regulatory authority is likely to greet the posture of resistance with either defensiveness or antagonism, such negativity on the part of authority is not justified. In a democracy, resistance is much-needed feedback. When the posture of resistance is displayed by at least half the taxpayers (most of whom have already indicated commitment to the system), a signal is being sent to authority that all is not as it should be, most particularly that the authority is not meeting its obligations satisfactorily to the community. As reported in the previous chapter, research findings suggest that resistance subsides when an authority takes responsibility for improving its performance. Resistance does not necessarily mean that the public does not share the goals of the regulatory authority in principle. Resistance is more likely to reflect misunderstanding, a mutual loss of trust and respect, and little responsiveness from the authority to rectify the situation.

The motivational postures that are least pervasive in the community are disengagement and game playing. Both postures are regarded as reflecting a degree of generalized contempt for taxation; to use the language of previous research, disenchantment with goals, not merely processes (Braithwaite, V. 1995). Disengagement is the posture that is the least commonly endorsed, and also the one that on the basis of past research appears to be most difficult for regulators to manage (Braithwaite, V. et al. 1994). Those who choose to disengage cut themselves off psychologically from attempts at persuasion or influence. In contrast, game playing demands engagement, but not in a way welcomed by authority. Game players remain a small segment of the population, probably because the resources required to use the letter of the law to circumvent the spirit of the law are accessed through relatively elite groups (Braithwaite, J. 2005).

As tax avoidance schemes become increasingly available and acceptable to the general public through mass marketing, the temptation to gameplay is expected to increase. In time, game playing is likely to lead to the redesign of the regulatory institution itself, and will possibly threaten the high levels of commitment and capitulation. But for the moment, these motivational postures seem to fit with expectations of the relative popularity of different kinds of responsiveness to authority, particularly a tax authority, in a politically stable Western democratic society. Commitment and capitulation dominate in the population, resistance is the next most prevalent (although substantially behind the front-running postures), and disengagement and game playing are minority codes for responding to taxation demands. In terms of face validity, the postures seem to be doing their job.

The next question addresses validity at a deeper level: is there evidence to support the claim that the postures reflect social distance? In Chapter 2, social distance from an authority was defined in terms of (a) positive or negative evaluation of the authority and (b) readiness to defer to the wishes of the authority.

CONSTRUCT VALIDITY ON POSITIVE OR NEGATIVE EVALUATION

In order to test the assertion that the motivational postures measure the degree to which respondents evaluated the tax authority positively or negatively, two measures were selected from the 'Community Hopes, Fears and Actions Survey', one focusing on the tax system, the other on the administration of the tax office.[5] First, respondents were asked how much they wanted to see the tax system abolished, and second, how good a job they thought the tax office was doing. The following hypotheses were tested by correlating the least socially distant postures (commitment and capitulation) and the most socially distant postures (resistance, disengagement and game playing) with attitudes to the tax office and tax system:

Hypothesis 4.1(a) Respondents who rejected the idea of abolishing the tax system and praised the job that tax officers were doing were expected to adopt the less socially distant postures that placed them close to the authority, that is, the postures of commitment and capitulation.

Hypothesis 4.1(b) Respondents who favoured abolishing the tax system and were not satisfied with the job the tax office was doing were expected to identify with the more socially distant postures of resistance, disengagement and game playing.

The results reported in Table 4.2 show support for these hypotheses. The postures of commitment and capitulation accompany perceptions that the tax office is doing a good job and that the tax system should not be abolished. The results for the postures of resistance, disengagement and game playing are generally in the opposite direction. Resistance, disengagement and game playing were all associated with a desire to abolish the tax system. The tax office was not doing a good job in the view of those with postures of resistance and disengagement.[6]

Table 4.2 Pearson product–moment correlation coefficients between motivational postures and the social distance indicators of evaluation

Social distance: evaluation	Commitment	Capitulation	Resistance	Disengagement	Game playing
The tax office does its job well	0.36	0.56	−0.44	−0.17	0.08
We should abolish the tax system	−0.39	−0.15	0.27	0.26	0.17

Note: Positive or negative evaluation is measured by asking respondents to use a rating scale from strongly disagree (1) to strongly agree (5) in relation to each statement. 'The tax office does its job well' had a mean of 3.26 and a standard deviation of 0.83. 'We should abolish the tax system' had a mean of 2.26 and a standard deviation of 1.01.
All correlations are significant at the 0.001 level.

CONSTRUCT VALIDITY ON DEFERRING TO THE AUTHORITY

The second test for demonstrating that the motivational postures measure social distance is to find out how well they reflect willingness to defer to authority. Taxpayers were asked about where they would ideally go for help with their tax return. Around three-quarters of Australian taxpayers use a tax agent or tax practitioner (77 per cent in 1999–2000, Australian Taxation Office 2002b: 10). Tax practitioners and taxpayers of like minds appear to find each other (Karlinsky and Bankman 2002; Sakurai and Braithwaite 2003). For those unwilling to defer or be cooperative, the first port of call is likely to be an aggressive tax practitioner or, at the very least, a shrewd tax minimizer. In contrast, those who wish to cooperate will favour a tax practitioner who will provide advice that is in accord with the intention of the law. Willingness to defer was inferred from seeking an honest no-risk practitioner; reluctance to defer was inferred from seeking a cautious minimizing or aggressive tax practitioner.

In the 'Community Hopes, Fears and Actions Survey', respondents were asked to imagine themselves in the market looking for a tax practitioner and consider the qualities that they would be looking for. They were then asked to rate a set of items describing each type of ideal practitioner (Sakurai and Braithwaite 2003). Those looking for an honest, low-risk, no-fuss service responded favourably to the following items: (a) someone who does it honestly with minimum fuss; and (b) someone who does not take risks and claims only for things that are clearly legitimate. Those who were clever at finding ways to minimize tax while avoiding trouble with the tax office were likely to endorse these items: (a) someone who knows their way around the system to minimize the tax I have to pay; and (b) someone who will take advantage of grey areas of the law on my behalf. Finally, those who reduced their tax payments through creative accounting and aggressive tax planning were positively disposed to the following: (a) someone who can deliver on aggressive tax planning; (b) a creative accountant; and (c) someone who is well networked and knows what the tax office is checking at any particular time.

The following hypotheses were tested by correlating the least socially distant postures (commitment and capitulation) and the most socially distant postures (resistance, disengagement and game playing) with preferences for an honest no-risk practitioner, a cautious minimizing practitioner and an aggressive tax practitioner:

Hypothesis 4.2 (a) Respondents who rejected the idea of a cautious minimizing or an aggressive tax practitioner and favoured an honest no-risk

Table 4.3 Pearson product–moment correlation coefficients between motivational postures and social distance indicators of willingness to defer

Social distance: willingness to defer	Commitment	Capitulation	Resistance	Disengagement	Game playing
Honest no-risk practitioner	0.22	0.13	NS	−0.23	−0.15
Cautious minimizing practitioner	−0.18	−0.08	0.24	0.15	0.18
Aggressive tax practitioner	−0.17	NS	0.23	0.15	0.33

Note: Willingness to defer is measured by asking respondents what priority they would place on particular qualities in a tax agent or tax adviser – low (1), medium (2), high (3) or top (4). The qualities were grouped into scales. Relevant scores were summed and divided by the number of items in the scale. The honest no-risk practitioner scale had a mean of 3.27, standard deviation of 0.63 and alpha reliability coefficient of 0.75. The cautious minimizing practitioner scale had a mean of 2.33, standard deviation of 0.78 and alpha reliability coefficient of 0.70. The aggressive tax practitioner scale had a mean of 2.22, standard deviation of 0.79 and alpha reliability coefficient of 0.79.
All correlations are significant at the 0.001 level with the exception of those marked not significant (NS).

practitioner were expected to adopt the less socially distant postures that placed them close to the authority, that is, the postures of commitment and capitulation.

Hypothesis 4.2(b) Respondents who favoured a cautious minimizing or an aggressive tax practitioner and rejected the idea of an honest no-risk practitioner were expected to identify with the more socially distant postures of resistance, disengagement and game playing.

From the results in Table 4.3, we see the positive postures of commitment and capitulation accompanying a preference for an honest no-risk practitioner. Aggressive tax planning and cautious minimizing, on the other hand, were the most popular choices among those displaying the negative postures of resistance, disengagement and game playing. These results confirm expectations that motivational postures reflect that aspect of social distance that we might call willingness to defer to authority.

Two correlations in Table 4.3 are not significant, and therefore do not fit the expected pattern. Those high on capitulation tended to be neither for nor against having a practitioner who specialized in aggressive tax planning, while those high on resistance tended to be neither for nor against having an honest no-risk adviser. In both cases, there are likely to be conflicting pulls. Capitulation is likely to involve fear of the system should one be caught, along with flirtation with the thought of a risky adviser. Resistance is likely to involve a degree of defiant bravado but also a desire not to be on the wrong side of the law. These conflicting reactions to the issue of deference to the tax office would explain non-significant correlations.

The absence of significant findings in these two instances does not undermine the case for interpreting the motivational postures as indicators of social distance of one kind (liking) or another (deference) from the tax authority. Overall, the motivational postures correlate in predictable ways with measures of liking for taxation and willingness to defer to the tax authority's power (see Tables 4.2 and 4.3). We can conclude that the motivational postures tell us something about the social distance that individuals place between the authority and themselves.

HIGHER-ORDER CONSTRUCT VALIDITY

So far, we have found support for interpreting motivational postures as indices of social distance: the postures correlate with variables that reflect social distance. There is also evidence of significant correlations among the motivational postures. The next question for empirical analysis is whether a single social distance ordering is implied along one dimension from the most sympathetic to the least sympathetic posture. One way of testing this hypothesis is by factor-analysing people's scores on commitment, capitulation, resistance, disengagement and game playing. The results of this analysis appear in Table 4.4.

A principal components analysis with varimax rotation produced two clear factors, together explaining 65 per cent of the variance in the scale scores.[7] Finding two separate factors in this analysis was the first statistical evidence that emerged from motivational postures research to support the distinction between resistant and dismissive defiance. Liking for an authority and willingness to defer to an authority appeared to be two separate dimensions of social distance, contributing to two different kinds of defiance with different etiologies.

The definition of the first factor was provided by commitment and capitulation at one pole and resistance at the other. Commitment and capitulation are compatible in so far as they are most likely to coexist in individuals. Where they are strong, the posture of resistance is less likely to be found. The factor might be described as the degree to which the

Table 4.4 Results of a principal components analysis with varimax rotation on five motivational posture scales

Motivational postures	Factor 1 Cooperation–Resistance	Factor 2 Dismissiveness
Capitulation	**0.81**	0.32
Commitment	**0.72**	−0.20
Resistance	**−0.68**	0.26
Game playing	0.05	**0.88**
Disengagement	−0.47	**0.64**

Note: The criteria for factor rotation were eigenvalues greater than or equal to 1.0 and the scree test. Both indicated a two-factor solution.

individual evaluates the tax authority in positive or negative terms. Factor 1 is labelled *Cooperation–Resistance* and appears to correspond to the traditional attitude to authority that underlies much of the research described in the previous chapter.

On Factor 1, authority is accepted: the variation relates to whether or not the authority is regarded favourably and sympathetically or unfavourably and critically. On the second factor, the authority of the tax office is open to question. Whereas Factor 1 reflects the degree of liking, Factor 2 reflects the degree to which status is conceded to the tax authority. Factor 2 is defined primarily by the motivational postures of disengagement and game playing. The feature that is distinctive about these two postures is the way in which the authority of the tax office is dismissed as being 'absent', or for all practical purposes, not effectively in the business of regulating activity. Those displaying disengagement and game playing adopt a position in the regulatory culture where they operate outside the controls of the regulatory institution. Those rejecting disengagement and game playing are subservient to authority looking for leadership and guidance. Factor 2 is labelled *Dismissiveness.*

The emergence of this factor in the analysis highlights the dangers of a regulatory institution losing its capacity to influence regulatees. In particular, those who are alienated from the system, referred to here as the disengaged, need not remain powerless at the margins of regulatory culture. Those who are disengaged simply need to find a way of successfully challenging the regulatory institution. In the domain of taxation, the successful challenge is encapsulated by the posture of game playing.

At this point, the question is whether we need to measure five motivational postures, or whether we should be content to measure the two higher-order dimensions of *Cooperation–Resistance* and *Dismissiveness*. The principal components analysis reported in Table 4.4 provides justification for combining the scales to form two supra-posture measures.

The answer is probably that we need to measure both motivational postures and supra-postures. Which will be most useful depends on the situation and the question being asked.[8] For purposes of understanding defiance, particularly the differentiation of resistant and dismissive defiance, the supra-postures are attractive options. With this in mind, two new scales were formed: *Resistance(–Cooperation)*, or *Resistance* for short, and *Dismissiveness*. The commitment, capitulation and resistance scales were combined after rescoring items such that low scores indicated cooperation and high scores resistance. Responses to the disengagement and game-playing items were combined to produce scores from low through high on *Dismissiveness*. We will return to these supra-posture scales at the end of the chapter. For the analyses in the next section, however, attention will remain focused on the original five postures and how they vary across time and across different groups in the population.

THE RELIABILITY OF THE POSTURE SCALES

Motivational postures have been conceptualized as dynamic phenomena that are responsive to the changing demands of a tax authority as well as to the changing role of citizens in relation to government. But does this mean they are will-o'-the-wisp phenomena that appear and disappear in the context of scientific enquiry almost at random? Ideally, the profile of the motivational postures of commitment, capitulation, resistance, disengagement and game playing measured in situation A should bear a strong resemblance to the profile observed in situation B, if situations A and B are sufficiently similar.

The opportunity to test for stability of the motivational postures came about in 2002 when 1161 respondents who had completed the survey in 2000 took part in the second wave of the study. Over the 18-month interval between the first and second surveys, there had been changes in the tax system, most notably the introduction of a goods-and-services tax (the GST). In one sense, there was reason to expect change in motivational posturing over this period; in another sense, not so much. The government had been returned to office on the understanding that a GST would be introduced, and at the end of the day the implementation of the GST was handled without disaster (Editorial, *The Australian Financial Review*, 11 November 2005).

To find out how stable the postures were over time, two strategies were used. First, attention focused on whether the postures strengthened or weakened in the group of taxpayers from 2000 to 2002. Mean scores were compared for the 1036 respondents who could be identified as completing both the 2000 and 2002 surveys. A statistically significant increase in commitment was found from an average score of 3.89 to 3.97, along with a statistically significant decrease in game playing from 2.39 to 2.29. The other postures were stable. This marked some, but not substantial, change in posturing over an 18-month period.

As the group increased or reduced its displays of a particular kind of posture over time, a separate question is whether or not individuals maintained their relative position. This second test used a correlation analysis to find out about the stability of the relative standing of individuals on each of the postures. The question was whether those scoring high (low) on a particular posture in 2000 continued to be just as high (low) scorers in 2002, relatively speaking. Correlations were calculated between scores in 2000 and scores in 2002 for each of the motivational postures. The strongest coefficients were found for commitment ($r = 0.63$) and resistance ($r = 0.60$), followed by game playing ($r = 0.56$), capitulation ($r = 0.54$) and disengagement ($r = 0.53$).

The stability of these coefficients over 18 months was impressive. But could it be that they were too stable to be useful? Were the measures too insensitive to detect change as individuals 'danced' their postures in response to the demands and enforcement practices of the tax authority? The answer may be that the authority, being a large, complex bureaucracy, is not able to change its demands and *modus operandi* too quickly or often, in which case taxpayers would not have any reason to change their posturing en masse from 2000 to 2002. But this explanation needs to be put to a further empirical test.

A time gap of five years provided a more robust test of the problem of measurement insensitivity. In 2000 to 2002, with the introduction of the GST, the focus was on education and persuasion; but by 2005, publicly announced enforcement actions and 'crackdowns' were under way (ABC Television, 24 July 2005; Australian and New Zealand Banking Group 2004; *Moore Tax News* 2005; *Sydney Morning Herald* 8 October 2005; *The Age* 16 August 2005). Peter Nicholson's cartoon for *The Australian* newspaper, 24 September 2003 captured the change of climate post-tax reform as the tax authority moved to a more enforcement-oriented mode (see Figure 4.2).

A comparison of the 583 respondents who could be identified as completing both the 2000 and the 2005 surveys showed change in the mean scores of all postures over the five years, except capitulation. Commitment decreased from 3.90 to 3.76 and resistance increased from 3.16 to 3.21. Disengagement fell from 2.29 to 2.22, as did game playing from 2.38 to 2.31. These findings were consistent with a strengthening of the ATO's enforcement activities after the GST had been bedded down (Roche 2006) and of a concerted effort to rein in investments in mass-marketed tax avoidance schemes that had mushroomed in popularity (Murphy 2003a; Braithwaite, J. 2005).

Source: Nicholson (www.nicholsoncartoons.com.au).

Figure 4.2 Cartoon from The Australian *newspaper*

The relative strength of the postures of individuals in 2000 was carried through to 2005. The correlations were a little weaker than those reported for the 2000 to 2002 period, but not markedly so. Those who were more committed in 2000 also tended to be more committed in 2005 ($r = 0.57$), followed by resistance ($r = 0.56$), game playing ($r = 0.52$), disengagement ($r = 0.48$), and capitulation ($r = 0.46$).

Taxation motivational postures were informative in tracking changes in the way in which the Australian population positioned themselves *vis-à-vis* the tax authority. The changes were meaningful when the public pronouncements of the ATO over this period were considered. The postures changed en masse in response to major shifts in the enforcement message of the tax authority. These data suggest that the motivational postures were sufficiently sensitive to track the ways in which the Australian public aligned themselves and then moved away from the tax authority over time. Such fluctuation is important if one adheres to the basic proposition that government should be responsive to the people, and the people to government. Motivational postures provide the signal: 'You need to listen.'

Along with evidence of the group reducing and increasing its social distance at various times is evidence that people tended to keep fairly close to their ranked position in the group, what we might think of as their relative position in the pack. This means that any one of us could have become more resistant to the tax authority over the five years of the study, but our resistance relative to those around us is likely to stay much the same. What has happened is that we have all become more resistant together. Thus those who were most (least) resistant in 2000 were likely to be the most (least) resistant in 2005 although their absolute levels were much higher in 2005 than in 2000.

At this point, the meaning of 'dynamic' needs tailoring to this research context. The dynamic relationship that was envisaged earlier was one in which people would be 'dancing', showing relatively high resistance at one point in time, and relatively low resistance at another, depending on how the tax office was affecting their lives. Clearly this movement across the range of motivational posturing for each individual depending on their experience and circumstances was not borne out by the data. The relatively high levels of stability suggest two interpretations about motivational postures in the tax context. First, they are remarkably stable because the actual interaction that individual taxpayers have with the tax office is remarkably stable (and limited). Second, the consistency we are observing in motivational postures implies some set of enduring beliefs or worldviews holding postures in place: perhaps the anchor for the postures is basic values, or beliefs about political systems, or location in the social structure (Rokeach 1968, 1973). These two not incompatible explanations for the stability of motivational postures in the tax context are considered below.

ENGAGING WITH THE TAX AUTHORITY: THE AUSTRALIAN EXPERIENCE

Most Australians pay income tax and, if they are wage and salary earners, have tax deducted from their pay automatically. At the same time, those earning more than a threshold level (A$6000 per year at the time this research was conducted) must lodge an annual income tax return. Individuals declare the income they have received in the past financial year and they claim deductions against their taxable income. More often than not, Australians engage in this self-assessment process with the expectation of receiving an annual tax refund. In the 'Community Hopes, Fears and Actions Survey', respondents were asked to consider the tax returns that they had lodged over the preceding four years: 72 per cent were owed money by the tax office on at least two of the four occasions (Braithwaite, V. et al. 2001).

Thus the major 'interaction' with the tax office involves lodging the annual income tax return, with the response from the tax office being either a tax refund, or an invoice, or an amended assessment. The amended assessment informs the taxpayer that the tax office has detected an anomaly or error in the self-assessed return. The taxpayer is informed of money owing, interest and possibly a penalty. If the taxpayer wishes to contest the amended assessment, he/she may do so in writing, and through this process, the amended assessment may be revised.

The inference that can be drawn from this is that the annual exchange between the tax office and taxpayer is either routinized, resulting in limited surprise, or adversarial, with taxpayers being put on the defensive, deciding whether to pay up or fight back. In most cases, however, the exchange will be uneventful. Thus it may be that the interactions between the tax office and the community are so minimal that little happens to dislodge the motivational postures of most individuals from one year to the next. That said, undoubtedly hidden in the samples who completed the 2000, 2002 and 2005 surveys is a proportion of Australians who have more extensive interaction with tax officials and who may have experienced the full gamut of postures over the period of their involvement.

The fact that nothing happens for most taxpayers explains some of the consistency in motivational posture scores over time. But the degree to which individuals held to their relative position on all motivational postures from 2000 to 2005 demands further exploration: what is actually holding the relative strength of a person's postures in place over such a long period of time? Are the postures anchored in ideological or value systems that are relatively enduring across time? Or do the postures come to be 'owned' by various subcultures in the regulatory community, for instance, are there social demographic differences? These were the questions that were next examined using the survey data.

DO THE POSTURES DIFFER BY SOCIAL DEMOGRAPHIC GROUPS?

First, six basic social demographic variables were selected for analysis: (a) age; (b) sex; (c) highest educational level attained; (d) marital status; (e) number of children living at home; and (f) country of birth.[9]

The data yielded little evidence of community divisions along social demographic lines in how people related to the tax office. The greatest differentiation was between age groups, with older respondents scoring higher on commitment and capitulation ($r = 0.22$, $p < 0.001$, in both cases). One of the most consistent findings in tax research has been that young people are less compliant and more tax resistant than older people (Mason and Calvin 1978; Jackson and Milliron 1986; Andreoni et al. 1998; Orviska and Hudson 2002). The finding is not specific to taxation. In general, we tend to age into or become socialized into law-abiding practices and work cooperatively with authority (Tittle 1980; Gottfredson and Hirschi 1990; Inglehart 1997; Watts 1999; Putnam 2000).

Lower education levels were associated with higher scores on capitulation ($r = -0.19$, $p < 0.001$). This finding underlines Kelman and Hamilton's (1989) warning of the need for society to educate against blind and ill-informed obedience to authority. Other postures were linked with socially peripheral populations. Younger, unmarried men were somewhat more likely to endorse the disengagement posture ($r = -0.08$, $p < 0.001$ for age; $r = -0.08$, $p < 0.001$ for marital status; $r = -0.10$, $p < 0.001$ for sex). Game playing was associated with lower educational attainment ($r = -0.14$, $p < 0.001$) and being born outside Australia ($r = -0.10$, $p < 0.001$). Qualitative data have provided evidence of game playing among self-employed migrants (Rothengatter 2005).

The social demographic correlates of the motivational postures are relatively weak in magnitude, but nevertheless they resonate with other knowledge we have about social distancing from authority among social demographic groups. The less educated are unlikely to question authority if all appears to be going well and can readily be enrolled in the agendas of powerful others who 'look good'. In other cases, people keep their distance possibly because they are marginalized in day-to-day social institutions such as work and family that link into systems of governance. Participation in such institutions is likely to be less regular and more difficult for young, unmarried men, and people who are poorly educated and non-Australian. People's social distance from the tax authority may mirror their social distance from authority more generally.

While of interest in their own right, these findings need to be put to one side for the moment. What has become clear from these analyses is that a person's social demographic background does not provide the answer to the most burning question for this chapter. The social demographic correlates are not sufficiently strong to be compelling anchors for stabilizing postures over time. We need to look elsewhere for consistency anchors for the postures.

DO THE POSTURES DIFFER IN TERMS OF BASIC VALUES?

Values, it will be recalled from Chapter 3, are among the basic building blocks in the value–attitude–belief system. Values are part of our self-conception of who we are and who we would like to be. As such they give direction to our actions and shape the way in which we interpret the world, what we see as threatening or helpful, what we like and dislike, and how we construe the actions of others. It is plausible that our basic values frame the way in which we think about taxation and that the values that are most important to us place constraints on our capacity to rethink our relationship with tax authorities.

Rokeach (1968, 1973) has provided a model of the value–attitude–belief system that assigns values a distinctive role. Values are goals in life and ways of behaving that are personally and socially preferable to alternative goals and ways of behaving across specific contexts. An example of a value, therefore, might be freedom. It represents a goal or a state of being; it transcends situations in that it is important in speech, in musical tastes, at work, in the family, in politics, to name but a handful of contexts; and it is reasonable to assert that the vast majority of people would consider being free to be a preferable state to not being free. Values include our hopes for the world – a world at peace for example; our hopes for the community – reward for individual effort perhaps; and our hopes for ourselves – possibly wealth and influence, or inner calm and happiness, or cheerfulness and good humour. Values of the kind proposed by Rokeach attract wide consensus in the community (Braithwaite, V. and Blamey 1998). They are shared principles that are overarching. As such, they guide and justify how a person behaves in specific circumstances. It would not be surprising to find that values form an important part of our personal narratives, explaining why we adopt certain postures in our dealings with the tax authority.

Rokeach (1968, 1973) proposed 18 terminal values (goals) and 18 instrumental values (modes of conduct) as a comprehensive list of the most important human values. Rokeach's goal was to have his values overlapping as little as possible. Another approach is empirically to generate a list of values that people think cover the important areas of goals in life and modes of conduct and then group the overlapping items into value scales. Braithwaite, V. and Law (1985) developed 19 such scales based on 125 values. On the basis of a series of statistical analyses (Braithwaite, V. 1982, 1994, 1997, 1998b, 1998c; Braithwaite, V. and Law 1985; Blamey and Braithwaite, 1997; Braithwaite, V. and Blamey 1998), these value scales reduced to a much smaller set of dimensions, two of which were particularly important in explaining how we engaged with political institutions. One was concerned with strength, safety and predictability, the other with human concerns of care, equality and peaceful coexistence.

These dimensions were theorized as manifestations of two value systems that we all subscribe to at some level and that our institutions often require us to trade off: the security value system and the harmony value system (Braithwaite, V. 1998b). Security values provide signposts for activity in which there is competition for limited resources. They guide us in what we have a right to defend and fight for, and place constraints on how we should do this.

Security values have been measured through a set of multi-item scales representing national strength and order, propriety in dress and manners, competence and effectiveness, and social and economic status. The values comprising each scale appear in the left-hand column of Table 4.5.

In the right-hand column of Table 4.5 are the scales that make up the harmony value system. Harmony values are guiding principles for establishing social bonds and cooperation with others in the society. The focus is on the quality of relationships, knowledge, understanding and human dignity; and the overarching goal is a social order that is peaceful, inclusive of others and shares resources. The harmony scales are international harmony and equality, personal growth and inner harmony, and having a positive orientation to others.

The value scales in Table 4.5 were stable over a three-year period and predicted many of the preferences people have for how society should resolve the tensions between a social order where resources are limited, competition is rife and security concerns high, and a social order founded on cooperation and sharing of the resources available, in particular providing for those in need (Braithwaite, V. 1998b; Braithwaite, V. et al. 2003). Taxation is a social institution that is enmeshed in this tension because it rests on the premise that being cooperative and paying tax provide government with resources to deliver security to the community. As such, motivational postures may be telling us less about a malleable phenomenon like social distance from a specific tax authority and more about the deeply engrained personal values of individuals.

Pearson product–moment correlation coefficients were calculated to find out if security and harmony values could be the anchors accounting for the consistency in the motivational postures displayed to the tax authority. The results supported this hypothesis. The key significant findings were as follows:

1. *Harmony values underpinned the commitment posture.* Those who prioritized a positive orientation to others, personal growth and inner

Table 4.5 Items comprising scales measuring security and harmony value systems

The security value system	The harmony value system
Social and economic status (M = 4.50, SD = 1.00, alpha = 0.81)	*Personal growth and inner harmony (M = 5.69, SD = 0.82, alpha = 0.84)*
Economic prosperity (being financially well off)	Wisdom (having a mature understanding of life)
Recognition by the community (having high standing in the community)	The pursuit of knowledge (always trying to find out new things about the world we live in)
Authority (having power to influence others and control decisions)	Self-knowledge/self-insight (being more aware of what sort of person you are)
Competitive (always trying to do better than others)	Self-respect (believing in your own worth)
Ambitious (being eager to do well)	Self-improvement (striving to be a better person)
	Inner harmony (feeling free of conflict within yourself)
Propriety (M = 5.62, SD = 0.86, alpha = 0.89)	*A positive orientation to others (M = 5.55, SD = 0.85, alpha = 0.88)*
Conscientious (being hardworking)	Forgiving (willing to pardon others)
Polite (being well mannered)	Trusting (having faith in others)
Patriotic (being loyal to your country)	Giving others a fair go (giving others a chance)
Prompt (being on time)	Generous (sharing what you have with others)
Refined (never being course or vulgar)	Understanding (able to share another's feelings)
Clean (not having dirty habits)	Helpful (always ready to assist others)
Self-disciplined (being self-controlled)	Cooperative (being able to work in harmony with others)
Reliable (being dependable)	
Neat (being tidy)	
Competence and effectiveness (M = 5.50, SD = 0.83, alpha = 0.85)	*International harmony and equality (M = 5.72, SD = 0.84, alpha = 0.87)*
Efficient (always using the best method to get the best result)	A good life for others (improving the welfare of all people in need)
Showing foresight (thinking and seeing ahead)	Rule by the people (involvement by all citizens in making decisions that affect their community)
Resourceful (being clever at finding ways to achieve a goal)	International cooperation (having all nations working together to help each other)
Knowledgeable (being well informed)	
Logical (being rational)	
National strength and order (M = 5.64, SD = 0.97, alpha = 0.83)	
National greatness (being a united, strong, independent and powerful nation)	

Table 4.5 (continued)

The security value system	The harmony value system
National security (protection of your nation from enemies)	Social progress and reform (readiness to change our way of life for the better)
Rule of law (living by laws that everyone must follow)	A world at peace (being free from war and conflict)
National economic development (having greater economic progress and prosperity for the nation)	Human dignity (allowing each individual to be treated as someone of worth)
Reward for individual effort (letting individuals prosper through gains made by initiative and hard work)	A world of beauty (having the beauty of nature and the arts: music, literature, art)
	Equal opportunity for all (giving everyone an equal chance in life)
	Greater economic equality (lessening the gap between the rich and the poor)
	Preserving the natural environment (preventing the destruction of nature's beauty and resources)

Note: Respondents were asked to rate each statement on a seven-point asymmetrical scale from reject as important (1) to accept as of the utmost importance (7).

harmony, and international harmony and equality in 2000 were more likely to express a commitment posture in 2000 ($r = 0.21, p < 0.001$; $r = 0.16, p < 0.001$; and $r = 0.18, p < 0.001$ respectively). These same value measures taken in 2000 were just as strongly related to the commitment posture measured five years later in 2005 ($r = 0.19, p < 0.001$; $r = 0.16, p < 0.001$; and $r = 0.18, p < 0.001$ respectively).

2. *Security values were linked with the posture of capitulation.* Those who placed value on propriety in dress and manners and national strength and order in 2000 were more likely to align themselves with the capitulation posture in 2000 ($r = 0.19, p < 0.001$; and $r = 0.17, p < 0.001$ respectively). These 2000 value scales remained significantly correlated with capitulation in 2005 ($r = 0.20, p < 0.001$; and $r = 0.17, p < 0.001$ respectively).
3. *Security values provided a base for resistance.* Social and economic status was the value priority in 2000 that underpinned the motivational posture of resistance in 2000 ($r = 0.16, p < 0.001$). Pursuit of social and economic status in 2000 predicted resistance in 2005 ($r = 0.17, p < 0.001$).

4. *Being uninterested in harmony and security values was the hallmark of disengagement.* Those who downplayed the importance of personal growth and inner harmony, positive orientation to others, international harmony and equality, propriety in dress and manners, and national strength and order in 2000 were more likely to adopt the posture of disengagement in 2000 ($r = -0.16$, $p < 0.001$; $r = -0.14$, $p < 0.001$; $r = -0.15$, $p < 0.001$; $r = -0.12$, $p < 0.01$; and $r = -0.11$, $p < 0.01$ respectively). The relationships extended across time with 2000 harmony and security values being negatively correlated with levels of disengagement in 2005 ($r = -0.18$, $p < 0.001$; $r = -0.21$, $p < 0.001$; $r = -0.10$, $p < 0.01$; $r = -0.16$, $p < 0.001$; and $r = -0.11$, $p < 0.01$ respectively; in addition, $r = -0.11$, $p < 0.01$ with competence and effectiveness).
5. *Security values underpinned game playing.* Placing value on social and economic status, national strength and order, propriety in dress and manners, and competence and effectiveness in 2000 predicted stronger displays of the game-playing posture in 2000 ($r = 0.31$, $p < 0.001$; $r = 0.13$, $p < 0.001$; $r = 0.12$, $p < 0.01$; and $r = 0.11$, $p < 0.01$ respectively). These 2000 values also predicted game playing in 2005 ($r = 0.24$, $p < 0.001$; $r = 0.12$, $p < 0.01$; $r = 0.14$, $p < 0.001$; and $r = 0.11$, $p < 0.01$ respectively).

These findings show that the motivational postures have some important anchors in the values that people hold, and these anchors endure over time. Tax authorities and tax systems will meet with a more positive reception and find commitment from people whose values promote being other-oriented, who want a world where there is a more equal sharing of resources, and who place a priority on non-material aspects of well-being. Importantly, where values are less oriented to cooperation, all is not necessarily lost for tax systems. In cases where commitment is not forthcoming, capitulation or tolerance of a tax system can be expected among those who value probity, have a strong sense of the importance of doing the right thing, and can put the security of the nation first.

By way of contrast, tax authorities and tax systems will meet with opposition from those whose values are more materialistic or who have cut themselves off psychologically from a humanistic worldview. The quest for status appears at the heart of social distancing from the authority. Wanting wealth, influence and social presence appeared to fuel the postures of resistance and game playing. It was as if humanity were being placed on hold until success had been achieved. Lack of interest in principles of any kind characterized disengagement. The disengaged had less time for idealism, efforts to improve the welfare of others and all matters spiritual. They exuded an aura of giving up on humanity.

Linking societal and personal values to tax posturing means that motivational postures measure more than social distance generated by the way in which a tax authority engages with its constituents. We do not approach taxation as if it were an island detached from other parts of our lives or our system of governance. Value differences that predispose us to engage with taxation in distinctive ways mean that we are bound to have robust debate within the democracy over taxation and its purpose. Moreover, when it comes time to pay our tax, some of us will send signals that make us easier to manage than others.

In spite of our value differences, tax authorities must find the skills to manage us all inclusively, responsively and with professional indifference. Their successes and failures will be apparent in the social distancing that occurs in response to tax authority actions. Values may limit the movement in our posturing, but there is no reason to assume that values will displace the more dynamic form of social distancing that occurs between taxpayers and their tax authority. Both may be important determinants of motivational postures, although clearly this proposition needs to be tested empirically.

DO THE POSTURES DIFFER ON HOPES FOR AUSTRALIAN DEMOCRACY?

If values have a bearing on motivational postures, so too will other beliefs and observations about the system of governance. Motivational postures are likely to be influenced by our hopes for the democracy, along with our assessment of how well the democracy is functioning (Dryzek and Braithwaite 2000). Social aspirations were represented by two measures in the 2000 survey. One represented the desire to have (a) a more caring society, the other the view that peace and prosperity can be delivered through (b) free markets and small government. Progress towards desired goals was measured on two scales. The first assessed the belief that basically (c) the democracy was OK, even if it wasn't perfect. The second focused on the degree to which individuals felt that they no longer had a part to play in the democracy, with most of the say residing in big business and those with money. This was called (d) the disillusionment with the democracy scale. Items for the scales and details about how these concepts were measured are provided in Table 4.6.

This section tests the following hypotheses:

Hypothesis 4.3(a) Respondents who hoped for a more caring society and reported that they believed that the functioning of the democracy

Table 4.6 Statements comprising scales representing hopes for Australian democracy

A more caring society (M = 4.08, SD = 0.59, alpha reliability coefficient = 0.72)

Our community and nation should appeal to a spirit that each person is important, and has a way of influencing things.
Our society will be more secure and more attractive if it is also more equitable and humane, as well as more productive and more efficient.

Small government, free markets (M = 3.14, SD = 0.80, alpha reliability coefficient = 0.43)

Free markets work because individual people, cooperating peacefully and voluntarily through markets, can achieve much that politicians and bureaucrats cannot achieve using compulsion and direction.
The true function of government is to maintain peace and justice: this does not include interfering in national or international trade or commerce, or in the private transactions of citizens, save only as they threaten peace and justice.

Disillusionment with the democracy (M = 3.76, SD = 0.61, alpha reliability coefficient = 0.77)

Democracy is a term that has lost much of its original meaning.
There's a dollar democracy that runs through our supposed democracy.
In Australia, the rich have virtually unlimited access to the legal system and the capacity to use it to achieve their own ends.
I don't think we have enough input into legislation and the decisions that are important.
Our government is attempting to mould our society to the needs of a profit-oriented market.
I'm always cynical about government processes.

The democracy is OK (M = 3.26, SD = 0.70, alpha reliability coefficient = 0.49)

In our democracy, we can hold our representatives accountable.
You don't have to wait three years to say 'I'm not happy with the government': you can apply pressure, and enough people writing to the local member can turn the situation around.
Our form of democracy is not perfect, but it beats by a long shot any other alternative we have been shown.

Note: Respondents were asked to rate each statement on a five-point scale from strongly disagree (1) to strongly agree (5).

was OK were expected to identify with the less socially distant postures of commitment and capitulation.

Hypothesis 4.3(b) Respondents who hoped for a political system with smaller government and free markets and who reported being disillusioned with the state of the democracy were expected to identify with the more socially distant postures of resistance, disengagement and game playing.

These four scales measuring hopes for and opinions about the state of the democracy were correlated with the motivational postures measured concurrently in 2000 and five years later in 2005. The results of the correlation analysis supported the hypotheses for the most part:

1. People who believed that we needed a more caring society and that the democracy was basically OK were more likely to display the posture of commitment. The correlations for 2000 were 0.22 ($p < 0.001$) and 0.28 ($p < 0.001$) respectively. When predicting commitment in 2005, the correlations were weaker, but still significant, with coefficients of 0.14 ($p < 0.001$) and 0.15 ($p < 0.001$) respectively.
2. People who believed that the democracy was OK were more likely to display the posture of capitulation ($r = 0.37, p < 0.001$). When predicting capitulation in 2005, the correlation remained strong ($r = 0.31, p < 0.001$).
3. People who were disillusioned with the democracy and believed in free markets and small government were more likely to adopt a posture of resistance ($r = 0.37$, $p < 0.001$; and $r = 0.23$, $p < 0.001$ respectively). These same attitudes predicted resistance in 2005, with coefficients of 0.36 ($p < 0.001$) and .21 ($p < 0.001$) respectively.
4. People who were disillusioned with the democracy and saw little need for a more caring society were more likely to adopt the posture of disengagement ($r = 0.12, p < 0.001$; and $r = -0.14, p < 0.001$ respectively). When predicting disengagement in 2005, the coefficients were much the same ($r = 0.09, p < 0.01$; and $r = -0.08, p < 0.05$ respectively).
5. People who believed in free markets and small government were more likely to adopt the game-playing posture in 2000 ($r = 0.19, p < 0.001$) and also in 2005 ($r = 0.16, p < 0.001$).

These findings show that the hopes we have for the world and the degree to which we see government working to support the democracy affect the ways in which we orient ourselves to taxation, not only at one moment in time, but also into the future. The analyses relating postures to values and hopes for the democracy revealed some coherent and familiar themes. Ideals and hopes that promote generosity of spirit, concern for the collective and a certain indifference to material possessions provide us with a sympathetic lens for evaluating the tax system. In contrast, ideals and hopes that are individualistic and private, that relish the competitive struggle and applaud the triumph of one over another provide us with a negative lens for appraising the role of taxation in our lives. On the basis of the findings so far, motivational postures have some important anchors in our value–attitude–belief system that are part of our definition of who we are.

DISSECTING THE MOTIVATIONAL POSTURES CONCEPT

Because motivational postures were developed with the purpose of chunking together a number of more discrete psychological concepts, it is not surprising that these postures are influenced by broader principles for governance and social living. Indeed, it would be surprising if there were not a range of factors, both tax and non-tax related, that contribute to the form that a motivational posture will take. Beliefs are interconnected, and when individuals are exposed to politicized and shared discourses about various institutions, ideas are taken on board from various sources and woven together, often in support of each other.

This being the case, the critical question becomes not whether motivational postures are purely one thing or another, but rather: can motivational postures be envisaged as the product of both values and hopes for the democracy and an individual's preferred social distance from a tax authority? The former would explain the stability and consistency of the postures while the latter would account for movement in the postures within the individual's predispositional constraints. For example, imagine a child brought up in a stable and happy home that was rudely thrown into chaos and trauma when his father, who did not believe in governments or paying tax, was prosecuted and jailed. It would be understandable for such a person not to look favourably on the institution of taxation throughout life. Yet, within the constraints that early childhood experiences impose, the individual nevertheless may be cooperative enough to file a relatively honest tax return regularly, if treated with sufficient respect and care. If not treated considerately, resistance might flare up. The proposition being put forward here is that values and beliefs about government may constrain our responses to authority, but there will always be a range within which we can be more or less cooperative, depending on how the authority treats us. We now turn to the data to find out if this proposition has validity.

VALUES AND HOPES FOR THE DEMOCRACY OR SOCIAL DISTANCE FROM A TAX AUTHORITY?

In order to find out how far motivational postures are shaped by general worldviews and how far by actions on the part of the tax office, a hierarchical multiple regression analysis is used. The statistical question is framed as follows: once social demographic characteristics, values and hopes for the democracy are controlled, is there any variation remaining that can be explained by the social distance indicators (wanting to abolish the tax system; praising the tax office for the job they are doing; preferring an honest no-risk practitioner; a cautious minimizer; or an aggressive practitioner)? This question was examined with each posture in turn. The results were substantively similar to those obtained with the supra-postures of *Resistance* and *Dismissiveness*. The results for the supra-postures are reported below. Final models included only those variables that made significant contributions.[10] The data are from the 'Community Hopes, Fears and Actions Survey' (2000).

PREDICTING THE DEFIANT SUPRA-POSTURE OF RESISTANCE

The beta coefficients for Model 1 in Table 4.7 show how important broader cultural factors (social demographic variables, values, hopes for the democracy) are in the prediction of resistance. To the cultural predictors of Model 1 are added the tax-focused social distance indicators (evaluation of the tax system and tax office, preference for an honest tax adviser or deference to a tax minimizer or aggressive tax planner) in Model 2. Model 2 results are described below.

Resistance as Cultural Background

The defiant supra-posture of *Resistance* was expressed more strongly among the young, the better educated, those with children, those disillusioned with the state of the democracy, and supporters of small government and free markets. The opposite pole of the dimension, *Cooperation*, was higher if the democracy was seen to be basically OK and if personal values gave priority to showing concern and support for others.

Table 4.7 The results of a hierarchical regression analysis predicting Resistance *from (a) social demographic characteristics, values and hopes for the democracy in Model 1 and (b) social demographic characteristics, values, hopes for the democracy and social distance indicators in Model 2*

Predictors of *Resistance*	Beta coefficients predicting *Resistance*	
	Model 1	Model 2
Social demographic variables		
Age	−0.20***	−0.10***
Educational level	0.02	0.04*
No. of children at home	0.04*	0.04*
Values		
A positive orientation to others	−0.15***	−0.11***
Hopes for the democracy		
Small government, free markets	0.14***	0.06**
Disillusionment with democracy	0.23***	0.11***
The democracy is OK	−0.27***	−0.14***
Social distance indicators		
Abolish tax system		0.20***
Praise tax office		−0.44***
Honest no-risk practitioner		−0.10***
Cautious minimizing practitioner		0.05**
Aggressive tax practitioner		0.11***
Adjusted R^2	0.26***	0.52***

Note: * $p < 0.05$; ** $p < 0.01$; *** $p < 0.001$.

Resistance as Social Distance from Authority

While cultural and value differences were important, so too were the social distance indicators. *Resistance* was associated with being open to abolishing the tax system, and having a tax practitioner who would minimize or use aggressive tax strategies. *Cooperation*, on the other hand, was associated with praise for the tax office and a preference for an honest no-risk adviser. These relationships remained important after controlling for social demographic and value differences.

A comparison of the beta coefficients from Model 1 to Model 2 shows that the contribution of the broader cultural factors remained significant but weakened when the social distance indicators were included in the regression model. This suggests that the cultural factors that we know to be stable and bedded down in the value–attitude–belief system of individuals frame the way in which individuals respond to taxation. Later chapters will return to this issue. For the present, the important finding is that both cultural factors and tax-specific social distance indicators shape the supra-posture of *Resistance*.

Further evidence for this conclusion comes from the change in the amount of variance accounted for in *Resistance* as we move from Model 1 to Model 2 in Table 4.7. The social distance indicators increased the variance accounted for in *Resistance* from 26 per cent to 52 per cent, an increment of 26 per cent. Both the bigger picture of governance and the smaller picture of tax office functioning make up the supra-posture of *Resistance* to tax authority.

PREDICTING THE DEFIANT SUPRA-POSTURE OF DISMISSIVENESS

As was the case for *Resistance*, the findings show that both cultural factors and social distance indicators play an important role in shaping *Dismissiveness* (see Table 4.8).

Dismissiveness as Cultural Background

The defiant supra-posture of *Dismissiveness* was more commonly observed among the unmarried, those born outside Australia, those who valued social and economic status, and believed in small government and free markets. Those who were dismissive were not particularly engaged with values such as personal growth and inner harmony, and national strength and order, nor did they wish for a more caring society. *Dismissiveness* tended to go hand in hand with a belief that the democracy was basically OK, but this did not rule out the opportunity to express a degree of disillusionment.

Dismissiveness as Social Distance from Authority

Dismissiveness was associated with being sympathetic to abolishing the tax system, being unimpressed by the prospect of having an honest no-risk practitioner, and being attracted to seeking help from those who could minimize their tax, in particular aggressive tax planners and creative accountants.

Social distance indicators played a major role in explaining dismissive-

Table 4.8 The results of a hierarchical regression analysis predicting Dismissiveness *from (a) social demographic characteristics, values and hopes for the democracy in Model 1 and (b) social demographic characteristics, values, hopes for the democracy and social distance indicators in Model 2*

Predictors of *Dismissiveness*	Beta coefficients predicting *Dismissiveness*	
	Model 1	Model 2
Social demographic variables		
Marital status	−0.06**	−0.04*
Australian born	−0.07**	−0.07**
Values		
Social and economic status	0.35***	0.25***
National strength and order	−0.09***	−0.07**
Personal growth, inner harmony	−0.20***	−0.16***
Hopes for the democracy		
A more caring society	−0.15***	−0.09***
Small government, free markets	0.15***	0.08***
Disillusionment with democracy	0.09***	0.05**
The democracy is OK	0.05**	0.08***
Social distance indicators		
Abolish tax system		0.15***
Honest no-risk practitioner		−0.19***
Cautious minimizing practitioner		0.07**
Aggressive tax practitioner		0.19***
Adjusted R^2	0.17***	0.27***

Note: * $p < 0.05$; ** $p < 0.01$; *** $p < 0.001$.

ness after controlling for social demographic variables, values and hopes for the democracy. The indicators of social distance of taxpayers from the tax authority accounted for an additional 10 per cent of variance above and beyond the 17 per cent predicted by social demographic characteristics, values and hopes for the democracy. The beta coefficients for cultural background variables weakened from Model 1 to Model 2 in Table 4.8, suggesting that values in particular may be important in framing the posture of *Dismissiveness*. Like the supra-posture of *Resistance*, *Dismissiveness* has anchors in social demographic background, personal values and hopes for the democracy. *Dismissiveness*, however, also reflects the relationship between taxpayers and the tax authority, in this case a relationship defined by a desire not to defer and to find an alternative authority to challenge the tax office.

SUMMARY AND CONCLUSION

Three findings are important both for providing closure on our conceptualization of motivational postures and for guiding the direction of subsequent chapters. First, motivational postures are part of how we see self and others, and are linked to our non-tax-related beliefs about the world we live in. Second, motivational postures can be understood as signals of how much distance separates the taxpayer from the tax authority and how that distance can be sustained through the help of tax practitioners. Third, motivational postures are also shared cultural phenomena: they are linked to demographic variables and to social discourses of a political nature. In this sense they are examples of what C. Wright Mills (1940) has termed 'vocabularies of motive'. If we were to apply Mills's ideas to the motivational posture concept, we would expect the postures to be socially constructed so as to be adaptive in particular social situations. For instance, an adaptive response (a response that protects or furthers the interests of the self) would be one that provided a plausible rationale for our actions, one that is credible to us as well as to others. The social distance indicators suggest that motivational postures lend themselves to being socially coherent narratives that justify why we do what we do.

This chapter established the measurement credentials of the motivational posture concept. The postures of commitment, capitulation and resistance can be measured with an impressive level of consistency and represent social distance of a traditional kind – the degree to which respondents regard the authority sympathetically and favourably or critically and unfavourably. These postures can be measured individually or together depending on the research context. Together, they form the supra-posture of *Resistance(–Cooperation)*: in subsequent chapters, *Resistance* is used to represent resistant defiance.

The postures of disengagement and game playing also display considerable consistency in their measurement, and tap into a different facet of social distance – the degree to which the authority is denied the right to exercise control over the individual's tax-related activities, that is, the degree to which taxpayers are unwilling to show deference to the authority. These postures can be used individually, but in the present research will be combined into the supra-posture of *Dismissiveness*. *Dismissiveness* will be used in subsequent chapters as our measure of dismissive defiance.

The stability of the postures over time, while probably stronger than anticipated on theoretical grounds, has been interpreted as a sign that transactions between the tax office and Australian taxpayers are routinized for the most part. Even when things go wrong, it would not be surprising to find stability in the postures. An individual's conflicts with the tax office tend to be handled in an impersonal way, and are usually mediated by tax practitioners. Nevertheless, change in motivational posturing was evident in the measures taken in three surveys in 2000, 2002 and 2005. There were encouraging signs that such changes coincided with changes in the policies and enforcement actions of the tax office. The case has been made elsewhere for how the ATO has become a more effective regulator since Grabosky and Braithwaite (1986) appraised its performance as part of a national study of regulatory agencies two decades ago (Braithwaite, J. 2005). The argument for greater effectiveness focuses in particular on the tax office's attention to dealing with tax avoidance. This observation is consistent with measured decreases in disengagement and game-playing postures. The increase in resistance and decrease in commitment suggest that a degree of good will in the community may have been sacrificed for enforcement effectiveness; but this remains an empirical question to be addressed in subsequent chapters.

In conclusion, the supra-posture scales, constructed in this chapter by combining the basic measures of motivational postures, behaved in predictable ways when relationships were examined with social demographic characteristics, values, hopes for the democracy, and other measures of social distance. Relatively few insights were lost when comparisons were made between the findings based on the supra-postures and those based on the basic motivational postures, with the gains in parsimony being substantial. The supra-posture scales of *Resistance* and *Dismissiveness* appear to be sound measuring instruments for testing propositions about how the community responds to threats from taxation, and the part that perceived integrity plays in drawing people back into a more cooperative and respectful relationship with the tax authority and the tax system. *Resistance* and *Dismissiveness* can now be used to empirically differentiate resistant and dismissive defiance.

NOTES

1. Psychological research has demonstrated that the prediction of individual behaviour is greatly improved when contextual factors are taken into account (see, e.g., Ajzen and Fishbein 1980) and theoretical developments in psychology mirror this advancement in scientific knowledge. Awareness of the importance of context, however, while improving explanatory capacity, can lessen the usefulness of the research to practitioners when

their capacity to tailor treatment to context is limited. The present research attempts to draw on past learning to generalize across contextual variables over which regulators have little control, and to develop theory at a level that can guide practical intervention. In pursuit of this objective, some degree of explanatory capacity may be forfeited.

2. Panel sample statistics were also compared with population parameters provided by the Australian Bureau of Statistics. Previously reported biases from the individual samples were present in the panel sample though were less marked: an underrepresentation of the young, of the unmarried, of people in occupations involving labouring, elementary clerical, transport and production work; and an overrepresentation of older people, professionals and those with post-secondary education.
3. The number of factors for rotation was decided *a priori*. The eigenvalue cut-off of 1 and the scree test did not produce a clear decision as to the number of factors for rotation: they pointed to five or six factors being most appropriate.
4. For full results, see supplementary statistical appendix at http://vab.anu.edu.au/defiance/sup01.pdf.
5. It is important that one of these questions focused on the tax system, the other on the tax office. In this way, an empirical check can be made of the assumption that underlies the measurement of the postures, that they reflect views both about the tax system and those who administer it.
6. The unexpected and small positive correlation between game playing and having a positive evaluation of how the tax office is doing its job is likely to be due to game players seeing the tax office as being a good gaming partner, moving in directions that meet their expectations and suit their interests.
7. A varimax rotation was used to produce a solution that provided maximum differentiation between the factors, although subsequent analyses revealed that the two factors were interrelated. The scales of resistant defiance and dismissive defiance developed on the basis of this analysis correlated 0.25 ($p < 0.001$).
8. Commitment and capitulation are closely related in the tax context, possibly because it is difficult to envisage how one could empirically disentangle doing the basics that are asked for by the regulator (capitulation) and going beyond the call of duty in taxpaying (commitment). In other contexts such as environmental regulation, one would expect that capitulation and commitment would be more easily disentangled (see Gunningham and Grabosky 1998). Because they would be associated with different behavioural outcomes, one would expect a more differentiated belief system to be built around each posture.
9. The measures used were: (a) age in years; (b) sex (male = 0, female = 1); (c) highest educational level attained (primary school or less = 1, year 10 = 2, year 12 = 3, diploma or trade certificate = 4, tertiary = 5); (d) marital status (not married = 0, married = 1); (e) number of children living at home; (f) Australian born (no = 0, yes = 1).
10. For the full regression model, see supplementary statistical appendix at http://vab.anu.edu.au/defiance/sup01.pdf.

5. Approaching defiance through threat and coping

> Stress is best regarded as a complex rubric . . . reflected in the person's appraisal of a relationship with the environment . . . relevant to well-being and taxing or exceeding his or her resources . . . [We ask] what it is about the person, in interaction with a given environmental situation, that generates appraisals of harm/loss, threat, or challenge . . .
>
> Richard Lazarus et al. 1985: 776

This chapter begins the journey of understanding the psychological drivers of resistance and dismissiveness, and more particularly, the differences between the two. The starting point in this journey is threat of taxation. Social distancing is purported to be a reaction to threat. Our different ways of coping with threat may explain why we adopt a social distancing response of dismissive defiance as opposed to resistant defiance. This chapter sets out a conceptual model for understanding how people cope with the threat of taxation and empirically tests the role of coping styles in shaping the defiance supra-postures of dismissiveness and resistance.

To sum up the argument, the social distance that individuals place between themselves and an authority can be observed in their motivational postures. These social distancing responses can be collapsed into two dimensions: liking and deference. When we distance ourselves from an authority because we don't approve of the authority's use of its power, we display defiance through the supra-posture of resistance. When we distance ourselves because we will not defer to the authority, irrespective of how it uses its power, we display defiance through the supra-posture of dismissiveness. In both cases, defiance is understood as something that we all experience, albeit to different degrees, because authority threatens us at the most basic level of our freedom. Authorities take away our freedom and can at any time demand our compliance, thereby threatening our independent identity, and possibly our well-being.

In Chapter 4, we gained some insight into the social values and goals that people hold that might affect the distance they place between themselves and the tax authority. The relative strength of allegiance to these values and goals leaves some more open to taxation defiance than others.

If we share collective values and hopes for the democracy, we are more likely to see some purpose in taxation and be less likely to display defiance to the tax authority. If we subscribe to individualistic values geared towards economic and social status and see little purpose in collective undertakings, we are more likely to see taxation as unnecessary and express defiance.

Defiance, however, is determined not only by an absence of the 'right' values. Regardless of the compatibility of our values with taxation, some choose to distance themselves, while others choose to align themselves with authority. Institutional norms, practices and social allegiances are able to override our personal values and preferences, shifting our willingness to cooperate or defy. Without such social processes, communities in a democracy could not be mobilized to act collectively.

Conceptualizing defiance in this way makes it a mixture of the emotive and the rational. The emotive makes its presence felt as we search for feelings of comfort or safety from the threat, through modelling others who know how to protect themselves or through joining up with others who are willing and able to protect us. Perhaps we feel safer when we are doing what everyone else does, an instinctive sense that safety lies with others and not with being alone (see Chapter 7). The rational plays out in other ways. We need reasons for overcoming our fear. In the taxation context, three loom large: benefits, social justice and obligation (Cullis and Lewis 1997; Tanzi 2001; also see more general reviews by Smith and Kinsey 1987; Slemrod 1992; Alm et al. 1995; Andreoni et al. 1998; Hasseldine and Li 1999).

Convincing ourselves that the tax authority collects revenue that the government then uses to improve the quality of our lives or at least our community's life alleviates some of the doubts we may have about the authority's interference and insistence that we pay tax. Tax for benefits is the avenue that governments commonly pursue in order to smooth ruffled feathers. Or we may ameliorate a sense of threat by resorting to arguments about justice, asking questions such as: are we all contributing our fair share and are there fair processes that ensure that everyone is treated with respect? When accepting that conditions of benefits and justice prevail, the threat of interference may seem more acceptable as a cost of communal living that requires accommodation to others. When a tax authority tries to improve the delivery of benefits and of justice within the government it serves – that is, when it practises integrity – our sense of threat should be relieved (see Chapter 6).

We may vacillate in our thinking about both the benefits and justice of taxation because of political differences with 'the system' (Kagan and Scholz 1984), or because we lack confidence in the authority's means of administering the system (Tyler 1990); but then most of us are given a little nudge in the right direction when we think of the law. We are socialized into valuing the rule of law and accepting that authorities can and should sanction those who knowingly break it (Braithwaite, V. et al. 2001; Braithwaite, V. et al. 2006; Maguire et al. 2007). Closely associated with accepting an authority's right to sanction for law violation is moral obligation and self-perceptions of being law-abiding citizens (Sykes and Matza 1957). Without such perceptions, most of us would have no way of discounting the threat we feel from a tax authority. We need to manage any sense of threat by believing that we will not be harmed because we are law abiding and because we live in a society that upholds the rule of law. This chapter focuses on moral obligation and the integral role it plays in reconciling the dual interests of closing the gap with authority and avoiding coercion.

MORAL OBLIGATION – DESIRED, BUT NOT THE ONLY RESPONSE TO THREAT

Institutional norms and practices keep defiance at bay by persuading individuals to enter into a cooperative relationship with authority – with coercive measures in the background should anyone withdraw consent, try to 'renegotiate' the law or simply assert their freedom. At this point, it should not go unnoticed that democratic governments walk on a knife's edge when they fall back on coercion rather than moral obligation to achieve the outcomes they desire. Governments have the power to coerce, but individuals have power to retaliate. Without moral obligation, individuals may defy. When individuals defy collectively, governments are at risk of destabilization.

In developing the argument that authority threatens freedom even in a democracy and defiance is a possible response, a definition of threat is useful. Generally speaking, a threat is a signal that something undesirable is about to happen. Most people associate threat with the sanctions that are waiting should they fail to comply with government rules. But when they do this, they overlook the more fundamental threat. The objective and universal threat in the tax context is that the law requires individuals to contribute a portion of their wealth to the government. We are not free to decline the government's request; we give up that freedom as members of the society.

Loss of freedom is undesirable. In the best of possible worlds, we would opt for having freedom of choice over our actions rather than being forced to hand over that freedom to others. In this sense, Rokeach (1973) has argued that freedom is a basic value that we all share – its presence is preferable to its absence for most people most of the time. It is also reasonable to assert that embedded in social life is regulation, and regulation similarly requires us to give up our freedom so that we march in step with others. At one level, regulation of any kind can be conceived as a threat. But such an analysis fails to recognize the human dimension. Sometimes regulation by others is 'no problem', sometimes it is 'a hassle', and sometimes it involves serious 'sacrifice'. How offensive we find our loss of freedom depends on circumstances. An important element of threat is subjective – it depends on our perceptions and the meaning the regulatory intervention has for us.

When asked to pay tax, individuals with similar backgrounds may respond quite differently. A person on a modest income may pay tax without misgivings, while another person on the same income in similar life circumstances may go to extraordinary lengths to learn how to avoid doing so. The surveys we conducted in the course of this research illustrate how threatening taxation can be. Our population surveys asked people about their civic engagement, what they thought of taxation, their treatment by the tax authority, and how they, in turn, responded to tax office expectations. In spite of our assurances to participants that the surveys were voluntary, their purpose was scientific, they were being overseen by the University Ethics Committee, and were conducted independently of government, surprising responses were encountered. In one case I received a personal note with a cheque for $100! The subjective meanings that we attach to what we might describe as the routinized and universal threat of taxation will vary considerably within the community.

The central purpose of this chapter is to understand the different ways in which we cope with the threat of taxation and how this shapes our motivational posturing (our defiance). In order to understand how we go about dealing with the threat, we need a theoretical framework that tells us how people think about the daily hassles that engulf them: the everyday things like traffic jams, tensions at work, insufficient time, family disagreements, illness in the family, financial hardship and so on. We are familiar with the unthinking responses we make to threat of harm: the adrenalin rush, elevated heartbeat, sweaty palms, and the automatic reaction of flight or fight. Not all threatening circumstances, however, require such an immediate response. When threat is ongoing and not life-threatening, our responses can be more deliberative and structured. We enter a process of appraisal and develop matching coping responses (Lazarus and Folkman 1984). The concept of coping styles from the stress and coping literature (Pearlin and Schooler 1978) can be usefully adapted to understand responses to loss of freedom in the regulatory context.

There can be little doubt that for most people taxation is a yearly hassle involving a degree of analysis and appraisal, privately and publicly. During this process, individuals consider how badly they feel about taxation, what their future losses are going to be, any associated gains, their capacity to meet expectations, and their feelings of self-worth. Through the appraisal process, individuals develop coping responses, the purpose of which is to restore balance to their psychological system and get rid of feelings of fear, pressure, tension or distress. Three coping styles that span appraisal and response have been identified as occurring in a wide range of stressful situations, and are of particular interest in the present research context: an emotion-focused style, a problem-focused style and a cognitive-reframing style (based on Pearlin and Schooler 1978). These are not the only coping styles, nor do they represent a universal taxonomy of how we cope with stress (see Carver et al. 1989 and Skinner et al. 2003 for more fine-grained accounts of coping strategies). They are, however, robust coping styles that have theoretical value for understanding why people place more or less social distance between themselves and authority. Some of us approach, some draw back, and some transcend authority's control. Which we do depends on the coping style that makes us feel most comfortable about how we want to define ourselves in relation to authority and shapes our motivational posturing.

COPING STYLES – EMOTION-FOCUSED, PROBLEM-FOCUSED AND COGNITIVE REFRAMING

When individuals are emotion-focused, they become preoccupied with loss and feel oppressed by their situation. They are likely to think that there is nothing they can do to make things better. They retreat in despair in the face of an authority that is believed to be ready to hurt them badly. Such a coping style of 'feeling oppressed' is likely to increase social distance and manifest itself in a posture of resistance rather than cooperation.

According to the second style, individuals can be problem-focused and favour taking control of the situation to hold the threat at bay. Individuals can command all the power and resources at their disposal to challenge the demands of the authority. A coping style of 'taking control' suggests a refusal to defer to authority and a posture of dismissiveness.

The third way of coping with threat, most suited to situations when we face a threat that we cannot do anything about, is to change the way we think about the situation. We cognitively rearrange the salient features of the situation, a simple example being to focus on seeing the glass half full, rather than half empty. Individuals can reframe the threat, reducing a sense of loss or harm. 'Thinking morally' about taxpaying and embracing it as an honourable activity exemplifies coping through reframing. Individuals take the threat out of taxation by constructing the authority as a benign presence to those citizens who are 'honest and law-abiding', perhaps even believing that authority is their protector.

This third coping style requires a narrative that deals convincingly with external sanctions for wrongdoing as well as a narrative about the correctness of what the government is asking of its taxpayers. In addition, the narrative needs to integrate external definitions of 'wrongdoing' with internal definitions of 'wrongdoing'. The way individuals build this narrative and the pins that give it coherence will be explored later in this chapter.

Within a democratic society, government agencies assume that their legitimate power automatically elicits the reframing coping style from citizens. We shall see that for the most part their assumption is well founded. But for some, questions arise about whether it is safe to reframe the threat of tax authority as benign. The tax authority remains a sinister force capable of and willing to undermine personal and community well-being. For these individuals, coping styles give direction to their unease and defiance becomes defensible.

MEASURING TAXATION COPING STYLES THROUGH SURVEYS

In order to have a coping style in response to taxation threat, we need to assure ourselves that taxation makes its presence felt in people's lives. None of this would make much sense if they did not know they were being taxed. Australian taxpayers appear to be very aware of the contribution they make, not always in dollar terms, but in terms of obligations (Rawlings 2003). In the 'Community Hopes, Fears and Actions Survey', 80 per cent considered it necessary to file an income tax return (Braithwaite, V. et al. 2001). For those who did not, taxation was not irrelevant. In survey comments, retirees spoke of their lifelong contribution to the tax system. To those who had yet to file a tax return because their income was below the threshold, tax entered their consciousness through the goods-and-services tax (GST). At the time that the surveys were conducted, the Australian tax system was undergoing major reform, introducing a value-added tax for the first time. Taxation was a very visible and controversial public policy issue (Braithwaite, V. and Reinhart 2005a). The increased demand for tax dollars, the threat of change imposed from above, and short-term financial costs due to the changeover were intertwined at the time the surveys were conducted.

FEELING OPPRESSED – THE EMOTION-FOCUSED STYLE

The style that stress researchers refer to as emotion-focused is a passive response to impending adversity. We feel that there is nothing that can be done, we vent our emotions, and focus on the awfulness of our situation. A key aspect of responding in an emotion-focused way is loss of personal agency to contain, reduce or modify the threat conditions that are engulfing us.

Such a response, marked by distress, outrage and a sense of hopelessness, is encountered not infrequently in the taxpaying community (Cartwright 2009). An emotion-focused response is likely to involve complaining about the unfairness or awfulness of a tax situation, without having sufficient personal agency to remove the threat. An emotion-focused style will find expression among those who feel that the system has them under its thumb – that is, among those who feel victimized or oppressed by the system.

Taxation most commonly makes its presence felt in an oppressive way by hurting people's 'pockets'. The amount of tax paid can have opportunity costs of which people are painfully aware and about which they sometimes feel resentful. It may mean forgoing a holiday, or not expanding a business, or raiding the children's education fund to pay the tax bill. It is also possible that taxation has little effect on disposable income and quality of life, causing an inconsequential amount of angst for the taxpayer. The extent to which people harbour regrets over what they are missing is the first measure of tax oppression. The scale measuring belief in being *economically deprived due to tax* asked survey respondents if they felt they just couldn't get ahead because of the tax they had to pay and whether taxation destroyed their incentive to work harder (Braithwaite, V. 2001).

Even if taxation is not causing financial hardship, individuals are likely to feel threatened if they are unable to take advantage of the opportunities that others use to work the system and minimize their tax loss. In Australia, those who do not minimize their tax have been made to feel that they are not keeping up with others: Australia's media mogul, the late Kerry Packer, made the news in 1991 when he declared to a print media parliamentary enquiry that 'Of course, I am minimizing my tax. Anybody in this country who does not minimize his tax wants his head read' (cited by Barry 1993: 382).

Feelings of being victimized, without capacity or opportunity to minimize tax, were measured in two ways. The first was the degree to which respondents thought they were *paying more than their fair share*, being lumbered with the tax burden of others who paid less than they should. Insights into the way in which some people, particularly those who are wealthy, can reduce their taxable income circulate widely in the community. Resulting perceived inequities were the source of much complaint in our surveys on how the tax system was travelling over a five-year period (Braithwaite, V. 2003c; Rawlings 2003; Braithwaite, V. et al. 2006).

The second measure focused on the degree to which individuals felt that, in the main, they had received *unfavourable decisions* – that is, they had been unsuccessful in protecting their financial interests from the 'taxman'. The concept of distributive justice is concerned with outcomes; the lack of distributive justice is seen in the extent to which individuals were losing out to the tax authority.

The three measures of the coping style of feeling oppressed were taken

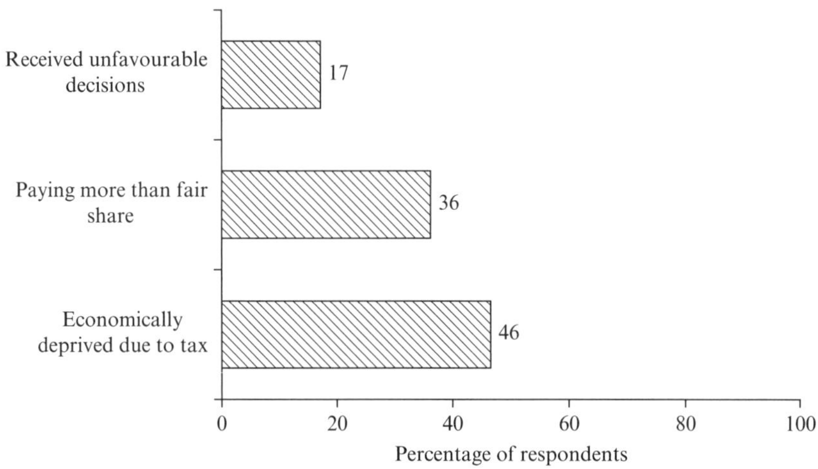

Notes:
1. The numbers used to construct the bar chart were obtained by calculating the percentage of cases scoring above the scale midpoint.
2. The measure of economic disadvantage is adapted from Sutton (1997) and is calculated by averaging strongly disagree to strongly agree ratings 1–5 on the items: (a) I would be better off if I worked less given the rate at which I am taxed; (b) Paying tax removes the incentive to earn more income; (c) Paying tax means that I just can't get ahead (alpha coefficient = 0.76).
3. The measure of paying more than one's fair share was taken from a set of questions asking 'do the following groups pay their fair share of tax?' Respondents were given the category, 'you, yourself' with response options ranging from much more to much less than their fair share. For present purposes, the 1–5 rating scale was scored so that 5 represented much more than their fair share.
4. The index of decisions going against one's interests comprised the average of almost never (1) to almost always (5) ratings in response to two interrelated questions (r = 0.63, $p < 0.001$): (a) How often do you agree with the decisions made by the tax office? (b) How often are the decisions of the tax office favourable to you? Scores are reversed for present purposes so that a high score of 5 represents almost never favourable.

Figure 5.1 Percentage of respondents reporting a feeling oppressed *coping style*

in the 2000 survey. Details of the specific questions asked in the survey are given below Figure 5.1. The graph in Figure 5.1 provides a summary of how people scored themselves on the oppression indicators. The percentage of Australians who saw themselves as being economically deprived because of tax was 46 per cent. Those who thought they were paying more than their fair share of tax amounted to 36 per cent. And as for coming out on the worst side of tax office decisions, the percentage was lower than expected at 17 per cent. This may reflect good tax administration, or it may say more about the tax system. It may be difficult for individuals to know how tax decisions affect them in many cases because of the complexity of the system. A further consideration in the Australian context is that around 85 per cent of taxpayers receive refunds (Australian Taxation Office 2002a: 2). As long as the refund comes, they may feel quite forgiving of the odd claim that is disallowed.

In all, it is reasonable to conclude that feelings of oppression were not overwhelmingly high in the Australian taxpaying population. Certainly, a significant proportion of people reported feeling oppressed by tax, but this response struck a common chord with less than half the population.

As expected, the three measures of feeling oppressed were correlated. Those who felt disadvantaged on one indicator tended to feel disadvantaged on others. Economic deprivation correlated 0.26 ($p < 0.001$) with paying more than one's fair share and 0.27 ($p < 0.001$) with receiving unfavourable tax office decisions. Paying more than one's fair share and receiving unfavourable tax office decisions correlated 0.17 ($p < 0.001$).[1] For the purpose of later analyses, these three measures of oppression were combined into one scale called the *feeling oppressed* coping scale.

TAKING CONTROL – THE PROBLEM-FOCUSED STYLE

The negative emotion-focused state of feeling oppressed will not appeal to everybody as a coping style. Individuals who have a strong sense of their own mastery in the world require another response. The desire for an alternative, more empowering approach to the taxation threat has already created a newly expanding market for the financial services industry in tax minimization. Financial planners have been quick to lend a helping hand to those who feel weighed down by their tax bills.

Tax minimization and tax planning exemplify the second coping style. Stress researchers who have uncovered this style across a range of contexts define it as a problem-focused approach. To be problem-focused is to subject the threat to hard analysis. Obstacles are delineated, and we devise an action plan to bring the threat under control or contain the damage. In practice, this may involve eliminating obstacles or finding alternative pathways to restore financial well-being. For example, a problem-focused style would consider an action plan that brings experts into the 'game' to reduce the tax bill, thereby indirectly giving the taxpayer greater control over the tax situation.

The problem-focused style in the tax context means working the system, or finding ways around perceived obstacles – legally or illegally – to protect one's assets. Working the system reflects high personal agency, but it is not of the kind that signals that the threat has been removed. In the domain of taxation, a win against the tax office is a transient event, and the threat will re-emerge in another form all too soon. Being able to work the system is more about keeping the threat at bay than extinguishing it completely. In order to measure this problem-focused style, it was necessary to measure regularly applied effort and the resources that individuals were drawing on for support.

The first measure focused on activities associated with completing the annual income tax return for the tax authority. Respondents were asked the degree to which they put in *effort to minimize their tax* – that is, how much work went into planning their financial affairs in order to legally pay as little tax as possible. They were also asked whether or not they considered *different ways of doing their tax return* to control the impact of different financial arrangements on the tax they had to pay. In order to assess the resources they had available, respondents were asked about *having a professional tax minimizer*, a tax adviser who was expert in tax minimization and creative in accounting.

The popularity of the taking control style in the 2000 survey is shown in Figure 5.2. Usage was consistently well below the 50 per cent mark. A total of 32 per cent of Australians reported that they put 'some', 'quite a bit' or 'a lot of effort' into planning their financial affairs so that they legally had to pay as little tax as possible, while 22 per cent looked at several different ways of doing their tax return in order to minimize their tax. When attention was turned to resources, 26 per cent of those who were using tax agents to lodge their tax returns had the support of an effective professional tax minimizer.

These three measures of the problem-focused style of taking control were highly related. Effort in financial planning correlated 0.50 ($p < 0.001$) with trying several different ways of arranging finances to minimize tax and 0.30 ($p < 0.001$) with having the support of a professional tax minimizer. Trying different ways of arranging one's finances correlated 0.27 ($p < 0.001$) with having a professional tax minimizer.[2] The quest for tax autonomy was not something delegated to others. It required concerted

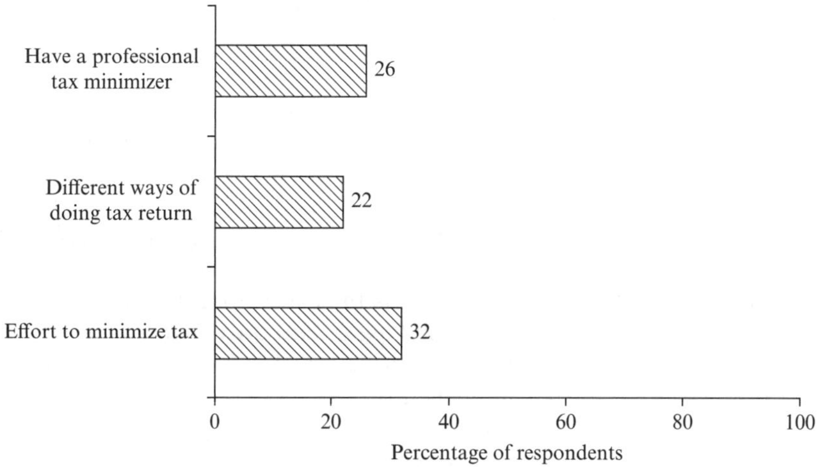

Notes:

1. The numbers used to construct the bar chart were obtained by calculating the percentage of cases answering in the affirmative or the percentage of cases scoring above the scale midpoint.
2. Effort to plan financial affairs in order to legally pay as little tax as possible was measured on a 1–5 rating scale from 'a lot' to 'none'. For present purposes, the scale has been reversed so that 5 means 'a lot'. In the graph, the categories 'some', 'quite a bit', and 'a lot' were combined to represent effort to minimize tax.
3. Trying several different ways of arranging finances to minimize tax was measured dichotomously as 'yes' or 'no'. For present purposes, 'yes' has been scored as 2, 'no' as 1.
4. Having a professional tax minimizer comprised the average of responses on a 1–5 strongly disagree–strongly agree rating scale to the following three items: (a) I have a tax agent who is clever in the way he/she arranges my affairs to minimize tax; (b) My tax agent helps me interpret ambiguous or grey areas of the tax law in my favour; (c) My tax agent has suggested complicated schemes I could get into to avoid tax (alpha coefficient = 0.55).

Figure 5.2 Percentage of respondents reporting a taking control *coping style*

effort on the part of the taxpayer as well as support from professional experts in tax minimization. The *taking control* coping scale was formed from these three measures for later analyses.

THINKING MORALLY – THE REFRAMING STYLE

Being distressed by taxation or wanting to fight against taxation are emotion- and problem-focused responses that continue to acknowledge taxation as a threat. The third coping style of cognitive reframing involves the construction of a narrative around our experience that makes our fears less intense and, therefore, more manageable. By constructing a narrative and reframing our experience, we can come to terms with our situation and let go of our grievances and distress (Antonovsky 1972, 1990; McAdams 1985, 1993; White and Epston 1990).

Reframing negates the threat, turning taxpaying into 'the right thing', a personal loss certainly, but one that we should bear together. In order to accept or accommodate the tax authority's demands, individuals must find a way to attach positive meaning to them. In order to cognitively reframe the taxation threat, the individual must have some credible scaffolding to fall back on. Part of this scaffolding is the expectation that the government will be honest, accountable, and use its authority legitimately for the benefit of all. In return, individuals are expected to be good, law-abiding citizens, which means paying their taxes (Maguire et al. 2007). Through cognitive reframing, paying tax comes to be seen in a positive light as an institutional requirement with which we all should comply voluntarily. Accepting taxation in this way means stepping up to the plate to do one's duty. Such a construction of taxation dampens its threat.

In a self-assessment tax system, much depends on cognitive reframing strategies that turn taxpaying into an honourable activity. With this in mind, four measures were taken of how taxpayers reframe the threat of taxation by thinking morally. First, the value placed on being an honest taxpayer was assessed through an *honest taxpayer identity index* that involved pride in being a member of the honest taxpaying group as well as placing importance on being part of this community. The second measure was targeted to taxpayers with an *ethical taxpaying norm* – they believed it was wrong to cheat on tax and that the authorities should take action to catch tax cheats. The third was designed to measure how much individuals *disapproved of tax cheating* – more specifically, how much they rejected the idea that tax cheating is smart if you can get away with it. The fourth measure, willingness to *report and confront tax cheating*, was pitched at taxpayers who wanted to call tax cheats to account by reporting the matter to the tax authority.

These measures assumed some relationship between believing one had a moral obligation to obey the law and expressing a moral conviction that everyone should obey tax laws. In practice, we have the capacity to step back from imposing our own standards on others. At an attitudinal level, however, it is common for people to extend their personal standards of behaviour to others, believing that such standards should be shared (Scott 1965). Together, these four measures represent the coping style of thinking morally, tapping into personal morality as well as the belief that others should follow suit.

Endorsement of these different facets of thinking morally showed up in the 2000 survey sample to different degrees. From Figure 5.3, an

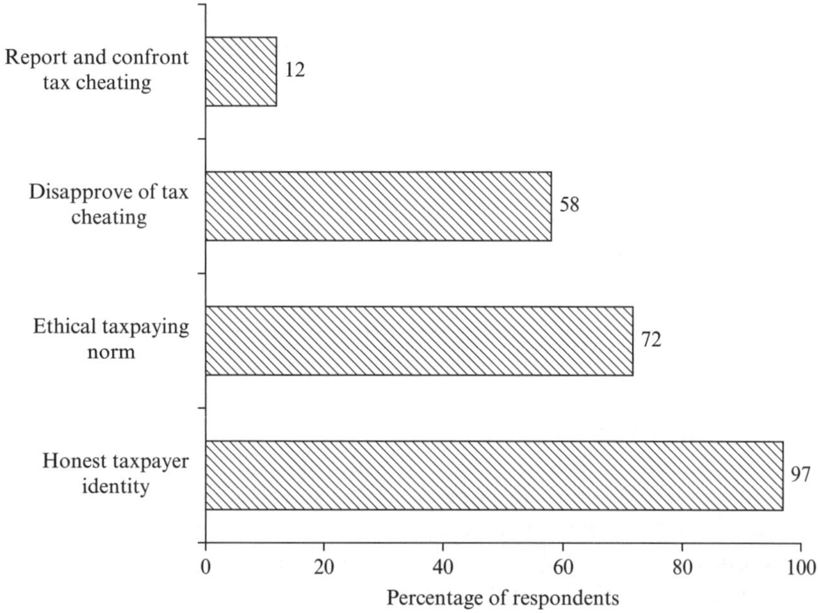

Notes:
1. The numbers used to construct the bar chart were obtained by calculating the percentage of cases scoring above the scale midpoint.
2. The honest taxpayer identity index was the average of responses to two items: On a 7-point 'do not agree at all' to 'agree completely' scale, how would you respond to the statement 'Being an honest taxpayer is important to me' and 'I feel a sense of pride in being an honest taxpayer' ($r = 0.76$).
3. An ethical taxpaying norm was the average of responses given on a 1–5 (no!! through yes!!) scale to the following items: (a) Do YOU think you should honestly declare cash earnings on your tax return?; (b) Do YOU think it is acceptable to overstate tax deductions on your tax return? (reverse scored); (c) Do YOU think working for cash-in-hand payments without paying tax is a trivial offence? (reverse scored); (d) Do YOU think the government should actively discourage participation in the cash economy? (alpha coefficient = 0.62).
4. Disapproving of tax cheating was measured by averaging responses given on a highly unlikely to highly likely 1–5 scale to the following questions: If you found out that an acquaintance was working for cash-in-hand payments, how likely is it that you would respond in the following ways – (a) I'd think they were clever (reverse scored); (b) I would not care (reverse scored); (c) I'd think it was wrong (alpha coefficient = 0.57).
5. The same rating scale as was used for disapproving of tax cheating was used to measure reporting and confronting tax cheating with the following two items: (a) I'd let them know I disapproved; (b) I'd report them to the tax office ($r = 0.48$).

Figure 5.3 Percentage of respondents reporting a thinking morally *coping style*

Table 5.1 Pearson product–moment correlation coefficients among the four measures representing thinking morally

Measures	Honest taxpayer identity	Ethical taxpaying norm	Disapprove of tax cheating
Honest taxpayer identity			
Ethical taxpaying norm	0.30***		
Disapprove of tax cheating	0.26***	0.50***	
Report and confront tax cheating	0.18***	0.28***	0.40***

Note: *** $p < 0.001$.

extraordinarily high 97 per cent of the sample laid claim to an honest taxpayer identity – feeling pride in the identity and considering such an identity as important. Adopting a moralistic stance towards taxation proved somewhat less attractive, particularly when respondents were questioned about calling people to account and reporting offences to the tax authority. A substantial 72 per cent of respondents displayed an ethical taxpaying norm, believing that it was wrong to cheat on tax, and 58 per cent disapproved of tax cheating. The proportion that would 'dob in' an acquaintance for tax cheating or call that person to account was only 12 per cent.

Despite their differences in capturing the moral zeal of Australians in relation to taxation, the four measures were positively and significantly intercorrelated (see Table 5.1), suggesting that all were relevant to reframing taxpaying as an honourable and normatively desirable activity.[3] The reframing exercise involves taxpayers in aligning personal beliefs about dealing with taxation with the expectations of authorities and the honest taxpaying community. The four measures were combined into the *thinking morally* coping scale for later analyses.

SUMMARY OF THE COPING-STYLE APPROACH

The above analyses provide support for the proposition that taxation threat can be managed much like any other stressor or hassle, by adopting a coping style and creating a narrative around it. The dominant style appears to be reframing as we mould ourselves in the image of the honest taxpayer. The flagship index for this coping response is identification with those in the community who are honest taxpayers – 97 per cent identified with this way of thinking. For all our huff and puff about taxation, the vast majority of us feel some pull towards the authority. Huff and puff, however, cannot be discounted as 'just hot air'. The coping styles of feeling oppressed and of taking control, while less prevalent, occupy the thoughts of a substantial proportion of taxpayers at one time or another. While recognizing potential sources of defiance when coping styles such as feeling oppressed or taking control take hold, the more immediate concern is to unpack theoretically the psychology behind what is arguably the tax authority's strongest weapon in containing defiance – thinking morally (Schwartz and Orleans 1967; Grasmick and Scott 1982; Gorsuch and Ortberg 1983; Jackson and Milliron 1986; Grasmick and Bursik 1990; Porcano and Price 1993; Andreoni et al. 1998; Richardson 2006).

SOCIAL INFRASTRUCTURE: EXTERNAL SUPPORT FOR THINKING MORALLY

The social distancing approach to defiance presumes that we withdraw from authority when threatened; we approach when the threat is reduced. Consistent with this premise is the prediction that those who are thinking morally about taxation have put threat to one side and will close the social distance. But this presents a theoretical inconsistency: how can the social distance approach explain an individual aligning themselves with authority and thinking morally, while at the same time fearing sanctions? Previous research has shown that sanctioning is most feared by those who take a moral stance on taxation (Grasmick and Bursik 1990; Smith 1992; Scholz and Pinney 1995). Given that they hold such knowledge, surely individuals when thinking morally would be wise to keep a degree of social distance? Or does this mean that the taxpayers who cope by thinking morally are deceptive, putting on a moral face to hide non-compliance that they fear will be punished if seen by the authorities? Or are we all tarred with the brush of the snitch to some extent, recognizing the potential for personal gain through ingratiating ourselves with power?

All accounts without doubt have some truth for all of us at some time in some place. It is important to remember that we have multiple selves that respond to the demands of the context in which we find ourselves (Goffman 1956, 1983). Within this framework, we should also remember that while thinking morally may be at the forefront of our minds, feeling oppressed and taking control are in our back pockets – access to one coping style does not mean we are unable to access the scripts of the others. The important point, however, is that scripts that engage us in conflict, tension and pretence with authority are unlikely to provide the peace of mind required to close social distance. This is after all what the reframing exercise should accomplish – a sense of comfort and ease in the midst of prospects of threat and coercion.

A plausible psychological account of how peace can be found in the eye of the storm is provided in part by social identity theory (Turner et al. 1987). We become part of a group that enables us to see ourselves as worthy and acceptable members of society – in our own eyes and in the eyes of significant others. By joining the authority's group, or a group to whom the authority shows benevolence, we assume that the authority will see us in a favourable way too, and will not be a danger to us. This, however, does not provide a sufficiently compelling account of how we, even as a group, can close the gap with authority while holding knowledge of sanctioning clearly in our minds. In today's democracies, we are not captives of the state: we can increase social distance from authority substantially without repercussions. Indeed, it was argued in Chapter 3 that some social distance is desirable for robust debate and a flourishing democracy.

One way of understanding the paradox of an individual's fear of sanctioning yet willingness to align is through the theory of possible selves (Markus and Nurius 1986; Oyserman and Markus 1990; Cross and Markus 1991). The deterrence threat posed by an authority's capacity to sanction is contingent on a person undertaking certain kinds of action. This means that the threat of sanctions is one step removed from the individual: it is *not* inevitable, unlike the loss of freedom or money on paying tax. This is not to deny that some people construe deterrence more potently, perhaps because they have experienced deterrence directly through being caught and sanctioned. But for the vast majority, sanctioning for tax noncompliance is something that they hear about through friends or as news circulates through the media. The message takes a familiar form: anyone entertaining the thought of non-compliance should think again, because they are likely to be caught and penalized if they become involved in illegal activity.

What is noteworthy about the form of this message is the subtle distinction it makes between a *possible* self and an *actual* self (Markus and Nurius 1986). The actual self describes the kind of person we see ourselves being right now, whereas a possible self describes the kind of person we might like – or might not like – to become in the future. We have both hoped-for and feared possible selves (Markus and Nurius 1986). Threats from authority in a democracy generally appeal to both kinds of possible selves. They warn us not to go in certain directions. Authorities demonize the path of defiance, and those who follow it. In past centuries, witchcraft became a useful symbol for distinguishing the 'good soul' from those who had gone astray (Geis and Bunn 1997). These days, military authorities have reinvented the technique with the depiction of foreign enemies as 'evil'. Following the attack on the World Trade Center, President Bush rallied the US nation around this theme: 'We will rid the world of the evil-doers' (www.cnn.com, 16 September 2001). If the population is sceptical of politics and rhetoric, the language may be more homely. For instance, in the regulatory context, it is not uncommon to hear talk of 'bad apples' and 'good apples'. (This usage, for example, is adopted in the 2003 Canadian documentary film, *The Corporation* by Mark Achbar, Jennifer Abbott and Joel Baken.)

While creating a possible self to be feared, authority offers us, and indeed counts on us adopting, their hoped-for law-abiding possible self. The psychology of these manoeuvres is clear. Authority shapes our identity for us, offering us a 'good possible self' or a 'bad possible self'. We align ourselves with the 'good possible self' and with this, the authority. We feel comfortable in embracing the exemption clause that the authority has offered us: 'You have nothing to fear; the sanctions won't be used against you if you do the right thing. They are designed to punish those who do the wrong thing and put us all at risk.'

The adaptability of the human mind to reframe events and experiences allows individuals to simultaneously accommodate both the threat of taxation and the fear of deterrence. Individuals who have managed to negate the threat of taxation through reframing can readily dismiss deterrence on the grounds that they are honest and dutiful taxpayers who are happy to play their part in building a better community. This sensibility allows them to live comfortably with the authority and its deterrence measures.

WHAT KEEPS THINKING MORALLY AT THE FOREFRONT OF OUR MINDS?

There are undoubtedly occasions when external sanctions prevent us from breaking the law. When a tax deduction or benefit is ruled illegitimate and the tax office announces a crackdown, the opportunity for tax evasion is dealt a serious blow. But much of the time, ambiguity surrounds what we can get away with and what we cannot, both because the law is unclear and because surveillance is inadequate (Long and Swingen 1988; Tanzi and Shome 1994; Brand 1996; Rossotti 2002; Picciotto 2007). In such circumstances, why don't we give in to temptation? Why don't we use the very adaptability that allows us to reframe taxation threat to reframe our temptation into a perfectly legal act? The answer is we do – but not without constraints. The constraints work so well that most of us most of the time do not take advantage of the illegal opportunities that present themselves, at least not to the extent that economists would predict if we were rational human beings seeking to maximize our financial well-being (Alm et al. 1995; Andreoni et al. 1998). We seem to think morally, even if the tax authority is 'asleep at the wheel'.

The way this happens is that we have an internal regulatory system of shame and guilt (Wikström 2002, 2004; Tangney et al. 2007). Generally speaking, this system echoes the ways of behaving that are deemed ethical and lawful in the broader society. Socialization theorists have long referred to the mapping of social prescriptions onto individual conscience as internalization. From childhood we learn the scripts and codes of our social group that are rewarded, and come to view them not as arbitrary edicts, but rather as ways of behaving that are intrinsically worthwhile and desirable, scripts that we want to follow because we believe they are 'best' and 'right'.

These are the aspects of our person in which we feel some pride. When we observe ourselves not doing as well as we should in our pride-generating endeavours, we feel disappointed, guilty and ashamed. We may also feel insecure because we have data that tell us that we may not be the kind of person who we think we are. Our ethical identity, as Harris (2007) calls it –the conception we have of our self at its best – is threatened. Often this insight comes about when we see ourselves through the eyes of others, the phenomenon that Cooley (1902: 179–85) referred to as the 'looking glass self'.

SHAME–GUILT: THE THREAT OF SANCTIONS FROM WITHIN

Because ethical identities are states of being that we believe we *should* live up to, any situation that alerts us to our failure to do so is likely to elicit emotional feedback of a negative kind. This negative feedback we refer to as shame–guilt. Following past practice (Ahmed et al. 2001), we make no distinction between shame and guilt. We follow Harris (2001, 2007), who brings shame and guilt together as intertwined, powerful and mutually reinforcing emotions that tell us our ethical identity is under threat. When our ethical identity is not implicated, the emotion we feel is much milder and is more likely to be a simple case of embarrassment. Harris (2001) debunks old distinctions between shame as an emotion that others *impose* upon us for breaking social norms and guilt as an emotion that we *generate* ourselves because we know we did not live up to our own standards.

Drawing on the work of philosopher Bernard Williams (1993), and psychology's Henri Tajfel (1972: 272–302), Harris (2001, 2007) points out that the evaluations we hold of ourselves and the evaluations that our significant others and reference groups hold of us are mutually reinforcing. Our values and standards are not peculiar to us; they are shared with our group – indeed they are acquired through our interactions with our group, and reinforced by them through our social exchanges. When we fail to live up to these values and standards, we need others to help us make sense of what we have done. 'Did I really do that?' 'Was it as bad as I think – or as bad as you think?' This social validation process is something that we all do, even if the other we are talking to is an imaginary figure in our head. In the process of deciding whether we have or have not done wrong, we need others to affirm our standards ('yes, you do hold that value, as do we') and validate our behaviour ('yes, you did act in a way that breached that standard'). If in the process we fall short as the person we think we are, we feel bad about ourselves, and we do so because we have failed in our own eyes (what many call guilt) and in the eyes of our reference group (what many call shame). Our eyes and our group's eyes are interconnected. Ethical identity, according to Harris, is the link between self and the group, and brings shame and guilt together.

Feelings of shame–guilt need to be managed. They may be managed in such a way that we are full of remorse for our actions; or we may feel outrage at the actions of the authority and believe that what we have done, although unlawful, was right and proper. Needless to say, remorse is what authority wants us to feel, but their needs are not the dominant concern of the individual coping with shame–guilt. Whatever the context, whatever the view of the authority, the objective of shame management strategies is to rid the self of shame and restore our psychological equilibrium so that we can feel good about ourselves again. Two such strategies are of interest in the present context, shame acknowledgement and shame displacement (Ahmed 2001).

Shame acknowledgement occurs when individuals admit and accept responsibility for wrongdoing and set about making amends for the harm done. The strategy is one of realizing one's shame and guilt, and finding the courage to get the problem out into the open, fix things up as best one can, and move on. One of the possible and desirable outcomes of shame acknowledgement is that it provides the opportunity to restore social relationships with significant others within one's group. Also restored is a sense of inner peace, of no longer feeling guilt-ridden or overwhelmed by concerns of who will find out. As such, it is a natural ally of the reframing coping style of thinking morally.

Shame displacement is a response that allows individuals to escape from the source of their shame. The most notable feature of shame displacement is anger and blame. Individuals will often explain their wrongdoing to themselves and to others in terms of the faults and shortcomings of other people; they become angry at the world and may even portray themselves as victims of circumstance or ill will. Shame displacement is a natural ally of the emotion-focused coping style of feeling oppressed.

The responses of acknowledgement and displacement should not be conceptualized as alternatives or as incompatible responses. The self-regulatory system allows us to flip from one to the other as we seek to regain psychological equilibrium. For example, if we were confronted with an image of ourselves on national television as someone who cheats on tax, we might vacillate between thinking how foolish we were to deal with our tax in that way, and being furious with the media for portraying us so unsympathetically. Anger and disappointment with ourselves is often confused with anger at others. We can do both, acknowledging and displacing shame almost simultaneously, trying one, then the other in a bid to decide which works best.

So how does the internal regulatory system operate to keep the coping style of thinking morally at the forefront of our minds? Let us suppose we are privy to the thoughts and feelings of Anne, a young corporate executive. Having worked her way through university as a tax investigator, Anne has become both familiar and comfortable with the coping style of thinking morally. In the corporate world, however, she enjoys the cleverness of tax avoidance schemes, schemes that she can readily use to reduce her own tax with a very good chance of not being detected. Anne is tempted. But then she remembers who she is – she believes in paying tax, she takes pride in being an honest taxpayer, she believes that people who don't pay tax should be prosecuted. On the other hand, the scheme she is tempted to buy into may be tested in the courts in time and found to be legal. But what if it is not? What if there is a crackdown? What would her family and friends say should she be caught? A feared-possible self enters Anne's consciousness. This feared-possible self makes her feel sick inside, she feels uncertain – she will leave buying in to the scheme for another day.

For Anne, and for most of us most of the time, the internal regulatory system, the external regulatory system and the coping style of thinking morally work in tandem to keep us law-abiding. As the media parades before us opportunities for saving tax, we imagine possible selves and possible scenarios. Those who cope with the taxation threat by thinking morally hold an ethical identity of being an honest taxpayer. They believe that without honesty on their side, they run the risk of being caught and sanctioned by the tax authority. With this realization comes a 'shot' of shame–guilt on considering something that might be tantamount to cheating. The discomfort of the anticipated emotion needs to be resolved (Lewis 1971; Scheff 1990; Retzinger 1991). There may be a period of indulgence in protective excuse making: avoidance is not necessarily illegal; others do it and get away with it; or, if something went wrong, it would be others' fault – the tax office, financial planners or tax advisers. After a period of vacillation, however, the internal regulatory system prevails. The discomfort subsides when the individual steps back from temptation and reaffirms commitment to being an honest taxpayer by saying 'I did the right thing.' Shame acknowledgement and shame displacement are the internal sanctioning agents of the tax system, triggered by thoughts of being caught and sanctioned, and fears of losing a prized ethical identity.

In using psychological theory to provide this account of a coping style of thinking morally, a coherent explanation has emerged of why tax morale is at the heart of tax compliance in stable, well-established democratic societies. Tax morale has been the term used by Swiss researchers who have pioneered the importance of obligation and state–citizen relations in bringing about compliance, and have for a decade been challenging the idea that deterrence is the single most important regulatory tool available to authorities (Frey 1997, 2003; Frey and Feld 2001; Torgler 2003; Feld and Frey 2005, 2007). In this chapter, the coping style of thinking morally, akin to the Swiss concept of tax morale, is proposed as a self-regulatory mechanism blocking expressions of defiance. Perception of deterrence is conceived as part of the process of arriving at a coping style of thinking morally. The next question, then, is: does deterrence play a different role for those who can't or won't think morally about taxation?

WHEN THINKING MORALLY FAILS

Authorities should not assume that their followers always will or should opt for the coping style of thinking morally about taxation. Authorities are not always fair, reasonable and right. While institutional scaffolding might work well in keeping authority and the community on the same page, it is inevitable that, at times, authority loses its place and has difficulty getting back on the right page. The same may be said for the community. As we saw in Chapter 4, there will always be people who have serious reservations about taxation. This is not to say that they are not aware of the social pressures on them to comply. They are aware of the pronouncements of tax practitioners and experts, approving of some ideas for reducing tax payments, not approving of others. We are all subject to social environs that niggle and shape actions, that kick-start guilt and shame, and that make us question whether or not we are living up to our ethical identity.

But if we don't believe in taxation, or we think the tax system has lost its way, we are less likely to resolve taxation threat by thinking morally. Feeling oppressed and taking control are more attractive options.

Those who have constructed the threat of taxation as an act of government oppression or as a battle for control are likely to have their own strategies for managing external (deterrence) and internal (shame–guilt) sanctioning systems. For these actors, awareness of deterrence measures and inklings of shame–guilt are likely to be resented as yet another form of oppression or domination imposed from outside. The moral or normative framework that would normally be triggered when confronted with the prospect of being caught for wrongdoing is unlikely to be 'switched on' voluntarily when defiant individuals think about their dealings with the tax authority. Yet a sanctioning authority is not easily dismissed, especially when it can stigmatize and ostracize those who do not submit to its power. Social rejection is unnerving (Braithwaite, J. 1989; Benson 1990). How we cope with rejection, however, depends on how we interpret it, and how others who are important to us interpret it (Braithwaite, J. 1989; Maruna 2001).

For this reason, sanctioning may produce unexpected outcomes; and the tax research to date tends to support this conclusion (Hessing et al. 1992; Scholz and Pinney 1993 cited in Andreoni et al. 1998; Wenzel 2004a; Braithwaite, V. et al. 2007). The work of Brehm and Brehm (1981) warns against thinking that people will kowtow to authority when they are threatened with sanctions. Those who view taxation as oppressive or resent its hold over them may react against the authority by asserting their freedom, and acting in ways that are the direct opposite to what the authority intends. Taylor (2003) found that hotbeds of reactance are more likely in some groups than others. Reactance is likely to be strong among people who fail to identify with the tax authority – in this case, those who are more likely to feel threat from the authority and remain socially distant.

This raises the question: can sanctions work with those who are already threatened and socially distant? Brehm and Brehm (1981) found experimentally that when deterrence was increased, eventually a point of capitulation to authority was reached. In the tax context, Wenzel (2004a) found deterrence was associated with less tax evasion when personal ethical norms were weak and when social norms were perceived to be supportive of the sanctions. In this case social distance from authority was offset by how the individual perceived the relationship of others with the tax authority. Influence from significant others, however, depends on willingness to take this perspective on board: if people are locked in battle with the tax authority, nothing else may enter their line of vision.

In a study on the effectiveness of deterrence in regulating nursing home care, perceived deterrence worked to increase compliance in one group of managers, but had a counter-deterrent effect in the other (Braithwaite, J. and Makkai 1991; Makkai and Braithwaite 1994b). The managers in the group in which perceived deterrence did not work were powerfully swayed by their emotions: they described themselves as hot-headed, being unable to control their anger, and taking a long time to calm down about things that upset them. With heightened emotions, deterrence was associated with deteriorating compliance.

These findings suggest that when the authority's preferred self-regulatory option, the 'good-self' pathway, is out of action, the effects of sanctioning are likely to be unpredictable. If sanctions are substantial enough, some may come into the fold through fear of the consequences; but other socially distant taxpayers may find comfort in dismissing the sanctioning process as bluff, or as underresourced and ineffective, or as not overly aversive in its consequences. They may comfort themselves with stories that give them a sense of technical or moral superiority over the tax authority. There is no reason why the socially distant can't neutralize threat just as they can neutralize accusations of wrongdoing. If sanctioning lacks credibility in their eyes, the defiant will maintain social distance from the authority.

TESTING THE COPING WITH TAXATION THREAT MODEL

The ideas that have been set out in this chapter require empirical testing. Data from the 2000 national random survey, the 'Community Hopes, Fears and Actions Survey' (n = 2040) will be used for this purpose. The analyses are organized around four questions and their associated hypotheses.

Question 1 Is there empirical evidence to support three styles of coping with taxation threat?
Hypothesis 5.1 The measures selected as representative of the coping styles of thinking morally, taking control and feeling oppressed will define three relatively independent factors in a factor analysis.

The expectation is that these factors will have non-significant and/or low correlations with each other, suggesting that people can cope using any of these styles; in other words, preference for one does not preclude the use of others.

Question 2 How does the social infrastructure of external and internal regulatory systems support the coping styles?
Hypothesis 5.2(a) Perceptions of high deterrence will accompany a coping style of *thinking morally* about taxpaying and tax evasion.

While recognizing various factors at work in shaping the deterrence effect, cognitive consistency theory would predict that where deterrence is recognized, fear would invite a sense of victimization; where deterrence is not recognized, absence of fear would invite testing of the boundaries. In this spirit, the following hypotheses are proposed:

Hypothesis 5.2(b) Perceptions of low deterrence will be linked with *taking control.*
Hypothesis 5.2(c) Perceptions of high deterrence will be linked with *feeling oppressed.*
Hypothesis 5.2(d) *Thinking morally* will be associated with an internal regulatory system that favours shame acknowledgement over tax cheating and discards the option of displacing shame on to others.
Hypothesis 5.2(e) The coping styles of *taking control* and *feeling oppressed* are more likely to be associated with the reverse pattern of high shame displacement and low acknowledgement.

Question 3 Are the ways in which individuals cope with the threat of taxation useful in differentiating resistant defiance and dismissive defiance?
Hypothesis 5.3(a) *Thinking morally* will be negatively associated with both resistant and dismissive defiance.
Hypothesis 5.3(b) Of the remaining coping styles, *taking control* is likely to be a stronger predictor of dismissive than resistant defiance; and
Hypothesis 5.3(c) *Feeling oppressed* is likely to be a stronger predictor of resistant than dismissive defiance.

The rationale for Hypotheses 5.3(b) and 5.3(c) is that the ideas behind both taking control and dismissive defiance involve a challenge to or disregard for authority. The ideas behind both feeling oppressed and resistant defiance involve opposition to recognized authority.

Question 4 What role does deterrence play in a coping with threat model of defiance?
Hypothesis 5.4(a) The role played by deterrence within the coping with threat model is to buttress the coping style of *thinking morally*, which, in turn, reduces the likelihood of both resistant and dismissive defiance.
Hypothesis 5.4(b) Deterrence may reduce *taking control*, which in turn, will reduce defiance, particularly dismissive defiance.

Hypothesis 5.4(c) Deterrence may increase *feeling oppressed*, which, in turn, will increase defiance, particularly resistant defiance.

Question 1: Three Coping Styles and Taxation Threat

The hypothesis is that the three coping styles of *thinking morally*, *taking control* and *feeling oppressed* are coherent ways of thinking about taxation that can be distinguished from each other. Furthermore, they are not mutually exclusive – that is, an individual may use any of the styles in response to taxation threat, without a preference for one precluding the others. We can entertain thinking morally and feeling oppressed simultaneously, or we can try our hand at taking control, while thinking morally and feeling oppressed. Practically, this means we are familiar with these ways of coping with taxation threat, we know people who talk about taxation threat in these terms, and we are versatile, choosing the style that suits the time and place. The first step toward subjecting this assumption to empirical verification is to factor-analyse the ten measures selected to represent the three coping styles. A factor analysis should produce three clear factors reflecting thinking morally, taking control and feeling oppressed.

A principal components analysis with varimax rotation was performed on 2000 survey data. The findings produced three well-defined factors to support the hypothesized model, accounting for 53 per cent of the variance. From Table 5.2, Factor 1 represented the reframing coping style whereby any potential tax threat was seen through the lens of moral obligation to obey the law. Individuals took pride in having an honest taxpayer identity, held an ethical norm in favour of paying tax, disapproved of tax cheating, and were prepared to take action to stop others cheating on tax. Proponents of this response were a regulatory force in and of themselves. Factor 1 was therefore labelled *thinking morally*.

Factor 2 in Table 5.2 represented commitment to push against the system and stave off the taxman. Protective action included the amount of effort that they had put into financial planning to minimize tax, arranging their finances in different ways to find the best strategy for minimizing tax, and having a professional adviser who knew how to reduce the tax bill through creative accounting and aggressive tax planning. Factor 2 was labelled *taking control* because the individual was focused on asserting some level of independence from the authority.

Factor 3 in Table 5.2 represented feelings of losing out and being the victim of taxation. Paying more than others, unable to win against the tax office and unable to get ahead financially because of tax describe a coping style of *feeling oppressed* at the hands of the tax system.

Thinking morally, *taking control* and *feeling oppressed* emerge as three

Table 5.2 Results of a principal components analysis with varimax rotation of ten variables measuring coping with taxation threat

Coping with taxation threat	Factor 1	Factor 2	Factor 3
Feeling oppressed			
Being economically deprived due to tax	−0.06	0.13	**0.73**
Paying more than fair share of tax	0.02	−0.12	**0.71**
Received unfavourable decisions	−0.21	0.11	**0.63**
Taking control			
Effort to minimize tax	0.02	**0.81**	0.04
Different ways of doing tax return	0.08	**0.79**	0.07
Have a professional tax minimizer	−0.21	**0.62**	0.01
Thinking morally			
Honest taxpayer identity	**0.52**	−0.03	−0.19
Ethical taxpaying norm	**0.74**	−0.15	−0.11
Disapprove of tax cheating	**0.80**	−0.08	−0.05
Report and confront tax cheating	**0.68**	0.13	0.05

Notes:
1. The criteria for factor rotation were eigenvalues greater than or equal to 1.0 and the scree test. Both recommended a three-factor solution.
2. The measures that contributed principally to each factor in the analysis (in bold) were combined to produce aggregate scores that represented *thinking morally*, *taking control* and *feeling oppressed*. Before being averaged, the measures were standardized to have a mean of zero and standard deviation of 1.

coherent, yet distinct, factors that represent coping styles that individuals use to deal with the threat of taxation. On the basis of these findings, composite scales were formed for testing Hypotheses 5.2 and 5.3. The scores of respondents on scales representing *thinking morally*, *taking control* and *feeling oppressed* were intercorrelated. The highest correlation was –0.25 ($p < 0.001$) between *thinking morally* and *feeling oppressed*. Those who were most attracted to the *thinking morally* coping style were least likely to adopt the coping style of *feeling oppressed*. This correlation suggested that the coping styles were not quite as independent as expected. Other relationships, however, were weaker and more in line with expectations. *Thinking morally* correlated –0.08 ($p < 0.001$) with *taking control*, and *taking control* correlated 0.10 ($p < 0.001$) with *feeling oppressed*. The low to modest correlations do not prevent us from concluding that individuals can be *thinking morally* at one moment in time and *taking control* or *feeling oppressed* at another. One coping style does not lock out another.

Question 2: Social Infrastructure and Coping Styles

The external and internal regulatory systems were measured in the surveys by asking respondents what they thought would happen if they were caught for tax evasion. All measures were based on previously developed instruments (Braithwaite, J. and Makkai 1991 for deterrence and Ahmed 2001 for shame management). Respondents were required to imagine two scenarios, one in which they were caught for not declaring all their income, and the other in which they were caught exaggerating their work-related deductions (see Note 1, Table 5.3). It is important to emphasize that the external regulatory system was measured at a perceptual and subjective level. The key question was not whether people knew about the deterrence measures that were actually in place, but rather what people's fears were should they cheat on their tax. Respondents estimated the chances of being caught and the likelihood of being sanctioned. They also indicated how big a problem being caught and sanctioned would create for them (see Note 1, Table 5.3).

These same scenarios were used to assess the internal regulatory system. Respondents were asked to think about being sanctioned with a penalty, and to turn their attention towards their internal emotional responses. A series of questions was asked to measure shame management strategies. The items in the acknowledgement scale captured the negative feelings of personal failure (e.g. shame, guilt, embarrassment, humiliation) that are experienced when we know we have not lived up to standards of competence and morality, combined with a desire to put things right and learn from our mistakes. The items in the displacement scale redirected negative feelings of blame and anger on to others, in particular the tax office (see Note 2, Table 5.3).

Relating coping styles to perceived deterrence and shame management

The findings reported in Table 5.3 are partially consistent with expectations. Deterrence had most credibility among those who favoured a coping style of *thinking morally*. More detailed analyses showed that those who scored high on *thinking morally* were systematically more fearful on all components of deterrence – they estimated their chances of being caught as higher, their punishment as more severe, and they regarded the problems resulting from being caught and punished as more serious. External sanctioning, therefore, provided a consistent and coherent buttress for those who coped with taxation threat through *thinking morally*. Hypothesis 5.2(a) was supported.

Hypothesis 5.2(b) was also supported. The credibility of deterrence was low among those who favoured *taking control*, mainly because they

Table 5.3 Pearson product–moment correlation coefficients for coping styles with perceived deterrence and shame management (acknowledgement and displacement)

Coping with taxation threat	Overall deterrence	Acknowledgement	Displacement
Thinking morally	0.26***	0.42***	–0.22***
Taking control	–0.08**	–0.09***	0.16***
Feeling oppressed	0.04	–0.20***	0.30***

Notes:

** $p < 0.01$; *** $p < 0.01$.

1. The following two questions were asked of respondents: (a) Imagine you have been paid $5000 in cash for work that you have done outside your regular job. You don't declare it on your income tax return. What do you think the chances are that you will get caught?; (b) Imagine you have claimed $5000 as work deductions when the expenses have nothing to do with work. What do you think the chances are that you will get caught? First, respondents were required to estimate the chances of being caught in each case. Responses were made along a five-point continuum, a horizontal line with the following points marked – 0 per cent (about zero), 25 per cent, 50/50, 75 per cent, 100 per cent (almost certain). Estimates were averaged across the two scenarios.

   Second, respondents rated the chance of four legal consequences occurring on the same five-point scale used above. Chances of being sanctioned was the average (over the two scenarios) of assessments of the following legal consequences: (a) taken to court + pay a substantial fine + pay the tax you owe with interest; (b) taken to court + pay the tax you owe with interest; (c) pay a substantial fine + pay the tax you owe with interest; (d) pay the tax you owe with interest. Third, the magnitude of the problem associated with each of these legal consequences was measured. Ratings were made on a four-point scale from 1 (no problem) through 4 (large problem). Scores on the magnitude of the problem created by sanctions were obtained by averaging these ratings over the two scenarios.

   The overall deterrence term was the average of the deterrence scores for the two scenarios. The deterrence term for each scenario was calculated as follows: Deterrence $= (C \times P_1 \times S_1) + (C \times P_2 \times S_2) + (C \times P_3 \times S_3) + (C \times P_4 \times S_4)$ where C = likelihood of being caught; P_1 = likelihood of having to pay tax with interest; S_1 = severity of the problem created by having to pay tax with interest; P_2 = likelihood of having to pay tax with interest + penalty; S_2 = severity of the problem created by having to pay tax with interest + penalty; P_3 = likelihood of being taken to court and having to pay tax with interest; S_3 = severity of the problem created by being taken to court and having to pay tax with interest; P_4 = likelihood of being taken to court and having to pay tax with interest + penalty; S_4 = severity of the problem created by being taken to court and having to pay tax with interest + penalty. The mean of the overall deterrence measure was 189.13, standard deviation 105.09.

2. Respondents were asked to imagine how they would feel after being caught and given a substantial fine in the two scenarios mentioned above.

   Shame acknowledgement was measured by asking respondents to rate on a four-point scale how likely they were to feel the following: (a) that you had let down your family; (b) ashamed of yourself; (c) angry with yourself for what you did; (d) concerned to put matters right and put it behind you; (e) that what you had done was wrong; (f) bad about the harm and trouble you'd caused; (g) humiliated; (h) embarrassed; (i) guilty. The shame displacement items were: (a) feel unable to decide, in your own mind, whether or not you had done the wrong thing; (b) feel angry with the tax office; (c) feel bothered by thoughts that you were treated unfairly;

Table 5.3 (continued)

(d) feel that you wanted to get even with the tax office. Responses were summed for acknowledgement and displacement over the items in each scenario and then an average score was calculated. The acknowledgement scale had an alpha reliability coefficient of 0.95 in scenario 1 and 0.95 in scenario 2. The scale correlation between scenarios was 0.91. The displacement scale had an alpha reliability coefficient of 0.71 in scenario 1 and 0.75 in scenario 2. The scale correlation between scenarios was 0.83. The mean for the combined shame acknowledgement scale was 3.06 (standard deviation = 0.81), for shame displacement 1.87 (standard deviation = 0.66).

estimated chances of being caught as low and any problems resulting from being caught as minimal. Perceived deterrence was not related to *feeling oppressed*, although more detailed analysis showed that one component of deterrence was more highly endorsed by this group. *Feeling oppressed* was associated with anticipating more significant problems if one happened to be caught and sanctioned. This finding was consistent with seeing taxation as a regime that inflicts suffering. Overall, however, Hypothesis 5.2(c) was not supported, at least not at the bivariate level of analysis (support is found at the multivariate level in Figures 5.4 and 5.5).

These results show that the ways people cope with taxation threat are associated with their expectations of how the tax authority uses deterrence. Those who find it most convincing are those most committed to doing the right thing. But this still does not give a complete account of how people can confidently align themselves with authority, recognize deterrence from an authority and keep out of harm's way. Such composure is presumed to come about through reliance on a well-tuned internal regulatory system.

In accord with Hypothesis 5.2(d), a strong internal regulatory system characterized those who favoured the coping style of *thinking morally*. *Thinking morally* existed comfortably alongside the acknowledgement of wrongdoing through feeling guilt, shame and embarrassment. Those who favoured *thinking morally* about taxation threat were also less likely to imagine themselves getting angry with others or displacing shame in the event that they were caught cheating. In contrast, those who preferred to cope with taxation threat through *taking control* or *feeling oppressed* were more likely to displace shame and were less likely to show signs of acknowledgement over their evasion. These findings were in accord with Hypothesis 5.2(e).

These findings provide support for the proposition that how we view the threat of taxation is related to how well our internal regulatory system works. If we reframe taxation as an honourable activity and take pride in being an honest taxpayer, we are more likely to have an internal regulatory system that alerts us to impending danger through triggering high shame acknowledgement and low shame displacement.

If the threat of taxation cannot be neutralized, and as a result, feelings of oppression and interest in taking control dominate our thinking, the internal regulatory system is not likely to be tuned to a 'deterring frequency'. When such individuals consider scenarios of being caught and sanctioned for tax evasion, they deal with their discomfort by blaming others, including the tax authority. The shame–guilt that is critical to self-regulation does not necessarily kick in.

Question 3: Coping Styles and Resistant and Dismissive Defiance

The third question examines how theorizing responses to taxation in terms of threat and coping helps our understanding of resistant and dismissive defiance. From Table 5.4, Hypotheses 5.3(a), 5.3(b) and 5.3(c) were supported.

Thinking morally was associated with low levels of defiance both of the resistant and dismissive kinds. *Thinking morally* was therefore a regulatory process that would boost cooperation between taxpayers and tax authorities. *Taking control* and *feeling oppressed* were both linked to defiance; but as expected, coping through taking control was more strongly linked to dismissive defiance, while coping through feelings of oppression was more strongly linked to resistant defiance. The model of coping with taxation threat appears useful in teasing apart the narratives of resistance and dismissiveness.

Question 4: Deterrence, Shame, Coping and Defiance

The final question presents the challenge of putting all the parts together – the external regulatory system of deterrence, the internal regulatory system of shame management, the coping with threat responses, and defiance. The alignment of *thinking morally* with shame–guilt and deterrence provides authority with the regulatory process that it requires for containing defiance without recourse to coercion and brute force. The expectation is that *thinking morally*, shame acknowledgement and perceived deterrence will be associated with low defiance of both resistant and dismissive

Table 5.4 Pearson product–moment correlation coefficients for coping styles with resistant and dismissive defiance

Coping with taxation threat	Resistant defiance	Dismissive defiance
Thinking morally	−0.39***	−0.21***
Taking control	0.16***	0.29***
Feeling oppressed	0.55***	0.12***

Note: *** $p < 0.01$.

kinds. Theoretically, it might be postulated that perceived deterrence of law violation will signal that certain psychological processes over the law should take place – *thinking morally* and feeling shame at the prospect of breaking the law. These processes should then protect against resistant and dismissive defiance.

Defiance, however, is likely to increase in the presence of the other coping processes of *taking control* and *feeling oppressed*. Both are likely to be accompanied by displacement. Deterrence may keep *taking control* in check, but it is unlikely to be helpful in containing the coping style of *feeling oppressed*.

The starting point for testing how well these relationships hold together in the data set is the correlation matrix involving all the key explanatory variables (see Table 5.5). The next stage is to use a multivariate analysis to tease apart the important relationships and control for extraneous effects that can mask relationships of core interest.

To test the plausibility of the proposed accounts of deterrence within the coping and threat model of defiance, structural equation modelling (SEM) was used. SEM offered a number of advantages over regression and path modelling in the current situation. First, through the notion of a latent construct, SEM offered a method of ensuring that predictor variables were as parsimonious and coherent as possible, an important consideration given the sheer number of measures involved in the defiance modelling project overall (Chapters 4 to 8). Second, SEM offered greater prospects of controlling error variances that were likely to be significant in a project that relied on newly conceptualized variables and newly

Table 5.5 Pearson product–moment correlation coefficients among variables measuring deterrence, shame management, coping styles and defiance

Measures	1	2	3	4	5	6	7
1. Perceived deterrence							
2. Acknowledgement	0.39***						
3. Displacement	0.07	−0.01					
4. Thinking morally	0.26***	0.43***	−0.23***				
5. Taking control	−0.08**	−0.09***	0.16***	−0.08**			
6. Feeling oppressed	0.04	−0.20***	0.30***	−0.20***	0.10***		
7. Resistance	−0.10***	−0.34***	0.33***	−0.39***	0.16***	0.55***	
8. Dismissiveness	−0.08***	−0.21***	0.29***	−0.21***	0.29***	0.12***	0.25***

Note: ** $p < 0.01$; *** $p < 0.001$.

developed measures. Third, SEM was the procedure considered most likely to provide useful insights into the plausibility of hypothesized pathways. This information was important to the aspiration of understanding how defiance developed over time and how it might be constructively contained.

SEM models were developed using Analysis of Moment Structures (AMOS) version 6.00 with maximum likelihood estimation (Arbuckle 2005). Two methodological decisions that were taken in the course of developing the models concerned the handling of missing data and the formation of the latent variables. First, missing data were managed through Expectation Maximization (Byrne 2001: 296–7). This procedure allowed for the retention of as many cases as possible. Second, the variables used in the SEM analysis were slightly modified with the construction of latent variables to represent coping styles, shame management and defiance. Shame acknowledgement was collapsed into the latent construct, thinking morally and shame displacement into feeling oppressed. This decision, made on the basis of the SEM analysis, was consistent with the conclusions reached in a previous analysis of coping styles and shame management (Braithwaite, V. et al. 2007). Another change made in the course of the SEM process involved the latent construct, taking control. Only two component scales were used for SEM: different ways of doing tax and effort to minimize tax. Having a professional tax minimizer was omitted because of the problem of missing data.

A model of resistant defiance

The pathways to resistant defiance under the threat and coping model are set out in Figure 5.4. Perceived deterrence affected the coping responses of individuals in different ways, and through these influences became

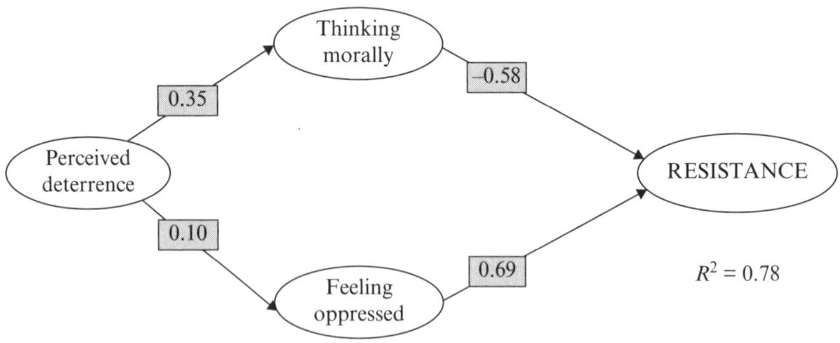

Figure 5.4 A structural equation model linking deterrence, coping styles and resistance (2000 measures)

indirectly relevant to resistant defiance. Perceiving a credible sanctioning system in operation strengthened commitment to doing the right thing and thinking morally. Less marked, but nevertheless significant, was a strengthening of the coping style of feeling oppressed.

A comparison of the main pathways and their effects on resistance focused attention on how perceived deterrence and feeling oppressed enhanced prospects of defiance, and how perceived deterrence and thinking morally contained defiance. When individuals believed that tax evasion would lead to negative consequences (being caught and punished, and suffering as a consequence), their resistant posture was torn in two directions: feeling oppressed tugged them one way, while thinking morally called on them to rein in their resistance. These two pathways dominated the shaping of resistance. In the SEM model, the latent construct of taking control failed to explain resistant defiance.

Taken together, the findings show that a large part of the negative posturing measured by resistance can be traced back to the coping styles of thinking morally and feeling oppressed. A substantial 76 per cent of the variance in resistance was explained by these styles of coping with taxation threat. The various indices of how well the data fitted the model were all satisfactory (see Appendix A for goodness-of-fit indices and squared multiple correlations for latent constructs).

A model of dismissive defiance

The SEM model representing the prediction of dismissiveness from coping with threat is depicted in Figure 5.5. All three coping styles of thinking morally, taking control and feeling oppressed contributed to explaining dismissive defiance. Taking control and feeling oppressed fuelled dismissiveness, while thinking morally reined it in. Deterrence

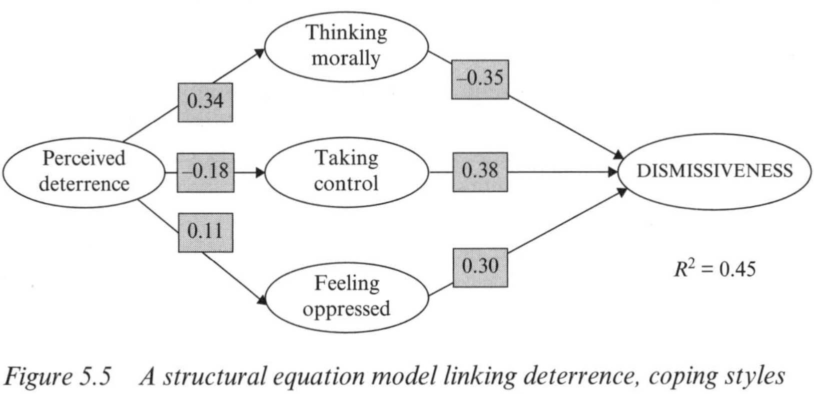

Figure 5.5 A structural equation model linking deterrence, coping styles and dismissiveness (2000 measures)

strengthened the coping styles of thinking morally and feeling oppressed, as occurred in the resistance model. At the same time, perceived deterrence weakened the taking control coping style.

Deterrence shows signs of being a means of reasserting the control of the authority through making a taking control coping style less attractive and a thinking morally style more attractive. Dismissive defiance can be constrained when individuals are subjugated to the rule of law. But the unintended consequence should not be discounted too readily. Congruent with the authority's agenda of control and subjugation, individuals who were aware of tax office deterrence felt oppressed. Oppression then strengthened dismissiveness, just as it strengthened resistance.

The variance in dismissive defiance accounted for by the threat and coping model was 45 per cent, much lower than in the case of resistance. Understanding dismissive defiance requires another level of theorizing (addressed in Chapter 7). Nevertheless, the hypothesis as to how coping with taxation threat was related to the posture of dismissiveness was confirmed. Dismissiveness of authority was most likely to be found among those who were taking control in dealing with taxation threat. Dismissiveness was also associated with the rejection of thinking morally and the acceptance of feeling oppressed. Goodness-of-fit indices for the model were satisfactory. These statistics, together with the squared multiple correlations for latent constructs, appear in Appendix A.

Summary of findings for Question 4

Hypothesis 5.4 with its three parts was supported: perceived deterrence was connected with coping styles, which in turn were connected with the defiance postures. As predicted, the strength of these connections differed for the two forms of defiance. Although the coping with taxation threat approach held more explanatory potential with regard to resistant than dismissive defiance, the model was useful for teasing apart defiance in its two forms.

When individuals are disenchanted with the coping style of thinking morally, they may choose either the resistant or dismissive pathway. Resistance is more likely when individuals cope with the taxation threat by feeling oppressed. Dismissiveness is more likely when the preferred coping style is taking control along with feeling oppressed.

From the analyses so far, deterrence appears to shape outcomes differently depending on the circumstances. When deterrence is perceived to be high, thinking morally appears to gain a boost and defiance of both the resistant and dismissive kinds is contained. Thinking morally is the most important single lever for reducing defiance across its two forms. But deterrence has other effects. Perceived deterrence promises to curtail a taking control coping style, but this assists only in dealing with dismissive defiance, not resistant defiance. While reining in the way in which taking control may fuel dismissiveness, greater perceived deterrence could inflame feeling oppressed. The outcome is that an increase in oppression will strengthen both forms of defiance, in particular resistant defiance. Perceived deterrence is therefore associated with varying outcomes, depending on which coping style comes to the fore in the mind of the individual who fears sanctioning.

CONCLUSION

Taxation threat is created by the tax authority's claim on an individual's freedom and income. Individuals cope with the experience of taxation threat by thinking morally, taking control or feeling oppressed. In the process of coping with the threat of taxation, individuals appraise the sanctioning that is in place for dealing with evasion. Sanctioning can deter through penalties or through arousing internal feelings of shame–guilt.

How individuals cope with the threat of taxation and how they appraise and manage the risks of sanctioning are interconnected. The links between coping response and the internal sanctioning system in the event of tax evasion are uncomplicated. Those who have reframed taxpaying as the right thing to do (thinking morally) are able to self-regulate temptation to evade tax through shame–guilt, and are therefore able to feel comfortable aligning themselves with the authority. Those who are unable to discount their concerns about taxation (feeling oppressed, taking control) do not have an effective internal self-regulatory mechanism (their negative feelings about being caught and penalized turn into anger and blame rather than shame–guilt). They have every reason to distance themselves from the authority, because they do not have the necessary social-psychological infrastructure to feel safe in close proximity to the authority.

The role that the external sanctioning system (perceived deterrence) has on the social distancing response depends on the coping style adopted. Awareness of the likelihood of deterrence is strongest among those who are thinking morally about taxation. In other words, it is strongest among those who have least social distance from the authority. Paradoxically, we would infer from this that those who were thinking morally were the least threatened. The explanation offered for this seemingly contradictory state of affairs is that awareness of deterrence among those so close to the authority is pronounced because, psychologically, they have freed themselves from the sanctioning threat. They rely on shame–guilt to self-regulate. Providing they feel no shame–guilt, they are good people. Their virtue is their protection from the authority's sanctions – the sanctions are a threat to others who are not thinking morally. Thus perceived deterrence brings the internal shame–guilt sanctioning system and the thinking morally coping style to life, and as a result defiance is put on the back burner, at least until the strength of this pathway begins to erode as the system loses credibility and respect from those it regulates. Effective and legitimate social regulation enables individuals to align themselves with authority rationally (doing what is right and proper) and emotionally (being good and virtuous).

Such an approach to fear reduction is not an option for those who cope with taxation threat by taking control or feeling oppressed. They see the tax authority as their adversary and place themselves at a comfortable and discernible social distance. Perceived deterrence can increase the threat and the social distance, particularly in the case of resistance, by exacerbating a feeling of being oppressed by the system. Perceived deterrence can also provide the useful service of reminding people that they are not free agents who can step outside the system entirely. Perceived deterrence dampens the intent of taking control. Perceived deterrence offers some pay-off to authorities that risk a challenge to their authority, but less pay-off to those who are dealing with a community that feels unfairly treated and under the thumb of oppression.

Living harmoniously together in society means succumbing to a social process that allows us to consent to the will of the democratically elected government. At a macro level, we accept that a democratic government should be responsive to the will of the people. At a micro level, we accept the corollary: on many occasions, government will act against our personal wishes. We must then have strategies in place in order to be comfortable with acquiescing to the dominant and democratically supported view. Centrally important to the process are moral beliefs and feelings (thinking morally). In this chapter we see a thinking morally coping style at work that protects authorities from the adverse effects of both resistant and dismissive defiance.

Regulators are sometimes sceptical of suggestions that they can improve compliance through appealing to people's 'better' selves (the thinking moral self), but these data demonstrate the pivotal role played by this key plank of the responsive regulatory tradition (Ayres and Braithwaite 1992). Central to the work that integrates responsive regulation and restorative justice (Braithwaite, J. 2002) is the assertion that within the minds of those being regulated, a battle rages between competing selves over how to deal with authority. Regulators too often zero in on the 'evil' self, virtually denying the existence of a better self that might respond positively to regulatory demands. In the context of the analyses of this chapter, one wonders what such regulatory intervention hopes to accomplish, apart from a general assertion of superiority. As regulators focus on 'beating' the evil self into submission, little wonder that an individual's coping responses come to the fore to protect through the persona of an oppressed self (see Braithwaite, V. et al. 2007).

When credible legal institutions make their presence felt through sanctioning, we should have confidence in the relevance of individual conscience to getting things back on track. When combined with credible community support for the disapproval expressed by the authorities, those in the firing line of an authority may start seriously to question whether or not their actions were reasonable after all, and the process of shame acknowledgement may start to kick in. As Harris (2007) has argued so cogently, along with Williams (1993) and Elias (1978), our judgements about what is fair, reasonable and morally right are not made in a social vacuum but rather require a social validation process, whereby we attend to what others in our social world think. Actions that cut us off from receiving these messages through reinforcing coping mechanisms that numb our conscience serve neither the interests of the regulatory agency nor the community nor the individual.

From the findings in Chapter 4, it might be conjectured that the dismissively defiant are more likely to cut themselves off from feedback from the collective about their actions. The dismissively defiant may have stepped outside the square of thinking morally. Maintaining this position rests on holding to a mindset that blocks out socialization and puts conscience and the shame emotions on ice. If dismissively defiant individuals were to experience some self-reflective moments that led them to accept responsibility for breaking the law and harming others, the challenge they were mounting against the tax system would become less gratifying. For many tax authorities this may be cold comfort. For a pocket of Australians and world citizens, challenging the tax system is a noble cause. It is worth noting at this point that challenge to a system is not in and of itself bad in a democratic society – we have praised challenge from outside the system at various times in history when the system has become corrupt and despotic. In this particular instance, however, few have confidence that tax avoidance by the rich and powerful is a form of heroism that will restore a system of good governance to nation states.

If tax authorities are to be advocates of the people and flip a tax avoidance market in vice into a market in virtue (Braithwaite, J. 2005), they need ultimately to change the actions and understandings of those who promote dismissive defiance. Challenge presents itself at two levels. Tax authorities need to understand the alternative authorities that are fuelling defiance and to reinvigorate a public conscience that involves respect for law (McBarnet and Whelan 1999). With this will come self-regulatory processes created by shame–guilt and discomfort about doing the wrong thing (see Chapter 7). At a second level, however, the challenge is to set one's own house in order before ordering another's. The bigger challenge facing tax authorities may be to scrutinize critically their own integrity, honestly and publicly. By so doing, tax authorities in the longer term will raise their profile as respected and valued authorities and will have greater confidence that indeed they are serving the public and acting in the interests of the democracy.

It does no harm at this point to emphasize that processes of social validation for both taxpayers and tax authorities need to be based on multiple voices and deliberative processes, not on crude campaigns designed to smear, ostracize and bully 'the wayward' into subservience. When we see authority being used in a bullying or coercive fashion, it is highly likely that the authority has already lost its integrity in the eyes of the public. Once the public's perception of the integrity of the authority has gone, thinking morally and shame–guilt are also likely to 'exit the psyche'. The findings of this chapter therefore provide no comfort for an authority ready to embark on shaming rhetoric, deceptive spin or domination. Rather, they are a reminder that morality on the part of taxpayers matters, as does integrity on the part of tax authorities (see Chapter 6), and both warrant considered, open and authentic deliberation.

NOTES

1. The internal consistency presumed to underlie the six items contributing to the *feeling oppressed* scale was confirmed by a standardized alpha reliability coefficient of 0.72.
2. The internal consistency presumed to underlie the five items contributing to the *taking control* coping scale was confirmed by a standardized alpha reliability coefficient of 0.63.
3. The internal consistency presumed to underlie the 11 items making up the *thinking morally* scale was confirmed by a standardized alpha reliability coefficient of 0.78.

6. Approaching defiance through integrity and trust

> When an institution is charged with lack of integrity, the charge always contains an implicit conception of what the institution is or should be.
>
> Philip Selznick 1992: 324

Authority engages in domination. Yet social constraints curb an authority's activities in a democracy, with the community consenting to the principle of domination in certain domains but not in others (Selznick 1992). Such authorities, therefore, use their regulatory power mindful of the limits of their legitimacy, and tax authorities are no exception. When tax authorities overstep their bounds and use powers that the public finds excessive or overly intrusive, government enquiries commonly follow (see, e.g., Joint Committee of Public Accounts 1993 in Australia and National Commission on Restructuring the Internal Revenue Service 1997 in the USA).

Enquiries of this kind target weakness. The resolve that accompanies them, however, draws strength from the belief that something important is absent in the manner in which the authority has conducted itself. We expect that when we place ourselves in the hands of authority, that authority will know how to respond with soundness of purpose and process. Views on what constitutes soundness in the sense of what is best for the community are likely to vary across the democracy. We see more convergence in public opinion, however, around worst practice. In this chapter it will be argued that the common element unifying communities is the perception of disrespect. The soundness of an authority's purpose and process, its integrity, is therefore seen to hinge on how well the authority is able to communicate respect for those it serves. Expressed in these terms, integrity becomes a state to which authorities are expected to aspire. Their failure to do so provides a breeding ground for defiance.

The notion of integrity is introduced in the first section of the chapter by looking at how tax authorities internationally have addressed public criticism and implied 'shortcomings' in their operations. Then follows an excursion through philosophical, organizational and regulatory literatures to open up our understanding of integrity and what it is that a disillusioned public might be looking for in a tax authority that wishes to improve its integrity. Finally, a composite measure of integrity is assembled and the overarching hypothesis of the chapter that integrity builds trust and reins in defiance is empirically tested.

1. HOW TAX AUTHORITIES HAVE MANAGED THEIR INTEGRITY

The Public Fears, Authority Protects

Doubts persist over whether the public can be assured that tax authorities will use their extraordinary powers only in the name of fair and reasonable administration (IRS Customer Service Tax Force 1997; Freeman 2002; McCracken 2002). In response to concerns that tax authorities were overstepping the mark, tax ombudsmen and formal complaints mechanisms were set up early in many OECD countries (Committee of Fiscal Affairs 1990). The pressure to adopt taxpayers' charters and bills of rights speaks to the importance that the public places on making tax authorities accountable, ensuring that they act with the utmost integrity in their pursuit of tax dollars (Centre for Tax Policy and Administration 2003). Documents of rights, principles of procedural justice and administrative codes of practice have been disseminated widely to inform taxpayers as to how they can expect to be treated by tax authorities. Some charters go further to stipulate mutual responsibilities, highlighting the benefits in establishing a cooperative relationship between the taxpayer and the tax authority (Centre for Tax Policy and Administration 2003; Australian Taxation Office 2007).

Not surprisingly, opinions differ on the appropriate balance of rights and obligations. Bentley is among those who express concern that authorities will relegate rights to a subordinate position to enforcing the obligation to pay tax (2007: 44–8). Others have argued that rights provide opportunity for abuse of the tax system. Game players use them to undermine the capacity of tax officers to enforce the law (Greenbaum 1998). Jurisdictions differ in how enthusiastically they have embraced the rights discourse. The USA has been particularly strong in promoting taxpayer rights (IRS Customer Service Task Force 1997). The UK has been far more wary in recent years, preferring to promote service standards (Williams 1998; James et al. 2004). Possibly rights' shyness is the result of a history of providing 'easy opportunities for avoidance and evasion' (Schmölders 1970: 303). Schmölders described the British tax system in 1970 as operating harmoniously, but ineffectively 'treat[ing] businessmen and professionals with great caution, dispensing with every form of administrative auditing and offering a rich reservoir of 'loopholes" (ibid.: 302). This is not to suggest that taxpayer rights are generally left on the shelf; rather they are allowed to nestle under service. The Canada Revenue Agency offers as its code of practice 'fairness through service' (Canada Revenue Agency 2003a, 2003b).

Tax Outreach through Rights, Service and Partnership

The service model has become a popular vehicle for tax authorities needing to boost public confidence and cooperation. They have sought to reform arcane inward-looking tax culture by researching taxpayer needs and tailoring services to their different client groups, the intention being to make it simpler and easier for all groups to comply (Conference Board of Canada 1998; Office of Public Affairs 2002; Commissioner of Taxation 2003). The message being sent to the public is: 'We are committed to taking a user-centred approach, creating products and services that are easier, cheaper and more personalized; . . . we are committed to building a shared understanding of intent, ensuring that . . . the user experience reflects that intent [and] we are committed to mapping the user pathway . . . to create [coherence]' (Body 2008: 61–3). The new deal is that taxpayers need no longer put up with a cumbersome and unintelligible tax system, and can rely on their tax authorities to help them meet their obligations efficiently and easily, with queries and problems reviewed and resolved in a timely and transparent fashion.

When tax authorities issue a message to the public about their standards of service they are addressing what have been called trust norms – the norms that authorities need to honour if they are to be trusted by the public (Braithwaite, V. 1998d). The service message above puts into practice the communal norms of 'understanding the position of others' and 'treating people with respect' – norms that allow people to trust because they realize that they share a social identity with the authority; they are part of a community of honest taxpayers who can be trusted to do the right thing and cooperate.

When taxpayer rights form the centrepiece of communications to the public in an effort to win trust and build the tax authority's integrity, an appeal is being made to trust norms of another kind – the trust norms of exchange. These trust norms, unlike the communal trust norms above, have little to do with shared identity and shared goals. Exchange trust norms are more about contractual certainty. Tax authorities that pledge themselves to a rights agenda address tax norms of 'acting in a predictable fashion' and 'keeping to the cautious, well-trodden path'. In embracing rights discourse, tax authorities are trying to win trust by promising essentially to do nothing unexpected or unorthodox – not to shift the goal posts. This is at times possibly a debilitating promise in a climate where tax avoidance is rife and is achieved by creatively redefining what the law means (McBarnet and Whelan 1999).

Australia has adopted a hybrid of the rights–services discourse (Braithwaite, J. 2005; Australian Taxation Office 2003b, 2007; Bentley 2007). At the same time, Australia has prioritized the building of a partnership between the Australian Taxation Office (ATO) and the taxpaying public defined by mutual respect, trust and cooperation (Commissioner of Taxation 2003; Bentley 2007). Rights, service and partnership are all appropriate objectives for a tax authority that operates within a democracy (The Commission on Taxation and Citizenship 2000). By bringing them together, the ATO sought to build its integrity in the eyes of the public. In this chapter, the effectiveness of these efforts in reining in defiance will be tested.

From Taxpayer Charters to Integrity

Charters and bills of rights follow a standard form, setting out conditions for engagement with taxpayers, among them that taxpayers be treated as honest in their tax affairs, that confidentiality be observed and privacy protected, that they have access to information that the tax office holds about them, that they be given advice and information they can rely on, and professional service and assistance. Should their tax affairs be investigated, taxpayers are entitled to representation, to an outside review, and to fair and reasonable treatment.

In these respects, charters represent minimal standards for transactions between the taxpayer and the tax authority. They cannot guarantee trust or cooperation, and in some cases may even be no more than the contractual safety net for enabling transactions to proceed when trust and cooperation break down. The quest for a cooperative relationship and a strong voluntary taxpaying culture requires more than an assurance that these basic performance standards are met. In order for taxpayers to trust and cooperate with an authority, they also need to be assured of benefits associated with taxpaying, that the system and procedures for tax collection are just, and that the tax authority is sensitive to public concerns and responsive where appropriate. These qualities are a manifestation of a tax authority's integrity, the subject of this chapter. The question is how, when and why would institutional integrity increase trust in the tax authority, thereby 'softening' the defiant posturing of taxpayers as they deal with the threat of taxation. In particular, can integrity and trust work with both resistant and dismissive defiance? The suspicion is that dismissiveness is less easily turned around by integrity than resistance.

2. OPENING WINDOWS ON INTEGRITY

Defining Integrity

Institutional integrity has an internal and external face. Internally, institutional integrity refers to how well the tax system is designed: does it achieve expected outcomes for tax collection; is the system integrated and coherent; where are the internal contradictions; and how does the tax system perform against Adam Smith's four canons of taxation – equity, certainty, convenience and economy? One meaning of integrity therefore is the degree to which the tax system is characterized by alignment of rules, practices, tasks and goals to achieve a common purpose in a manner that adheres to accepted principles.

Generally speaking, tax systems do not perform well on these criteria. While there is agreement on what the gold standards of tax design should be, there is also agreement that much work needs to be done to bring the world's tax systems up to standard (Tanzi and Shome 1994; Brand 1996; Tanzi 2001). Unfortunately, the gap between the highly complex set of laws and rules that constitute many tax systems and the understanding that citizens have of taxation is enormous (Long and Swingen 1988; Burton 2007; Picciotto 2007). Arguably, integrity as coherence in tax law and practice is beyond reach at this stage in the evolution of tax systems, although this is not to deny that some authorities are putting their shoulder to the wheel to improve tax coherence and intelligibility (Body 2008).

While the internal face of tax system integrity befuddles experts as much as ordinary taxpayers, the public can readily assess the external face of integrity. By this is meant the degree to which the community regards an authority as acting with soundness of purpose, executing its operations competently, reasonably and fairly with awareness of and consideration for those affected by them. In the context of taxation, a high-integrity tax authority will be conscientious in collecting taxes, abide by the Taxpayers' Charter, be fair in its processes, and respectful of and responsive to taxpayers, making or recommending corrections to the system when falsehood, injustice and/or inefficiency become apparent. All of this would take place within a values framework that recognized the pivotal role that a tax authority plays in enabling the democracy to function, and its responsibilities at all times to uphold and advance democratic principles of governance.

The origins of this conceptualization of integrity are varied. It draws on works of philosophers in uncovering what lies at the heart of personal integrity, on works of organizational and management scholars whose concerns revolve around the avoidance of corruption, fraud and inefficiency, and the work of Bernstein (1955) and Selznick (1992), who provide rich analyses of how government agencies can either lose their relevance and effectiveness or provide valuable leadership for a moral and civil society. In the accounts of both Bernstein and Selznick, issues of integrity loom large.

Philosophical Contributions on Personal Integrity

Dictionary entries for integrity equate the term with a state of wholeness; in psychological terminology as a state of integration manifesting itself in consistency and coherence in thinking and action (English and English 1958). Personal integrity, however, has been the subject of considerably more theoretical analysis against the backdrop of popular understandings of what it means to be a person of the highest integrity (for philosophical readings on personal integrity see Winch 1972; Williams 1973; Taylor 1981; McFall 1987; Halfon 1989; Davion 1991; Babbitt 1996; Ramsay 1997). Interest in these writings stems from the common observation that personal standards of integrity do not always translate into organizational integrity and even less so, institutional integrity (Argyris and Schön 1988; Calhoun 1995; Adler and Borys 1996). The challenge is to discern the defining features of personal integrity, track its translation to the collective level and identify the features of organizational culture that facilitate and retard the development of institutional integrity.

Coherence has always been considered important for personal integrity, although this coherence should not slide into rigidity. Early writing emphasized coherence: to display personal integrity was to follow through on beliefs and commitments in behaviour and be true to oneself across contexts (Winch 1972; Taylor 1981; Halfon 1989). A deeper psychological analysis linked integrity with self-identity. Integrity involved defining the self in terms of a coherent and stable set of principles that a person would fall back on to deliberate upon decisions, judgements and actions (Williams 1973). Accompanying the idea of principled deliberation was a moral dimension. For Ramsay (1997), integrity was not indifferent to whether a person was committed to doing good things in the world or being destructive of human goodness. A person could have a very coherent personal narrative, but integrity would be absent if that narrative were one of moral visciousness (ibid.: 16–17).

A second layer of understanding surfaced with concerns that personal integrity might be mistaken for being set in one's ways, unwilling to listen and negotiate with others, and denying the reality of complex moral dilemmas. Benjamin (1990) proposed capacity for compromise as a key to understanding integrity. Openness to new knowledge would unavoidably lead to changing values and commitments, but integrity would not necessarily be sacrificed. If change evolved through a personal narrative that made the journey intelligible and reasonable, the person's wholeness of character and integrity might be preserved.

The way in which integrity came to be understood was as an adaptive personal quality, one that merited recognition as a quality of leadership. The metaphor desired for integrity was not of a rock in a turbulent sea, but of a boat, navigating a course around swirling currents, inspiring other boats in the process, and showing the way to calm waters. The person of integrity stood apart from the ideologue and dogmatist in having 'the capacity for self-criticism and ability to reassess one's roles and relations' (Halfon 1989: 19). Once integrity was allowed to incorporate processes of growing self-awareness and changing commitments and values, it became a facilitator for moral development on the one hand, and social and political change on the other (Halfon 1989; Babbitt 1996). These developments were appealing and were consistent with popular usage. Individuals of high integrity recognized complexity, navigated their way through conflicting moral imperatives in a principled way, and provided the leadership required to pull disparate voices and warring factions together.

The contributions of Benjamin (1990), Babbitt (1996), Davion (1991) and Halfon (1989) drew out the social face of integrity. Ramsay built on their work to present a highly social perspective on integrity, maintaining that to put 'personal psychological unity' ahead of 'responsibilities to others' was not integrity at all. This work paved the way for applying the principles that defined personal integrity at the collective level. Before discussing Selznick's (1992) work and the antithesis of his vision of integrity as described by Bernstein (1955), a brief detour through the organizational literature will serve to demonstrate the practical concerns around fostering integrity in the workplace.

Organizational Integrity

In the organizational literature, integrity has been embraced as a key element in containing corruption, fraud, impropriety and low morale (Srivastva 1988; Frederickson and Ghere 2005). Integrity has primarily been associated with executive officers engaging in ethical decision making (Menzel 2007), but there is also a burgeoning literature on how integrity needs to be embedded in leadership styles and infiltrated through the organization's culture, changing the work climate from one that tolerates moral bankruptcy and disinterest to one that insists on employees being responsible and ethically aware. This literature confronts the challenge of ensuring that workplace practices match the rhetoric of moral responsibility (Petrick and Quinn 2000). The journey is considered to be dialogic: 'The development of integrity . . . is carried forward through the initiation of mutual *dialogue*. . . . [N]ew forms of responsiveness to the other . . . reduce asymmetry (schisms) and enhance the relational life of the whole' (Srivastva and Cooperrider 1988: 6).

While urging organizations to strike a healthier balance between 'an achievement oriented culture' where there is a collective will to achieve a shared purpose and 'a support culture' where there is a striving for caring and responsive connections (Harrison 1988: 59), neither consultants nor academics underestimate the difficulties of change. Dialogue that brings to the fore values of social responsibility, issues of moral complexity and awareness of harm done jars with the ethos of individualism and competitive aggressiveness that lives in the engine room of most organizations (ibid.). Practically speaking, dialogue also brings forward the very different priorities of various parts of a complex organization, many of which have a value or moral base (Heimer 2008), and which need to be juggled, not resolved in pursuit of a harmonious whole. In spite of these difficulties, building stronger organizational integrity remains on the agenda of most businesses and government agencies.

One recurring theme in the organizational literature has been to unpack the stumbling blocks to developing organizational integrity: to understand the impediments to 'deliberating about what is worth doing' and the 'powerful deterrents to speaking and acting on one's own best judgment' (Calhoun 1995: 259). At the heart of the problem is unwillingness to deliberate and share the complexities of moral decision making and a desire to script the responses that should be made should certain contingencies arise. The work of Argyris and Schön (1988), Wolfe (1988) and Adler and Borys (1996) provides insights into the issues that hamper the progress of large complex organizations like tax authorities when they take on the challenge of building a culture of integrity not only internally but also externally in their relationship with the public.

Argyris and Schön (1988) have argued that organizations are poor venues for promoting integrity because they lack the norms for dealing with dialogue over conflicting values and competing priorities. Organizations either allow differences to polarize their workforce, or in order to avert conflict, differences are pushed underground through adopting 'defensive routines' (Argyris 1985). Defensive routines purportedly help people save face and avoid threat and embarrassment, but in practice result in mixed messages and disempower individuals. They also

> trigger all kinds of unintended consequences: Unreliable information gets passed along, people say one thing in meetings and just the opposite in the halls,

> mistrust abounds, the rumour mill begins generating 'noise,' and more and more participants feel increasingly helpless, and hence distance themselves from personal responsibility for dealing with the situation. (Srivastva and Cooperrider 1998: 20)

Wolfe (1988) has described a different set of defensive routines common to complex organizations. Integrity at both the individual and institutional level is compromised by denial of complexity. Denial is made possible through a number of strategies. One is to build an edifice of slogans that demand and justify simplification. Evidence is found in commonly used organizational catch-phrases: 'cut to the chase', 'time is money', 'the bottom line', 'the quick fix', 'see what you can get away with', and 'that's not my responsibility', all of which demand a simplification of the problem and become code for a shared understanding that anyone who flags complexity, or worse still wants to manage it, is out of order.

A second strategy for simplification is to turn to public relations experts to create the image of integrity: 'If you have a good PR agent, you don't have to clean up your act. You only have to sell it' (Wolfe 1988: 153). The technology of managing people's consciousness and beliefs, like many technologies, can be exploited – in this case by those who mistakenly believe that changing people's minds adequately substitutes for changing the organization's actions.

A third strategy described by Wolfe (1988) involves restructuring or segmenting the functions of a workforce differently, supposedly to clean up and better align responsibilities. Wolfe has argued that such an approach does not necessarily enhance institutional integrity: indeed the reshuffle is often misguided. Pretending messiness and complexity do not exist does not rid the organization of the problem, as has become all too apparent in organizational responses to human catastrophes. Examples include the US federal government's intelligence-gathering capability before 9/11, its response to Hurricane Katrina in New Orleans and the United Nations response to genocide in Rwanda. Admittedly, policy and not structures are implicated in big events such as these. But once we extend Wolfe's analysis to policy implementation, the significance of the problem takes on an even more troubling dimension. The Rwandan case, in particular, reveals failures of integrity over policy definition and implementation. While the UN was holding firm to the idea that it had no role as a peacekeeper until political leaders enforced a peace, Rwandans were suffering terribly because of lack of policy flexibility and responsiveness.

The fourth strategy of simplification detailed by Wolfe (1988) is the mentality of 'it's all a game'. Decisions are made in a psychological bubble, and the problem is stripped down to a few elements of which one can be certain, so that the decision can be made in a straightforward and undisputed way. The justification for the simplification is that problems are just too complex to make it worth even trying to look for a responsible, integrative solution. The problem becomes worse when norms are weak and the shared view is that 'anything goes'. The 'it's all a game' oversimplification abstracts decision making to a level 'that seems to have little to do with real people, real communities, or real consequences other than wealth' (ibid.: 148).

Without understanding of or interest in local circumstances and contexts, people are dehumanized and stereotyped. Wolfe has linked this disconnected game mentality to a preoccupation with winning and losing, so much so that everyone comes to be seen as 'a potential opponent, a rival who may be playing the game more craftily and whose efforts must therefore be countered' (Wolfe 1988: 149). Such a mentality effectively screens out any opportunity for empathy and responsiveness to the problems that others may be having. The kind of dialogue about social responsibility and ethical decision making advocated by Srivastva (1988) is likely to be dismissed as of little value by those locked into Wolfe's game mentality.

In spite of these impediments to the development of integrity within organizations, models of change are continually being developed and fine-tuned in workplaces, including tax administrations (Centre for Tax Policy and Administration 2001, 2003; Job and Honaker 2003; Job et al. 2007; Body 2008). Part of this process has involved a rethinking of the capabilities of complex bureaucracies.

Adler and Borys (1996) have challenged the idea that bureaucratic workflow formalization necessarily leads to top-down command-and-control work practices and the kinds of information asymmetry that stifle creativity, demotivate employees and generate dissatisfaction. The starting point for their argument is acceptance that bureaucracies formalize workflow – that is, they set in place a structure in which the rules governing behaviour are precisely and explicitly formulated and roles and role relations are prescribed independently of the personal attributes of individuals occupying positions in the structure (Scott 1992: 31–2).

From this point of common agreement, Adler and Borys (1996) argued that how employees feel and respond to these rules and to the structure depends on whether they find them coercive and restrictive or enabling and motivating. If rules are good in so far as they help people do their jobs and contribute to the organization's goals, they are likely to be accepted. If rules are bad in so far as they strip work of its meaning and purpose, they are likely to be resented, if not bypassed or ignored.

Adler and Borys (1996) concluded that formalization does not hold bureaucracies back from being productive workplaces peopled by committed staff. The critical factor is whether the rules, work norms and procedures are enabling and allow staff to perform at a high level or whether they are coercive, asking employees to 'check their brains at the door' (ibid.: 83). The central thesis is that complex bureaucracies with their much-needed formalization can nevertheless be enabling workplaces that 'deliver efficiency without enslavement' (ibid.: 85), and can provide committed employees with opportunity to do their jobs more effectively, building stronger commitment in the process.

While the struggle for integrity proceeds, seemingly against the odds, the basic reality for democratic governments is that their incentive for success is high. Governments and tax authorities may well fall back on their traditional legitimate power – and legal coercion – when they find themselves facing public criticisms of low integrity. But there can be no question that in a democratic society, governing through the use of power is no substitute for a situation in which people cooperate because they trust their government (Culbert and McDonough 1988).

The Quest for Integrity by Regulatory Authorities

The organizational literature has focused on how integrity can enrich workplace culture and improve ethical decision-making processes. This literature also examines why this is so difficult to achieve, while dismissing suggestions that it is too difficult. Looking at integrity in a state-funded regulatory authority from the perspective of the public presents the same basic challenges but with some twists. Many of the features are the same – soundness of purpose, competence, willingness to listen, responsiveness and respect for the public – but some of the problems encountered in an effort to establish integrity are different.

A central issue when we think about state–citizen relations is authenticity: is the state authority genuine and committed to serving the community or are its interventions designed to serve its own interests or those of powerful others (Inglehart 1977, 1990, 1997; Mathiesen 2004)? Cynicism about government more broadly is rampant (Inglehart 1977, 1990, 1997; LaFree 1998; Comstock 2001). In the Australian context, political rhetoric and spin have given rise to widespread public disillusionment (Maguire et al. 2007). Reported findings, for instance, suggest that Australian taxpayers may harbour reservations over how authentic the ATO's commitment to the Taxpayers' Charter really is (Braithwaite, V. et al. 2007).

When we consider the integrity that individuals see or fail to see in their democratically elected governments and their agencies, we are picking up on something deeper than just how well people are doing their jobs, although undoubtedly this is part of it. The institution itself is in the firing line – the soundness or authenticity of its purpose, as well as the norms and attitudes that accompany officials doing their duty. It is to the question of perceptions of institutional integrity that we now turn. Trust and willingness to cooperate are presumed to be contingent on the degree to which the public perceives integrity in the way the authority goes about its work.

The regulatory literature provides any number of accounts of the quest by regulatory authorities for integrity in the eyes of a sceptical, if not hostile, public. A persistent theme is regulating with emotional intelligence, reasonableness and fairness, while guarding against capture and meaningless auditing and inspection. Bardach and Kagan (1982) warned of the dangers of 'going by the book', and instead promoted the importance of listening and thinking about the reasons for non-compliance, offering solutions that fit the problem; Hawkins (1984) warned of the dangers of regulators being captured or exceeding their mandate as they used their initiative to get the job done; Rees (1994) identified the importance of communitarian regulation based on values and goals with which members were familiar and to which they were committed; Heimer (1998) emphasized the importance of regulating through understanding and utilizing routines valued within the organization as opposed to imposing routines from outside; Ayres and Braithwaite (1992) laid the foundations for republican regulation operating responsively through regulatory pyramids; Black (1998) injected regulatory conversations into the regulator's repertoire; and Braithwaite, J. et al. (2007) pointed to growing tendencies towards ritualism that may engulf both regulators and regulatees in the least authentic of regulatory exercises.

While all these contributions assert the importance of integrity to effect constructive and lasting change, two other classic texts are used to develop a framework for how integrity is conceptualized and measured in relation to the ATO. Bernstein (1955) has provided a meticulous account of the ways in which regulatory authorities compromise their authenticity, integrity and ultimately legitimacy. Selznick (1992), on the other hand, articulates what a regulatory authority needs to do to demonstrate authenticity to the public, and thereby advance the cause of integrity and legitimacy.

Learning from Bernstein's Regulatory Commissions

In tracing the evolution of regulatory commissions in the USA, Bernstein (1955) provided an account of the thinking of the day on the ideal structure and function of regulatory institutions. Because regulation, particularly of an economic kind, was antithetical to Americans' commitment to freedom and capitalism, regulatory activity was doomed always to face a legitimacy crisis.

In order to secure legitimacy in the eyes of sceptical interest groups, the commissions modelled themselves on the judicial system. They were to be impartial and aloof from the political process and from the regulatory community. The value they added beyond the courts was that they could focus on issues that required detailed and specialized knowledge, and they could be flexible enough to deal with intricate cases that might require persistent, time-consuming effort to bring to resolution (Bernstein 1955: 36–7). In a bid to prevent corruption, fend off political interference, and assist in restoring decency and fairness to the world of commerce, regulatory commissions were set apart to construct a pristine world of what might be.

The picture that Bernstein (1955) paints of early regulatory bodies is a reasonably accurate account of one conception of how tax authorities are thought to operate to demonstrate integrity and preserve their legitimacy in the eyes of the public. Until recently challenged, it was common practice for tax authorities to remain detached, to be guarded in the information they disclosed to the public, and to slavishly adhere to administrative principles of consistency, the letter of the law, and clarity through detail (Job and Honaker 2003).

The character of Harold Crick in the Hollywood film, *Stranger than Fiction*, depicts the traditional image of a high-integrity taxman. Dedicated, focused, a whizz with numbers and obsessed by punctuality, he is responsible for auditing the Harvard law drop-out turned baker, Ana Pascal, who has refused to pay 22% of her taxes in defiance of the government's use of public monies for 'national defence, corporate bail-outs and campaign discretionary funds'. Harold executes his duties with detached impartiality, understanding Ms Pascal's defiance as unworldly, ill-considered anarchism. As his self-contained auditing style increases Ms Pascal's ire, Harold explains: 'IRS agents – we are given rigorous aptitude tests before we can work, but unfortunately for you we are not tested on tact or good manners.' Harold finds himself totally incapable of responding graciously to an offer of freshly baked cookies from Ana Pascal – a woman whom he desperately wants to romance – because it would break the well-established rule of 'no gifts' in the auditor–auditee protocol. In the film, as in life, the tax auditor zealously fends off capture by adopting the persona of a 'human-proofed' individual who cares about nothing beyond the case file.

A quest for integrity that requires regulators to insulate themselves from the highly politicized and conflict-ridden environment in which they operate is doomed, according to Bernstein (1955). All that comes from a determined non-engagement in the politics of regulation is a constriction of the regulatory mission to the point where it becomes so specific and so technical that the public is completely unable to relate to its activities in a meaningful way. Having lost connections with the public and any sense of how the actions of the regulatory agency might further the democratic will, regulators become locked in battle with the powerful interests that they are trying to regulate. Bernstein depicted this course of action as one leading to the demise of the regulatory institution. Isolated, performing a thankless task that no one understands except their adversaries, dominated by powerful interest groups intent on regulatory capture if not complete control, regulatory institutions move acquiescently along a path of capture or incapacitation, if not ruin.

While tax authorities appear to have been spared this fate, they are not spared criticism from those who object to government telling them what to do. A proportion of people, in Australia and elsewhere, are openly defiant of tax authorities (Rawlings 2004; Braithwaite, J. 2005; Roche 2006). Associated with the defiance is a refusal to grant them legitimacy.[1] At one level we may consider a tax authority as having the right to 'rule', 'govern', or 'command' because the law states that it is entitled to control actions in a prescribed fashion (Reus-Smit 2007). But as Reus-Smit goes on to point out, legitimacy in any meaningful sense depends on social perceptions. People have to believe that 'the actions of an entity are desirable . . . within some socially constructed system of norms, values, beliefs, and definitions' (Suchman 1995: 574). If we don't accept the same socially constructed system, it will be difficult for us to accept the authority of the tax office as legitimate, regardless of how much integrity it displays.

That said, the central premise of this research programme is that integrity matters. Perceived lack of integrity is considered an important factor in breaking down trust and fostering defiance. Integrity is also a quality of governance that an authority offers to the public to win their respect and ultimately to win their acceptance as a legitimate authority.

Learning from Selznick's Moral Commonwealth

Selznick's view of integrity is akin to Ramsay's (1997) in that it is less concerned with 'coherence of every sort' and more with 'moral coherence' in the sense of soundness of purpose (1992: 322). Responsibility is central to Selznick's view of integrity, where responsibility represents a responsiveness to the social function of the organization, 'to those upon whom the institution depends; and to the community whose well-being it affects' (ibid.: 338). Selznick associates integrity with a tussle between conflicting forces: 'Established structures, rules, methods, and policies are all open to revision, but revision takes place in a principled way, that is, while holding fast to values and purposes' (ibid.).

Selznick is mindful of how a regulatory agency 'will shortchange the public interest by narrowing its perspectives' (ibid.: 343) – to 'specialize', in Bernstein's terms (1955). A related problem is that of goal displacement, whereby the means for accomplishing a particular purpose dissociate from the ends. The means take on a life of their own, thereby undermining the institution's capacity to achieve its purposes. Means–end disjuncture has resulted in a proliferation of routines, often performed mindlessly and serving little purpose.

As Heimer (2008) points out, however, we should not be too harsh or hasty in criticizing routines or mindlessness. Both can be adaptive and productive in complex organizations. Heimer causes us to pause and consider which one of us would prefer to have our surgeon scouting around looking for equipment rather than focusing on what she is about to do to our body. Routines, checklists and assistants have their place.

Of critical importance, however, is recognizing limitations and making judgement calls about when a routine is not serving its intended purpose; what to do when a routine is considered invaluable in one part of the organization but trivial or counterproductive in another; and when tasks require thoughtful engagement, as opposed to functioning on automatic pilot (Heimer 2008). The lack of process for reflecting on these institutional issues is a major concern of Selznick (1992). Maintaining or achieving institutional integrity demands that an agency take responsibility for and regularly review its 'fidelity to self-defining principles' while 'respect[ing] the autonomy and plurality of persons and institutions' (ibid.: 322).

Another dimension of Selznick's (1992) work that is so informative for regulatory agencies such as tax authorities is his insistence that integrity does not mean applying rules meticulously and rigidly; nor does it imply ritualistic consistency in decision making; nor does it connote impersonal communication. These patterns of activity, although common in bureaucracies and associated with order and structure, are destructive of human capital and human relations, and, in turn, weaken the social fabric of the society (ibid.: 256).

Selznick's (1992) view of integrity has been used by Waller (2007) to evaluate the performance of the ATO as it set out to implement its compliance programme based on a responsive regulatory approach (see Braithwaite, V. 2003a, 2007 for a description). Consistent with Selznick's depiction of integrity, Waller's tax administrators had internalized the importance of developing positive relationships with their taxpaying communities as a way of building trust and eliciting voluntary compliance. The community of interest at the time of Waller's study was used-car dealers. For the tax officials, the objective of establishing a working relationship with these businesses based on respect and trust was a challenging one. It required thoughtful engagement on the part of the tax officials and preparation based on awareness that the business owners would be suspicious of their presence, perhaps even hostile. The response of the tax officials, however, was not as one might have hoped. They entered the establishments of used-car dealers with checklists, collecting data that according to the dealers, the ATO already had in its records. The means did not suit the desired ends.

Selznick's vision of integrity involved a thoughtful and ethical meshing of means and ends, what he referred to as 'principled conduct' (1992: 323); and not 'mechanical or mindless following of rules or procedures, without regard for purposes and effects . . . [thereby losing] the substantive aims of justice and public policy' (ibid.: 330). As Waller illustrated, this was precisely where the ATO's bid to build integrity with its taxpayers came unstuck. It was trained to work from procedural manuals; it was poorly equipped to work at the desired level of process that defined Selznick's conception of integrity.

To Waller (2007), the state aspired to – of arriving at a set of practices that were aligned with the organization's philosophy – seemed beyond reach. Tax administrators wanted to embed their integrity in prescribed scripts and manuals; implicitly they rejected Selznick's plea to reflect on means–end processes and to resist the temptation to seek integrity through 'consistency – doing the same thing in apparently similar cases, sticking to accepted rules, practices, or categories' (Selznick 1992: 323).

Waller's (2007) study revealed some of the difficulties of bringing a complex operational concept like integrity into the regulatory workplace. But by identifying difficulties, it also revealed future directions. Conversation and dialogue of the kind recognized by Black (1998) had not occurred with these tax administrators. In other parts of the organization, conversation was far more readily embraced as part of the job and appeared to be producing the desired outcomes with building and construction workers (Shover et al. 2003). But in the case of the used-car dealers, the tax authority acted out one of Argyris's (1985) defensive routines. Field officers were required to implement the new responsive compliance model, but at the same time follow the procedure manual – they were given a mixed message (Waller 2007). To the tax office field staff, it did not make sense. As Waller found through her interviews with taxpayers, it did not make sense to them either.

While Waller (2007) tells a story of failed implementation, she also confirms the importance of institutional integrity, in Selznick's (1992) terms, for a tax authority. Taxpayers ask and notice how means are connected to ends; they expect to see their tax inspectors – no matter how unwelcome – operating with purpose and competence. Their regulatory activities need to be meaningful and resourced efficiently, and they need to be transparent and honest. To mesh a procedural manual with an integrity initiative did not produce the ends required to satisfy taxpayers that their tax authority had institutional integrity. According to Waller, trust in the authority seemed to be less, if anything after the visit, and certainly not more.

3. EMPIRICALLY TESTING INTEGRITY, TRUST AND DEFIANCE

Measuring Integrity

Institutional integrity demands correspondence between how things are and how they appear to be to the public, which for a public institution means having soundness of purpose, reasonable and fair processes, competence in implementation, willingness to listen and, at all times, responsiveness and respect for others. In a mature democracy, we expect these things – when present, we take them for granted. As the chapter's opening quote from Selznick (1992) reveals, we become most aware of the reliance we place on integrity when we witness shortcomings and failures.

Against this backdrop, the approach taken to measuring integrity started with the challenges facing the ATO at the time that the study was conducted. The more persistent issues involved underspending by government on social infrastructure, the introduction of a tax reform, a mass-marketed schemes debacle and tax dodging by the wealthy. In its pursuit of sound purpose and process, the ATO struggled with the integrity dimensions of providing benefits, treating the community with respect, showing commitment to the Charter and upholding shared principles of justice. The relevance of these dimensions to the context in which the ATO was operating is elaborated upon below. Corresponding measures from the survey were selected for hypothesis testing and analysis.

Benefits and Respect

At the time that the present study was conducted (2000–2005), survey findings were showing that Australians were concerned about public social infrastructure, in particular health and education, and wanted the government to invest more in these areas, even if it meant they had to pay more taxes (Braithwaite, V. et al. 2001; Wilson and Breusch 2003). The value-added tax (GST) introduced as part of the 'New Tax System' by the federal government meant that there should have been more tax dollars in the system to enable discernible improvements to occur, providing the ATO did a good job in collecting the tax.

The introduction of the 'New Tax System' caused complaint and upheaval, but given the magnitude of the change, the transition proceeded remarkably smoothly (Editorial, *The Australian Financial Review*, 11 November 2005). A central plank of the ATO's change programme was consultation with the community, and a substantial investment was made in recruiting tax field staff with expertise in human relations, education and communications (Job and Honaker 2003; Job et al. 2007). This represented a marked shift in employment practices from the accountants, economists and lawyers who were traditionally recruited by the tax office.

The ATO's massive education and persuasion campaign to implement the 'New Tax System' took place against other initiatives to build a more cooperative relationship with the community (Bentley 2007: 106–7). The ATO had developed a compliance model with the assistance of its community consultative body, the Cash Economy Task Force (Cash Economy Task Force 1998) in which it proposed a responsive regulatory compliance strategy to be rolled out across the tax office (Job and Honaker 2003; Job et al. 2007). The ATO compliance model emphasized the authority's commitment to education and persuasion before imposing sanctions and penalties. The ATO also launched a 'Listening to the Community' project to improve its service delivery (ATO 2003c; Webb 2006) and initiated the release of an annual Compliance Program so that taxpayers knew where the tax authority would be focusing its compliance investigations in the coming year (ATO 2002a). The ATO was actively pursuing an improvement in its integrity ratings at the time this study was conducted by being more communicative, responsive and sympathetic to the problems experienced by taxpayers.

Justice and the Charter

As effort was poured into bedding down the 'New Tax System' and relationship building with the Australian public, the enforcement side of the ATO's activities was taking a turn for the worse. For some time, the tax authority had been charged with not tackling tax avoidance and evasion among the very wealthy and at the big end of town (Braithwaite, V. et al. 2001; Braithwaite, J. 2003; Rawlings 2003; Evans 2005). Indirectly, the GST was addressing this problem. A value-added tax broadened the tax base and provided a register of businesses that could either be evading tax through the shadow economy or avoiding tax through complex schemes involving off-shore tax havens. But the public wanted more direct action and the tax reform considered most important by the community involved making the wealthy and corporations pay their fair share of tax and getting rid of the grey areas of tax law. These reforms ranked in the top three while 'keeping taxes as low as possible' ranked sixth (Braithwaite, V. et al. 2001). The priorities expressed so forcefully by the community were about the need for better government-funded social infrastructure, justice and more effort to collect tax from the well-to-do.

The community's rawness surrounding the seemingly protected status of Australia's rich and powerful had shown signs of festering in 1998 when the ATO announced a crackdown on mass-marketed tax avoidance schemes. Murphy (2003a, 2003b, 2004) has provided a detailed account of how people were affected by the ATO's crackdown and how they fought back to effectively eliminate penalties and interest charges in many cases. The key events as outlined by Murphy are summarized below.

With the realization that scheme-related tax deductions had increased from A$54 million (1993–94 income year) to over A$1 billion (1997–98 income year), the ATO took enforcement action against 42000 participants in 1998. The targeted group was not only large but covered an unusually broad spectrum of people, from middle-income taxpayers (e.g. school teachers, miners) to the wealthy (e.g. professionals, sports celebrities). Amended assessments required participants to pay tax on their investments, in some cases going back six years, as well as interest on the tax shortfall and penalties. The interest charge of 13.86% per annum applied retrospectively and increased debts substantially, particularly among those with six years of tax to repay.

Participants responded angrily to the ATO's actions. They resented the implication that they were 'tax cheats'. Their defence was that accountants and financial planners had sold them the schemes as a way of legitimately minimizing tax, while still enabling them to make a long-term investment. The investors virtually declared war on the tax authority. Complaints were made to the Commonwealth Ombudsman, various legal fighting funds were set up, and the majority refused to pay back their scheme-related tax debts. The dispute between the taxpayers and the ATO culminated in a parliamentary inquiry (Senate Economics References Committee 2002).

In response to both the Senate Committee's report and persistent taxpayer defiance, the ATO backed down. In February 2002, a resolution was reached. The ATO acknowledged that many investors had been the victims of bad advice. Naïve participants in the schemes (accountants, financial planners and tax lawyers were excluded) were given a generous offer: interest charges and penalties dropped and a two-year interest-free period in which to repay, providing the offer was accepted within two months. The offer was extended for a further three weeks, during which time the tax office won two relevant court cases. After four years of active resistance, 87 per cent of all investors finally agreed to settle their debt (ATO 2002c).

Unfairness both in terms of applying the law retrospectively and targeting end-users of the schemes rather than the promoters and boutique investors who had profiteered from them cast one shadow over the integrity of the tax authority. The other shadow was cast by the question: what was the tax authority doing all that time; why didn't it act sooner? Either through lack of wherewithal to take on the scheme promoters or simply slowness to act, the ATO compromised its integrity through its handling of the 1998–2002 crackdown on mass-marketed tax avoidance schemes (Senate Economics References Committee 2002; Editorial, *The Australian Financial Review*, 11 November 2005). Moreover, the Taxpayers' Charter, the document that promised taxpayers fair and reasonable treatment, appeared to be put to one side by the tax office. It was left to a government inquiry to remind the ATO of its obligations under the Charter (Senate Economics References Committee 2002).

The integrity battles that the ATO had on its plate at the time of conducting this research were therefore substantial. First, there was the question of the community receiving the benefits it expected – a responsibility of the democratically elected government admittedly, but in this regard tax system integrity was bound inextricably to the willingness of the government to be responsive to taxpayer needs. Second, there was the question of whether the tax authority displayed integrity by implementing change to the tax system through a process that was respectful of the community. Third, there was the question of fairness in shouldering the tax burden: were the well-to-do getting away with paying less tax than they should? Fourth, there was a question mark over the tax authority's commitment to its own Taxpayers' Charter during the much-publicized crackdown on mass-marketed tax avoidance schemes.

With integrity questions surrounding benefits, respect, commitment to the Charter and justice at the time of the research, three hypotheses were formulated:

Hypothesis 6.1 The concepts of benefits, respect, commitment to the Charter and justice point to a relevant set of measures to test hypotheses around the role of integrity in the development of defiance.

Hypothesis 6.2 The integrity measures of benefits, respect, commitment to the Charter and justice will increase trust and will be associated with less defiance.

Hypothesis 6.3 These relationships will be stronger in the case of resistant defiance than dismissive defiance because dismissiveness is likely to be the preferred posture of people who regard tax integrity and trust (even if present) as unimportant.

The reasoning underlying the third hypothesis is that integrity and trust will be superfluous to the interests of those who do not share the socially constructed system of values and norms that makes the collection of taxes acceptable and desirable (see discussion of Reus-Smit 2007 earlier in this chapter). In other words, a person who is dismissive of authority might say, 'Yes, the ATO does a good enough job, its integrity and trustworthiness are OK. But in my world, it is irrelevant to the main game.'

Before testing these hypotheses, the research design will be described, as will the measures used.

Research Design

Four measures of integrity – *benefits*, *respect*, *commitment to the Charter* and *justice* – were measured in 2002, 18 months after the initial survey. All respondents who had completed the 'Community Hopes, Fears and Action Survey' in 2000 (the data set used for analyses in Chapter 4 and 5) were sent the 2002 follow-up, the 'Australian Tax System: Fair or Not Survey'.

The further round of data collection undertaken in 2005 with the 'How Fair? How Effective? Collection and Use of Taxation in Australia Survey' provided measures of *trust* in the tax authority and *resistance* and *dismissiveness* in the community. The defiance measures of *resistance* and *dismissiveness* were identical to those used in 2000. By using measures of integrity taken in 2002 and trust and defiance taken in 2005 we gain greater insight into how integrity contributes to the long-term building of trust and cooperation in the taxpaying community.

The number of respondents who completed all three surveys conducted in 2000, 2002 and 2005 was 511. It is this panel (described in more detail in Chapter 4) that will be used for testing the hypotheses of this chapter.[2]

Taxation as a Benefit to the Community

Two questions were asked to gauge people's perceptions of how appropriately their tax monies were spent: (a) Do you think that the tax you pay is fair given the goods and services you get from the government? (b) Overall how dissatisfied or satisfied are you with the way the government spends taxpayers' money? Answers were given to each question on a five-point scale. Of the panel respondents, 43 per cent conceded some degree of fairness in the tax paid for the goods and services received, and 22 per cent expressed some level of satisfaction with government spending of taxpayers' money. The majority of respondents, however, were either uncertain or unimpressed by performance on these integrity measures.

Responses to the two questions about benefits were not surprisingly, quite strongly correlated ($r = 0.47$, $p < 0.001$): those who believed the exchange of tax for goods and services was unfair were also likely to be dissatisfied with how government spent taxpayers' money. In subsequent analyses, the measures will be combined into one, representing *satisfaction with collective benefits*.

Paying Respect and Being Consultative

A six-item scale was used to measure the concept of *showing respect* for the community. Procedural justice (Tyler 1990, 1997, 2001) provided the theoretical underpinnings of the scale, in particular that aspect of procedural justice that has been referred to as interactional justice. The term has been used in the context of interpersonal relationships, particularly in organizational contexts (Cropanzano et al. 2002) but also in consumer complaint situations (Blodgett et al. 1997) to capture the degree to which the person controlling resources and rewards treats the justice recipient with politeness, honesty and respect (Bies and Moag 1986; Tyler and Bies 1990; Cohen-Charash and Spector 2001).

In the current research the idea is extended beyond the interpersonal dyad to the relationship a regulatory agency has with its community. Agencies can and do nurture broad-based relationships through dealing with members of the regulatory community in a way that is respectful, consultative, responsive and dialogic (Selznick, 1992; Braithwaite, J. 2005: 68–100, 156–66). Engaging in relationship building with the public is fundamental to countering the cultures of disrespect that can engulf a society, deepening cleavages between privileged and disadvantaged groups (Rawlings 2003) and creating mistrust that rebounds on the authority itself (Braithwaite, V. 1998d; Job and Reinhart 2003).

The *showing respect* scale comprised two items that measured (a) the degree to which respondents believed the tax office treated ordinary taxpayers with respect; two that measured (b) the degree to which the tax office treated taxpayers as being trustworthy; and two that measured (c) the degree to which taxpayers believed that they had been consulted about changes in the system (see items in Table 6.1; see Braithwaite, V. 2001 for more details on the origins of these measures). Respondents rated these items on a five-point scale from strongly disagree to strongly agree.

The percentage agreeing with the statements in Table 6.1 suggests that the tax authority had greatest success in communicating passive respect – respecting individual rights, trusting, and *not* forcing people to

Table 6.1 Percentage of panel respondents agreeing with the items on the showing respect *scale*

Items for the *showing respect* scale	% in agreement
The tax office . . .	
respects the individual's rights as a citizen	61
is concerned about protecting the average citizen's rights	40
treats people as if they can be trusted to do the right thing	56
treats people as if they will only do the right thing when forced to*	27
consults widely about how they might change things to make it easier for taxpayers to meet their obligations	20
goes to great lengths to consult with the community over changes to their system	19

Note: * This item was reverse-scored before aggregating scores for the *showing respect* scale.

do the right thing. Taxpayers less often saw tax officers taking respectful initiatives. For example, consulting with taxpayers was not seen to be a common practice, nor was going the extra mile to protect a taxpayer's rights. When the responses were combined into scale scores representing *showing respect*, 53 per cent of the sample considered that, on balance, the tax authority showed respect in their interactions with the community.

The six items in Table 6.1 were strongly interrelated, with correlations ranging from 0.31 to 0.70 (median = 0.42). The alpha reliability coefficient for the scale was 0.83. An aggregated measure of *showing respect* will be used in subsequent analyses.

Commitment to the Taxpayers' Charter

The Australian Taxpayers' Charter is in accord with OECD guidelines (Centre for Tax Policy and Administration 2003) and covers (a) the instrumental needs a taxpayer may have (for information, advice and explanations for decisions or expectations); (b) taxpayers' expressive needs (to be treated fairly and reasonably, as someone trying to do the right thing); and (c) protection against wrongful domination (respecting taxpayer privacy, allowing taxpayers the support of an independent tax adviser of their choosing, and abiding by confidentiality requirements set out in law). In a more general context, the Charter might be considered a measure of procedural justice, a concept that has great importance for ensuring that people obey the law and cooperate with authority, even when the outcomes are not as favourable to them as they personally would like

Table 6.2 Percentage of panel respondents reporting that the ATO honoured the Charter 'most times' or 'almost always'

Charter standard	% in agreement
Keeping the information they hold about you confidential, in accordance with the law	72
Treating you as honest in your tax affairs unless you act otherwise	68
Accepting that you have the right to be represented by and get advice from a person of your choice regarding your tax affairs	65
Respecting your privacy	64
Offering you professional service and assistance to help you understand and meet your tax obligations	52
Giving you access to information they hold about you, in accordance with the law	53
Treating you fairly and reasonably	55
Explaining to you the decisions they make about your tax affairs	52
Giving you advice and information that you can rely on	51
Giving you the right to an independent review from outside the tax office	42
Being accountable for what they do	42
Helping you to minimize your costs in complying with the tax laws	32

(Tyler 1990, 1997). Murphy (2003b, 2004, 2005) has shown how important procedural justice is for the credible operation of the tax system.

In 2002, survey respondents were asked to report on how well the ATO performed on each of the 12 standards of the Taxpayers' Charter (see Table 6.2). Each standard was rated on a five-point scale from 'almost never' through to 'almost always'. The majority of respondents believed that the ATO honoured its commitments to confidentiality, privacy, accepting tax advisers, and accepting taxpayers as honest through the self-assessment system. The tax office performed best on the technical 'rights' standards.

Performance on what might be called human relations standards was substantially lower. Only about half of the respondents thought that the tax office consistently provided information, advice, support, good service, and reasonable and fair treatment. The tax office performed most poorly on standards that presupposed that it was not infallible and criticisms should be addressed. The ATO performed poorly on accommodating independent reviews, on being accountable, and reducing taxpayers' costs of compliance. These data suggest that the public may perceive the tax authority as 'closing ranks' or being defensive when under scrutiny.

The ratings of the 12 standards were correlated with each other. Those who were relatively high scorers on one standard were relatively high on others. Correlations ranged from 0.42 to 0.74 (median = 0.52). The alpha reliability coefficient was 0.93. Ratings were aggregated to form a scale measuring *commitment to Charter*.

When the distribution of aggregated scores was examined, 72 per cent of the sample rated the tax office as being more often in compliance with its own standards than not. Given that the standards were developed and 'owned' by the tax office, it is reasonable to conclude that the tax authority fell short in practising what it preached. The tax authority's performance on *commitment to Charter* as well as *showing respect* calls into question the agency's integrity in the eyes of the public.

Justice – Fairness in Tax Collection from Rich and Poor

Survey participants reported on the degree to which they believed that each of 11 occupational groups paid their fair share of tax. For each of the targeted occupations, survey participants were required to say whether this group paid much more tax than they should, a bit more, about their fair share, a bit less than they should, or much less than they should. For convenience of analysis, the occupational ratings were collapsed from 11 to three categories based on a factor analysis (Braithwaite, V. 2003c): (a) the first targeted category represented high-wealth managers and professionals (chief executives of large national corporations, owner–managers of large companies, senior judges and barristers, surgeons, doctors in general practice, tax agents and advisers); the second targeted category comprised the self-employed in smaller enterprises (small business owners, farm owners); and the third targeted category represented low-income wage earners (unskilled factory workers, farm labourers, waitresses).

Each of these groups at times has come under criticism for their taxpaying. High-wealth individuals have been criticized for their tax avoidance, small business owners for their cash economy activity, and poorly paid wage earners for working for cash in hand while receiving government benefits. If the tax authority were meeting the integrity standard of collecting tax justly, Australians ought to think that these groups generally were paying their fair share.

The percentage of panel respondents who considered that high-wealth managers and professionals were paying about their fair share[3] was 24 per cent, compared with 62 per cent who thought that the self-employed were paying their fair share, and 50 per cent who thought that low-income wage earners were paying their fair share. Public reservations about managers and professionals and low-income wage earners were then explored further. Were they paying too much or too little?

When the data were examined to find out who Australians thought were paying less than their fair share, 71 per cent of panel respondents identified the high-wealth managerial and professional groups as failing to meet their tax obligations. Only 17 per cent of survey respondents believed that the self-employed were paying less than their fair share, and an even smaller 6 per cent judged low-income wage earners as falling short.

These findings show that perceptions of vertical tax inequity are rife in Australia: the wealthy and powerful are seen to escape the tax net, while ordinary Australians are left behind to shoulder the burden. In subsequent analyses, an index of vertical inequality based on the work of Kinsey and Grasmick (1993) will be used to represent this aspect of *justice*.

The finding of low institutional integrity in the system with respect to who is shouldering the tax burden is in accord with other analyses conducted around this time (Braithwaite, V. et al. 2001; Rawlings 2003; Roche 2006). If the tax authority loses integrity because of perceptions of vertical inequity in tax collection, government needs to accept part of the blame through its legislative and policy development function. But this is not the complete story. Tax authorities' willingness and capacity to implement and enforce the law is just as important. Tax authorities rationalize their resources. While the principle of rationalization does not undermine integrity in itself, practices associated with rationalization of resources often do. Complaints have been made of tax authorities increasing their revenue collections by 'picking the low-hanging fruit'. Cases that can produce an outcome easily are far more likely to receive attention than those that are less clear-cut or labour-intensive. Enforcement activity therefore gravitates towards the easy pickings, and cases that are less likely to improve performance statistics for the tax authority or the public prosecutor are put on the back burner (Roche 2006). In the tax context, this means that taxpayers who are caught red-handed without the economic and social resources to fight back receive disproportionate prosecutorial attention.[4] Such rationalizing strategies undermine the integrity of the tax system.

Trust in the Tax Authority to Act in the Collective Interest

Definitions and understandings of trust are varied and numerous (Levi and Braithwaite 1998). For present purposes, trust is defined as an attitude that has a rational or emotional base and that describes a relationship between actors or groups, in which one party (A) adopts the position that the other party (B) will honour commitments and live up to expectations of protecting or enhancing A's well-being (Braithwaite, V. 1998d; Job 2005).

Table 6.3 Percentage of panel respondents trusting and distrusting the tax authority

The ATO . . .	% in agreement
trust items	
has acted in the interests of all Australians	32
is trusted by you to administer the tax system fairly	49
is open and honest in its dealings with citizens	34
has met its obligations to Australians	33
distrust items	
takes advantage of people who are vulnerable	37
has caved in to pressure from special interest groups	34
has turned its back on its responsibility to Australians	29
has misled the Australian people	19

The measure chosen to reflect trust in the ATO was adapted from the organizational trust work of Cummings and Bromiley (1996). Three facets of trust were assessed within the one scale: (a) the degree to which respondents believed that the tax authority shared and acted on the interests of the Australian people; (b) the degree to which respondents believed that the tax authority was honest and open in its dealings with citizens and taxpayers; and (c) the degree to which respondents believed that the tax authority was fair and responsible in its administration of the system.

The *trust* scale comprised eight items that respondents rated on a five-point scale from strongly disagree to strongly agree. The items appear in Table 6.3. At the level of individual items, the percentage of panel respondents agreeing with items expressing distrust and trust is roughly the same. About a third of survey respondents were inclined to endorse items that suggest that the tax authority should be trusted, while about a third endorsed items suggesting that the tax office is untrustworthy.

The *trust* scale was calculated by averaging responses to the four trust items and the four reverse-scored distrust items. The items had intercorrelations ranging from 0.24 to 0.61 (median = 0.45) and produced an alpha reliability coefficient of 0.88.

Overall, the percentage of panel respondents who found themselves either agreeing or strongly agreeing that the ATO was an authority that they could trust to represent their interests was 47 per cent. Levels of community trust declined over the period that the surveys were conducted (2000–2005) (Braithwaite, V. and Braithwaite 2006).

Are the Integrity Measures Telling a Consistent Story?

The four measures of integrity – *benefits*, *respect*, *commitment to the Charter* and *justice* – all located the integrity of the tax authority in 'middling territory', and did so relatively consistently. Under half thought that government spent tax monies responsibly to benefit the community and under half believed that the system shared the tax load fairly by ensuring that the rich paid their fair share of tax.

Just over half believed that the tax authority consulted taxpayers, treated them with respect and trusted them to do the right thing. The best (and outlying) score was for how well the tax office complied with its own Taxpayers' Charter, with an approval rating of 72 per cent. Trust, however, measured two years later was more in line with the other integrity measures, with 47 per cent giving a nod of approval.

If the measures of integrity are reliable and valid, they should be positively correlated with each other. Moreover, they all should be positively correlated with *trust*. A tax authority that is part of a democratic governance structure that offers benefits, collects tax fairly from rich and poor, treats people respectfully and is committed to the Charter is likely to be trusted as a tax authority that is honest and acts with probity in the interests of all Australians. In the context of the present study, perceiving integrity and placing trust seem to go hand in hand.

While trust is the likely outcome of integrity, it is important to note that it is not the inevitable outcome. Taxpayers may regard the tax authority as having integrity on all the listed criteria – they may see benefits from taxation, they may see respect being given to the people, they may see the Charter being honoured, and they may think that various groups are paying their fair share of tax. But they may not proceed to the next step of trusting the authority if they think integrity is unimportant – or if they think of integrity simply as meaning that a tax authority should live up to its 'tough cop' image using any means possible to catch those who are cheating the system. Such a person might see toughness, perhaps even going by the rule book, as the only way that a tax officer could act in the interest of all Australians and earn their trust. For such people, integrity as defined here would do little to improve their trust in the tax authority.

Table 6.4 shows the correlations among the integrity and trust measures. For completion, the defiance postures of resistance and dismissiveness measured in 2005 are also included. In accord with expectations, *trust* in the tax office in 2005 was found to be higher for those who, in 2002, perceived the *benefits* greater ($r = 0.42$, $p < 0.001$), *respect* from the tax office as stronger ($r = 0.43$, $p < 0.001$), *commitment to the Charter* as more consistent ($r = 0.41$, $p < 0.001$) and greater *justice* in contributions from

Table 6.4 Pearson product–moment correlation coefficients among the integrity, trust and defiance measures

Measures	1	2	3	4	5	6
Integrity 2002						
1. Collective benefits						
2. Showing respect	0.40***					
3. Commitment to Charter	0.38***	0.72***				
4. Rich–poor justice	0.36***	0.24***	0.22***			
Trust 2005						
5. Trust in the tax authority	0.42***	0.43***	0.41***	0.28***		
Defiance 2005						
6. Resistance	−0.39***	−0.51***	−0.49***	−0.20***	−0.56***	
7. Dismissiveness	−0.08	−0.06	−0.08	0.00	−0.20***	0.34***

Note: *** $p < 0.001$.

the rich and the poor ($r = 0.28$, $p < 0.001$). The correlations among the integrity measures were all significant and positive.

The findings provide reasonable support for Hypothesis 6.1, that all these measures are relevant to the concept of integrity, with the possible exception of justice in collecting tax from the rich and poor. For the justice measure, correlations were consistently lower.

Preparatory Regression Analyses

Before we tested the remaining hypotheses using structural equation modelling, a set of regression analyses was undertaken to provide a richer base for understanding just how these variables were working in isolation and in relation to each other. Details are reported in the supplementary statistical appendix.[5] Two conclusions are important to note.

First, a possible source of confounding in the proposed analyses and the interpretation of findings is that defiance posturing before the measurement of integrity in 2002 is likely to predict defiance in 2005. The question is whether integrity can account for change in earlier levels of defiance – that is, did integrity lower defiance between 2000 and 2005, or increase it, or bring about no change at all?

This possibility was tested using hierarchical multiple regressions in which defiance in 2000 was first entered into the regression equation to predict defiance in 2005, followed by the integrity measures taken in 2002, and finally, the trust measure taken in 2005. As expected, defiance in 2000 was a very strong predictor of defiance in 2005, but both integrity and trust were also significant. Those who reported integrity in the system in 2002 and trust in the authority in 2005 expressed less resistant defiance by 2005. Integrity explained 6 per cent of the change with the significant work being done by collective benefits and respect. An additional 7 per cent of variance was explained by trust. In the case of dismissiveness, trust but not integrity predicted a lowering of this form of defiance over the five years (2 per cent). The findings from these regression analyses were in accord with the structural equation models presented below.

The second insight gained from these preliminary analyses, and confirmed by the structural equation modelling exercise, was that justice in collecting taxes from the rich and poor did not contribute in its own right to explaining defiance. Furthermore, as was evident from Table 6.4, it was only weakly connected with the other integrity measures. The integrity measure of justice in collecting from the rich and poor is omitted in subsequent analyses, not so much because it is viewed as conceptually flawed, but because of suspicions that the measure is not strong enough for present analytic purposes.

The measure of justice in collecting from rich and poor involved asking survey respondents to consider different occupational groups and then to indicate on a rating scale whether the group was paying less or far less than their fair share, the right amount, or more or far more than their fair share. The measure contained no evaluation except for that implied by the word 'fair'. Some might say that what we were measuring was agreement with facts since the tax avoidance opportunities of those with money were widely acknowledged and tacitly endorsed. In retrospect, what we should have been measuring was the following: did respondents feel angry about rich–poor injustice, believe they had been let down by the government or feel dissatisfied with the tax authority's performance? Failure to measure a respondent's evaluation of rich–poor tax injustice was picked up in part through the trust measure. This may explain why the highly evaluative measure of trust rendered rich–poor tax injustice non-significant in the regression analyses.

The measure of justice in collecting tax from rich and poor has been retained up to this point because it is central to how integrity has been theorized and there is no evidence that it should be jettisoned on these grounds. Empirically, however, it makes sense to use only three integrity measures (benefits, respect and commitment to Charter) to represent the latent trait of institutional integrity in subsequent analyses.

Before moving to the results of the structural equation modelling, an explanation is warranted for the general approach to model building. The analyses presented at the end of each chapter are pared down to present as clearly as possible the core dynamic that is being theorized in the chapter. The models below involve three key latent variables (integrity, trust and defiance). No attempt has been made here to integrate the threat and coping model with the integrity and trust model – this is the purpose of Chapter 8. The goal of this chapter is simply to find the most parsimonious set of variables to tell the story of how institutional integrity might be expected to affect defiance.

A Model of Resistant Defiance

The role that integrity is expected to play in the defiance story is an ameliorating one. We may not like the tax authority or the officials that preside over the system, we may all feel like Ana Pascal in *Stranger than Fiction* as she meets Harold Crick for the first time, but we shall contain our defiance if we see signs of integrity in the authority. The signs may involve our satisfaction with collective benefits, the tax authority showing respect for taxpayers or showing commitment to its own Taxpayers' Charter. When we can discern such signs of integrity, trust that the agency will serve the interests of all Australians is expected to increase. We accept and share their purpose, and on this basis become a little more cooperative and a little less resistant to the power they hold over us.

Figure 6.1 tells the story of how integrity increased trust and trust reduced resistant defiance using structural equation modelling. The variance accounted for in resistance was 57 per cent. These findings provide

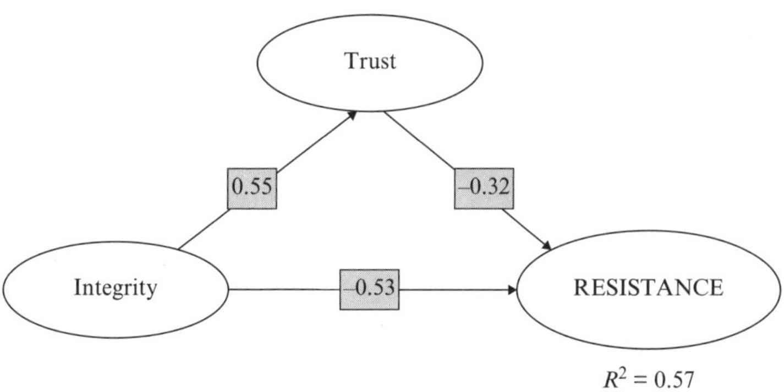

Figure 6.1 A structural equation model linking integrity (2002), trust (2005) and resistance (2005)

support for Hypothesis 6.2 in relation to resistant defiance. The goodness-of-fit indices and squared multiple correlations for latent constructs were all satisfactory and are presented in Appendix B.

Of considerable interest is the pathway going from integrity to resistant defiance. While not hypothesized, the pathway would be of no surprise to scholars of procedural justice and group identity theory (Tyler 1997; Wenzel 2002). A very large part of integrity is procedural justice in the sense that taxpayers are acknowledged as valued members of the taxpaying community. This simple act of inclusiveness and affording of status is likely to elicit a positive, cooperative and reciprocating response from taxpayers.

A Model of Dismissive Defiance

Integrity and trust behaved in the predicted manner in the structural equation model explaining dismissiveness (see Figure 6.2). Trust was the variable through which integrity was able to make its presence felt on dismissiveness. There was no direct link between integrity and dismissiveness, however. If integrity could not make its presence felt through improving trust in the tax office, the opportunity for containing dismissiveness through institutional integrity was lost.

While the model provided a good fit to the data (see goodness-of-fit indices in Appendix B), the variance accounted for in dismissiveness was not high (8 per cent). Indeed, it indicates a remarkably weak explanation for a large set of theoretically credible variables. The finding casts doubt on the usefulness of integrity as a leverage point for managing dismissiveness. On the basis of the findings in Figure 6.1 for resistance and Figure 6.2 for dismissiveness, we see different pictures emerging of resistant and dismissive

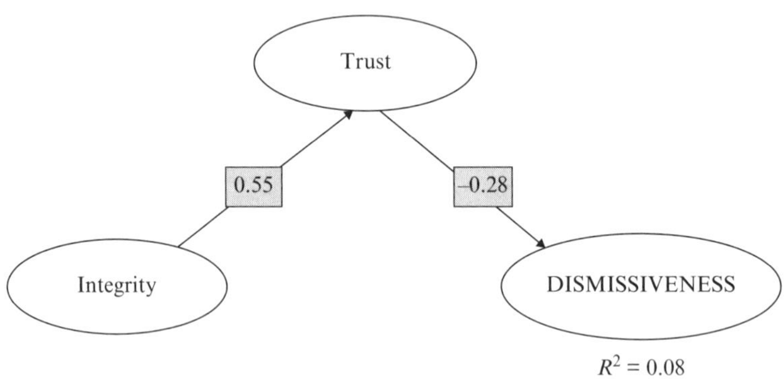

Figure 6.2 A structural equation model linking integrity (2002), trust (2005) and dismissiveness (2005)

defiance. Resistance can be contained through integrity, dismissiveness barely at all.

Resistance can be thought of as a relationship between taxpayers and the authority that is tense and in need of repair through efforts that demonstrate openly the authority's integrity and its trustworthiness. Dismissiveness, on the other hand, sets in when there is no longer interest in protecting or strengthening the relationship. Dismissiveness may be contained a little if we believe that the authority is working in all our interests, but we might conjecture that those who are dismissive need some hard evidence before them if they are to be convinced.

SUMMARY

This chapter sets out a way of viewing institutional integrity in the context of a tax authority. Institutional integrity is an umbrella term for the coherence, responsiveness, fairness and commitment that an authority displays in the performance of its duties. The problem of coherence is one of huge proportions for the tax systems of most developed countries. Australia attempted a large structural reform with the introduction of the 'New Tax System' in 2001. As significant as this change was for Australians and for the ATO, it did not resolve the layers of complex and conflicting tax law that had accumulated over decades.

But shortcomings at the structural level of tax system design need not and should not affect a tax authority's commitment to collect taxes from all taxpayers, abide by the Taxpayers' Charter, be fair in its processes, respectful of and responsive to taxpayers, and clear and sound in its purpose, making or recommending corrections to the system when falsehood, injustice and/or inefficiency become apparent. This is the face of integrity as authenticity as opposed to integrity as coherence of tax design.

As the new century began, Australia attempted to build greater integrity on both fronts, recognizing that the structural reform could not be achieved without the good will of taxpayers. In a bid to build a more authentic relationship with the Australian community, the ATO reaffirmed its commitment to the Taxpayers' Charter; endorsed a responsive regulatory model – the ATO compliance model that emphasized consultation, persuasion and education as tools for compliance that would be tried before sanctioning and prosecution; and introduced a clearly articulated Compliance Program detailing enforcement priorities. Good intentions at times went awry, however. While the introduction of the new tax system was generally hailed a success, the tax authority's handling of mass-marketed tax avoidance schemes involving tens of thousands of Australians faltered, weighed down by tax authority decisions that appeared to the public to be unfair, poorly explained and justified, incompetent and punitive.

Against the background of these events, this chapter reviews data on the public's perceptions of how the tax office was travelling on integrity in late 2001 to early 2002. The focus was on integrity as authenticity – how was the ATO performing in the eyes of the public? Survey respondents were divided on the extent to which the ATO was showing respect and could be trusted to represent the interests of all Australians. They were more of one mind on three other integrity measures: that taxes were not being collected fairly from rich and poor, that taxes were not being used to benefit the community as a whole, but that, most of the time, the tax authority was acting in accordance with its Taxpayers' Charter in its treatment of taxpayers. Despite differences in ratings on where the tax office was doing well and where it was doing poorly, there was coherence among the measures, suggesting that they were all reasonably reliable and valid measures of integrity. That said, weaknesses emerged in the measure of justice in collecting tax from the rich and the poor. This measure was omitted from the final analyses that mapped the role of integrity in shaping postures of resistance and dismissiveness.

The core hypothesis of this chapter was that integrity as authenticity would build trust in the tax authority, and trust, in turn, would curb defiance. This hypothesis was supported. A structural equation model showed support for pathways linking integrity in 2002 to trust and defiance in 2005. Moreover, supplementary regression models revealed that integrity and trust accounted for a change in defiance from 2000 to 2005. Integrity and trust together gave the tax authority leverage for containing defiance, but the effects were not uniform across the two forms of resistance and dismissiveness.

The effects were much stronger for resistance than for dismissiveness. Integrity was strongly linked directly with trust and resistance, and trust was strongly linked to resistance. The variance explained in resistance was 57 per cent. In contrast, the links between integrity, trust and dismissiveness were weaker. Integrity had no direct significant link to dismissiveness. The only way it could influence this form of defiance was through trust. Integrity and trust were weaker leverage points, accounting for only 8 per cent of variance in dismissive defiance.

CONCLUSION

The significance of the findings of this chapter need to be interpreted in the context of other major advances in our knowledge about regulation, particularly the contributions of procedural justice researchers. When we consider the three key variables in this chapter – integrity, trust and defiance – it would not be unreasonable to suggest that integrity is an embellished version of procedural justice. Its relationship with trust therefore follows a well-trodden research path. Moreover, to find that both integrity and trust are related to defiance is also a variation on an old theme: procedural justice builds trust and increases obedience to the law and cooperation with its enforcers. This is the appropriate starting point for appreciating the significance of the findings of this chapter.

Most significant is the finding that the integrity story is strong for resistance but not for dismissiveness. The group-value model of Tyler (Lind and Tyler 1988; Tyler 1989; Tyler et al. 1996; Tyler 1997) and the social exchange models of Smith (Smith and Stalans 1991; Smith 1992) and Scholz (Scholz and Pinney 1995; Scholz and Lubell 1998a, 1998b) both provide explanations for why this may be the case. Tyler's work focuses attention on shared identities. If taxpayers do not share the identity of an honest taxpayer, for example, the status afforded to an individual through respectful treatment and responsiveness from the tax authority will not change that individual's sense of belonging or pride in being a member of the group. They may enjoy the authority's display of respect in a superficial way, but not in any deep or meaningful sense – it is irrelevant to their ethical identity (Harris 2007). For this reason, within the framework of the group-value model, the integrity of the tax authority may not matter to the socially distant and dismissive taxpayer. Those who are dismissively defiant may even interpret some aspects of the integrity of the tax authority as a display of weakness – the authority's Achilles' heel in the event of a challenge (Braithwaite, J. 2005).

In terms of the conceptual framework of Smith and colleagues (Smith and Stalans 1991; Smith 1992), the failure of integrity to shift dismissiveness is just as explicable. Integrity is being used in effect as a positive incentive for taxpayers to comply, and the principle expected to swing into play in response is reciprocity: the tax authority is offering to trust and cooperate with taxpayers, and therefore taxpayers should reciprocate that trust and cooperation. But the extent to which the incentive is actually regarded as positive should not be assumed. As Smith and Stalans (1991) and Feld and Frey (2007) have pointed out, in order for positive incentives to work, they need to strengthen moral resolve to do the right thing, not become tools for undermining the authority of the tax office or be seen as bribes by an intractable government under pressure. A culture of scepticism about the legitimacy of taxpaying makes it particularly difficult for authority to increase commitment through positive inducements (Nagin 1990). It is likely that, for the dismissively defiant, integrity is not the positive incentive that will change the frame of reference for engagement with the tax authority. Something is needed to encourage the dismissively defiant to switch from a competitive, adversarial frame that is predominantly about protecting assets to a cooperative, altruistic frame that is hopeful about finding win–win outcomes (Smith and Stalans 1991). The findings of this chapter suggest that integrity – as measured here at least – is not the something that is required.

Is Integrity Irrelevant to Dismissiveness?

To move at this point to conclude that integrity will not dislodge dismissive defiance is premature. It is more appropriate to take a critical look at how integrity was operationalized in this research, and by the tax authority at this time. A plausible argument might be that integrity reform needs to go deeper; it needs to address the concerns of the Ana Pascals of this world (of the political left and right), and not just tinker at the edges. The fundamental problem may be that the institution of taxation needs to acquire relevance in the minds of the dismissively defiant.

This is the point that Gibson has made in his criticism of procedural justice: 'that citizen's general views of institutions – including highly symbolic and diffuse views – have more to do with directing their behavior than do . . . perceptions of procedures employed by institutional decision makers' (1991: 634). This position comes close to that of Scholz and his colleagues (Scholz and Pinney 1995; Scholz and Lubell 1998a, 1998b), who have pursued the idea of a 'trust heuristic' that similarly is diffuse in so far as it spans a lot of territory including the political, but that seems very practical for individuals wishing to keep a finger on the pulse of the democratic process.

The intention was for integrity to be a construct that was closer to the things an authority must do to score well on Gibson's (1991) diffuse institutional support and Scholz and Lubell's (1998a, 1998b) 'trust heuristic'. A similar and equally diffuse understanding of integrity of the Selznick (1992) kind can be read into the regulation literature (Bardach and Kagan 1982; Kagan 1989; Braithwaite, J. 1985, 2002) where the concept is taken well beyond procedural justice to the idea of responsiveness (sometimes forsaking consistency in the process).

Working Integrity Harder

Procedural justice is at the heart of the measure of integrity used in this chapter, but so too is interactional justice (Aryee et al. 2002; Barling and Phillips 1993) and good governance plays a small role. What all three have in common is that they represent ways in which authorities demonstrate respect for the people they govern. Together they represent the justice of respect, meaning that respect is something to which every individual is entitled and justice is the delivery of that respect without discrimination. In the Taxpayers' Charter, many of the standards are highly procedural, addressing impartiality and the right to voice and review, as well as fairness and respect. In this way, each person must be treated with dignity and consideration, regardless of background. The *showing respect* scale reflects how an authority with integrity communicates to the public that relationships based on trust and mutual respect matter, cemented by processes of consultation. The contribution of individuals is welcomed and considered valuable, regardless of background. For respect to be consummated, however, the gestures must serve some worthwhile objective that benefits the collectivity, regardless of background. Thus authorities with integrity prove their respect for the community by generating benefits without fear or favour, which will be reflected in community appreciation.

Through identifying the core of integrity as the justice of respect, there is room to push the concept further than has been the case in the current research. The justice of respect speaks to our ethical identity in the same way as the group speaks to our self-worth in the group-value model. Our ethical identity is created, nurtured and damaged by the groups to which we belong and with which we identify, but it is a personal construct, existing in our minds and able to engage with entities in abstract ways (Harris 2007). We can frequent cultures of disrespect and suffer at their hands locally, nationally or internationally – perhaps more commonly these days in cyberspace (Grabosky 2007). If we consider shame, for instance, and the way in which our ethical identity can suffer as a result of a harsh judgement, that harsh judgement can be communicated face to face or through an intimate friendship group. Or the interaction may occur with distal entities by means of a letter from the government, a text message from source unknown, a television advertisement or an image of our ancestors. We bask in the positive messages that are sent to us – or we wither in response to negative messages. Importantly, the senders of these messages need not be people we know; they can be faceless authorities outside our circle of contacts. We are all vulnerable to their message, however, providing it conjures up the image of a group with which we identify and is a symbol of a moral judgement that matters to us. That moral judgement may relate to the processes that we believe we deserve as well as the resources to which we believe we are entitled. The justice of respect therefore is procedural, interactional and distributive. How the message is delivered – as processes or outcomes, in personal or mass communication – is less important than what it says: 'We respect you for who you are and what you do.'

This brings us to a clearer understanding of the limits of integrity as the tax authority implemented it and as this study measured it, and why it could not explain dismissiveness in this particular context. To a disillusioned taxpayer who is disturbed by the waste of public money or the government's engagement in unjust wars or its short-termism or corrupt practices, being afforded respect by an authority is inconsequential. Nothing short of a fundamental rethink of governance structures will satisfy such a taxpayer. Such a 'rethink' was not part of the integrity package that either the ATO or the Australian government offered to taxpayers. The message was 'trust us', not the more respectful message of 'let us share and work with you on our strategic vision for taxation and governance in this country'.

Delving More into Dismissiveness

Public disillusionment with the government's integrity efforts is not the only line of enquiry that should be pursued in understanding the development of dismissiveness. The above findings and their interpretation give rise to a second line of enquiry. The direct link between integrity and resistance should provoke a degree of alarm from the perspective of those who value good governance. In Chapter 3, concerns were raised in light of research that has shown the willingness of citizens to follow authority uncritically. It is a disturbing thought that superficial respect in the form of treating people nicely or going through the motions with the Charter can be reciprocated as cooperation from taxpayers. But what if the respect is not so superficial and ritualistic? What if the respect seems authentic and takes the form: 'we understand what you need, we understand that this is a worry for you, we can offer you a plan that will help you survive and prosper'; and what if this voice of apparently genuine respect does not come from government, but from the financial services sector, from financial planners, accountants and advisers?

In an era of nodal governance, there are many who can compete with tax officials for authority and influence (Braithwaite, J. 2005, 2008). The tax authorities of nation states have readily placed their trust in outside professionals (tax practitioners, auditors, criminal investigators, the courts) to ensure that their tax systems function smoothly. Moreover, there is no shortage of overseers to monitor the activities of tax authorities to ensure that they meet expected standards of integrity (ombudsmen, taxpayer interest groups, politicians, government audit offices and productivity commissions). It makes perfect sense that, in such an environment, taxpayers will be open to any number of influences and will recognize multiple 'authorities', particularly taxpayers who are not tied into a 'mutually satisfying' tax compliance routine with the tax authority. Taxpayers who are keen to maximize their own gain or are disenchanted with the tax system are prime candidates for being attracted to alternative authorities and to the path of dismissiveness (Smith and Stalans 1991).

Those scouting around for an alternative authority may connect up with others whose interests are in opposition to those of the tax authority (Tan 1999; Karlinsky and Bankman 2002; Sakurai and Braithwaite 2003; Braithwaite, J. 2005; Braithwaite, V. and Wenzel 2008). These ideas raise the important question of whether the dismissive posture of defiance has little to do with the quality of the relationship between the taxpayer and tax authority. This particular relationship may have become irrelevant as other relationships have taken its place. New relationships may shape tax posturing in adversarial and non-compliant directions. Dismissive defiance may exist almost within a psychological bubble set apart from the tax authority, where talents and resources of like-minded players are pooled in the spirit of Wolfe's (1988) 'it's all a game'. The next chapter explores the contours of the tax game bubble, while continuing to track disillusionment with the democracy as the irritant that turns people towards defiance.

NOTES

1. Legitimacy in the sense of whether people regard an authority as deserving of obedience is an overarching concept for this research project. The motivational postures in Chapter 4, coping styles in Chapter 5 and integrity and trust in Chapter 6 all speak to the legitimacy question: does this authority deserve to be obeyed as the law says it should?
2. By having data collected at three points in time, the research design enabled empirical examination of this question: does integrity displayed in 2002 change the relationship between coping styles adopted in 2000 and the motivational posturing (or defiance) individuals show with regard to tax matters in 2005? This question is addressed in Chapter 8. For consistency the panel data are used in this and all subsequent chapters.
3. Respondents rated whether or not an occupational group was paying less than, an OK amount or more than its fair share on a five-point scale where the midpoint of 3 represented an OK amount. For scales representing high-wealth managers and professionals, the self-employed and low-income wage earners, anyone scoring between 2.5 and 3.5 was classified as thinking that the group was paying its fair share.
4. In 2006, the ATO and the Australian government showed signs of shifting this bias when they announced Operation Wickenby, the largest investigation of tax fraud and money laundering ever conducted in Australia, with a special focus on the misuse of tax avoidance schemes. The initiative was announced in the Treasury budget papers of 2006–07, under the heading 'Maintaining the Integrity of the Tax System'. http://www.budget.gov.au/2006-07/ministerial/html/treasury-06.htm.
5. See http://vab.anu.edu.au/defiance/sup01.pdf.

7. Approaching defiance through social modelling

> Learning would be exceedingly laborious, not to mention hazardous, if people had to rely solely on the effects of their own actions to inform them what to do. Fortunately, most human behavior is learned observationally through modeling: from observing others one forms an idea of how new behaviors are performed, and on later occasions this coded information serves as a guide for action.
>
> Albert Bandura 1977: 22

Evidence is accumulating to support the initial proposition that resistant and dismissive defiance represent different styles of motivational posturing. But the evidence provides greater insight into the psychological processes that lead to resistance than to dismissiveness. It seems that a different approach is needed theoretically if we are to glimpse the heart of dismissiveness.

In the preceding two chapters, defiant posturing has been approached through two theoretical lenses, one focusing on threat to the taxpayer, the other focusing on the integrity offered by the tax authority to quieten taxpayer misgivings about possible injustice and unreasonableness. As different as the theoretical lenses are, they share an important element. Both assume that the tax authority matters to people and that complaints and unease over taxation lend themselves to meaningful dialogue – threat and injustice can be talked through, preferably to a resolution that is acceptable to both parties. The argument that has been constructed to date is that, through cognitive reframing and institutional reform, individuals are in a position voluntarily and thoughtfully to desist from defiant posturing. Desisting from defiance is, in effect, a decision made in a relational context, where the authority is re-evaluated as a power that deserves cooperation.

In this chapter, an alternative perspective is explored. Defiance may not be as thoughtful or deliberative a reaction to taxation as assumed. Defiance may be a mode of adaptation to authority that is intuitive and has more to do with following influential voices than thinking through the rights and wrongs of the tax system.

Within this context it is worth noting that, in the ideal world, authentic deliberation is considered important for building cooperation and eliciting compliance, but sometimes it is not practicable, nor does it guarantee resolution of compliance problems – it depends on who is at the table, the knowledge at hand and how the deliberative process unfolds (Young 2000; McFarland 2001; Irvin and Stansbury 2004). Complexity and information asymmetry sometimes result in insufficient data to arrive at an agreed course of action through deliberation, made more difficult by individual differences in willingness to fill in knowledge gaps with principles and heuristics (Scholz and Pinney 1995; Braithwaite, V. 1998b; Day 2006). Deliberation may also serve little purpose if it is not possible to bring to the fore mutual trust or cooperation among participants (Young 2000; Irvin and Stansbury 2004).

In institutional contexts, problems of complexity and lack of knowledge can be dealt with by setting clearly defined boundaries on what is relevant to task completion (Wolfe 1988; Day 2006); and routines and checklists socialize us into dealing with just enough information so that we can perform tasks almost on automatic pilot. Ideally, these constraints help free up cognitive capacity to focus on more important issues (Heimer 2008), but often the expectation is that we will leave thinking to others (Adler and Borys 1996). Even in the absence of scripts and rules, there is an easy path to arriving at an action plan. We have access to role models whom we can follow without too much cognitive overload (Bandura 1977), to say nothing of the guidance provided by advertisements that set standards and market products that promise to deliver the outcomes we want (Klein 2000).

The circumstances of our lives are such that if we choose not to deliberate on an issue or if we believe that such deliberation is a waste of time, we are capable of action that is 'light on thought'. The submissions made to Australia's inquiry into mass-marketed tax avoidance schemes revealed a tax planning culture heavily influenced by marketing, a deeply entrenched belief in individualism and self-sufficiency, and the desire to succeed (Senate Economics References Committee 2002). In pursuit of these goals, many people had been gullible in accepting the word of high-status and high-profile Australians on how to minimize their tax legally (Hobson 2002; Braithwaite, J. 2005: 50–51). The observable by-product of poor-quality deliberation on tax matters intrigues in so far as it raises the question of how this could occur. Surely at some point warning bells would have been heard, signalling to taxpayers that they should consider the possibility that they were defying authority and that there could be consequences.

Defiance at the outset was defined as an attitude or behaviour used by individuals to signal to self and others that they are either knowingly departing from a prescribed path, or are in the process of questioning the path laid out for them by an authority. This definition of defiance implies deliberation and thoughtfulness. How can we then articulate a narrative of defiance as we see in the motivational postures of disengagement and game playing without really being able to engage in a regulatory conversation about how we got there? The answer lies in thinking about defiance as a response that involves input from actors outside the tax office–taxpayer dyad. As Bandura (1977) and many of the institutional design theorists (Tversky and Kahneman 1974; Scott 2001; Scholz and Pinney 1995) have pointed out, people take short cuts in their thinking and action, picking up from others bits and pieces that sound plausible and seem to work. There are many occasions when we leave 'the thinking' to others. Taxpaying may be a private and confidential matter from the tax authority's perspective, but the narratives surrounding taxpaying are highly public and constantly in creation through financial networks, blogs, advertising and the media. The argument that narratives of defiance are constructed outside the relationship between the taxpayer and tax authority is explored in this chapter. A model is developed and tested that identifies external lures and influential role models as factors shaping defiant posturing. The argument is grounded in three bodies of research – surveys tracking cultural change from materialism to postmaterialism (Inglehart 1990, 1997; Inglehart and Welzel 2005), work on nodal governance and regulatory capitalism (Shearing and Wood 2003; Gordon 2007; King 2007; Braithwaite, J. 2008) and studies that look at the culture of competition and its links with white-collar crime (Benson 1990; Beams et al. 2003; Gobert and Punch 2007; Shover 2007).

POSTMATERIALISM, REGULATORY CAPITALISM AND HIERARCHIC SELF-INTEREST

Inglehart (1997) has observed that a postmaterialist worldview has become increasingly prevalent in mature democracies where the public no longer harbours concerns about their vulnerability and insecurity. He has argued that with postmodernization in the mature democracies have come generations who have not known hunger, nor the loss of family, home, possessions and nation state on a scale commensurate with that experienced by many Europeans during World Wars I and II. Taking prosperity for granted, the postmaterialist approach to life contrasts with that of materialists. They are less likely to trust institutions and are more likely to challenge authority, particularly authoritarian institutions. In Inglehart's words, 'conditions of prosperity and security are conducive to greater emphasis on individual autonomy and diminishing deference to authority' (1997: 296).

Inglehart's (1997) conception of postmaterialism provides an interesting background against which to consider the posture of dismissiveness in particular. Perceiving the tax office as irrelevant and/or as a fair target for citizen challenge is consistent with Inglehart's postmodernist perspective. There does not need to be much deliberation about the tax system: awareness of how it might interfere with future plans would suffice.

The decline in deference to hierarchical institutions dovetails with increasing awareness of the many sites of governance in our society and the accompanying diversity in networks of trust and obligation (Shearing and Wood 2003). From a nodal governance perspective, tax officers are not only likely to come under scrutiny as the postmaterialist age makes its presence felt, but also are likely to fade in importance as other experts in financial and tax planning assume the mantle of trusted advisers and standard-bearers.

No assumption can be made as to whether such governance networks are anchored in or run counter to the interests of the democracy (Sørensen and Torfing 2005). The goods and bads that arise in the markets generated in an era of regulatory capitalism are open to contestation and deliberation in the democratic tradition (Braithwaite, J. 2008: 202–7). Some tax planning networks will act responsibly, contributing to a stronger economy; others will be 'fiscal termites' undermining tax systems (Tanzi 2000). Dismissiveness may be a manifestation of what is problematic in regulatory capitalism. Markets are created in tax planning and tax avoidance that flourish outside an arena that allows for public contestation and deliberation (Braithwaite, J. 2005, 2008). Dismissiveness may be symbolic of neither having nor wanting a relationship with the tax authority or the democratically elected government of the day; instead it may be an expression of pursuing actions that are rewarding when regulatory constraints can be safely ignored and when a tax authority is marginalized in people's consciousness.

Distaste for hierarchical institutions and a rich array of alternative authorities in a nodal governance tax network explain why a tax authority may become irrelevant, obsolete or sidelined in the consciousness of taxpayers. Neither, however, quite satisfactorily explains the defiance of dismissiveness as described in Chapter 1. Dismissive defiance was conceived as an individual's assertion of freedom from authority, an expression of individual agency in which there was no need to deliberate or argue with a so-called authority about the why and wherefore of the action. A person does *X* because she feels entitled and able to do *X* – there is no justifiable regulatory constraint and that may extend to law.

When such freedom is exercised under the purview of authority, it challenges that authority. Exercising freedom says 'you can't touch me' or 'catch me if you can or dare'. When authority is challenged in this way, its response will involve a reckoning of the importance of asserting its control. In some circumstances, the authority and the individual may go their separate ways, both acknowledging, covertly if not overtly, that one need not have any kind of relationship with the other. But if the costs of looking the other way are too high, authority may come to a different view. When authorities try to exert control over those who persist in asserting freedom, competition for dominance is likely to develop. This competitive mindset is hypothesized as lying at the heart of dismissive defiance.

The battle for dominance – a battle that takes place over the individual's right to be free to do as he or she chooses regardless of what the law demands – is a domain of enquiry tackled by criminologists. Shover (2007) has profiled the culture that nurtures white-collar criminals. He attributes white-collar criminality to fluctuations in the business cycle, the culture of work organizations and belief that credible oversight is lacking. The business cycle is relevant at both ends of the spectrum. When the economy is taking a downward turn, the temptation may come from the fear of going under if corners are not cut. When there is an economic upswing, an equally tempting mentality may come into play – everyone else is getting rich on this, why shouldn't I?

Shover argues that the privileged citizens who engage in white-collar crime 'are aware of whether or not and how closely overseers are paying attention to them' (2007: 95). When authorities are looking the other way, predispositions come to the fore, nurtured particularly strongly in the materially comfortable social classes (Lareau 2002; Shover 2007). These generative worlds for criminality instil an 'unbridled competitive thrust' for individualized success (Hagan et al. 1998: 317) and an insatiable appetite for winning (Gobert and Punch 2007), arrogance and rhetoric 'to neutralize obeisance to law' (Shover 2007: 93) and an ethic of entitlement to success, status and respect, whatever the cost to others (Hagan et al. 1998; Shover 2007).

The account of pride in white-collar criminality provided by Gobert and Punch (2007) usefully contrasts with the image of the honest law-abiding taxpayer portrayed in Chapter 5. The successful tax evader might be expected to show a passion for being a 'winner', with 'pride . . . from identifying and exploiting loopholes in the law, outwitting law enforcement personnel, and massaging regulatory systems to . . . financial advantage' (ibid.: 100). Such image making is condoned in the name of 'the abstract entity commonly referred to as "the market"' (ibid.: 101).

Hagan et al. (1998) have progressed a research programme that examines the social consequences of having a market culture that places the goal of material success ahead of the rule of law. They introduced two concepts, hierarchic self-interest and anomic amorality, to explain how a culture of competition (Coleman 1987) can promote criminality. Hierarchic self-interest is found in advanced market societies and incorporates attitudes about competitiveness, success and individualism. To this value set, Hagan added indifference to conventional morality. Anomic amorality captures an attitude of cynicism, relativism and opportunism towards rules and law, particularly where these rules and the law are not entirely clear. While Hagan's work focused on group delinquency, the parallels with corporate culture are striking.

Within the white-collar crime tradition, Geis (1967) and Vaughan (1996) have brought many of these elements together in their descriptions of how illegality can become so commonplace within corporate culture that it comes to be accepted as the normal way of doing business. Simpson and Piquero (2002), however, have placed an important caveat on the influence of corporate culture – or in the current context, culture-led defiance. When individuals believe that an act is highly immoral, they are likely to be unwilling to even contemplate that course of action. Even when 'forced' to meet the expectations of an unethical corporate environment, the moral self is not entirely extinguished from a self-regulating deliberative process (Yeager and Reed 1998; Braithwaite, J. 2005: 111).

Even in the midst of unethical activity, we are able to connect with role models that communicate different kinds of messages. The role models that emerge in competitive markets may be antagonistic or sympathetic to the tax system. In spite of the salience of the tax minimization market, with its mixture of aggressive and more cautious advice, it is important not to lose sight of the fact that the greatest demand is for tax advisers who offer a basic, honest and competent service (Tan 1999; Sakurai and Braithwaite 2003).

LOOKING TO MODELLING TO EXPLAIN DEFIANCE

Behaviour is often executed without much thought. Acts of desire, fear, anger, curiosity, risk or fun may be 'spontaneous' in this sense (Massey 2002). They are not necessarily grounded in a consciously held coherent belief set. In retrospect, such acts may appear rational or irrational, and trigger much deliberation after the event. At the time, however, they may be based on very little thinking, understanding or knowledge of the situation. This is not to deny occasional brilliance and the agile minds of those who spot opportunities for defiance. Innovators and early adopters, as Gladwell (2000) called them, show considerable insight and perceptiveness in recognizing opportunity and leading the way. The subsequent process, however, in which others jump on the bandwagon, has more to do with modelling, the appeal of populist ideas, and not wanting to be left behind. Thoughtful analysis of the virtues of the course of action is unlikely until the action is challenged.

Defiance, even when we can converse about it – as we can with taxation – may follow principles of social modelling and contagion. When we see someone doing something, we are curious, we try it, and if it works for us, we try it again. The phenomenon of modelling has been extensively theorized, empirically tested and broadly applied in the social sciences. Just as particular behaviours are copied, so too are ideas and attitudes. We learn to be like others. More than mere imitation, modelling is defined as 'action(s) that constitute a process of displaying, symbolically interpreting and copying conceptions of actions (and this process itself)' (Braithwaite, J. and Drahos 2000: 581). Models for how things might be done are launched (model missionaries), sold (model mercenaries), floated without compatibility checks (model mongers), borrowed not always appropriately (model misers), and adopted for reasons of legitimacy and status (model modernizers). The important point is that rarely are ways of doing things thought out from first principles. In the competitive world of financial planning and tax minimization, it is not difficult to understand how modelling of various kinds by advisers and taxpayers creates narratives of defiance that are reactive and not necessarily consistent or coherent criticisms of the tax system and the tax authority.

THE BASIC SOCIAL MODELLING PARADIGM

Theories of social modelling derive from learning theory. We observe an association between an action and an outcome, and, depending on whether the outcome is a reward or punishment, we learn to perfect its accomplishment or avoid it. Learning takes place sometimes through direct experience, but more often than not through observing others (Bandura 1986). The 'others' who most frequently capture our attention and teach us how to respond to our environment have special significance in our lives: they may care for us, control our access to resources, make us feel good, be a companion, or represent who we would like to be. Significant others or role models shape our actions – they lead us by example. It is not necessary for us to talk about what they do or why we want to follow in their footsteps. We observe and pay attention to them, we abstract ideas of cause and effect, and we act.

Social learning theory has spawned a variety of accounts of how we are influenced and why (Rotter 1954; Sutherland 1947; Burgess and Akers

1966; Bandura 1977; Akers 1998). For present purposes, one basic principle from Chapter 3 requires revisiting. When we identify with another person or group, we are susceptible to taking on their values, attitudes and ways of behaving, in part because we want to belong and receive approval from the group, and in part because we rely on others to give us confidence that our understanding of the world is true (Turner et al. 1987; Hogg and Abrams 1988). Following the lead of others satisfies our need for affiliation (Schachter 1959; Gump and Kulik 1997) and our need for certainty and knowledge (Turner et al. 1987).

Moreover, acting and thinking as a unified group creates momentum for social change. When a critical mass assembles in defiance, the 'weak' gain capacity to undermine the agenda of dominating powers (Braithwaite, V. 1994). At the less disruptive end of the regulatory spectrum we see enforcement swamping, in which authorities lack the resources to rein in the undesirable behaviour because so many are now doing it without a second thought. At the most disruptive end of the regulatory spectrum is change in the authority structures, with the regulatory agency being decommissioned or radically restructured.

MODELLING AND RULE FOLLOWING

McAdams and Nadler (2005) have explored the ease with which individuals follow a certain course of action in order to receive monetary rewards. Using a spinner in a game to signal to a group of players that they may want to follow a certain decision path, experimental participants quickly fell into line, accepting the recommendation of the spinner as if it were a leader. The findings were comparable when a random leader replaced the spinner, and were only marginally improved by a leader who had been assigned a degree of legitimacy. McAdams and Nadler have used their experimental laboratory-based evidence to argue that law (regardless of its legitimacy or its sense) becomes a focal point around which individuals coordinate their efforts to receive positive outcomes. The depth of commitment – or faith – that may come about through McAdams's (2000) analysis was apparent in a recent response to a survey on citizen obligations to government (Maguire et al. 2007): '[My job is] to obey the law, even if an imbecile is in charge.'

The application of this experiment to the area of tax avoidance is intriguing. If actors in the marketplace of tax planning can 'capture' law and use it to 'authorize' their actions, they place themselves in a very advantageous position. McAdams's work explains how the tax planning industry has grown its market share in Australia by associating its products with credible legal authorities and by providing access to advisers who purportedly can share the tricks of the tax minimization trade with ordinary taxpayers. The result has been that aggressive promoters have become the alternative authority, leading an unsuspecting public into the domain of non-approved mass-marketed tax avoidance schemes (Braithwaite, J. 2005: 44–6).

UNCERTAINTY, FEAR OF LOSING OUT AND RULE BREAKING

When knowledge is restricted and competition is rife, the capacity to scan the environment and adapt quickly becomes a valuable asset. If we are not constantly vigilant, being a member of a group that offers security makes sense. Signing up to mass-marketed tax avoidance schemes, for instance, could be seen as joining a large, respectable group of investors with knowledge and skill to create financial rewards. Safety comes through backing from distinguished legal experts and from the sheer numbers involved in the schemes. This form of social contagion, be it emotionally driven (the excitement of the chase) or cognitively driven (the expected pay-off), has survival value. Bikhchandani and Sharma (2000) have argued that it can be economically rational to follow others when information is truncated – herding both into markets and out of them.

The contagion that affects money markets has been used to explain the way in which taxpayers enter and exit mass-marketed tax avoidance schemes (Braithwaite, J. 2005). In *Markets in Vice, Markets in Virtue*, John Braithwaite draws upon interviews with top-level tax lawyers and accountants to show that while aggressive tax planning involves meticulously crafted and clever game plans for the wealthy elite, ordinary taxpayers experience something quite different. Schemes that had met with some success at elite levels were repackaged, in the process losing some of the niceties that protected against challenges from tax authorities. They were then marketed to an unsuspecting public eager to save tax by jumping on the next financial planning bandwagon. Not until the mass-marketing stage were tax authorities confident that they had the ammunition to challenge the schemes and take action to close them down. By this time, scheme promoters had made their financial killing, and small investors were left to their own devices to fight their case against the tax authority.

The growth of the aggressive tax planning market proceeds in cycles. Schemes become attractive as they acquire reputation as smart and legal investments. When the tax authority takes action against investors, activity dies down. The cyclical theory of tax avoidance contagion assumes an environment where there are significant periods of uncertainty about what is permissible under the tax law. Because tax law is unclear and unwieldy, those who are sharp enough to seize opportunities can exploit the grey areas in the law to substantially reduce the tax they should pay. Contributing just as much to the uncertainty is the fact that tax authorities are stretched to the limits of their technical competence in providing rulings on when tax breaks apply and when they do not. A loophole to one taxpayer may be a genuine business expense to another as governments encourage innovation by nudging more cautious businesses into seeking a competitive edge with tax concessions. It is not difficult to appreciate why there is scope for alternative authorities to emerge for taxpayers looking for direction.

Uncertainty creates opportunity that attracts public interest, and closure of the uncertainty by the authority kills off interest. But it is social contagion that explains the build-up in support for an action and the subsequent defection from that action (Bikhchandani and Sharma 2000). Human beings follow a critical mass of others into activities that they assume will produce a favourable outcome; and they charge out again when they catch sight of unfavourable outcomes or when they see others abandoning the activity. Such understandings of human behaviour guide market research (Neal et al. 2004). In the marketing context, demand is built by creating or appealing to an emotional need in individuals that can be satisfied intermittently through supply of the good or service in question. The appeal increases as the product gains rational substantiation: the product works, it gives us what we want. When it no longer works, interest wanes and activity subsides until new opportunities are spotted and the cycle starts again.

TAX ADVISERS AS ROLE MODELS AND ALTERNATIVE AUTHORITIES

The need for knowledge, fear about uncertainty, distaste for or lack of confidence in government, and the desire to be a law-abiding taxpayer or a clever tax minimizer or both lead taxpayers to the doors of professional tax advisers.

Tax researchers have a well-established literature examining the role of practitioners in 'leading' taxpayers into and out of compliance, and on the opposite phenomenon – taxpayers demanding aggressive tactics from their advisers, who then feel pressured into supplying riskier advice than they would otherwise give (see, e.g., Klepper and Nagin 1989; Klepper et al., 1991). There is evidence for both kinds of pressure, the outcome often being that taxpayers who are high risk takers find tax advisers who specialize in aggressive advice and creative compliance, while cautious, no-fuss taxpayers find advisers who deliver a competent and honest service (Karlinsky and Bankman 2002; Sakurai and Braithwaite 2003; Tan, 1999).

Drawing on the work of Wenzel (2002, 2004a, 2004b, 2005), an explanation for why some prefer aggressive advice and others honest, no-risk advice is that the groups with which we identify shape our taxpaying persona. If we are attracted to and identify with members of a group who spend a lot of time practising tax minimization, we are likely to learn a more competitive way of engaging with the tax authority. If, on the other hand, we align ourselves with a group that takes pride in paying tax and doesn't begrudge payment, our identification with that group is likely to lead to a more positive way of engaging with the tax authority. As Wenzel reminds us, we should not think of these identities as mutually exclusive. We have multiple identities. As contexts change, our group identifications change, along with our salient selves.

POSTMATERIALIST VALUES AND HONEST ROLE MODELS

An individual's worldviews are likely to result in the expression of certain preferences that direct the individual towards some groups rather than others. Postmaterialists with values such as wisdom, inner harmony, self-expression, tolerance and human rights (Inglehart 1997: 111–12, 210–11) might be expected to have a sympathetic spot for taxpaying if not for the authority itself. Postmaterialists might be expected to value the democracy and want to do their bit to keep it flourishing, while being wary of an overbearing, officious tax administration. Their ideal role model for taxpaying is likely to be competent, knowledgeable, willing to pay a fair share, and with integrity to challenge tax authority foolishness should it arise. Their ideal tax practitioner is likely to be the honest, no-risk adviser described in Chapter 4. Modelling this ideal means that any hint of defiance of tax office authority should be successfully contained. This model does not involve deep deliberation over tax, but rather an action plan of delegating tax matters to a trusted other.

Hypothesis 7.1 Support for postmaterialist values associated with personal growth and inner harmony is likely to lead to a preference for an honest adviser to mediate the relationship with the tax authority, resulting in less defiance than might have been assumed given the authoritarian nature of the institution.

STATUS VALUES AND A CULTURE OF TAX DEFIANCE

While values and worldviews can orient people on a cooperative path, they can also be the marketing hook for luring people towards aggressive tax planning. Internationally, financial planning has been promoted as savvy and sophisticated, and as the way of creating wealth and protecting one's assets from the government (see Box 7.1 for examples of advertisement captions when tax reform was under way). Financial planning agencies have worked to 'sell' tax defiance as legitimate and safe, if done cleverly.

The efforts of the ATO to contain tax avoidance have earned them media exposure as well, usually expressed in terms of dominance and coercion, although the ATO has taken the initiative on occasion, with warnings of

BOX 7.1 CAPTIONS FROM AUSTRALIAN ADVERTISEMENTS PROMOTING TAX MINIMIZATION PRODUCTS AND SERVICES IN THE LEADING FINANCIAL NEWSPAPER, 2000–2001

CAPITALIZE ON TAX REFORM WITH THE FIRM WHO WROTE THE BOOK (ARTHUR ANDERSEN)
The Australian Financial Review 5 June 2000: 14

TAX EFFECTIVE FORESTRY INVESTMENT AVAILABLE TO 30 JUNE 2000
The Australian Financial Review 7 June 2000: 12

SHIFT YOUR WEALTH CREATION INTO OVERDRIVE AND YOUR TAX INTO REVERSE
The Australian Financial Review 7 June 2000: 15

'FLICK GST'
The Australian Financial Review 10–12 June 2000: 43

THE BEST INVESTMENT ADVICE YOU'LL EVER GET, TAX CERTAINTY WITH TIMBERCORP'S 2001 ALMOND PROJECT (ATO PRODUCT RULING)
The Australian Financial Review 20 June 2001: 6

IF TAXATION ROBS PETER TO PAY PAUL, MAKE SURE YOU'RE PAUL
The Australian Financial Review 12 June 2001: 6

THE ONLY THING BETTER THAN YOUR SHARES GOING THROUGH THE ROOF IS YOUR TAX BILL GOING THROUGH THE FLOOR
The Australian Financial Review 12 June 2001: 37

KNOW YOUR MARKET AND BEAT THE TAXMAN
The Australian Financial Review 16–17 June 2001: 33

YOU'VE ONLY GOT 8 WORKING DAYS LEFT TO CUT YOUR TAX LIABILITY BY THOUSANDS OF DOLLARS THIS FINANCIAL YEAR . . . BUT HURRY LIMITED SUBSCRIPTIONS AVAILABLE!
The Australian Financial Review 20 June 2001: 16

OUR CLIENTS TELL US. 'I KNEW THIS INFORMATION WAS "OUT THERE", I JUST DIDN'T KNOW HOW TO GET IT' . . .
Learn how to dramatically reduce your tax burden . . . legally. We reveal how and why the government has tried to keep this information hidden from you . . . Pay little or no tax – legally . . . and with a clear conscience. The wealthy have done this for generations.
The Australian Financial Review 14–15 July 2001: 16

possible dangers that may lurk for unsuspecting investors in the financial planning sector (see Box 7.2). Examples of headlines from Australian dailies featured in Box 7.2 convey the message that the tax office is doing its job – albeit not with as much flair and sophistication as the promoters of tax minimization and avoidance. The headers and bylines feature words of a Wild West posse – 'fighting', 'chases', 'pursuing', 'closes in on', 'grabs', 'firing line' and 'hit'. Not surprisingly, some newspapers have taken on the role of protectors of taxpayer rights in a climate that suggests that a battle is under way (see Box 7.3).

The struggle of the ATO to earn public respect has been and continues to be a marathon event. Integrity reconstruction for a public institution is a process of continuous improvement, but often the journey seems to involve two steps forward and one step back. Newspapers are one source of collective storytelling that tell us what readers can relate to, find credible and want to hear (Cohen and Nisbett 1997). The public stories from Australian dailies that feature in Box 7.4 are reflections of, as well as contributions to, the narratives and culture that have surrounded Australian taxpaying and the ATO, a culture that is at odds with the desired ethic of integrity outlined in Chapter 6.

BOX 7.2 HEADERS AND BYLINES FROM AUSTRALIAN DAILY NEWSPAPERS REPORTING TAX OFFICE EFFORTS TO CONTAIN TAX AVOIDANCE, 2000–2005

Tax man comes out fighting/I shall not be moved, says commissioner
Tax Commissioner Michael Carmody has attacked what he claims is an unprecedented campaign to damage the Australian Taxation Office, promising that it will not deter him from delivering . . .
The Australian 31 March 2000 by Ian Henderson

Tax Office chases a new image
The Australian Tax Office has moved to clean up its image, employing an ethics counsellor and establishing an internal hotline for whistleblowers in the wake of recent damaging allegations.
Illawarra Mercury 3 May 2000

ATO vows: the GST won't stop us pursuing tax cheats
The Australian Taxation Office has begun executing search warrants against the promoters of aggressive tax avoidance plans after forging closer links with the Federal police to stop the rapid growth of such schemes.
Sydney Morning Herald 10 June 2000 by Tom Allard and Sherrill Nixon

Tax office closes in on rich
The Auditor-General yesterday called for a continuing attack on rich tax cheats after the tax office identified more than 250 high wealth individuals at risk of being tax avoiders.
Daily Telegraph 14 June 2000

If benefits look too good to be true they usually are
As the financial year draws to a close you may see advertisements for investment arrangements which claim to be 'tax effective' and which promise 'big tax breaks' [warning issued by the ATO]
Canberra Times 11 June 2001

ATO grabs $1bn from rich dodgers
Twenty-four of Australia's 600 richest people repaid the tax man almost $1 billion last financial year. By tightening auditing procedures on big business and wealthy individuals, the Australian Taxation Office . . .
The Australian 1 November 2002 by Luke McIlveen

Rich in the firing line for ATO
The Australian Taxation Office said yesterday it would continue to focus its energies on big business and wealthy people to ensure they paid their share of tax.
Daily Telegraph 12 December 2002

Pay your share! Wealthy hit with tax bill for $6.7bn
Large companies and wealthy individuals have been hit with $6.7 billion in amended assessments following Tax Office audits in the past two financial years . . .
Sydney Morning Herald 18 March 2005 by John Garnaut

If we consider the advertising materials and journalists' accounts of tax activity shared with the Australian public through the print media in the period of this study and during the period of tax reform, two conclusions seem inescapable. First, taxpaying is governed nodally through networks that have different perspectives on the worthiness of the taxpaying enterprise. Second, within this governance network, there is scope for the financial planning industry to occupy a position that makes it a respectable and successful alternative authority for taxpayers wishing to pay as little tax as possible.

This overview of the public storytelling of taxation is sufficient for establishing that tax planning has an influential and legitimate place in Australian taxpaying culture. The credibility of tax planning professionals, in particular the attraction to tax avoidance schemes, has been aided by the fact that privileged and respected classes, including Australia's political, business and entertainment elites, are reputed to have been beneficiaries (see Box 7.5). Moreover, schemes of questionable legality have been widely promoted by eminent lawyers and sporting stars (Braithwaite, J. 2005). The images promoted in the media link social and economic status with tax avoidance. The message has been that the wealthy and privileged can defy authority and get away with it, as can the ordinary taxpayer if he/she has enough money to invest in tax avoidance schemes and retain the services of a clever and efffective tax adviser.

Taxpayers who place a premium on economic and social success are likely to be drawn to this web of tax defiance. The attraction is likely to be strengthened if such taxpayers also subscribe to norms of competition and winning, described by Hagan et al. (1998) as hierarchic self-interest. A shared ethic of economic and social success and winning would increase the likelihood of risk taking and trying new ways of

BOX 7.3 HEADERS AND BYLINES FROM AUSTRALIAN DAILY NEWSPAPERS SUPPORTING TAXPAYERS' RIGHTS TO MINIMIZE TAX, 2000–2007

Mastering tax an early lesson in survival
Thousands of new entrants to the job market will be paying tax for the first time. But a little knowledge of the tax system can reduce how much they will have to pay according to Paul Drum, CPA Australia's senior taxation consultant.
Herald-Sun 23 December 2002

Don't be bullied by the taxman – 04–05: the year ahead
This is the time of year when people carefully gauge their tax obligations, and residential property investors should take particular care.
The Australian 1 July 2004 by Bina Brown

Avoid tax but don't evade it, businesses told
Big business should do everything it can to minimize its tax bill, the Business Council of Australia has declared, as it resumed its push yesterday for lower corporate and personal tax rates.
The Australian 16 June 2005 by Katharine Murphy

Plan to start now for a tax-effective year
It's time to dig out that shoebox and start sorting through your tax paperwork. But if you're tired of seeing your dollars go to the tax office, take action now to minimize the loss.
The Courier-Mail 2 July 2007 by Erica Thompson

Don't confess tax sins yet: accountants
Accountants and industry bodies have praised the Australian Taxation Office's move to provide a year-long amnesty to admit 'past mistakes' to private companies that make tax-free distributions of profits.
Australian Financial Review 1 August 2007 by Marsha Jacobs

avoiding tax. People who hanker to be part of this scene will not want to be left behind socially or economically. They will emulate the actions of those who successfully save on their tax: they will seek the expertise of aggressive tax planners.

BOX 7.4 HEADERS AND BYLINES FROM AUSTRALIAN DAILY NEWSPAPERS REPORTING TAX OFFICE FUMBLES AND COMPROMISED POSITIONS, 2000–2005

Taxing times for 60 sacked workers
William Thomas is one of 60 sacked textile workers who stand to lose thousands of dollars after Fabric Dyeworks in Coburg was forced to close its doors when the tax office recovered outstanding debt.
The Age 18 March 2000 by Andrea Carson

Taxman blamed for big avoiders
One of Australia's most senior tax advisers has strongly criticized the Australian Tax Office, saying technical opinions and rulings by the ATO helped spawn a $1 billion-plus avoidance industry, and should never have been issued.
The Age 11 May 2000 by Malcolm Maiden

Drug dealer's tax win
ATO rules stolen money legitimate – Taxpayers had the green light to rort the system after a drug dealer was allowed a tax deduction for $220,000 stolen from him during a drug deal, a tax expert said yesterday.
Adelaide Advertiser 12 August 2000 by Mark Russell

Tax debt lawyers on payroll
Bankrupt barristers with huge tax debts have been paid by the Commonwealth to represent it in courts around Australia. Some have even received income to appear on behalf of the Australian Taxation Office . . .
Herald-Sun 24 March 2001 by Keith Moor

Dodging tax, according to ATO manual
A leaked tax office manual has exposed the tricks the taxman will use to cut his own bill this year while he's processing yours. The Salary Packaging Manual contains scores of tips for tax officials to cut their own tax, by having the . . .
The Australian 25 August 2001 by Duncan Macfarlane

Taxing times at the ATO
With a federal election looming, the Australian Taxation Office is increasingly caught between what it thinks is right and what the Government wants.
Adelaide Advertiser 8 September 2001 by Phillip Coorey

Tax whiz misused influence, court told
Nick Petroulias, the whiz-kid who supervised the tax schemes of the nation's wealthiest for Commissioner Michael Carmody, was secretly using the powerful position to promote his own lucrative tax venture.
The Australian 6 November 2001 by Martin Chulov

Tables turn as ATO grovels to tax cheat
The tax office has begun paying a convicted tax cheat more than $1.4 million plus interest of at least $200,000 after a tribunal ruled it had penalized him too much.
Courier-Mail 28 November 2001 by Chris Griffith

Poor taxed more as rich enjoy cut
Australia's lowest paid workers are paying almost $700 more tax a year than they were when Peter Costello became federal Treasurer. Figures reveal below-average wage earners are being hurt the most by tax.
Daily Telegraph 26 November 2005 by Scott Murdoch

BOX 7.5 NEWSPAPER REPORTS OF CELEBRITIES AND HIGH-PROFILE CITIZENS ENGAGING IN CONTENTIOUS TAX MINIMIZATION STRATEGIES AND SCHEMES

Packer tax victory sparks wide anger
Ordinary taxpayers pay almost 600 times more in tax than Mr Kerry Packer and have no hope of exploiting the same loopholes because they cannot afford the expensive advisers who assist Australia's richest man.
Sydney Morning Herald 15 October 1998 by Tom Allard

Professionals 'among biggest tax debtors'
Lawyers, accountants and medical practitioners are among the country's biggest tax debtors, owing nearly five times the national average in unpaid taxes, the Audit Office has found . . .
Canberra Times 21 December 1999 by Kirsten Lawson

Packer firms win against Tax Office
The Australian Tax Office has failed in its epic 12-year battle to claw back hundreds of millions of dollars of tax allegedly unpaid by companies controlled by Australia's richest man, Kerry Packer.
The Age 1 June 2001 by Josh Gordon

Former Minister liable on $1m 'gift'
A former federal Minister, John Brown, had deliberately sought to evade paying tax on what he had claimed was a $1 million gift from a prominent Gold Coast developer, Brian Ray, a Federal Court judge has found.
Canberra Times 2 June 2001 by Roderick Campbell

The QC who paid NO tax for 40 years
One of the nation's leading barristers told a bankruptcy hearing yesterday he had not filed a tax return since the early 1960s – almost his entire working life. John Cummins, QC, who declared himself bankrupt in December and now claims to . . .
Daily Telegraph 7 June 2001 by Martin Chulov

PM seeks tax audit to defuse scandal
Prime Minister John Howard has called for a full GST audit of the Queensland Liberal Party in a bid to end continuing fallout over claims of an organized tax scam.
Courier-Mail 27 August 2001 by Dennis Atkins

Rafter living in land of Oz
Australian-of-the-year Pat Rafter is a Queenslander again, his father said yesterday. 'I am sure Pat would think that as far as he is concerned he has clarified this issue that he is no longer a resident of Bermuda,' Jim Rafter said . . .
Herald-Sun 5 February 2002

A taxing time for Hoges
It could be the plot for a new Crocodile Dundee film, in which the rough-neck innocent abroad is caught up with murky Caribbean tax havens, high-flying accountants and a top-secret crime commission. This time, however, actor Paul Hogan, a . . .
Canberra Times 13 September 2005

Tax office studies Crocodile Hunter's offshore scheme
Crocodile Hunter Steve Irwin and his wife, Terri, personally signed off on a plan to send a share of their Australia Zoo profits offshore in a tax scheme that allowed them to obtain significant deductions.
The Australian 3 April 2008 by Susannah Moran

Hypothesis 7.2 Valuing social and economic status will result in attraction to the competitive ethos of winning and, in turn, to aggressive tax advisers and defiance.

DEMOCRATIC EXPECTATIONS AND DEFIANCE

The third and final hypothesis is derived from analyses of how political and economic institutions may have disappointed the public in delivering the postmaterialist outcomes of an enriched democracy, greater respect for civil liberties and equal opportunity. From Inglehart's (1997) work the inference can be drawn that community hopes and expectations for democracy have grown and are high. Democratic ideals have captured people's imagination to the extent that they have become less accepting of discrimination and failure to observe human rights and lack of accountability and transparency by governments and corporations. Rules abound in mature democracies to protect the public from such abuses. At the same time, the practices of governments, corporations and individual citizens do not always match aspirations, or even minimally comply with the rules. The work of Karstedt (2006), Karstedt and LaFree (2006) and LaFree (1998) has sought to explain the breakdown of social order and cooperation when hopes and expectations are not realized.

Styles of democratic governance that adhere to the promotion of equal opportunity and individual freedom tend to yield lower crime rates (Karstedt 2006). Crime rates have of late been rising in mature democracies (Karstedt and LaFree 2006). LaFree has attributed increases in crime in the USA to failing legitimacy of some key institutions. In particular, he has pointed to loss of trust in political institutions and the use of law to impose change from the top to the detriment of community social capital (ironically, LaFree argued, in pursuit of postmaterialist aspirations of civil liberties). Added to this has been failure to attend to certain kinds of growing inequalities: '[I]nequality will only be accepted when 'most people have an equal chance to aspire to that inequality' [citing Charles Handy 1994: 41]' (LaFree 1998: 181). Connecting with all three elements is the purpose of law to restore a sense of order and security for the community. In the work of Karstedt and LaFree (2006) 'the rule of law is a cornerstone of the institutional regime of democratic societies. All actions of citizens, the state and government are equally subject to legal scrutiny, independent of position, status, and power' (ibid.: 11–12). When the public perceives democratic values and standards as being compromised and legal institutions as failing to protect them, it is likely that mentalities of disillusionment, anomie and defiance will flourish. On the basis of Inglehart's (1997) work on postmaterialist hopes and La Free and Karstedt's work on failing democratic legitimacy and rising crime (LaFree 1998; Karstedt 2006; Karstedt and LaFree 2006), a third hypothesis is proposed:

Hypothesis 7.3 Disillusionment with democracy in so far as it has failed to meet community expectations of justice, equal opportunity and freedom is likely to give rise to generalized anomic amorality (Hagan et al. 1998) or legal cynicism (Sampson and Bartusch 1998). In particular, it is likely to lead to idealizing aggressive tax planners and defiance of an authoritarian institution like the tax authority.

This hypothesis envisages a link between becoming disillusioned with the quality of the democracy and succumbing to the view that rules can be manipulated to achieve a desired outcome. This might be thought of as the dark side of postmaterialism, a result of the failure of traditional, particularly authoritarian, institutions to be responsive in a time when their integrity has been challenged. The confidence crisis in democracy and its institutions is likely to bring about general legal cynicism. The disillusionment and cynicism that permeate society beyond taxation will inevitably affect how people see the tax system and its authority. The expectation is that, regardless of a tax authority's efforts to improve integrity, this more generalized form of disenchantment with the system of governance will strengthen defiance.

RESEARCH DESIGN

Measures of the postmaterialist values of *personal growth and inner harmony* and the competitive ethos of *social and economic status* were measured in 2000 in the 'Community Hopes, Fears and Action Survey'. Also measured in this survey was *disillusionment with the democracy*.

All other measures were taken in the final round of data collection in 2005 with the 'How Fair? How Effective? Collection and Use of Taxation in Australia Survey'. At this time measures were taken of *legal cynicism* and *winning*, mentalities that reflected how individuals were engaging with the democracy and the culture of competition. *Legal cynicism* and *winning* were considered to be the vehicles by which individuals change gear and turn abstract values into preferences that lead to defiance. The decision that was important in actioning preferences was to whom individuals would turn for advice on tax matters – an *honest tax adviser* or an *aggressive tax adviser*? Because use of an adviser is not universal, and because we don't always have the advisers we want, the question asked was not about current use, but rather 'who is your ideal tax adviser?' This measure, while one step removed from behaviour, was more in keeping with the theoretical ideas being advanced. The focal point of this chapter is the way in which an alternative authority can provide role models for defiance, offering attractive possible selves to taxpayers. The final two measures from the 2005 survey used in the analyses below were of defiance – resistance and dismissiveness, as in Chapter 6.

As in the previous chapter, the analyses were based on the panel sample of 511 respondents who completed all three surveys conducted in 2000, 2002 and 2005. The following sections provide details of the measures that were used and map the sentiments of Australians at the time the study was conducted with regard to their values and disillusionment with democracy, their competitive and moral attitudes, and their role models. The hypotheses are subsequently tested using structural equation modelling, as in the previous chapter.

Individual Values

Among the scales used in Chapter 4 to assess how much of posturing was stable and connected to personality was *personal growth and inner harmony*. Values of *personal growth and inner harmony* may shield people from tax defiance because, essentially, these values are cooperative, conflict-avoidant and humanistic. It was hypothesized that placing priority on this postmaterialist form of self-expression and individuality would lead taxpayers down a non-confrontational path, towards honest tax advisers and away from defiance. *Personal growth and inner harmony* involved prioritizing the following values: (a) wisdom (having a mature understanding of life); (b) the pursuit of knowledge (always trying to find out new things about the world we live in); (c) self-knowledge/self-insight (being more aware of what sort of person you are); (d) self-respect (believing in your own worth); (e) self-improvement (striving to be a better person); and (f) inner harmony (feeling free of conflict within yourself). Respondents rated each value in terms of its importance on a seven-point rating scale. When responses to these values were aggregated, the value constellation *personal growth and inner harmony* was considered important, very important or of the utmost importance by 92% of respondents.

In order to measure the importance placed on the value cluster *social and economic status*, survey respondents were asked to pass their judgement on five values (as measured in Chapter 4): (a) seeking economic prosperity (being financially well off); (b) being recognized by the community (having high standing in the community); (c) having authority (having power to influence others and control decisions); (d) being ambitious (being eager to do well); and (e) competitive (always trying to do better than others). Such values were expected to draw people towards defiance and towards the alternative authority of an aggressive tax adviser through a preference for being a winner. Again, these personal values were rated on a seven-point scale by respondents in terms of how important each was as a guiding principle in their daily lives. Scores were aggregated to produce a scale on which 51% of respondents considered striving for *social and economic status* as important, very important or of the utmost importance.

Disillusionment with Democracy

In the social modelling approach adopted in this chapter, the attraction to role models who constitute alternative authorities needs to be understood in terms of a broader picture of governance. Global economic forces have created opportunities for financial planning and tax avoidance that were not so readily accessed in the past. These industries have become a magnet for 'success seekers'. Equally important may be the goal of survival for those who do not fall into this category. They cannot ignore the fact that they are enmeshed in a market economy, even if they disapprove of its impact on society. The attitude scale used in Chapter 4, *disillusionment with the democracy*, captures dissatisfaction with inequalities in wealth, status and power that are perceived to have distorted democratic processes and the justice system. Those who are disillusioned may be turning their back on ethical norms and established institutions, drifting towards a more defiant way of being.

Disillusionment with the democracy was measured by six statements, all of which convey a sense of the ordinary citizen being excluded from the democratic process and being sidelined as the rich and powerful exercise their control over legal and political systems (see Table 7.1 for items). Respondents indicated how strongly they endorsed each statement on a five-point scale from strongly disagree to strongly agree. The percentage of respondents who had concerns about the state of the democracy was high; for four of the six statements in Table 7.1, the percentage expressing *disillusionment* approached or exceeded 70%. Averaging over the six items, the percentage of respondents who agreed that they were disillusioned was

Table 7.1 Percentage of panel respondents agreeing with the items on the disillusionment with the democracy *scale*

Items for the *disillusionment with the democracy* scale	% in agreement
Democracy is a term that has lost much of its original meaning	53
There's a dollar democracy that runs through our supposed democracy	70
In Australia, the rich have virtually unlimited access to the legal system and the capacity to use it to achieve their own ends	89
I don't think we have enough input into legislation and the decisions that are important	67
Our government is attempting to mould our society to the needs of a profit-oriented market	70
I'm always cynical about government processes	59

87%. The widespread unease with the state of the democracy is likely to create opportunities for aggressive tax planners trying to increase their market share. Those who are disillusioned are likely to lend their ear to anyone suggesting that there are more cost-effective ways for taxpayers to satisfy the unreasonable demands made on them by government. *Disillusionment with the democracy* may neutralize obligation, making it easier to follow defiant others: It may fuel contagion.

Competitiveness, Winning and Legal Cynicism

A display of defiance to the tax authority may reflect the aspirations and preferences of taxpayers, but it may also signify caving in to new pressures to provide for one's own economic security in the future. Whether extremely disillusioned with their system of government or struck by the rhetoric of individualism and economic self-sufficiency, individuals are likely to accept new norms for transacting business. Competitiveness, winning and bending rules may be 'soaked up' as codes for how we should behave if we want to survive in a world that rewards those who are economically productive and abandons those who cannot look after themselves.

The measures of *winning* and *legal cynicism* involved survey participants responding to a set of statements on a five-point strongly disagree to strongly agree scale. The items were adapted from measures used earlier by Hagan et al. (1998) and Sampson and Bartusch (1998). A factor analysis of the items produced two clear dimensions, one representing competitiveness and the need to win at all costs, the other representing moral acceptance over bending rules and lack of concern about law-abidingness.

Table 7.2 Percentage of panel respondents agreeing with the items on the winning *scale and* legal cynicism *scale*

Items for the *winning* scale and *legal cynicism* scale	% in agreement
Winning	
Winning is everything	10
It is not so important how one wins, but that one wins	7
To make money, there are no right and wrong answers, only easy ways and hard ways	34
Legal cynicism	
It is never OK to break the law, not even minor ones*	65
I do not care too much if other people think that I sometimes 'bend' the rules	14
It feels good to bend the rules and get away with it	9
Even if I had the chance to cheat I wouldn't do so. It is morally wrong*	77
Sometimes you need to ignore the law and do what you want to	11

Note: * This item was reverse-scored before aggregating ratings for the *legal cynicism* scale.

The intercorrelations for the items for the *winning* scale were strong (0.26, 0.29 and 0.42), producing an alpha reliability coefficient of 0.58. The items of the *legal cynicism* scale correlated well with each other, with coefficients ranging from 0.21 to 0.54 (median = 0.28), producing an alpha reliability coefficient of 0.70.

The percentage of respondents who agreed with the individual items in the scales are shown in Table 7.2. Ratings for items on each scale were averaged to produce scale scores for further analysis. The percentage of the sample committed to *winning* at any cost was a minority, 13% overall. The proportion of the sample expressing *legal cynicism* was relatively small also, 10% overall. *Winning* at any cost was hypothesized as being part of the pathway linking a desire for social and economic status to an aggressive tax planning adviser and defiance. *Legal cynicism*, on the other hand, was considered more likely to be part of the disillusionment pathway to defiance, a pathway defined by anger and disenchantment with governance generally.

Honest and Aggressive Tax Advisers as Role Models

In Chapter 4, preferences for an ideal tax adviser who was honest and for one who was aggressive were used as indicators of deference to tax authority. The same scales were used again in 2005. *The ideal of an honest adviser* and the *ideal of an aggressive tax adviser* represented attraction to an alternative authority that would be a tax-sympathetic role model and a tax-antagonistic role model respectively.

Attraction to these different role models was assessed by asking respondents to imagine that they were in the market for a tax adviser and whether they would place a low, medium, high or top priority on their prospective adviser having certain qualities. The honest no-risk qualities were: (a) someone who does it honestly with minimum fuss; and (b) someone who does not take risks and only claims for things that are clearly legitimate. Responses were highly correlated ($r = 0.61$) and were averaged to provide an overall score. A substantial 87% of respondents indicated that they would prioritize *an honest adviser*.

The aggressive tax planning qualities were: (a) someone who can deliver on aggressive tax planning; (b) a creative accountant; and (c) someone who is well networked and knows what the tax office is checking on at any particular time. Intercorrelations for this set of items were also high (0.33, 0.36 and 0.60), producing an alpha coefficient of 0.69. When scores were aggregated, a low 18% indicated that they would prioritize *an aggressive adviser*.

CORRELATING VALUES, ATTITUDES, ROLE MODELLING AND DEFIANCE

The correlation matrix provides a starting point for examining the central questions: (a) do postmaterialist values around *inner harmony* in 2000 lead to attraction to an *honest tax adviser* and less defiance in 2005? (b) Do *status* values in 2000 lead to being preoccupied with *winning*, attraction to an *aggressive tax adviser* and more defiance in 2005? And (c) does *disillusionment with the democracy* lead to *legal cynicism*, attraction to an *aggressive tax adviser* and more defiance in 2005?

The correlations in Table 7.3 are informative in a number of respects. First, it is of note that the 2000 measures – seeking *personal growth and inner harmony*, seeking *social and economic status* and *disillusionment with the democracy* tend to be positively interrelated. Values, by definition, are goals that we all would rather have than not have, although the relative importance will vary from one person to another (Rokeach 1973). The minority who place low importance on values generally adopt the view that they prefer not to think of options in terms of vague abstract principles – they are detail people and are wary of what they call motherhood statements and 'feel-good' messages (Braithwaite, V. 1998b). The majority, who are comfortable with more abstract principles, not surprisingly express disappointment when they don't see their government putting the

Table 7.3 Pearson product–moment correlation coefficients among variables measuring inner harmony and status values, disillusionment, attitudes to winning and legal cynicism, honest and aggressive role models and defiance

Measures	1	2	3	4	5	6	7	8
1. Disillusionment								
2. Seeking inner harmony	0.13**							
3. Seeking status	0.05	0.39***						
4. Legal cynicism	0.15**	−0.14**	−0.04					
5. Winning	−0.03	−0.19***	0.28***	0.22***				
6. Honest adviser	0.01	0.17***	0.02	−0.32***	−0.18***			
7. Aggressive adviser	0.01	0.02	0.21***	0.11*	0.24***	0.04		
8. Resistance	0.30***	−0.06	0.08	0.28***	0.11*	−0.25***	0.14**	
9. Dismissiveness	0.09	−0.17***	0.13***	0.36***	0.31***	−0.31***	0.32***	0.34***

Note: * $p < 0.05$; ** $p < 0.01$; *** $p < 0.001$.

society's shared values into practice, for example not respecting civil liberties, the rule of law or equal opportunity. Those with high scores on *inner harmony* and *disillusionment* might be depicted as life's hopefuls who feel let down by their system of governance.

If we examine the correlations to ask if there is evidence of linkages between the key concepts outlined in the questions above, the results are encouraging. Those who valued *inner harmony* were less likely to be drawn towards competitive and rule-breaking behaviour (*winning* and *legal cynicism*) and dismissive defiance. They preferred an *honest adviser*.

Those who valued *status*, on the other hand, were drawn to the competitive culture (*winning* and an *aggressive tax adviser*). Their form of defiance was more likely to be dismissive.

Those who expressed *disillusionment with the democracy* were more likely to embrace *legal cynicism* and were exponents of resistant defiance.

The correlations suggest that there may be three pathways to defiance that can be examined in more detail through structural equation modelling. The goodness-of-fit indices for the models of resistance and dismissiveness were satisfactory. These indices, together with the squared multiple correlations for latent constructs, are presented in Appendix C.

A Model of Resistance

In the model of resistant defiance in Figure 7.1, three pathways are important. At the top is a disillusioned, legal cynicism pathway to resistance. Two points of note here are the absence of either honest or aggressive advisers as role models and the direct link between disillusionment with the state of the democracy and resistance to the tax authority. This pathway seems to have less to do with the social modelling process outlined earlier in this chapter and more to do with a personal and deep resentment towards systems of governance. No solace appears to have been sought in alternative authorities.

At the bottom of Figure 7.1 is a pathway that reflects engagement in the culture of competition. It is an aspirational, winning pathway with a particularly strong link from status values in 2000 to an attitude of being preoccupied by winning in 2005. Those intent on being a winner looked to aggressive advisers as their ideal role models. Interestingly, the final pathway connecting the ideal of an aggressive tax adviser with resistant defiance was remarkably weak. Resistance appeared to be more the outlet for the disillusioned and disenchanted than the aspiring, must-win, can-do challengers of the tax system.

The middle pathway in Figure 7.1 involving inner harmony has more connections than the other two pathways mentioned above. This value constellation comprised wisdom, self-improvement, self-respect and

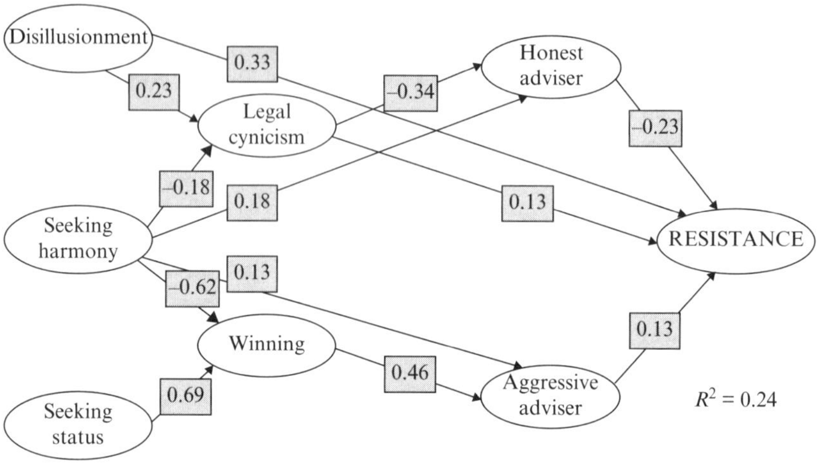

Figure 7.1 A structural equation model linking values and disillusionment (2000), attitudes to winning and legal cynicism (2005), ideal role models (2005) and resistance (2005)

self-insight. The pathways starting with inner harmony diverged, in the process conveying a struggle between doing the right thing and seizing opportunities for success.

Those who placed importance on personal growth and inner harmony stayed away from legal cynicism. Legal cynicism led to rejecting an honest tax adviser as an ideal. There was also a direct pathway from valuing inner harmony to preferring an honest adviser. As hypothesized, preferring an honest adviser was associated with less resistant defiance.

Consistent with this story of staying away from conflict and looking for a sense of personal well-being was a strong negative pathway from inner harmony to winning. To value inner harmony is to turn away from a winning-at-any-cost mentality. But the analysis suggests that those who value inner harmony are not immune from temptation. Their personal development can take many courses (Braithwaite, V. 1998c) and there are indications that when it comes to tax minimization, they don't want to be left out of the action completely. From Figure 7.1, those who value inner harmony can catch a glimpse of the aspirational, winning pathway by idealizing an aggressive tax adviser. Inner harmony exponents, therefore, may express a degree of resistant defiance. In so doing, they have avoided any psychological conflict by sending their thwarted aspirations 'off-shore' into the safe hands of an imagined aggressively oriented other.

The model confirmed for the most part the three hypotheses outlined earlier in the chapter. Inner harmony was the starting point for a moral pathway turning away from legal cynicism towards an honest tax adviser, thereby avoiding resistant defiance (Hypothesis 7.1). By the same token, there was evidence of the possibility of a dalliance with aggressive tax advisers, not hypothesized at the outset. The link was not strong. Status values were the starting point for a competitive pathway, with success values leading to importance of winning, and the desire to win leading to the ideal of an aggressive tax adviser and resistant defiance (Hypothesis 7.2). The major departure from the hypothesized relationships involved the disillusionment pathway that was linked to resistance directly and indirectly through legal cynicism. Disillusionment did not work through either role model, suggesting that this particular pathway was not as amenable to a social modelling interpretation of tax defiance as supposed.

The pathways to defiance shown in Figure 7.1 explained 24% of the variance in resistance, substantially less than the 78% explained in resistance by the threat and coping model and the 57% explained by the integrity model.

A Model of Dismissive Defiance

In the main, the pathways that emerged for the prediction of dismissive defiance mirrored those that emerged for resistant defiance, although overall the pathways to dismissiveness tended to be stronger (see Figure 7.2). For instance, the values of inner harmony and status both had direct effects on dismissiveness; personal preferences mattered for the expression of dismissive defiance. These direct effects did not emerge for resistance.

In the dismissiveness model of Figure 7.2, the competitive pathway was also more compelling than it was in the case of resistance, with status leading to an increased desire for winning and winning increasing preference for an aggressive tax adviser, which in turn fuelled dismissiveness. The link between idealizing an aggressive tax adviser and dismissive defiance was considerably stronger than in the case of resistant defiance. An additional pathway showing that those prioritizing winning were less likely to be attracted to an honest adviser made the competitive pathway to dismissiveness more distinctive than it had been for resistance. The findings were in accord with the social modelling account of how alternative, adversarial authorities are implicated in the expression of dismissiveness.

Counterbalancing the competitive pathway was the moral pathway, placing constraints on dismissiveness as it did on resistance, beginning again with inner harmony values and working through rejection of legal cynicism and preference for an honest tax adviser. To those following the moral pathway, rules matter and cannot be used creatively or manipulated to suit the desired outcome.

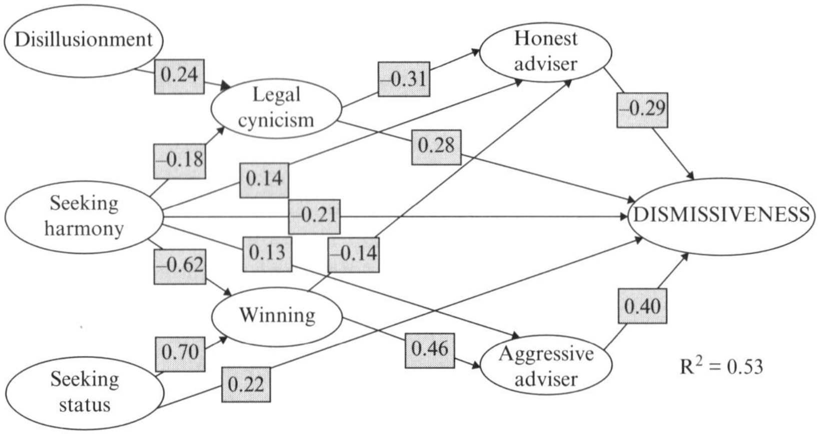

Figure 7.2 A structural equation model linking values and disillusionment (2000), attitudes to winning and legal cynicism (2005), ideal role models (2005) and dismissiveness (2005)

Finally, mention should be made of the fact that disillusionment had fewer connections to defiance in the dismissiveness model than in the resistance model. The pathway to dismissiveness that was fuelled by disillusionment and legal cynicism remained strong but there was no direct link between disillusionment and dismissiveness, as there was between disillusionment and resistance in Figure 7.1.

The pathways to defiance shown in Figure 7.2 explained 53% of the variance in dismissiveness, substantially greater than that accounted for by the threat and coping model (45%) and the integrity model (8%).

CONCLUSION

The social modelling approach examined in this chapter made different assumptions from previous chapters as to why defiance was occurring. The social modelling paradigm freed the research from the assumption that defiance was something that lent itself to dialogue about the way in which the institution threatened the individual or failed to deliver social justice. Previously, defiance was conceptualized as the signal for the tax authority to improve its relationship with the people and reassess the democratic will through the processes that the democracy has in place for such deliberation. If the relationship was worked at, defiance could be contained.

The findings from this chapter provide a critical rejoinder to this argument. It may still be the case that resistant defiance is a story of betrayal and disrespect of the people by government authorities, as told in Chapters 5 and 6; and in such cases, dialogue is fundamentally important to righting past wrongs and moving on. For dismissive defiance, however, the damaged relationship paradigm as it has been told up to this point does not fit the data well. The present chapter sought clarification on what was going on in the minds of the dismissively defiant. The social modelling paradigm remedies some of the previously observed deficiencies and ambiguities.

Those who display resistance and dismissiveness identify with aggressive tax advisers. They serve as an alternative authority that has the knowledge and expertise to help taxpayers win against the tax authority. For the dismissively defiant, deliberating about their relationship with the tax authority and thinking of how it might be improved is less important than turning attention elsewhere where their needs can be met. As was evident from the advertisements in Box 7.1, the tax planning industry markets itself as an authority on taxation that has style and flair and that is dedicated to helping taxpayers fulfil their desire to pay less tax. In a marketing sense, cautious and aggressive advisers are embedded in each other's territory: there is no black and white; the boundary between cautious and aggressive advice is permeable and 'grey'. The level of risk that is implied through the marketing styles represented in Box 7.1 fluctuates between 'certainty' to wealth creation in 'overdrive'. The range of risk is readily apparent across the advertisements. What is also noticeable is that the honest adviser misses out on an eye-catching spot on the advertisement – as do the words 'responsible' or 'obligated' or 'law-abiding'.

It can be argued therefore that accompanying the lure to aggressive tax advisers is an implicit turning away from advisers who work in a more 'compliant' way with the tax authority. As expected, marketing ploy appears to be responsive to taxpayer preferences. The reasons why the appeal of an honest adviser conflicts with the appeal of an aggressive adviser lies in the values that define individual identity. The tax planning industry has polarized taxpayers on these values, and has been successful in bringing over part of the honest no-risk market with tax-approved and tax-certain messages.

Hypothesis 7.1 initiated a search for pathways that oriented those with postmaterialist values of wisdom, inner harmony, personal development, self-insight, knowledge and self-respect away from the ideal of an aggressive tax adviser and away from defiance. A moral pathway placing constraints on both resistance and dismissiveness emerged from such a value base and worked through a refusal to subscribe to legal cynicism. Those who travelled the moral pathway said it was never OK to break the law or bend the rules or cheat, even if you could get away with it. The moral pathway with a postmaterialist anchor reveals the impetus for the advertising industry's use of well-known barristers and Queen's Counsels to give legal credibility to their products. Assurances of legality are necessary to entice people away from the moral pathway; it is not enough to point to the opportunities created by poor enforcement practices.

While postmaterialist values shielded individuals from entering potentially conflictual terrain, success values brought on the contest as proposed in Hypothesis 7.2. Individuals who value status and security subscribe to an ethic that endorses acquiring and protecting resources of a finite nature, thereby commanding a position of advantage should any competitive struggle for these resources ensue. The key psychological dispositions that defined the pathway to tax defiance were having values associated with achieving social and economic status and the desire above all else to be a winner in life's competition. This competitive pathway, leading both to resistance and dismissiveness through preference for an aggressive tax adviser, shows the psychological hooks that lie in readiness for an alternative authority that will challenge the tax regime. We should also bear in mind that challenge in and of itself is not a bad thing, particularly if the tax authority has lost its integrity.

Demonstrating empirically the importance of personal dispositions such as postmaterialist values, morality, success values and wanting to win in shaping defiance does not imply that institutions are unimportant. Central to the argument presented in earlier chapters is that institutions create defiance. Moreover, institutions that can be restructured in ways that build integrity can change the form that defiance against them takes. Defiance that is resistant rather than dismissive can be embraced as an asset of the democracy, and not rejected as a phenomenon that needs to be suppressed by fair or foul means. In the light of present findings, individuals and institutions should not be seen to trump each other in shaping defiance. They interact, in the best of times symbiotically, but too often destructively, to the detriment of both individuals and institutions.

The competitive pathway to dismissiveness might be construed as a personal preference pathway. It might be read as individual choice and, if we are comfortable with market culture, we shall applaud our society for enabling such a pathway to flourish. But if we think a little bit more about the choice, concerns about institutional failure cannot help but creep into our consciousness. The pathway that counters personal competitiveness is morality, requiring personal dispositions of good will on the part of individuals to be sure, but also requiring a belief that the law matters, that it matters to others and that society has respect for an honest tax adviser. It might be argued that the institutions that uphold tax law and that promote honest tax advisers are prone to be depicted as not altogether competent, perhaps a little old-fashioned, and, in the case of the tax authority, coercive and bullying. The question that needs to be asked then is: what kind of choice are Australians being presented with when we consider possibilities for social modelling of taxpaying within market culture?

The social modelling analysis of this chapter proved particularly useful for understanding defiance of a dismissive kind, although the approach also provided an adequate and meaningful account of resistant defiance. In previous chapters, the differences between resistant and dismissive defiance were marked. In this chapter the differences were more nuanced – the competitive pathway was more strongly linked with dismissiveness while the disillusioned pathway had more connections with resistance.

Possibly the most insightful finding for piecing together the story of resistance and dismissiveness involved the mapping of the disillusioned pathway. The findings for disillusionment with the democracy were surprising because those who were disillusioned and took on board legal cynicism (as in Hypothesis 7.3) nevertheless did not idealize the aggressive tax adviser. It is almost as if they were shunning the government and alternative authorities, be their marketing pitch pro-tax or anti-tax. Their resistance and dismissiveness of tax are societally generated, sourced from what they see as disappointing governance models that fail to honour their conception of democracy. The disillusioned do not appear to be open to being governed through social modelling. At this point, the story of the kind of governance to which they would concede remains untold.

Understanding the differences between resistant and dismissive defiance requires an integration of the different theoretical lenses that have been used to examine them. The integrity and trust model from Chapter 6 provided a compelling account of resistant defiance, as did the threat and coping model in Chapter 5. The social modelling approach revealed the workings of dismissiveness in a way that neither of the other models could. Yet parallels can be seen in the findings across chapters – similar insights surface despite different theoretical assumptions at the outset. The issues that were flagged in the integrity and trust pathways are echoed in the present chapter's pathway of disillusionment. All three coping styles from Chapter 5 are echoed in the social modelling results of the present chapter: the moral pathway connects with the 'feeling responsible' coping style, while the disillusioned and competitive pathways have parallels in the 'feeling oppressed' and 'taking control' coping styles respectively. Theoretically integrating and providing empirical support for models of resistant and dismissive defiance is the challenge addressed in the next chapter.

8. Integrative models of defiance

> The seeing of self as, with all other selves, creating, demands a new attitude . . . The fallacy of self-and-others fades away and there is only self-in-and-through-others, only others so firmly rooted in the self and so fruitfully growing there that sundering is impossible.
>
> Mary Parker Follett 1965: 8 [*c*. 1918]

The purpose of this chapter is to reconcile tensions and capitalize on synergies. The most important tension to resolve is the extent to which defiance is an expression of personal preferences and values, and the extent to which it is a response to an institution's unfairness and low integrity. At its most fundamental level, defiance has been considered a relational concept in so far as it occurs against the action or will of something or someone. The conception that was put forward in the early chapters implied conscious engagement, one with the other. The implication was that institution building would soften the desire of individuals to express their values in ways that did not serve collective interests. This conception needs to be revised in light of the data.

The model of defiance developed here needs to accommodate the not insignificant effects of personal values in the last chapter that led individuals to pursue other authorities who might deliver their wish list, rendering government authority almost irrelevant. It seems that defiance may be a reaction actively directed against authority (resistance) or it may be a reaction of active engagement with alternative authorities that promise liberation (dismissiveness). Defiance against an authority centres on institutional fairness and integrity. Defiance of liberation and alignment with alternative authorities centres on the advancement of personal values.

The challenge for government authorities is: how can they deal responsively with defiance where individuals' level of engagement with them appears to be minimal? By integrating theory and findings from previous chapters, it is argued that a 'declining' authority can reclaim relevance by addressing moral legitimacy, respecting individual advancement, and by persuasive appeals to a collective as well as individual self.

The argument is developed in four stages. First, the theoretical frameworks used in Chapters 5 to 7 are brought together to provide a coherent account of defiance for testing with the panel data. Three selves are implicated in defiance – a moral self, a status-seeking self and a democratic collective self. The case is made for why resistant defiance is a healthy response in the regulatory context and why it is a mistake for regulators to approach it with fear and trepidation. Dismissiveness, on the other hand, poses a more serious threat to democratic governance.

Next, in section 2, the connection of defiance to law-abiding behaviour is examined. Defiance has been conceptualized as a signal of how comfortable we feel about an authority. It is possible for individuals to send defiant signals to authority, yet draw the line at breaking the law. Resistant defiance proved to be in this category – there was no systematic relationship with tax evasion. On the other hand, dismissiveness was consistently associated with tax evasion.

Section 3 introduces the notion of a culture of disrespect that comes into play as government fails to engage appropriately with the individual identities implicated in defiance. Finally, Section 4 consolidates understanding of resistant and dismissive defiance through an analysis of qualitative data on how government should relate to citizens, citizens to government and citizens to each other. From the qualitative data, dismissive defiance could be differentiated from resistant defiance in terms of greater estrangement from government, absence of a collective democratic self, and advocacy for individualism. Even so, the individualism of the dismissively defiant incorporated a personal sense of responsibility to help those in need – the problem seemed to be more with systems than with people.

1. INTEGRATING THEORY AND DEVELOPING COMPOSITE MODELS OF DEFIANCE

Three Approaches to Defiance

Three theoretical approaches have been offered with different focal points for understanding defiance. The threat and coping model of Chapter 5 places individual cognition at the centre of analysis. The threat is loss of freedom and income to the tax authority. The person appraises the threat and adopts a coping response that will relieve their discomfort and restore equilibrium to their sense of being. The process of appraisal is not necessarily undertaken in concert with other people, yet the coping response is a shared narrative. Defiance is dampened by cognitively reframing – people cope by thinking morally and aligning themselves with the authority. Defiance is keenly felt, however, when loss of freedom and income translates into feeling oppressed or challenging tax office power. Those who cope through feeling oppressed or taking control prefer to maintain social distance from the authority.

The integrity and trust model of Chapter 6 locates the root cause of defiance in people's perception that their relationship with government has soured. The focus is not necessarily on individual hurts, but collective hurts. The failure of institutions to meet public expectations breeds discontent and creates social distance. The answer to defiance lies in institutional reform. The institution needs to critically evaluate its purpose and procedures, and to generate a new authenticity that is more acceptable to the public.

The social modelling approach of Chapter 7 makes alternative authorities the centre of the analysis, their attraction being that they promise desirable tax outcomes to those who seek their advice, and they offer status through their association with the rich and famous. Defiance becomes a statement of preferences and concedes greater status and legitimacy to alternative authorities than to government. Defiance will recede when government finds a way of respecting such preferences while reasserting its authority to regulate.

On one reading, our understanding of defiance communicates a disturbing message. It implies that defiance is snuffed out when individuals opt for cognitive reframing, once institutions receive a facelift and authoritative leadership wins back public support. The role envisaged for defiance is short-changed in this analysis. For defiance to be valued in the process of governance, the explanatory elements must be removed from their theoretical silos and allowed to mingle. Common to all approaches is the idea that defiance restores, defends or promotes a much-valued self-identity. If we approach defiance from this perspective, we gain insight into why defiance cannot be quelled by superficial tinkering, and why the quality of governance would be better if defiance became a learning platform from which authorities could adjust to new demands.

While there is a best-case scenario for how authorities might respond to defiance, the worst case must also be addressed. Authorities are known for their preoccupation with squashing, diverting, discrediting or ignoring that which challenges or threatens their futures (Turk 1982; Mathiesen 2004). Each theoretical perspective plays into the hands of authorities that want to avert their eyes to the value of dissent. It is important to recognize the dysfunctional responses that authorities can make to defiance, risking throwing out the baby with the bath water. Defiance may be difficult for an authority to manage, but squashing defiance can mean squashing the identity that the defiance is protecting. Robbing individuals of valued identities also robs the community of human and social capital that enables it to grow and flourish.

Irresponsible Responses to Defiance

Starting with the threat and coping approach, defiance can be controlled 'cognitively' by limiting individuals' options as to which path they should follow. A non-transparent authority will use subterfuge to make sure that the only viable path left open is the responsible law-abiding way. Architectural regulatory constraints can effectively rule out 'taking control' in many cases and marketing spin can numb the community's sense of 'feeling oppressed'. The law-abiding path can be made more salient through a signal of serious enforcement intent. At the end of the day, aligning with authority may be the only coping response that can promise safety and remove the sense of threat. All the while, very bad law may remain in place because criticism that could have led to improvements was 'silently silenced' (Mathiesen 2004). In such circumstances, the paucity of dialogue means we fail to appreciate what might be.

The integrity model has an equally dark side. It allows less than scrupulous authorities to buy off those who are defiant by offering a form of procedural justice that makes them feel included in a high-status group (Braithwaite, J. 2005). When group identity is strong, an attack on the integrity of the authority is an attack on the integrity of the group. This means that the authority cannot be criticized for low-integrity practices in terms of poor performance and questionable purpose without creating discomfort for the whole group. If the group collectively confronts their problem, no harm is done. But there is always the risk that by closing ranks around the authority, those who dared speak of performance problems are stigmatized as an out-group. If defiance is discredited, problems remain unaddressed and are allowed to deepen. We fail to appreciate institutional shortcomings and fix them.

Last but not least are the strategies for squashing defiance through social modelling. Authorities rely on social modelling when they manipulate human behaviour by changing incentives and disincentives for targeted groups. Government policy creates opportunities; the first wave of beneficiaries leads the way and others follow. In order to contain defiance, authorities need only to tinker with incentives to make certain pursuits non-productive and competing pursuits productive. In effect, government sends out a message that is noticed and that creates a market towards which people orient their response. A social modelling process begins.

Hamilton (2007) has shown how the Australian government, more than a decade go, engaged in the energy debate by reducing funds for renewable energy and increasing funds for the development of 'clean coal'. Whatever the merits of supporting the fossil fuel industry at the time, the outcome was that voices of defiance urging the development of renewable energies were discredited through government's failure to use financial backing to signal confidence in their mission. The advocates of renewable energy could not lead by example. Lack of market enthusiasm for renewable energy meant that it did not capture the public's imagination as a viable alternative. All the while the general public was unaware of or chose to ignore how government shaped popular thinking about the viability of the renewable energy market. Our tendency to rely on cues from the marketplace to discriminate desirable from undesirable pathways means that we abrogate our responsibility to obtain relevant information and thoughtfully arrive at an action plan. Social modelling means that we fail to think for ourselves.

When the worst-case scenario is considered, the downside of extinguishing defiance becomes apparent: (a) we fail to appreciate what might be; (b) we fail to appreciate institutional shortcomings and fix them; and (c) we fail to think for ourselves. The challenge in living successfully with defiance becomes twofold. One part engenders greater deliberation in the processes that people use to 'manage authority' and that governments use to 'manage defiance'. The second part expects individuals to engage seriously with a collective identity – that is, to accept responsibility for thinking in terms of what is good for the whole and the many subgroups it covers. Being accomplished in using this identity is not to the exclusion of personal or subgroup identities. In a democracy, individuals should be fluent in operating at all levels – at the levels of personal identity, subgroup identity or collective identity. There is ample evidence that we change our level of functioning as we move between groups and that others manipulate social cues to change them for us (Wenzel 2003). The important skill to learn, however, is how to manage these changes, knowing when collective or individual identities are expected and appropriate. If we could manage this kind of control over our identities, authorities could be confident of engaging the public at the collective level. By the same token, authorities should also be put on notice that a collective self is a gift that individuals offer when an authority has moral legitimacy and is authentic in its deliberation and policy making. It can be withdrawn as readily as it is given.

It has become apparent that the interventions that authorities often prefer to use to silence defiance yield unexpected consequences that do not serve them or the democracy well in the longer term. Governing effectively depends on authorities being able to engage with defiance, generate informed debate and harness human and social capacities to ensure that regulatory goals are accomplished with good will, positive outcomes and social justice. Why this pathway remains so underappreciated by regulatory institutions is something of a mystery. But as the next subsection shows, this has been the case for many generations at least.

Obsessing Institutionally with Control and Competitiveness

Mary Parker Follett (1965, *c.* 1918) issued a challenge for the post-World War I era – to reform our political systems so that the creativity of human beings could be unleashed to build a more participatory and vibrant democracy. She bemoaned the absence of positive principles in American politics, questioning a preoccupation that still exists today with regulation as constraint: 'The measure of our progress is never what we give up, but what we add. It may be necessary to prune the garden, but we do not make a pile of the dead branches and take our guests to see them as evidence of the [garden's] flourishing state' (1965: 8).

Parker Follett was equally disapproving of the way in which individualism was understood at the time, as a doctrine of egocentrism around which policy making and governance more generally could be formulated. A philosophy of 'every-man-for-his-own-interests', she warned, had 'little to do with true individualism, that is, with the individual as consciously responsible for the life from which he draws his breath and to which he contributes his all', a life that is inherently social (ibid.: 3). Central to Parker Follett's vision for society was that individuals would not be 'submerged, smothered, choked by . . . herd theory' (ibid.: 11) but rather be freed to develop a 'social mind' that allowed conscious self-determination (ibid.: 8). Government could reasonably be expected to represent the people if the people were enabled to integrate consciously their thought and will, so that proposals could be deliberated upon and prioritized with reason and good intent:

> All our ideas of conscious self-determination lead us to a new method: it is not merely that we must be allowed to govern ourselves, we must learn how to govern ourselves; it is not only that we must be given 'free speech,' we must learn a speech that is free; we are not given rights, we create rights; it is not only that we must invent machinery to get a social will expressed, we must invent machinery that will get a social will created. (Ibid.: 8–9)

Parker Follett's insights early last century have been superseded by the work of distinguished social scientists who have understood the importance of social capital to the well-being of communities (Putnam et al. 1993; Putnam 2000) and who have advocated deliberative and inclusive decision-making processes that give voice to different groups and ensure equality for those who are often marginalized or ignored (Dryzek 1990; Phillips 1991; Habermas 1996; Young 2000; Fung 2004). While these advances have been important at the institutional and political levels, the question remains as to how pathways of human understanding impede the realization of the visions of Parker Follett and those who have followed.

What is missing from our understanding of human psychology that prevents progress from being made in a practical sense? Specifically, why has it been so difficult for Western societies to implement more deliberative, engaged and thoughtful dialogue within our institutions, occasions that welcome difference to grapple with the issues that defiance raises, and that are inclusive of all stakeholders in the process? Part of the answer may lie in the threat that defiance poses to authority and the assumptions that authorities make about defiance and the need to bring it under control.

What We Now Know about Resistant and Dismissive Defiance

Resistant defiance was defined as motivational posturing that signalled to an authority that its actions were unacceptable to the individual. Resistance communicated an individual's objection to what the authority was doing with its power, rather than an objection to authority having power. In contrast, dismissive defiance was defined as motivational posturing that signalled to an authority that its interference generally was not welcome and that its insistence on wielding power was out of order.

In the course of the research, the position on dismissiveness has been modified. Dismissiveness is posturing that communicates the inappropriateness of power residing in the hands of an authority, but if such power is not being visibly exercised, the message is one of the authority's irrelevance. Inappropriateness and irrelevance are not incompatible messages to send to an authority. Irrelevance may precede the signal that the power being exercised is inappropriate. For instance, individuals and groups may go about their business under the purview of an authority that takes no interest. When the authority 'wakes' and asserts control by interfering in ongoing activities, perceptions of the irrelevance of the authority are challenged. Individuals and groups may flip into acceptance; or perceptions may graduate into opposition to the authority's presence. Dismissiveness incorporates responses of irrelevance as well as opposition to the authority's presence, depending on how much the authority engages with the public.

Regulatory institutions commonly move in the public's mind between states of irrelevance and relevance. Two examples of institutions that have become more relevant over the years are ethics committees and equal opportunity and anti-discrimination boards. At best in the early years they commanded lip-service, but with time they have acquired more relevance. Institutions move the other way too. For Australians, rule by England's monarchy has become less relevant over time. Should the Queen of England intervene in the country's governance, the response of the public would signal inappropriateness – that is, that the use of her authority was out of order. Australians' defiance would be of a dismissive kind, albeit kindly dismissive! And then there are institutions that assert their authority intermittently. The ATO appears to be on a long-term trajectory of sharing the regulatory stage with tax practitioners and advisers, but reasserts power in cycles as tax avoidance and tax evasion peak. The tax authority may be regarded much of the time as out of sight, approaching irrelevance, but it is clearly not out of mind. Anxieties linger over what might happen when the 'giant wakes up'.

Resistance and dismissiveness are forms of defiance that have been aligned with liking for authority and deference to authority, drawing on Bogardus's (1928) classic work on social distancing and attitudes to groups that threaten us. Lack of liking represents resistance. Lack of deference represents dismissiveness. Both resistant and dismissive defiance dwell in a comfort zone at some distance from authority, held in place by supporting attitudes and beliefs. Distance from authority reduces the threat to freedom that the authority poses. At the same time, relocation closer to the authority is not entirely impossible and not without compensations.

An Integrated Framework for Understanding Defiance

The starting point for putting together a framework for understanding defiance is self-worth. At the psychological level, a belief–attitude–value system is assembled that preserves self-worth through scripts of what we expect for ourselves and from government, of threat and coping, and of role models to follow should we be unclear as to how to proceed. At the institutional level, social identities are created for us, informing us of our role and value. If the identity suits us, we shall more than likely adopt a cooperative set of postures for authority. If we don't like the message that the institution sends, we fight back or turn away. Cooperatively, adversarially, or dismissively, we develop motivational postures for 'managing' authority.

On the basis of the research findings from previous chapters, defiance is proposed as giving expression to three kinds of individual identity. The first is an ethical self, a self that everyone, including authority, recognizes as being good and law-abiding. Second is a status-seeking self that strives for achievement and success. In the context of taxation this self is modelled on the rich and famous who avoid tax, choose to whom they will give money away and under what terms, and do not trust governments to disperse philanthropic funds as effectively as they can. In different contexts, the status-seeking self will take different forms, yet its nature is to transcend constraints imposed by authority. Third is a democratic collective self that believes in citizenship as a way of living in harmony with others and sharing benefits as part of a prosperous democracy. In the present research context, the democratic collective self that is of interest is one that is aggrieved by current government processes and outcomes, and expects better governance as a mark of respect for the electorate. Each of these selves is seeking to have its existence validated and supported. All of these may be manifestations of Harris's (2007) 'ethical identity'. Harris (2007) has argued that ethical identity is social. Without affirmation from significant others, the moral self, the status-seeking self and the democratic collective self will suffocate. The struggle for affirmation of these identities carves out pathways to defiance.

A Moral Self

Authorities impose requests and demand certain kinds of responses. They rob us of freedom. Through processes of socialization, however, we move towards accepting that loss of freedom does not necessarily mean loss of dignity. Authorities are not without psychological clout of an identity-affirming kind. They have their own status-ascribing capacity. For authority to say that a person is 'good' in a democratic system is to affirm the status of the person as a law-abiding citizen. It also signals to such persons that they are safe from authority's interference and sanctioning – they will be left in peace. In the analyses based on a threat and coping approach and in those based on a social modelling approach, this facet of authority's control is internalized in the pathway of moral obligation. Our sense of self-worth is reinforced by aligning ourselves with other good citizens and the morally obligated pathway provides self-regulation to keep us so aligned.

The morally obligated pathway, however, might be expected to work less well if the tax office's approval is not affirming for us, either in our own or our community's eyes; or if it leaves us unsure as to whether or not we are safe from tax investigations and sanctions. The strength of the pathway will depend on the tax authority's capacity to affirm our ethical self. As the morally obligated pathway strengthens, defiance should recede. As it weakens, defiance should strengthen.

The data suggest that the morally obligated pathway that incorporates the self-defining variable of thinking morally can be strengthened by credible deterrence and by role models who hold to standards of honesty and caution with regard to interpreting the law. Both these elements communicate societal expectations of high ethical standards on tax matters. Also part of the morally obligated pathway is a rejection of legal cynicism – holding firm to the principle of being honest and not cheating the system, even if detection is unlikely, and even if only some bending of the rules is involved. The data from the previous chapter reinforce the assertion that signing up to honesty and law-abidingness has popular appeal, particularly to the significant number of people who value personal growth and inner harmony. If it is important to know and feel at peace with who we are, we like being law-abiding. Most of us gravitate towards alignment between having inner peace and being at peace with authority for ensuring our well-being.

Table 8.1 provides a summary of the morally obligated pathway. It features the following variables in previous chapters: (a) *personal growth and inner harmony*; (b) *perceived deterrence*; (c) *thinking morally*; (d) rejection of *legal cynicism*; and (e) *idealizing an honest no-risk adviser*. These variables are milestones on the path of being at one with the institutional

Table 8.1 An integrative account of the variables defining the morally obligated, competitive and grievance pathways to defiance

Morally obligated pathway	Competitive pathway	Grievance pathway
Inner harmony values (Ch. 7)	Status-seeking values (Ch. 7)	Disillusionment with democracy (Ch. 7)
Perceived deterrence (Ch. 5)		
Thinking morally (Ch. 5)	Taking control (Ch. 5)	Feeling oppressed (Ch. 5)
Rejection of legal cynicism (Ch. 7)	Prioritizing winning (Ch. 7)	Low integrity of tax office (Ch. 6)
Idealizing an honest no-risk adviser (Ch. 7)	Idealizing an aggressive adviser over an honest no-risk adviser (Ch. 7)	Low trust in tax office (Ch. 6)
Low resistance and low dismissiveness	High dismissiveness	High resistance

Notes:

1. From the pathway of moral obligation, two variables were omitted in the composite defiance models: inner harmony values and rejection of legal cynicism. Both variables were considered unnecessary when deterrence and thinking morally were included in the structural equation models.
2. From the pathway of competition, two variables were omitted in the composite model: taking control and prioritizing winning. Taking control was conceptually not important as a process variable once status seeking was included in the model. Prioritizing winning was illuminating in defining the pathway in the previous chapter, but with improved understanding of the competitiveness pathway, seeking status and idealizing an aggressive tax adviser sufficed.
3. From the pathway of grievance, one variable was omitted: trust. Trust was very highly related to integrity. Conceptually, integrity was the preferred variable for inclusion in model building.

environment, of receiving affirmation for one's concordance, and feeling as if one is and is seen to be a 'good' person. The pathway of obligation was operational for both resistant and dismissive defiance, in the former case reining in expressions of complaint, in the latter, expressions of freedom.

A Status-seeking Self

Being 'good', honest and law-abiding represents one dimension of our identity that is critically important for us as individuals and for democratic governance. But there are more dimensions to human character – positive dimensions that generate productivity, creativity, cleverness, sociability, happiness and pleasure. Such dimensions and the identities associated with them lead people down pathways that are quite different from the morally obligated pathway and give them different perspectives on authority, the purpose it serves and its ways of operating.

These other identities are many and varied. Within the context of taxation, what we have called the social and economic value status cluster is a particularly important 'possible self' that lures taxpayers away from the orbit of control of the tax authority. This 'possible self' of seeking status aspires to being financially well off, having high standing in the community, being influential and occupying a position of authority, all the while engaging others with a hunger to get ahead. Such a self is well catered for in market culture. The status-seeking self sees and is attracted to opportunities for sidestepping taxation. Role models who are rich and famous are sprinkled across the newspapers and celebrity pages of magazines; financial planners offer deals with promises of emulating the rich and famous; and the status-seeking self is awakened by prospects of keeping ahead of the game.

The status-seeking self finds expression through a competitive pathway. This self may have felt oppressed by taxation, but without the intention of staying there. The objective is to be a winner, not a loser. The ambition to transcend the power of the tax authority will be enduring – first imagining how to take control, next arranging tax affairs in a way that is financially rewarding, and then continually improving tax savings with new schemes. The original coping style of taking control therefore becomes more of an outcome of a process of breaking free, one that can be achieved either through one's own resources or through finding someone with the skills to help – that is, an aggressive tax adviser. An aggressive tax adviser is defined as someone who knows how to do the accounts creatively, is well networked in the tax system, knows the investigative hot-spots and is skilled in avoiding detection. The process of following in the footsteps of successful tax minimizers and avoiders, who enrol the services of aggressive tax advisers rather than honest no-risk advisers, is the central dynamic at work in the competitive pathway.

The goal of the competitive pathway is to transcend mainstream authority, making its attempts to bear down on the self almost irrelevant to one's being. There is positive action and purpose initiated by the individual, but it is not envisaged as being invented from scratch, nor closely scrutinized by those who travel the path. It's a 'me-too' response that may be chosen to protect the self from grievance, but primarily aims to promote self-worth by being an economic and social success. Searching for status and engaging in competitive bouts of winning are likely to lead taxpayers to idealize the services of aggressive tax advisers, not honest no-risk advisers, and adopt postures of defiance to the tax authority.

In summary, the variables that have defined the competitive pathway in previous chapters are (a) placing a high priority on achieving a position of social and economic *status*; (b) *feeling oppressed* by taxation, but at the same time (c) *taking control* of one's tax affairs to reduce the tax bill; (d) believing in the importance of *winning* and being the best in any competition; and (e) preferring an *aggressive tax adviser* as an ideal, as opposed to an *honest no-risk adviser*. These variables represent milestones for the disruption of institutional complacency and the shaking up of the social order. Individuals meanwhile are restored any lost dignity and gain a sense of dominion and self-worth.

The competitive pathway is likely to be strongest in the context of dismissive defiance. Dismissiveness is more subversive than resistance in the sense that it involves escape from control, as opposed to simply changing the direction of that control. This is not to deny that escape may be the first step to reform for dedicated strategists; but in this particular case, convincing evidence has yet to be uncovered that the dismissively defiant had tax reform on their mind.

The competitive pathway is particularly interesting because it includes non-tax-specific variables that describe how a person approaches life generally – competitively with an appetite for winning and for status, both social and economic. As such, the individuals who exemplify the pathway that subverts the tax system are not necessarily targeting taxation; tax is more a casualty of their way of being, an approach that does not incorporate moral boundaries, or arguably boundaries of any kind.

This observation, of course, does not preclude the possibility of an ideological underbelly to the competitive pathway. There is evidence of appeal to those of a more libertarian persuasion. However, the competitive pathway did not appear to be dotted with calling cards from those opposed to the state. As might be expected, those who favoured *small government and free markets* and wanted to see the *tax system abolished* (measures used in Chapter 4) were more likely to be *status* driven ($r = 0.23$, $p < 0.001$ and $r = 0.12$, $p < 0.001$ respectively), to prioritize *winning* ($r = 0.22$, $p < 0.001$ and $r = 0.20$, $p < 0.001$ respectively) and to idealize an *aggressive tax adviser* ($r = 0.18$, $p < 0.001$ and $r = 0.19$, $p < 0.001$ respectively). But when all these variables were considered together in a set of regression models, political ideology was less important than personal preferences in mapping out the competitive pathway. The competitive pathway is therefore proposed as being opportunistic, jumping on a bandwagon, fuelled by a desire to get ahead and not be left behind, and blinkered from moral deliberation as in the mentality of 'it's all a game' described by Wolfe (1988).

The morally obligated pathway and the competitive pathway set out the psychological hooks that are used by individuals as they try to reconcile their moral and status-seeking selves with the demands of the tax authority. But neither can take the place of a collective self that guides efforts to collaborate and live harmoniously with others. Taxpaying is an institution that justifies its interference in our lives by appeals to a collective self, a self that values democratic governance and sees taxation as a means for providing it.

A Democratic Collective Self

Considerable debate has taken place over what democracy means in Western and non-Western cultures in terms of our political, economic, legal and social institutions (Sartori 1987; Dahl 1990; Dryzek 1990; Nye et al. 1997). While ambiguities surround the meaning of 'democratic', communities with long traditions of democracy are surprisingly articulate in their understandings of what it means. The meanings may be multiple (Kornberg and Clarke 1994; Dryzek 1994; Dryzek and Berejikian 1993) but they are part of people's coherent belief and attitude systems – what one expects of democratic governments, what one gives in return, and what is expected of fellow citizens (Maguire et al. 2007).

In a study of Canadians' beliefs about democracy, four dimensions were identified to capture people's thoughts on what democracy should deliver (Kornberg and Clarke 1994). Democracy was regarded as providing: (a) collective security and limiting individual rights for the benefit of all; (b) economic and political opportunity for everyone; (c) elections and capitalism; and (d) equal influence across groups. Where democracy was considered to deliver collective security, equal opportunity and equal influence, satisfaction was high. Dissatisfaction with democracy was strongest among those who believed that it had a restricted role, delivering an equal vote for the election of leaders along with economic opportunity through capitalism.

Research in Australia suggests similar conceptual maps of what democracy does and should deliver (Dryzek 1994; Dryzek and Braithwaite 2000; Maguire et al. 2007). The dimension of small government and free markets featured in Chapter 4 resembles support for a restricted view of democracy. Regret over the democracy's performance on protection, opportunity and representation is reflected in the disillusionment with democracy scale that first appeared in Chapter 4 and played a prominent role in the analyses of Chapter 7. Disillusionment captures the belief that profit making drives the government agenda, that the democracy and the legal system have been hijacked by the rich and powerful, and that people don't have an opportunity to have input into the decision-making process.

Disillusionment was strongly felt and openly acknowledged in the population under study. It was not a 'hoped-for possible self'; rather it represented the realization of a 'feared possible self'. The qualitative data presented later in this chapter revealed just how emotional and outraged people were by what they saw as a major departure from the democratic ideal – lack of honesty, neglect of social justice, and failure to meet community expectations on process and outcomes (Maguire et al. 2007).

Disillusionment with democracy was shown in Chapter 7 to have an effect on how people engaged with the authority of the tax system. Disillusionment bred legal cynicism and increased prospects of defiance. Disillusionment undermined the pathway of moral obligation, and encompassed feelings of oppression over the tax that must be paid. Interestingly, disillusionment did not directly predispose people to seek the advice of alternative tax authorities, but feelings of oppression did.

Disillusionment seemed to fit most comfortably in a pathway of grievance. Grievance embodies discontent with the delivery of social justice. Perceptions of social justice may originate in the democracy or be centred on the tax system. The grievance pathway also incorporates perceptions of the authority's failure to deliver integrity – someone who is disillusioned with the quality of the democracy is unlikely to be favourably disposed to the tax authority, even if it is trying to improve its performance. In reviewing the findings of previous chapters, the following variables can be identified as representing the grievance pathway: (a) *disillusionment with the democracy*; (b) *feeling oppressed* by the tax authority; (c) low regard for the institution's *integrity*; and (d) lack of *trust* that the institution is acting in the interests of the community as a whole (see Table 8.1).

The pathway captures the milestones of how institutions fail individuals by not living up to expectations, not delivering community benefits, and promulgating a culture of disrespect and social exclusion. The pathway is expected to be strongest in the case of resistant defiance because with this type of defiance, individuals accept the authority's position. They place themselves in a subservient role, and therefore allow themselves to be vulnerable to how the authority treats them and thinks of them. With this vulnerability comes a purpose in expressing grievance. Grievance may at best elicit a response of care, concern and making amends. At worst, the individual expresses grievance as self-protection, to assert personal dignity, to assure others that what has happened is not reasonable, and that such neglectful treatment is wrong. Within a democratic society, the expression of grievance is appropriate and necessary: it is the responsibility of authorities to respond constructively to such grievance.

These three pathways of moral obligation, competitiveness and grievance give expression to valued selves – that is, the identities of a moral self, a status-seeking self and a collective democratic self respectively. To build composite defiance models, we need markers of these three selves from the variables listed in Table 8.1. The variables chosen as proxy measures for these three selves have appeared in earlier analyses – *thinking morally* (Chapter 5), *status*-seeking values (Chapter 7) and *disillusionment with the democracy* (Chapters 4 and 7). They are expected to be linchpins for the proposed pathways in the newly developed structural equation models.

Building Composite Models of Resistance and Dismissiveness

The pathways of moral obligation, competitiveness and grievance summarized in Table 8.1 provided a base for constructing new composite models of resistance and dismissiveness. The hypothesized interrelationships among the final set of variables selected for the modelling exercise appear in Figure 8.1, based on the basic research model presented in Chapter 1. A broken line is used to show the special role that institutional integrity plays in the evolution of resistant as opposed to dismissive defiance.

Not all the variables from Table 8.1 were used in the new structural equation models developed around Figure 8.1. The objective was to keep the number of variables to a minimum for the purposes of model building. The notes below Table 8.1 provide explanations for why certain variables were omitted in the final models.

The process for building models involved thinking initially about the variables in terms of being instigators or mediators in the pathways of moral obligation, competition and grievance. The term 'instigator' refers to variables measured in 2000 that represented a mental state envisaged as the beginning of a path to defiance. *Disillusionment with the democracy*, perceived *deterrence*, and seeking *status* were instigators in so far as they were variables that explained why individuals might feel threatened just by the thought of government taxation.

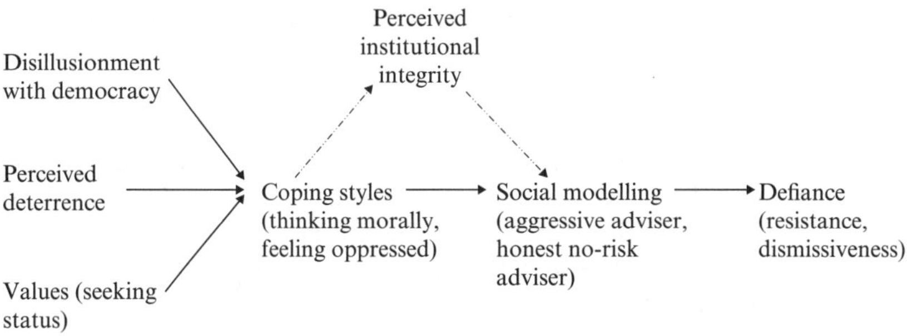

Figure 8.1 Concepts, variables and theoretical links used for building models of resistance and dismissiveness

Coping styles also were measured in 2000. They are the ways in which individuals dealt with tax after a period of appraisal of how taxation was likely to affect them personally. *Thinking morally* and *feeling oppressed* were expected to prove useful in fending off the trials and tribulations of tax reform. They were expected to be shaped by the more general sources of threat mentioned above as instigators – *status*, *deterrence* and *disillusionment* with government.

Perceptions of the integrity of the tax authority were measured in 2002, 18 months into the tax reform process. It was reasonable to suppose that, by this time, Australians would have formed some view of how the tax authority was performing as it implemented the tax reform package. Individual predispositions (*status*-seeking values, *disillusionment*, *feeling oppressed* and *thinking morally*) and perceptions of how the tax office operated (*perceived deterrence*) were assumed to function as a lens through which the tax authority's efforts to improve its performance would be interpreted; even so, perceptions of integrity were unlikely to be determined solely by perceptual bias. Interventions that affected integrity should have registered with the public and made a difference to how much defiance individuals felt.

By 2005, individuals were able to look at the tax reform process with some distance and perspective. They were in a position to decide whether they were on side with the tax authority or not. The 2005 measures included attraction to *honest no-risk advisers* or *aggressive tax planning advisers* and the measures of *resistant* and *dismissive defiance*.

In summary, from left to right, Figure 8.1 shows the instigator variables of disillusionment with the democracy, perceived deterrence and values setting the scene for how individuals cope with the demands of the tax authority. How individuals appraise and construe this threat sets them on a path that accepts subordination to tax office authority (resistance) or challenges its authority (dismissiveness). Acceptance of subordination brings tension between a desire to do the right thing and a disappointed democratic self – the problem can be resolved through leadership by the tax office showing its integrity and defusing defiance. Challenging tax authority occurs through a process of social modelling that exposes individuals to alternative authorities that forge paths that satisfactorily resolve the tension between being a 'good person' and acquiring status, while at the same time denying the tax authority of subservience – and presumably tax monies.

These theoretical propositions guided the building and testing of structural equation models for resistant defiance and dismissive defiance. Initially the aspiration was to integrate models of resistance and dismissiveness into one model that corresponded to that presented in Figure 8.1. The number of variables involved and the differences between the two forms of defiance, however, made the model too complex. The models of resistant and dismissive defiance, for purposes of clarity, have been presented separately in these analyses.[1]

A Composite Model of Resistant Defiance

Resistant defiance was best explained in terms of two pathways, one representing moral obligation, the other representing grievance. Grievance against injustice in the democracy and tax system increased resistance while moral obligation and the desire to stay out of trouble with the tax authority reduced it. The variance accounted for in resistant defiance was 58%. The model had satisfactory goodness-of-fit indices (see Appendix D). Support was not found for a competitive pathway to resistance; the competitive pathway was important only in the case of dismissiveness.

From Figure 8.2, it can be seen that the anticipated grievance pathway began with disillusionment. Disillusionment with the democracy was linked with feeling oppressed by taxation, which, in turn, lowered perceptions of integrity in the tax authority. Feeling oppressed and perceptions of low integrity contributed directly to greater resistant defiance. At every point, the grievance pathway reflected perceptions of injustice.

The pathway of moral obligation was represented in Figure 8.2 by thinking morally, which linked with preferring an honest no-risk adviser, associated, in turn, with lower scores on resistant defiance. Perceived deterrence did not work through thinking morally as anticipated. Instead it directly increased the likelihood of preferring an honest no-risk adviser as the ideal and, through this path, reduced resistance.

Of special interest in Figure 8.2 were the crossover variables – that is, variables that connected the grievance and moral obligation pathways.

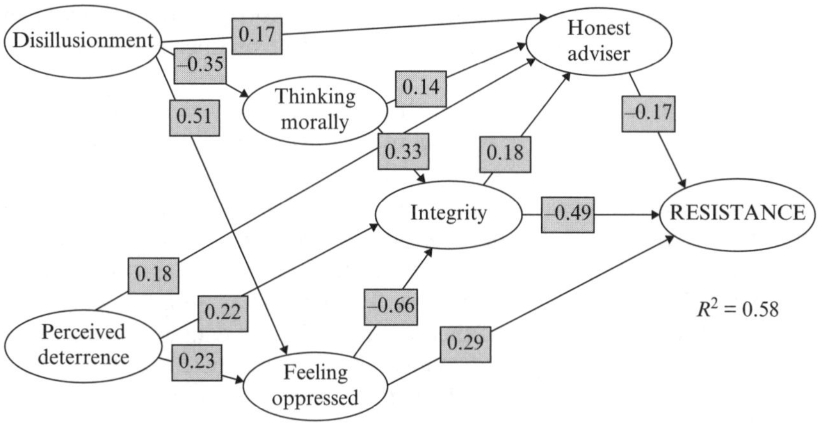

Figure 8.2 A composite structural equation model predicting resistance

Thinking morally was such a variable. When disillusionment with the democracy was high, thinking morally was low and this was predictive of perceptions of low tax system integrity. It is reasonable to suppose that individuals who perceive themselves as being excluded from a system abused by the rich and powerful will have more doubts about committing to an ethic of public tax morality. What is more surprising is that when confidence is dented in thinking morally, the integrity of the tax authority comes under suspicion. Different attitudes are brought into alignment to protect the ethical self – if a good person does not feel compelled to obey or morally comply, then it is possible that the enterprise is morally corrupt. Perceptions of good governance and a well-functioning democracy are therefore critical to both keeping grievance down to manageable levels and strengthening the self-regulating pathway of moral obligation.

Perceived deterrence was another important crossover variable. Perceptions of deterrence were associated with feeling oppressed by the tax system, a not surprising finding when these measures were taken concurrently. Over time, perceived deterrence positively affected perceptions of tax integrity and preference for an honest no-risk adviser. Deterrence may not be flavour of the month when one is struggling to find the money to pay a tax bill, but believing that a deterrence system is operating and that it is risky to cheat on tax appears to pay dividends for authorities in the long term. It places the tax authority in a good position for being ranked as having integrity in its operations, and it increases the desirability of choosing an honest, no-risk tax adviser. Deterrence strengthens the morally obligated pathway in the long term and the grievance pathway in the short term. The problem for a tax authority is that short-term resistance may overshadow and adversely affect prospects of long-term cooperation.

The third crossover relationship of interest involved disillusionment with the democracy. Those who were disillusioned with the democracy were more likely, five years later, to give as their ideal an honest no-risk adviser. These findings suggest that dissatisfaction with government does not necessarily find expression in a desire to hit out at tax authorities. Instead, responsibility is handed over to an agent who will ensure that tax obligations are properly met. The strategy is an interesting one. Individuals preserve a sense of their own probity by imagining themselves 'outsourcing' their taxpaying responsibilities to an expert who they know will do the right thing. Meanwhile, they withdraw from espousing the moral high ground themselves, and remain oppressed by the tax system. By suggesting an honest no-risk adviser as their preferred intermediary, these taxpayers are in effect imposing constraints on their path to defiance. In popular accounts of all kinds of social evils, much is made of how the squeamish (and/or powerful) find others to do their dirty work for them. In this instance, we observe the opposite phenomenon. Disillusioned Australians kept some kind of faith with the democracy by idealizing delegation of their duties of citizenship to a tax adviser who would do the right thing.

The crossovers serve to demonstrate the unexpected consequences facing tax authorities that try to raise their effectiveness through single point interventions. For instance, increasing deterrence may push taxpayers into the arms of an honest no-risk adviser and increase ratings of tax system integrity in time; but initially, perceived deterrence is likely to increase feelings of oppression that take individuals down quite a different path. Resistance may be given such a boost that chaos ensues before benefits to the system kick in.

A further case offering possible unexpected consequences is perceived integrity. From Figure 8.2, we see the number of influences on such perceptions and gain some insight into the malleability of these judgements. The protective value of integrity for an authority is also evident in so far as an honest adviser becomes an attractive option and resistance is curtailed. We begin to understand why authorities might be tempted to be opportunistic and invest in 'spin' – rather than do the job of improving integrity properly and working from within. But if the spin is recognized for what it is, disillusionment with the democracy will work indirectly to counteract any benefits. Authorities would be taking risks by trivializing integrity. Perceptions of institutional integrity play a central role in both grievance and morally obligated pathways to resistance.

A Composite Model of Dismissive Defiance

Two pathways are important for understanding the development of dismissive defiance in Figure 8.3; the pathways of competition and moral obligation. Absent from this model was the grievance pathway that was so important in defining resistance. In spite of a grievance pathway not emerging for dismissiveness, variables associated with grievance (disillusionment with the democracy and feeling oppressed) played a part in fuelling the pathway of competition. The structural equation model depicted in Figure 8.3 explained 50% of the variance in dismissiveness. The data fitted the model well (see Appendix D for goodness-of-fit indices).

The competitive pathway began with status-seeking values, which led to feeling oppressed by taxation. Tax oppression precipitated dismissiveness directly and indirectly by increasing attraction to an ideal aggressive tax adviser.

Strengthening the competitive pathway was perceived deterrence. Perceived deterrence increased feelings of oppression, as did disillusionment. But disillusionment with the democracy also halted recourse to an ideal aggressive tax adviser. In this sense, disillusionment showed itself to be an expression of grievance. It gave rise to tax dissatisfaction but could not pave the way for a counter-move of entering the territory of aggressive tax planning.

The morally obligated pathway looked much as it did in the model of resistant defiance. Thinking morally increased attraction to an honest no-risk adviser and lowered attraction to an aggressive tax adviser, thereby lowering dismissiveness. Moral obligation was strengthened by the link between perceived deterrence and increased attraction to honest no-risk advisers. It is of note that perceived deterrence also had a direct effect on lower dismissiveness. This direct link possibly reflects the fact that individuals who are mindful of tax office power are more cautious about how much dismissiveness they engage in.

Weakening the morally obligated pathway was disillusionment with the democracy. As with resistance, disillusionment with government more generally was associated with less commitment to thinking morally about taxation. These findings are reflective of the unravelling of Feld and Frey's (2007) psychological contract between government and the taxpayer – if the government does not take its responsibilities to the people seriously and abide by an honest code of conduct, why should the taxpayer feel morally obligated to abide by a code of honest taxpaying?

The variables that had interesting crossover roles in the dismissiveness model were disillusionment, thinking morally and deterrence. Disillusionment increased feeling oppressed and reduced thinking morally, thereby strengthening competitiveness. At the same time, disillusionment

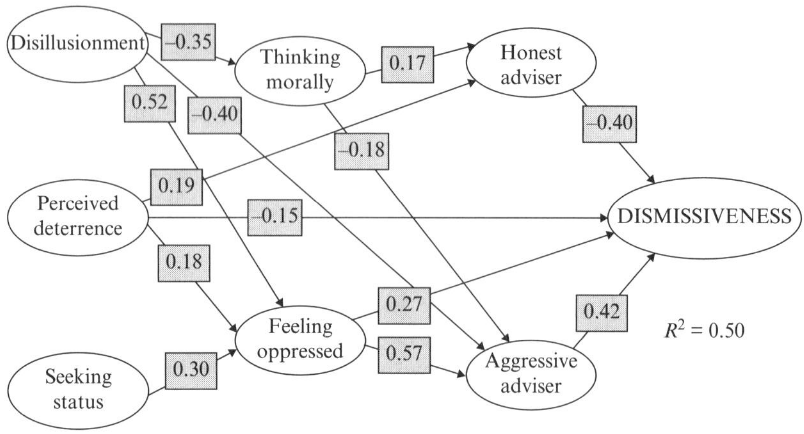

Figure 8.3 A composite structural equation model predicting dismissiveness

with the democracy behaved similarly to thinking morally and had a direct negative relationship with idealizing an aggressive tax adviser. It seems that those who are disillusioned struggle with moral ambivalence. As observed earlier, individuals who believed that their democracy was being inappropriately influenced by rich and powerful actors were likely to step back from being supportive of an ethos of tax morality. They may have disapproved of cheating the tax system in principle, but have been less willing to apply such standards to the real world – they may have been reluctant to condemn cash/black economy work when so much tax avoidance was going on at the 'top end of town'. Yet their personal views on tax morality did not interfere with their social persona. They shied away from those offering aggressive tax advice.

The third crossover variable that was associated with conflicting outcomes was perceived deterrence. In Figure 8.3, perceived deterrence emerged as a particularly attractive means of promoting honest no-risk advisers and curbing dismissiveness for an authority; but it could also lead to feelings of oppression and flight towards aggressive tax planning.

There is an argument from these data for seeing deterrence as the best option for managing defiance. That argument will be strengthened in the next subsection when dismissiveness is linked to tax evasion. But deterrence within a policy framework that sensationalizes such a regulatory intervention as a 'crackdown' (see Chapter 7) is fraught with danger. This is not to downplay the importance of deterrence. The public expect authorities to use deterrence to ensure that people take the rules seriously and obey them. But deterrence needs to be accompanied by integrity.

It is not unusual for regulatory authorities to use deterrence to correct a problem that government policy has created; unexpected consequences are commonplace. Tax in particular proceeds as a game of cat and mouse, as law is used for competitive advantage. In a practical sense, this means that deterrence should be introduced with a heavy dose of explanation for why certain actions are unacceptable at the level of principle. As Picciotto (2007) has pointed out, the sense of tax law is not evident to most people. While tax may be special in the amount of confusion it creates over what is legitimate and what is not, the legal system more generally is regarded with a degree of cynicism (Papadakis 1999). In these circumstances, explanation seems the least that authorities can offer when human initiative exceeds legal and acceptable bounds. Maguire et al.'s (2007) qualitative data have provided insight into the public's sense of abandonment by government as free market ideologies touched their lives. It is possible that dismissiveness is in part a response to this change.

For more than a decade now, Australians have absorbed institutional imperatives for productivity, material achievement and economic independence (Pusey 2003). Most Australians want to spend more time with family and friends and in leisure pursuits, but they believe that all of this depends on their being able to provide financial security for their families. Between 2000 and 2005, Australians grew to accept the idea of small governments and free markets and a more competitive, self-reliant ethos. They accepted responsibility to work hard and get ahead financially, and not rely on the public purse (Braithwaite, V. et al. 2006).

When the findings are analysed contextually, a more complex picture emerges of the competitive pathway to dismissiveness, and why people may be drawn to it. It could be argued that attraction to acting on status values with numbing of moral obligation to government is not just personal choice but also a result of neo-liberal economic philosophies implemented and advocated over more than a decade (Pusey 2003). Occurring alongside these social changes has been increasing disillusionment with government, bemoaning the way in which those with power and wealth have sidelined the interests of ordinary Australians (ibid.: 162–7). Institutional failures to support communities, therefore, may be something of a 'sleeper' contributor to dismissiveness. What is seen as a personal quest for status through engagement with the aggressive tax planning market may be little more than a creative cocktail adopted by individuals in response to the institutional blueprint promoted by economic elites for the future. If so, managing dismissiveness may mean not only using deterrence, but also going back to the basics of negotiating just what government's relationship with citizens should be.

2. DEFIANCE AND TAX EVASION

Dismissiveness: The More Serious Form of Defiance

Dismissiveness has been identified as the more serious form of defiance. The evidence presented to date has focused on the costly implications of managing dismissive defiance. Authorities have difficulty engaging with dismissive individuals to resolve problems. Those who are dismissive want to be free from constraint – the authority is either irrelevant or its actions inappropriate. In all likelihood, the dismissively defiant are not in the headspace for negotiating a truce or compromising with an authority; they want to win at any cost.

Putting management difficulties aside, the question to be asked is whether the dismissively defiant pose a threat by breaking the law. In theory we would expect this to be the case because they object to their actions being controlled by the tax authority. Resistance, on the other hand, is not an objection to control – just to how it is being done. Resistance is less likely to precipitate law breaking than dismissiveness.

Research Design Testing the Defiance–Evasion Relationship

In 2000, 2002 and 2005, participants were asked if they had lodged a tax return for the preceding year, and if so, had they failed to declare income, had they claimed deductions that might not be legitimate and had they earned money in the cash (black) economy that they had not declared to the tax authority. A set of 11 questions was used to elicit these data (see Braithwaite, V. 2001, 2003a; Ahmed and Braithwaite 2004, 2005, 2007 for discussion of measures). For present purposes, a summary of the prevalence of self-reported tax evasion is provided in Table 8.2 for the panel sample in 2000, 2002 and 2005.

The measure of overall tax evasion was a dichotomous variable: did the respondent fail to comply on any of the measures of tax evasion? If they did, they were coded as an evader. If they were compliant on every question, they were coded as a non-evader. This approach differentiated the scrupulously honest from others, rather than making discriminations among the group who were non-compliant. The reason for this choice was that it was the cleaner measure, even though the evasion category included non-serious as well as serious offenders. The alternative approach using a continuous measure based on aggregating the 11 measures risked confounding seriousness of evasion with having access to multiple ways of evading. For instance, a person may only reply 'yes' to one of the 11 indicators (e.g. cash economy), but be a more serious evader than someone

Table 8.2 Percentage of panel respondents admitting to non-compliance

	% in 2000	% in 2002	% in 2005
Not declaring income	11	10	9
Overclaiming deductions	15	15	19
Cash economy activity	6	6	8
Any one of the above	27	26	29

who had several 'yes' responses. Fiddling at the edges on a number of indicators may pale into insignificance compared with the one strategy that works so effectively that there is no need to evade on the other ten indicators.[2] To avoid this source of error, the dichotomous measure of evasion was preferred and is reported in the results below.

The approach taken to assessing whether resistance and dismissiveness were risk factors for tax evasion was to allow each person to serve as his or her own control and ask the question: are the defiant more likely to engage in tax evasion on a future occasion once their current evasion activity has been controlled? Three logistic regression analyses were undertaken with the following aims:

(a) predicting change in tax evasion status from 2000 to 2002 using measures of resistant and dismissive defiance from 2000;
(b) predicting change in tax evasion status from 2000 to 2005 using measures of resistant and dismissive defiance from 2000; and
(c) predicting change in tax evasion status from 2002 to 2005 using measures of resistant and dismissive defiance from 2002.

Increased Likelihood of Evasion among the Dismissive

The results presented in Table 8.3 show that those who were more dismissive were more likely to turn to evasion over time. The effect was significant between 2000 and 2002 when tax reform was being bedded down and the system was undergoing considerable upheaval, it was significant after tax reform from 2002 to 2005 when enforcement efforts by the ATO were significantly increased, and it was significant from 2000 to 2005 before and after the reform process. These findings are impressive in their consistency across different periods in the ATO's reform programme.

While dismissiveness was predictive of increased likelihood of tax evasion, resistance was not. Those who displayed high resistance were neither more nor less likely to have evaded at a later date.

These analyses confirm the hypothesis that from the perspective of

Table 8.3 Three logistic regression models over three different time periods predicting a change in tax evasion status with defiance

Predictors	b coefficients (Wald statistic)		
	2000 measures predicting 2002 evasion	2002 measures predicting 2005 evasion	2000 measures predicting 2005 evasion
	Model 1	Model 2	Model 3
Tax evasion (control variable)	2.17 (54.35)***	1.81 (43.54)***	1.56 (34.58)***
Resistance	0.22 (0.30)	−0.29 (0.64)	0.42 (1.35)
Dismissiveness	1.23 (11.02)**	0.69 (4.66)*	0.67 (4.43)*
Nagelkerke R^2	0.32	0.23	0.19
Overall percentage classified correctly	80	77	75

Note: * $p < 0.05$; ** $p < 0.01$; *** $p < 0.01$.

authority, dismissiveness is the more serious form of defiance. Not only is it difficult to manage but also it predicts an increased likelihood of tax evasion.

3. INDIVIDUALISM, DEFIANCE AND CULTURES OF DISRESPECT

Cultures of Disrespect

Through the structural equation models in Figures 8.2 and 8.3, we catch a glimpse of what Parker Follett (1965, *c.* 1918) referred to as the tragedy of individualism. Three selves provide the starting point for pathways to defiance. Not only are they expressions of who we are as individuals, they signal possible selves in terms of our relationship with government. All of them are at risk of being dealt with haphazardly, if not poorly, by authority. Regularly, they are neglected in favour of a conceptualization of individualism as narrow self-interest.

If we think of individualism more broadly as the right that we all have to grow and develop without hindering the right of others to do the same, governance no longer is framed by 'every-man-for-his-own-interests'. Instead, it is judged in terms of effectiveness in engaging with our moral self that promotes our sense of goodness (and thereby law-abidingness), our status-seeking self that promotes our sense of achievement, and our democratic collective self that enables us to feel part of a just society. When our moral self is engaged, we don't have to suffer the indignity of being coerced into action by authority. When our status-seeking self is rewarded, we don't feel held back by authority. When our democratic collective self is welcomed, we don't feel socially marginalized at the hands of authority or each other. By way of contrast, when these conditions are absent, the scene is set for posturing that is defiant, in terms of resistance and dismissiveness.

In reality, any society will struggle with nurturing moral selves, status-seeking selves, and democratic collective selves simultaneously. In a diverse society, many people will feel defiant at any one time – with good reason, from their individual perspectives. The social objective, however, is not to disparage defiance, but to have processes in place to understand and deal with it constructively. The processes will be discussed in the next subsection. The important point to make about these processes is that they contribute to creating a culture of respect – people feeling respected by government, government being respected by the people, and people respecting each other. Regulation should not be incompatible with this objective. Nor should regulation conflict with individual development. The normative contribution of regulation should be measured in terms of its promotion of the growth and development of individuals in ways that are personally satisfying and mutually beneficial.

Individualism and Platforms for its Development

In part, individualism means being one's own person and feeling comfortable with the unique configuration of strengths and weaknesses that separates each from the other. For humanistic psychology it means celebrating these differences and embarking on a journey of continuous improvement to develop strengths and compensate for weaknesses (Maslow 1968). Institutions that potentially serve this purpose are not in short supply. The ways in which institutions operate and engage human capacity, however, leave room for improvement.

A fundamental premise of those who focus on the development of the more positive aspects of human character (Fromm 1947; Maslow 1968; Seligman 2002) is that healthy, productive and fulfilled individuals are socially interdependent (McGeer 2004). For regulatory agencies, this means paying attention to supporting social infrastructure. Many have. Since Putnam's (2000) book, *Bowling Alone*, government authorities have become intent on building social capital in communities to both increase productivity and impose regulatory constraints. Building social capital, however, is not synonymous with communicating respect; particularly not when conformity is unilaterally demanded of community members.

Strazdins (2000) has used the term 'emotional work' to refer to the process of giving individuals a sense of their own worth by improving their emotional well-being. Emotional work is defined in terms of the behaviours of help, regulation and companionship. Strazdins examined emotional work in the institutions of the family and work. She argued that we do emotional work for each other without giving it much thought or attaching much importance to it – it is work that is responsive to need in others. Help is offered in the form of support, giving a helping hand when needed, assisting with tasks and sharing responsibilities. Regulation involves giving advice, pointing out pitfalls, suggesting better ways for dealing with issues and protecting against harm. Help and regulation repair and regulate negative emotions.

The third dimension of companionship builds positive emotions. It involves spending time with people, to listen and share pleasurable and recreational contexts.

Strazdins's (2000) thesis is that the emotional work we do for each other is neither self-indulgent nor wasteful, but is essential to human well-being. All three types of emotional work occur concurrently, one reinforcing the positive influence of the other. Doing emotional work is personally costly, however, particularly if not shared and rewarded within our institutions, which unfortunately is often the case. Emotional work is proposed as the most plausible and practical way of building cultures of respect within our institutions.

It is not difficult to appreciate why emotional work is undervalued and underperformed – it does not enhance the performance of the individual doing it. Emotional work does not lead to ticks in boxes of tasks to be completed, and often slows such progress down. There is no clear output from emotional work in a world that compartmentalizes individual accomplishment – the effort is invisible and the outcomes benefit others.

It is precisely because emotional work can slow down prospects of personal advancement that it can communicate respect for others in a compelling way. Respect is actioned by investing in another person's process of personal growth and development. The tragedy of individualism, therefore, is that the emotional work that is necessary to support the growth and development of individuals to fulfil their potential is left to chance or to informal networks: the formal platform for its delivery within our system of governance tends to operate exploitatively or not at all.

An institutionalized form of emotional work occurs in highly successful corporations. Personalized employment packages, recreational resources, health and well-being services, and lifestyle enhancement are offerings used by large corporates to communicate to employees how much they are valued and how much the corporation cares about them as individuals. Such companies see these human resource policies as giving them a competitive edge in recruiting and retaining the best staff. The downside, however, is that in market culture, emotional work is provided for winners. Emotional work is given as a reward to communicate that the firm wants to retain someone's services. It is a badge of respect not generally designed into systems as a healing balm to preserve the dignity of those not living up to performance expectations.

Platforms of Respect for Resistance and Dismissiveness

In light of this discussion, Figures 8.2 and 8.3 can be interpreted as a story of the risks of government failure to invest sufficiently in platforms of respect for citizens. Disillusionment with the democracy meant that the democratic collective self had no means of expression or validation. In its wake, the moral self was embroiled in indignity. Thinking morally seemed almost foolish when government failed to act morally itself. As in the Milgram obedience studies, those who felt torn between the authority's and their own conception of what was 'moral' expressed unease by grievance. Not surprisingly, the grievance was personal. They were coerced into paying tax while the wealthy avoided it. Less commitment to think morally in the interests of authority and greater readiness to feel oppressed by authority meant that citizens were less likely to see integrity in their tax authority. Cynicism – legal and otherwise – led citizens to turn away from government and find their authority figures elsewhere. The present study suggests that these alterative authorities can be found in the market where individualism is compartmentalized and advancement can be bought, and where one is safely cocooned from government infrastructure that disappoints and fails to deliver.

Tax defiance can be traced back to an impoverished democratic collective self – a self that needs to be acknowledged, created, shared, debated and nurtured. It is not a self that takes the same form across individuals. The various democratic collective selves will frequently be in disagreement, competing with each other for the distinction of being 'the self' that is heard and validated by the decision-making process. The democratic collective self can therefore be in alignment with the status-seeking self. This does not always have to be the case, but people need to believe that their chances of influencing outcomes are just as good as everyone else's. If the democracy can offer no prospect of this happening, status seeking will be actioned increasingly beyond spheres of government influence. Such choices may be beneficial for a society – or they may be harmful. From this psychological space, the interests of the democracy are blocked from view.

In the next section, as we review respondents' written narratives, we see that the situation is not as gloomy as might be anticipated among Australians. A democratic collective self seems to continue to reach out to government, at least in the case of resistant defiance, expecting an improvement in standards of governance while expressing in no uncertain terms disillusionment and grievance. A moral self is also present in the narratives of those displaying resistance and dismissiveness, albeit expressed more generously in relation to doing the right thing by fellow Australians than by government.

4. NARRATIVES OF DISMISSIVE AND RESISTANT DEFIANCE

Having spent the best part of this book using measures and statistical procedures that carefully disentangle governance concepts of defiance and link them to distinguishable psychological processes, the objective is now to blur distinctions, acknowledging that people's mental lives are intricately interconnected, complicated and socially nuanced.

In order to interpret the identified analytic processes in a way that sits comfortably with the narratives of respondents, written responses that individuals provided at the end of the 2005 questionnaire, 'How Fair? How Effective? Collection and Use of Taxation in Australia' were analysed. In this third-wave survey, 1406 respondents were asked three questions: (a) What do you expect the Australian government to deliver to you? (951 answered the question) (b) What are your responsibilities to the Australian government? (930 answered the question) and (c) What are your responsibilities to your fellow Australians? (922 answered the question). The subsamples chosen for the narrative analysis were the highest scoring 2% and the lowest scoring 2% on resistant defiance, and the highest scoring 2% and the lowest scoring 2% on dismissive defiance. From this base, the qualitative responses of six individuals were chosen to represent each group. The criterion for selection was the meaningfulness of the written answers. Text where ideas were connected was more useful for purposes of analysis than disconnected words.

Interpreting the Narratives

In interpreting the responses of those who scored at the upper end of the defiance scales, the responses of those who rejected defiance became the benchmark or the comparator. Most of the defiance that was detected in the sample was not so extreme.[3] What this means, practically, is that while Australian respondents were keen to register a modicum of defiance, they did not throw themselves into a full-blown state of defiance. They were in many respects much like anyone else, very much of the community, which was particularly apparent in the way they described their responsibilities to their fellow Australians. In their relationship to government, however, the defiant articulated very different points of view. Politically they were consistently more sceptical, more critical and more guarded about their contributions.

Comparing Narratives: High versus Low Resistance

'What do you expect the Australian government to deliver to you?'
Government was expected to provide direct benefits and assistance regardless of whether the resistance score was high or low (see Box 8.1). Government was seen to be responsible for watching out for groups within the Australian population who were 'doing it tough'. In addition, the government was expected to deliver everyone with a fair and just legal system, a safe environment, quality medical care and quality infrastructure. Those high and low on resistance seemed to converge in their views on how they wanted to be governed – they wanted honesty and openness from government.

So how were high scorers different from low scorers on resistance? The critical factor that differentiated responses in Box 8.1 was endorsement of tax reform. Those who expressed most resistant defiance considered that tax reform (in particular GST) unfairly hurt people, in particular rural taxpayers and low-income earners. Their expectation of government was that tax money should be better used, that services and assistance should be better targeted, and that the unfairness in the tax system should be corrected.

'What are your responsibilities to the Australian government?'
Those scoring high and low on resistance saw their responsibilities to government differently (see Box 8.2). High scorers varied from being 'detached' and non-committal to being active in questioning government claims. High scorers used terms such as 'pay just taxes', 'keep job' and 'be vigilant' with regard to both government and terrorism. Low scorers were more open and

BOX 8.1 COMPARING RESPONDENTS WITH HIGH AND LOW RESISTANCE ON 'WHAT DO YOU EXPECT THE AUSTRALIAN GOVERNMENT TO DELIVER TO YOU?'

High resistance

Reasonable taxation. More services for the dollar. Less red tape. Truth in delivery of services.

To get out to rural Australia, . . . and then provide all necessary services as quickly and efficiently as possible. Support rural Australia in droughts immediately. Change laws to allow rural people to run their properties efficiently as they have for hundreds of years without the red tape. Stop driving rural people off the land. Abolish GST immediately; it is crucifying rural Australia.

Tax cuts – better health care – more jobs. Better trade in Australia. Need a good look [at] jobs here, not overseas – Australia is big, give our people a good go!!! Instead of handing it to Asia!!!

A better tax system for low-income earners. Bracket creep has eroded my take-home pay.

Easier understanding of GST. Fairer tax between rich and poor. Make rich pay more. Help unemployed and homeless. More help for disabled. Keep fuel rebate going for farmers. More work to prevent terrorism.

Hospitals, emergency services (police etc.), roads, education, defence.

Low resistance

To follow through election promises. Advance details of changes planned, fairness.

I expect the honest administration of all departments and an openness to the wider community. The government should be charismatic, humane and imaginative in handling complex international situations.

A system of government based on sound and fair legal practices that allows for people to make the best of the opportunities that life brings. To provide a safety net for the vulnerable members of our community that gives them a reasonable standard of living. A safe country that makes the best of its opportunities.

A country I can be proud to call 'mine'.

A fair society for the poor as well as middle-income families. A safe environment. Medical services available free to all with no long waiting lists.

Protection, peace, justice.

BOX 8.2 COMPARING RESPONDENTS WITH HIGH AND LOW RESISTANCE ON 'WHAT ARE YOUR RESPONSIBILITIES TO THE AUSTRALIAN GOVERNMENT?'

High resistance

To be vigilant that they are never able to abuse their power.

To pay just taxes, act responsibly, make it aware where their policies are destroying the country.

Support??? Can you trust a politician??? NO!!!!

None.

Keep job. Pay taxes. Report any suspicious acts/ terrorism.

To pay my fair share of tax and to be an active, involved, law-abiding person.

Low resistance

To be honest in all dealings.

To be a loyal patriotic Australian. To be thoughtful about issues involving elections and be prepared to question and analyse proposed changes.

To pay my fair share of tax for redistribution for the greater good of Australia. To be a loyal Australian that supports a fair go to make the best of the opportunities provided by the system of government.

To be a law-abiding and honest citizen.

To vote when I have the right to. To pay tax. Keep an eye out on things such as terrorists. To bring my children up with manners as they are the future leaders of the country.

Contribute, work/play/financially build our nation. Keep them accountable.

generous in how they saw their responsibilities, mentioning being 'loyal', 'patriotic', 'honest', 'thoughtful' and being an engaged contributor to the nation. In spite of the differences, both high- and low-resistant respondents projected a responsible approach in dealings with government.

'What are your responsibilities to fellow Australians?'
High and low scorers on resistance saw their responsibilities to fellow citizen similarly (see Box 8.3). Just as they looked to government to provide help and support, so they believed their responsibility to their fellow Australians was to 'accept' and 'respect' them; to be 'fair', 'reliable', 'law-abiding' and 'honest', to be 'caring', give 'help' and be 'generous'; and to 'learn to understand differences' in order to work together for a better society for everyone.

Comparing Narratives: High versus Low Dismissiveness

'What do you expect the Australian government to deliver to you?'
Those who scored high on dismissive defiance did not refer to government as having 'in principle' responsibilities to the community (see Box 8.4). Instead, high scorers referred to specific needs that they personally had, such as 'more money', 'access to doctors and dentists without paying so

BOX 8.3 COMPARING RESPONDENTS WITH HIGH AND LOW RESISTANCE ON 'WHAT ARE YOUR RESPONSIBILITIES TO YOUR FELLOW AUSTRALIANS?'

High resistance

To treat them as I would like to be treated – as a fair and honest person.

To respect them and treat them honestly and fairly. To listen to their point of view, learn to understand differences and work towards a happy society where everyone is financially secure and not always struggling.

Honesty, reliable.

None.

Care for. Help. Listen. Support.

To pay my fair share of tax and to be an active, involved, law-abiding person.

Low resistance

To be open to ideas opinions. To accept them – what ever. To respect them. Help overseas if problems.

To be a caring citizen. Charitable and generous in dealing with less fortunate in our society. To support health, education and environment issues which will impact on our future generations.

To pay my fair share of tax. To give them a fair go to achieve. Support the vulnerable members, but not the people who do not want to work to make this country even better than it is.

To be a law-abiding and honest citizen.

Care for each other. Show each other love not hate.

Social justice. Support for needy.

much more' and 'listen to me when I object to their policies'. There was little sense that the highly dismissive saw themselves as part of a community that shared resources and outcomes, for better or for worse. They saw themselves as individuals who used and needed little from government. But when they did have something to say, they expected to be heard.

In contrast, those low on dismissive defiance (see Box 8.4) saw the government as having responsibilities for the provision to the collective of 'security', 'quality health services', 'support and assistance while unemployed', 'education', transport systems of 'a high standard' and 'good

BOX 8.4 COMPARING RESPONDENTS WITH HIGH AND LOW DISMISSIVENESS ON 'WHAT DO YOU EXPECT THE AUSTRALIAN GOVERNMENT TO DELIVER TO YOU?'

High dismisiveness

I would prefer to pay no income tax and only pay tax on goods and services which I use.

Am very content with the commonwealth government. Cannot believe a word of our local state government, feel that they 'rob' us all. Oh well, that's life.

More money please! Disability pensions are unfair!

I am working in a motel. I am a housemaid, I clean, make bed, I work in morning part time, I declare all my income, I pay taxes as every other Australian that is working just as I am working. I hope the Australian government can help me with my tax please.

Being single and employed full-time I receive very little in terms of services from the government (except for global/infrastructure services such as roads etc.). I pay full fares on public transport, receive no subsidies of any kind and only now getting some relief for education in the form of Fee-Help (and paid full fees up front a few years ago for my IT degree). If the government wasn't helping the medical insurers to rip off health consumers (high fees – bad return on claims), I'd be satisfied with that. But at least, I'd appreciate having access to doctors and dentists without paying so much more.

I expect them to listen to me when I object to their policies. I did not vote for this one and I do not consider they represent me or my view of responsible democracy.

Low dismissiveness

Fair and equitable laws and regulations. Honest and fair governance as per the values of the Australian society. Disband multiculturalism and in its place put an integration programme where immigrants become fully participating members of 'our society'. I am an immigrant and I strongly object to multiculturalism as a concept. I see too much abuse of the Australian way of life.

A fair and equitable tax system. Support and assistance whilst unemployed. Open and honest government. Border and internal security. Consistent laws in each state/territory. An affordable medical system.

Fair and equitable tax system for all must be a very simple system. The tax system must be revised. The present tax system is manipulated by the rich and with their clever accountants and lawyers can avoid paying their fair share. Overseas companies do not contribute their fair share of tax from the profits and benefits they rip from Australia due to the complicated tax laws. Overseas and local companies must be brought to account.

To fix up the railway system. To fix up the health care hospital system – amalgamation of hospitals was a drastic mistake . . . should have been left as it was with individual hospitals being accountable for themselves. To change the goods and services tax system. This is an unfair tax.

A secure environment to live in with an emphasis on health and education for all income levels. This combined with an obligation for those who can to pay their taxes. The government also has a duty to promote harmony among its citizens. Fair wages and fair trade are also important. Not business monopolies.

A defended country. Quality health services. Highways and roads of high standard. Good communication system.

communication systems'. It was striking that respondents with low dismissiveness scores expected government to act to curtail abuse of government systems, almost to guarantee a level playing field. There seemed to be particular interest in law and regulation that was 'fair' and 'equitable', and government was to act to keep things 'fair' (wages and trade), 'equitable' (tax) and 'consistent' (across states). On this same theme was the call to do away with multiculturalism to prevent 'too much abuse', to revise the tax system so that it was 'simple' and unable to be exploited by the rich, to ensure tax law was clear so that overseas and local companies were 'brought to account', and to make sure there were 'no monopolies'.

'What are your responsibilities to the Australian government?'

Responsibilities to government for those high and low on dismissiveness revolved around the individual and obeying the law (see Box 8.5). High scorers described their responsibility to government in terms such as 'to obey the laws', 'to keep out of trouble', to fill out surveys and 'pay my tax'. More active involvement with government meant 'to vote them out' and to 'complain often and publicly'. While there appeared to be a stand-off with government, there was no evidence of antagonism to the community. Contributing to the community seemed to be compatible with dismissiveness, without the government being part of it.

At the other end of the dismissiveness continuum, individuals made more positive noises about contributing to government, although the contributions were of a cautious nature (see Box 8.5). Those with low dismissiveness mentioned being 'law-abiding', 'openness and honesty', 'obedience', 'payment of required taxes' and of 'lawful taxes'. A little less cautious were the responses, 'uphold the values of Australia', 'cooperate when requested', 'protect the interests of Australia and encourage others to do the right thing', 'to respect other people . . . to watch out for other people' and 'to participate in the community'. Importantly, low scorers on dismissiveness felt the need to assert their obligation for 'self-sufficiency' and paying 'my own way – not expecting handouts'.

'What are your responsibilities to fellow Australians?'

For those with high scores on dismissiveness (see Box 8.6), the central theme of responsibility to others was not to be a burden or interfere in the lives of others: 'try to do the right thing'; 'keep to myself'; 'look after myself'; not 'make anyone else's life harder'; 'don't cheat' on tax; 'to maintain respectful, friendly relations'; and 'support the community . . . in maintaining a decent standard of living for all'.

For those low on dismissiveness (see Box 8.6), there was an emphasis on 'obedience' to laws, 'be honest', 'work hard', respect others – 'the person

BOX 8.5 COMPARING RESPONDENTS WITH HIGH AND LOW DISMISSIVENESS ON 'WHAT ARE YOUR RESPONSIBILITIES TO THE AUSTRALIAN GOVERNMENT?'

High dismissiveness

To obey the laws of the land.

Keep out of trouble.

Filling out forms! Filling out surveys.

That I pay my tax as other Australians that are working as well as myself.

To vote them out.

To contribute at a family and community level, to stay within the law and complain often and publicly when I disagree with government policies.

Low dismissiveness

Uphold the values of Australia (but this does not include multiculturalism). Abide by the laws and regulations passed by the Australian parliament. To be self-sufficient.

Openness and honesty in all dealings. Payment of required taxes. Lodgement of honest tax returns. Obedience to all Australian laws. Cooperate when requested.

To be honest in my dealings. To uphold the laws of the country. To keep an eye on what is happening around me and be informed. Protect the interests of Australia and encourage others to do the right thing.

To obey all laws. To respect other people. To earn my own living and pay my own way – not expecting handouts. To watch out for other people – to take care. To lodge a yearly tax return.

To be law-abiding (including pay taxes) and to participate in the community. At the moment the government has alienated me as it fosters monopolies, attempts to suppress workers' rights, panders to the USA and especially annoying: Iraq!!

Pay lawful taxes.

BOX 8.6 COMPARING RESPONDENTS WITH HIGH AND LOW DISMISSIVENESS ON 'WHAT ARE YOUR RESPONSIBILITIES TO YOUR FELLOW AUSTRALIANS?'

High dismissiveness

Always try to do the right thing.

Look after myself.

Keeping to myself! You asked!

That I don't cheat and declare all my income (I am working part time in mornings).

Not to make anyone else's life harder by not taking advantage of welfare services if I can. Support the community as a whole in maintaining a decent standard of living for all.

To maintain respectful, friendly relations in order to offset the role of 'enemy' in which this government casts us internationally.

Low dismissiveness

That they take more responsibility for the behaviour of their children. That the abhorrent rudeness and disregard for others be replaced by respect, courtesy and [being an] upright citizen. . . That the endemic unacceptable behaviour in schools by children who disrupt classrooms be dealt with not only by 'behavioural modification techniques' but by the full gamut of disciplinary measures including punishment strategies.

> Obedience of laws. Respect their opinions and the person, respect their property and thoughts. Be honest. Work hard. Help if possible.
>
> Be a good citizen, be honourable in my dealings with others. Respect others as I expect others to respect me. Get involved in helping others less fortunate. Voice my concerns when I see wrong being done.
>
> To obey all laws. To respect other people. To watch out for other people. To care for other people. To drive safely and carefully to avoid accidents.
>
> Contribute materially and socially on a local level, especially to make a better country for my kids. Promotion of the awareness of greenhouse dangers is also important to me. Essentially as a 55-year-old I believe that the Australian community has accelerated towards selfishness more since the Howard government came to power than any other period in my memory. A real shame and a danger to my children's happiness.
>
> Treat them as equals.

. . . their property and thoughts', and treat others as 'equals'. Alongside these standards was commitment to others: 'to care for other people'; 'voice my concern when I see wrong being done'; 'be honourable in dealings with others'; work 'to make a better country for my kids'; and 'help' others if possible or if needed. Those low on dismissiveness expected others to be respectful and good citizens, and standards to be maintained. Being highly dismissive appeared to echo some of these expectations: the difference was that the highly dismissive were not prepared to impose them on others.

SUMMARY

The qualitative responses of the most resistant and dismissive respondents reveal dissatisfaction with the performance of government. They see their responsibility to government in guarded terms, yet the most interesting aspect of the qualitative responses is that responsibility among the defiant is apparent. As a group, they neither discount obligation out of hand nor are they uninterested in the role they play in the process of governance. In cases of both resistance and dismissiveness, readiness to improve the quality of government is forthcoming, although not necessarily expressed in a way that would be comfortable for authority to hear.

Yet authority should hear these voices, an assertion based on another observation from the qualitative data. Those who are among the most defiant show a responsibility to others in the community that is as strong as that of their non-defiant peers. The qualitative responses are a reminder that authorities that automatically discount taxation defiance because such people are entirely self-serving are incorrect. Scepticism about government, even scepticism turned to cynicism and self-interested rhetoric, does not translate necessarily into irresponsibility with regard to community interests and needs.

Understanding tax defiance, then, involves casting a web that is wider than the narrow domain of taxation. The whole of government is implicated at a fundamental level. The quantitative analyses provide insight into why in these Australian data (see Maguire et al. 2007) there has been an unravelling of relationships with government, while local communities remain 'in contact' with each other. In the case of resistant defiance, the problem lies in government not providing care and support, and communities feeling abandoned and disrespected in the process. In the case of dismissive defiance, the problem lies in government intruding on their lives, creating conflict over the appropriateness of government intervention. Using both the quantitative and qualitative work, a culture of disrespect is thought to enshroud citizens and their government. In the case of resistant defiance, government communicates this disrespect through a withdrawal of responsibility to join in with and support Australians in their endeavours. In the case of dismissive defiance, citizens communicate disrespect by rejecting the authority's wish to 'regulate' through controlling behaviour. They reject the tax authority's efforts to keep them on the straight and narrow path. The dismissively defiant, unlike those who are resistant respond by challenging authority – and they will be more likely to evade their taxpaying responsibilities.

Through the quantitative analyses the pathways to resistance and dismissiveness shared some elements and were different in respect of others. Theoretically these analyses were interpreted within a framework of selves that individuals strive for as they deal with authority. Taxpayers seek meaning and safety in a moral self that they hope the authority will support, they pursue a status-seeking self that they hope the authority will condone, and they look to a democratic collective self that they hope contributes to a better, fairer society.

The analyses tracking pathways to resistant defiance showed that the pathway for the democratic collective self had been eroded. Instead a grievance pathway emerged. The pathway that in theory could have reined in resistance was the morally obligated pathway. It was weakened, however, by grievance about the state of the democracy. Resistance reflected disappointment and anger, but not loss of hope that things could be improved.

The pathways to dismissiveness were not dissimilar from those to resistance, but with a negative twist. The weakened morally obligated pathway was there, but grievance underwent a transformation. It became part of status seeking and contributed to the competitive pathway. It was as if the democratic collective self had become dormant at the level of citizen–government relations, and a new self that had been inspired by the financial planning industry had taken its place.

In comparing resistant and dismissive defiance, integrity plays different roles. Perceived lack of integrity is a central part of how government generates resistant defiance and executes recovery. If government is going to be able to reach out to dismissive defiance, however, a relationship needs to be first established. It is difficult to imagine that this is possible without integrity on the part of a tax authority. The first step may require deeper transformations and adjustments than were undertaken during Australia's tax reform process.

CONCLUSION

This chapter has provided a deeper and more nuanced understanding of resistance and dismissiveness, and how they connect with our understanding of democratic governance. By bringing together knowledge gained through the qualitative and quantitative analyses, it has been shown that those who display defiance, either resistance or dismissiveness, have mapped out different views of the future for their governance. There is good reason to expect conflict between them because each harbours a different feared possible self. The resistantly defiant fear an acceleration of government abandonment of the people and sacrificing the interests of ordinary Australians for macroeconomic and geopolitical agendas. Their future leaves the democratic collective self under threat. The dismissively defiant assume that such abandonment is inevitable, and focus their concerns on the intrusion of government regulation on their freedom. Their status-seeking self is under threat. Common to both resistance and dismissiveness is the sense that contact between government and citizens lacks respect.

In the case of resistant defiance, the disrespect takes the form of government lacking benevolence, appearing not to care about providing support and serving the needs of the community. Government is not finding the right balance for its emotional work with citizens. Not surprisingly, the enterprise of taxation to support government also loses credibility: taxpayers' money is not collected and distributed fairly. The battle for and against resistance revolves around government taking tax and purportedly giving goods, services and opportunity in return. The correct balance may be elusive, but public deliberation about what the balance should be is a moral imperative for democratic governments. Without proper deliberation and explanation for the structure and form of tax collection and expenditure, moral obligation to be law-abiding is readily compromised.

In the case of dismissive defiance, benevolence is not the governance issue of concern: the issue is control and regulation. Dismissiveness is a response to the community asking: 'Why isn't government taking charge here?' The dismissively defiant appear to accept this situation, perhaps condone it, and certainly take advantage of it. The highly dismissive have come to expect minimal intrusion on the rights and freedom of individuals. In contrast, those rejecting dismissiveness looked to government and law to restrain activities that were potentially damaging or harmful. On the dismissiveness dimension, individuals may accept that they have responsibility for looking after themselves and each other, but the question that divides them is how far government goes in making harmful behaviour unlawful, creating a level playing field, protecting against abuse of regulatory systems, preventing monopolization, and managing risks to themselves and the community.

The defiance dimensions of resistance and dismissiveness can therefore be seen as responses to two different kinds of regulatory intervention. Resistance triggers dispute about how much support government should offer the community. Dismissiveness triggers dispute about how much control government should exercise over the community. Resistance is a complaint about failure to enable; dismissiveness is a complaint about right to disable.

Importantly, among the defiant, be they resistant or dismissive, the social capital and infrastructure on which democratic governments depend appears to survive. But defiance means that it is not used to support government initiatives. Social capital is dedicated to providing mutual support at the informal community level. The agenda is decided by the many communities that share social capital and can access resources to effect plans for the development of their particular community. In the process, government is excluded. Short of coercion, government has to settle for following a multitude of social wills. When they must intervene, they will be resented and costs will be high. More tragically, the social exclusion of government means that democratically elected representatives are denied a proactive leadership role in their communities. As we struggle with global threats such as climate change, poverty, rapidly spreading diseases, nuclear weapons, the dislocation of populations and war, it seems an understatement to say that it is an unfortunate time for governments to be so careless as to risk losing contact with those they govern.

NOTES

1. Readers interested in the combined model are referred to the supplementary statistical appendix at http://vab.anu.edu.au/defiance/sup01.pdf.
2. In practice, the results obtained when using the continuous measure were similar to those obtained with the dichotomous measure.
3. Defiance scores fell in the range from 3 (neutral) to 4 (agree) on a five-point rating scale. Respondents rarely used the range from 4 (agree) to 5 (strongly disagree).

9. Reasoning with defiance

> To safeguard democracy the people must have a keen sense of independence, self-respect, and their oneness.
>
> Mahatma Gandhi, cited in Prabhu and Rao 1969: 339

Defiance is a complex and compelling expression of individualism that is commonly encountered and socially shared. The complexity seems to have caught us on the back foot. At a personal level, we avoid confronting defiance if possible. We either walk away, adopting a 'live and let live' philosophy, or we placate defiance – it is too resource-intensive to deal with otherwise (Maguire et al. 2007). Authorities respond similarly. They fail to see value in defiance. If their risk assessment indicates danger, action will be taken. Generally such action will be punitive. Authorities fear the organization of discontent for reasons of political and economic instability, mob violence, terrorism – and, sometimes, adverse publicity. If risks are low, however, authorities discount defiance as negative, emotional and counterproductive.

Stigma allows authorities to get away with their disregard for defiance (Goffman 1963), and discourses are created to discredit those who question how authorities govern (Mathiesen 2004). The 'politics of envy' discourse, for example, sought to dampen debate over whether growing inequalities in society are harmful and require redress. The rhetoric successfully excises from individual conscience a sense of responsibility for those less fortunate. By defining the problem as the attitude of the poor, the privileged are released from feeling they have too much. A vexed issue is simplified to become a non-issue. One hundred years ago the women's suffrage movement faced a similar battle with a power structure that refused to engage respectfully and reasonably with the position that women had a right to vote (Purvis 1995; Joannou and Purvis 1998). Things should be different. There is no acceptable reason for authorities not to step up to the plate and embrace defiance as an expression of individualism that needs to be heard respectfully: defiance has potential for strengthening democracy and the quality of governance.

The purpose of this book has been to uncover what it means when individuals defy. In this concluding chapter, a map of defiance is presented that provides a detailed analysis of those aspects that impinge on regulation and governance. How current practices of governance can engage defiance constructively is no small challenge, but the argument presented is that opportunities are opened up by decentred regulatory control. Nodal governance allows for a strengthening of expressions of defiance. Nodal governance is 'a way of thinking about possibilities for strategic regulatory action', action that emanates from places 'where resources, ideas, deliberative capacity, and leadership' come together 'to make networked governance buzz' (Braithwaite, J. et al. 2005: 9). Braithwaite, J. et al. (2007) found that many of the best nursing homes were nodally governed. They gave space to residents' councils to meet alone and get angry about nursing home policies, with opportunity to connect resident nodes of governance to the homes' management system. Power-sharing agreements were also decided with resident nodes of governance – thenceforth the residents' council would decide what the next outing would be, how the menu would be changed and so on.

Defiance needs to have an airing in settings at a distance from authority; and in the process, reasons for defiance can be analysed and adjudicated in terms of their worth. Those who are defiant can then present their best possible case for consideration supported by sound argument. In response, governments and authorities are challenged to raise their game. They need to consider the content of defiance more seriously and the degree to which it feeds into bigger social and political issues, all the while having high-integrity processes in place to deliver fair and desirable outcomes to those they govern.

MAPPING DEFIANCE

Defiance has elements that are both emotional and cognitive. Their balance varies with people and context. The emotional and reactive side of defiance has attracted considerable research attention under topics such as child disorders and behaviour problems (Kalb and Loeber 2003). A child will fight for her freedom against a parent's unwelcome instruction. The defiant reaction is not restricted to the authority. Others offering comfort may bear the brunt of defiance just as much as the parent exerting control. For this to occur occasionally is considered normal: it is understood that it takes time to find a social niche. It is when indiscriminate displays of hostility and non-compliance to basic demands of civility persist over time that assessments of behavioural pathology take hold.

While defiance can generate anxiety in a community, it becomes a symbol of courage when enmeshed in stories of oppression. Defiance seems to speak to both an inner and a collective self about the importance of freedom and its protection. At the time of writing, Wikipedia identified defiance as the title of two films and one play, two computer games, four books, three music bands and one album, no fewer than 19 British royal navy ships and three US navy ships. The US boasted place names that included the word 'defiance' in Iowa, Pennsylvania, Virginia, Arizona, Ohio, Missouri and New York. None of this should surprise. Psychologically, defiance defends the self against criticism and constraint from others. Defiance asserts individualism, and when reasons for defiance are shared, it represents our collective oneness against oppression and proclaims a right to liberation.

The degree to which defiance generates anxiety or inspiration depends on context. When the case for defiance against oppression is made, the cause wins legitimacy. When it is not, defiance means spoiling or creating trouble unnecessarily. Defiance ranges from being the most prosocial to the most antisocial of constructs. The significance of defiance at the collective level therefore depends on shared meaning – although almost always a display of defiance will prove emotionally cathartic for individuals.

Emotionally driven defiance hits out because of feelings of indignation, shame and humiliation. Criminal behaviour has been analysed through the emotional, reactive defiance lens. Sherman's (1993) theory of defiance explains how the most violent of crimes can be perpetrated against apparent innocents when individuals or groups who feel socially disconnected from mainstream society are sanctioned in ways that generate shame–rage spirals (Scheff and Retzinger 1991). In such circumstances, rudimentary support for emotional reactivity may come from cognitions – perceptions of injustice, discrimination and of not being understood. Nevertheless, the defiance that Sherman analyses is predominantly emotional and behavioural. It involves resenting the command of authority, experiencing denigration at the hands of authority, and expressing the psychological pain inflicted by the authority at a reactive, affective level. With few social bonds and significant others to provide comfort and exercise control, the defiant individual directs rage towards what is seen to be a hostile world, causing harm to others and introducing mayhem into their lives. Sherman's contributions have profound policy implications, calling for government to foster 'emotionally intelligent' justice to replace a crime management mentality of artless dominance and coercion (Sherman 2002).

Resenting commands and hitting out at authority is the essence of defiance – the emotional reactance is always there, but often defiance is clothed in sophisticated argument. Such arguments rest on superior knowledge, stylish rhetoric and communication technology to get a convincing message out to the world that the threshold has been crossed

– defiance has moved from the stand of selfish troublemakers to that of socially responsible heroes. To which of these sides particular acts of defiance belong, however, remains an enigma. We often struggle to comprehend the truth; should we get over that barrier, we often disagree on what is socially responsible. At critical moments in history, there has not been consensus on the defiance of George W. Bush against the international community over the invasion of Iraq, of the Burmese generals against the international community over human rights, of Nelson Mandela against South Africa's apartheid government, and of the Dalai Lama against China's domination of Tibet. In a postmaterialist world that has learnt to articulate interests for self and others, to value individual expression and development, to negotiate with power for desired outcomes, and to settle conflict with respect for others' rights, defiance has become an intriguingly complex social, cognitive and emotional phenomenon.

MOTIVATIONAL POSTURING THEORY

Motivational posturing theory provides one way of viewing defiance that guides more constructive engagement and responsiveness by authority. Motivational postures are signals that communicate to observers how we feel about the demands of an authority. Motivational postures include the cooperative signals of commitment and capitulation. They also include defiant signals of resistance, disengagement and game playing. Resistance conveys dislike for the demands that the authority is making and is the name given to the first defiant supra-posture. When individuals come to terms with the demands of the authority, they move away from resistant defiance towards capitulation, and, if won over, commitment. Disengagement and game playing are postures communicating a different kind of defiance – an unwillingness to defer to the authority. Disengagement and game playing are brought together to form the second defiant supra-posture of dismissiveness. It is not uncommon for both kinds of defiance to coexist, with individuals moving from one to the other in the course of an interaction, as did Sheikh Mohammed Omran in his 2005 television interview described in Chapter 1.

The five postures (commitment, capitulation, resistance, disengagement and game playing) and the supra-postures of resistant and dismissive defiance are generated empirically. This does not mean that they are without theoretical infrastructure. They follow the precepts of well-established theories of how individuals behave when faced with a threat of change. Motivational postures manifest in ways consistent with the ideas of

Pearlin and Schooler (1978) on threat and coping, Rokeach (1968, 1973) on value–attitude–belief systems, Bandura (1977, 1986) on social modelling, Bogardus (1928) on social distance, Goffman (1956) on face work, and C. Wright Mills (1940) on vocabularies of motive. Motivational postures have the following qualities:

1. They communicate identities for which understanding is sought from authorities.
2. They protect the self from potential harm at the hands of an authority.
3. They exist relatively independently of each other and fluctuate in salience depending on the actions of the authority.
4. They have not only a dynamic component that is driven primarily by the quality of the relationship with the authority, but also a stable component driven by the alignment of personal values and worldviews with those enunciated by the institution.
5. They reflect social distance from the authority that is legitimated through a shared discourse with like-minded individuals, providing the self with a zone protected from interference by the authority.
6. They may be used to bargain, threaten, justify actions, provide an escape route from authority when necessary, and assert one's intrinsic worth regardless of the opinion of the authority. They are both strategic and expressive.
7. They function in three domains: (a) psychologically, they are protectors of an individual's dignity in the presence of an authority that can coerce; (b) socially, they are signals that seek reinforcement from like-minded individuals about social truth; and (c) politically, they are signals to authority about how satisfied people are with its objectives or processes or both.

APPROACHES TO UNDERSTANDING DEFIANCE

The research in this book traces the pathways to resistant and dismissive defiance. Models of resistance and dismissiveness were developed around three ideas that have stood the test of time and scholarly scrutiny. The first approach focused on individual response to potential threat. The basic idea was that, either consciously or unconsciously, we are aware of how authority might engage with our needs and aspirations, and that the resulting appraisal of what might happen influences our motivational posturing (threat and coping model of Chapter 5).

Second, while government authorities have certain legitimacy within a democratic society, they do not necessarily have integrity as a regulator. In other words, they do not necessarily steer our behaviour with what we consider to be soundness of purpose, an appropriate sense of responsibility, reasonableness or justice. Therefore they do not earn our trust (integrity and trust model of Chapter 6). Integrity and trust, when earned by an institution, can lessen the threat of authority.

The third idea was that we arrive at our motivational postures not only through appraisal of our needs and analysis of how the authority functions, but also through a process of modelling those whom we admire and would like to emulate. Initial appraisals, be they thoughtful or intuitive, influence whom we model ourselves upon and to whom our attention is turned for steering the flow of events (social modelling approach of Chapter 7). This may be the least cognitively rational aspect of choosing motivational postures, as advertisers show, for example, when they link subconsciously a particular model of car to a defiant role model.

The models that were empirically tested around these ideas were useful in explaining resistant and dismissive defiance in terms of both similarities and differences. Theoretically, resistant defiance was understood as opposition to the way in which an authority uses its power. Resistant defiance is the feedback authorities need from time to time when a community says: 'You are not doing too well here – we expect you to improve your performance to better serve us.' Dismissive defiance, on the other hand, was understood not as opposition to how power is used, but rather to the authority having power. Dismissive defiance conveys a loss of hope that authorities can or will use their power well. Dismissive defiance is a message to authorities from a community saying: 'Let us be; there is no place for you here.'

The empirical analyses cast light on the emergence of resistant and dismissive defiance in the context of taxation. Resistance and dismissiveness are positively correlated. Nevertheless, the statistical analyses provided evidence of their distinctiveness in terms of the comparative importance of institutional and personal determinants. In the case of resistant defiance, judgements about the quality of institutional performance were paramount at both the broad level of the democracy and the specific level of the tax authority. Disillusionment with the democracy and perceptions of lack of integrity in the tax authority were conditions that fuelled resistant defiance in people regardless of personal desires and preferences. In the case of dismissive defiance, personal preferences and what other people were doing was of far greater significance than the institutions themselves – government leadership was not valued highly. Government institutions, and particularly the tax authority, were not worthy of respect in the thinking of the dismissively defiant.

BEST MODEL OF RESISTANCE

When the threat and coping, integrity and trust, and social modelling approaches were integrated, the best model of resistance highlighted the importance of grievance. Resistant defiance reflected tensions in the relationship between taxpayers and authorities surrounding obligations, justice and benefits. These three characteristics represent core concerns in the tax compliance literature (Braithwaite, V. and Wenzel 2008). Resistant defiance occurred when individuals personally felt victimized by the tax system as well as when they viewed the tax authority as not doing its job well, as lacking integrity. General disillusionment with democratic governance that came about when taxpayers perceived themselves as being pushed to one side while the demands of rich and powerful elites were satisfied also fuelled feelings of tax oppression and were a central part of the grievance pathway.

Countering the grievance pathway was a pathway of moral obligation defined by a personal commitment to upholding the law. The morally obligated pathway, however, was intertwined with issues of integrity at the level of the democracy and of the tax system. In order for the morally obligated pathway to fire up, answers were needed to the problem of disillusionment with the democracy and to failings in tax integrity.

The pathways to resistant defiance are signs of a democracy and tax system that may not be in good shape, but are capable of recovery. Citizens withdraw their cooperation from the state as they see shortcomings in how its institutions operate, but they have neither lost sight of possibilities nor hope that institutions can be reinvigorated. *Resistant defiance is best understood as an expression of grievance for personal loss or collective offence at the hands of the tax authority, grievance that has the capacity to undermine commitment to upholding the law, and that can be reversed through whole-of-government institutional reform.*

BEST MODEL OF DISMISSIVENESS

An integration of approaches revealed the superiority of social modelling for understanding dismissiveness. The tax planning industry with its aggressive as well as its more honest, no-fuss advisers was the alternative authority that led the way in igniting and dampening dismissive defiance. The role of the tax office was limited to that of a perceived deterrent force, which could be either effective in reining in dismissiveness or counterproductive. Disillusionment with the democracy also played a major role in shaping dismissiveness, strengthening it along one pathway, weakening it along another. Those who were disappointed with the quality of the democracy felt victimized by the tax system. When this was combined with personal values that pushed individuals toward achievement and status – social and economic – a competitive pathway emerged, setting the scene for a surge of interest in aggressive tax planning and dismissive defiance.

For others who were disillusioned with the democracy, modelling aggressive tax planning was not the answer. While this pathway to dismissiveness was rejected, it would be a mistake to assume this meant open commitment to upholding the law. The disillusioned who did not join the competitive pathway were lost in a system of governance that neither satisfied nor engaged them. The tax authority's powers to sanction seemed to be the only corrective that could boost moral obligation, and then only superficially through incentivizing reliance on an honest adviser. For any deeper effect on moral obligation to occur, a makeover of the quality of democratic governance was required. Such a makeover would delegitimize the aggressive tax planning market and curb social modelling, linking dismissiveness with an image of dodginess, rather than cleverness and success. For this to have authenticity, one might expect that a prerequisite would be clarification of tax law.

Dismissive defiance is the upshot of a person's preferences and resources, irrespective of the wishes of the state. The pathways to dismissive defiance involve adversarialism and taking initiative, if not risk. There is nothing in the findings to suggest that dismissive defiance is a highly deliberative process that could sensibly lend itself to constructive engagement with the tax authority to resolve differences. Dismissive defiance involves following leaders who successfully challenge the established authority, or it sleeps in a system ignorant of its presence. *Dismissive defiance is best understood as a socially sustained, yet individually focused, preference that has the effect of subverting the regulatory intention of the tax authority.*

FROM FINDINGS TO THEORY: RESISTANCE AND DISMISSIVENESS

Proposition 9.1 When authority threatens, three selves go forth to face a potential enemy. They are: (a) a moral self; (b) a status-seeking self; and (c) a democratic collective self.

The *moral self* declares its presence in pathways of wanting to do the right thing and honouring the law. It relies on the external infrastructure of deterrence and an honest no-fuss tax adviser, and on psychological infrastructure, the most important elements of which are shame, guilt and a personal quest to realize growth and inner harmony. Even the most competitive among us want to feel at peace with ourselves: that we have done our best, that we tried to do what is right and that others value us for our efforts. We all have a moral self, which makes its presence felt to a greater or lesser degree depending on its relevance to context.

The *status-seeking self* exists alongside a moral self, but is attracted to different institutional pathways. Status seeking is about standing out from the crowd – or rather doing better than the crowd in terms of material assets, social position, power and influence, and achievements in life. Our status-seeking self wants to be a winner above all else and seeks out the resources that will help that occur. Both within and outside the domain of taxation, advertising ensures that we are constantly exposed to images to remind us of the status to which we aspire. Advertising feeds the status-seeking self, enticing us to model ways of behaving that promise to deliver the specialness that we would like.

The *democratic collective self* is a manifestation of shared identity with others – a sense of oneness we have with communities to which we belong. Communities where connectedness is high use their social capital to work together to improve their collective well-being, with citizens and governments working cooperatively (Putnam et al. 1993; Putnam 2000; Lowndes et al. 2006). The democratic collective self expects to engage with government in the process of deciding what constitutes improved quality of life (Stoker 2005; Lowndes et al. 2006). The democratic collective self is acknowledged through government honouring principles such as honesty, fairness, respect, reciprocity, and treating others as you wish to be treated (Maguire et al. 2007).

Within the context of taxation, Wenzel (2003, 2007) and Taylor (2003) have identified an inclusive national identity from which people draw pride and a sense of belonging, and that predisposes them to think positively about taxpaying as a way of supporting the democracy. Collective selves are many and varied and need not be political (Taylor 2003; Wenzel 2003). In the context of regulation and governance, however, the relevant collective self is necessarily political. The collective democratic self involves sacrificing freedom and acquiescing to the coercive capacities of regulatory agencies in order to improve the quality of life for the community.

Proposition 9.2 When the moral self, the status-seeking self and the democratic collective self are denied the social infrastructure required for their expression by government authorities, defiance ensues.

Proposition 9.2(a) When government authority undervalues a moral self by failing to recognize its presence or by taking it for granted, the morally obligated pathway is weakened and the way is cleared for defiance.

Neglect of or carelessness with the moral self occurs when authorities lock themselves into a one-dimensional conception of human beings as self-serving or motivated simply by greed. By failing to recognize human motivations as complex and variable, authorities send a message about the language they speak and understand. If authorities don't understand moral obligation and refuse to engage with those they are regulating in such terms, it is little wonder that it has an out-of-order sign in the human psyche. If a moral self is not understood, it will not be activated in social encounters; or it will be hidden from view for fear of exposure to exploitation.

In interactions with authority, we may seek to change the discourse or assert our self-worth through claiming to be a 'good person'. Authorities sometimes become disconcerted at this point, because they 'don't know' if this is true or not. There is no reason for authority to be afraid of affirming a person in this way. If authorities expect individuals to use their self-regulatory capacities to control their actions, the signal must be sent that the moral self is relevant (Braithwaite, V. 2001). Moral selves need nurturing through acknowledgement (Braithwaite, J. 1989). Doing so does not translate into saying that we are not guilty of an offence – good people do bad things.

Proposition 9.2(b) When a status-seeking self cannot be expressed within a regulatory domain, a competitive pathway to defiance comes into being, strengthened by alternative authorities that provide resources to defeat the legitimate authority's agenda.

In the field of taxation, it is inevitable that a tax authority wanting to collect a proportion of a person's wealth will clash with the individual painstakingly accumulating that wealth. It is also inevitable that pursuers of wealth whose agenda is being frustrated will form coalitions to advance their interests. The clash will intensify as the amount of money that is involved increases. Herein lies the inevitability of conflict and political tussle. Conflict cannot be avoided; what can be avoided are practices that presume that it is acceptable to resolve such conflict through marketing images rather than informed debate.

In the research presented in this book, social modelling was at the heart of status seeking. Modelling others is how we learn. It makes sense that those who want to be winners will be astute observers of opportunity. But whether we learn good habits or bad is not a function of status seeking. Status seeking is neither good nor bad in itself. The good and bad come into play in our assessment of how that particular form of status seeking enhances or harms the opportunities of others.

The responsibility of governments is to monitor impact and lead quality debate that may underpin subsequent regulation. Tax authorities have given relatively free rein to status-seeking selves in the domain of tax avoidance. In this sense, they have failed their democracies, looking the other way as tax avoidance burgeoned. Financial practices that can undermine the quality of the democracy have developed, not because this is an inevitable part of status seeking, but because institutional constraints to contain it have not been effective. It should be acknowledged, as it has been in earlier chapters, that drawing the distinction between tax avoidance and a legitimate tax concession that strengthens the nation's economy is not always an easy call for tax authorities, courts of law or the business sector (Picciotto 2007). Uncertainty and flawed judgement are part and parcel of governance. Where criticism is warranted globally is towards governments' failure to revisit and reanalyse tax avoidance issues, and engage effectively with an industry that threatens the sustainability of tax systems (see, e.g., Rossotti 2002). Status-seeking selves can be, and in most cases think of themselves as being, honest, law-abiding selves. Poor public deliberation and inadequate regulatory engagement boost the likelihood that status seeking and law-abidingness follow separate paths.

Proposition 9.2(c) When a democratic collective self is betrayed, a grievance pathway comes into being that is shared with others and expressed as protest against the government.

Disappointing a democratic collective self is easily and frequently done (Irvin and Stansbury 2004; Lowndes et al. 2006). The democratic collective self potentially has as many agendas as there are people who engage with this identity. In collective undertakings of any kind, not everyone will be satisfied. It seems inconceivable that citizens have not adapted to this aspect of compromise in a democratic society. Betrayal of a democratic collective self is a little more than not satisfying the electorate on a particular issue.

Political revitalization to affirm the democratic collective self is well under way (Irvin and Stansbury 2004; Lowndes et al. 2006), but these developments have been relatively recent. In the past, authorities have been remiss in failing to acknowledge and appreciate the role of the democratic collective self. New public management models, like earlier Weberian models of bureaucracy, did not require negotiation with the democratic collective self (Stoker 2005). The task of engaging citizens in debate was regarded as the domain of politicians (Stoker 2005).

On the other hand, new public management has taken feedback on service delivery and client satisfaction very seriously, so much so that the identity of consumer–citizen has been popularized, possibly awakening discontent in the democratic collective self. Consumer–citizen implies an impoverished status beside the democratic collective self. Consumer–citizen gives choice within a range of offerings, not a say in deciding on the offerings and how they might be developed.

In this particular research context, evidence emerged of a democratic collective self that had been swallowed up in a culture of disrespect. Evidence was presented in the form of self-reports of feeling neglected and irrelevant in the political landscape. Knowledge of how to reverse this trend is advanced (Irvin and Stansbury 2004; Stoker 2005; Lowndes et al. 2006). According to Lowndes et al., people participate when they feel they are part of the deliberative process, when they have resources to enable them to participate, when they have supporting civic networks and organizations, when they are asked directly to contribute, and when they believe authorities will listen and that their engagement will make a difference. Also part of the agenda of participatory democracy practitioners (Irvin and Stansbury 2004) are institutional safeguards to ensure that particular interest groups, including government, will not dominate and that others, in particular individuals, are not marginalized or excluded from actively participating (Mansbridge 1996; Young 2000; Fung 2004). These advances provide opportunity to engage the democratic collective self, recognizing its worth and benefiting from its participation.

The alternative of satisfying the democratic collective self with spin and rhetoric is too deeply entrenched in political institutions to discount its influence and the dangers it presents. It is not difficult for an authority to create a democratic collective conscience around a person, idea, policy or ideology that is unsound, emotionally charged and antagonistic to dissenters. Interest groups, political parties and the media have become adept at fuelling fears about issues that threaten well-being (e.g. increases in crime, costs of transport, food, water or energy). There is no suggestion that these are not legitimate concerns, but it is questionable whether heightened emotionality paves the way for effective solutions. One of the challenges facing all who want more reasoned, evidence-based debate about social issues is learning self-regulation of mindset when we engage with defiance. This mindset is one that is attuned to the many layers of defiance, realizing some as being less productive than others. While all layers need to be recognized, not all need to be reinforced. We have the capacity to work towards changing the layer of our engagement. Instead of fostering the ascendancy of emotion, in-group conformity and out-group rejection, we can work to create an institutional space that channels defiance towards meaningful dialogue characterized by reason, reasonableness and respect.

Greater social distance creates space for defiance and non-compliance, and for questioning the legitimacy of legally constituted authority. Such space allows for defiance to be shared and discussed safely outside authority's reach. When that social distance reaches a point where empathy, self-doubt and acknowledgement of authority are absent, the risk of social fragmentation and competing social norms and expectations is high. By the same token, some social distance between citizens and authority is essential for an airing of issues – of the status-seeking self and the democratic collective self pitted against a moral self that draws us towards seeing virtue in playing by the rules. Deliberation – as opposed to undisclosed thoughts and unresolved shame over these tensions – constitutes the micro-foundations of a vibrant democracy. Safe institutional space for defiance therefore means not too close to authority, but not too far away either.

GOVERNING WITH RESISTANCE AND DISMISSIVENESS

Resistant defiance involves an internal dialogue between a moral self and a democratic collective self. Because a democratic collective self orients us to other citizens and to authority, the dialogue is easily externalized. Differences in views may divide and create heated debate, but in the process we gain a consciousness of what is important to our fellow citizens. We become attuned to other voices and calibrate our views in relation to them. In spite of differences of opinion, there is a common element that unites – the belief that what is at stake is a better way of life for the collective.

Dismissive defiance has no such underlying common element bringing together individuals and authority. A democratic collective self is abandoned as a valued identity. Dismissiveness is a posture that allows at best closed and guarded dialogue in keeping with protecting the interests of the status-seeking self. As such, dismissive defiance is not easily influenced. It is more prone to social distance that precludes empathy, self-doubt and exposure to the influence of lawful authorities. As well as a status-seeking self, dismissive defiance involves a moral self that may serve to rein in indulgence of harmful practices. Energizing the moral self, however, requires determined effort if appropriate social infrastructure is not close at hand. Family and friends may lack willingness or capacity to challenge a loved one who has excised a moral self in pursuit of a dream of status. The situation is likely to be worsened by the absence of a hopeful democratic collective self that could provide moral social infrastructure. A democratic collective self can shed light on group responsibility and arouse self-regulatory feelings of guilt and shame. Without these opportunities for self-correction, the moral self is likely to struggle to contain dismissive defiance. The moral self more than likely will not be engaged until called to account by the rule of law.

For these reasons, dismissive defiance is regarded as posing a greater threat to authority and democracy than resistant defiance. Consistent with this analysis is the persistent link of dismissiveness with tax evasion. No such link was established between resistance and evasion. It is dismissive defiance that goads authority to forsake dialogue and moral suasion, escalating to measures of coercive control. We have seen authorities follow this path most recently in the extreme measures they have taken to deal with terrorism, pushing to the side civil liberties and human rights.

The question of how to engage constructively with dismissiveness remains open. The best wisdom is prevention. When dismissiveness seems to be developing, the best option for authority is to work tirelessly to convert it to its more manageable companion, resistance. Clearly this is not always going to be possible: there are times when dismissive defiance cannot be 'talked through'. When this happens, dismissiveness should not be ignored. It may convey profound injustices about the way the society is working and it may genuinely threaten collective well-being.

Observation tells us that the threat that authority feels in the face of defiance commonly results in their resorting to three responses – avoid, crush or appease. When defiance registers with the authority as requiring a response, the assumption too often made by authorities is that they are up against dismissiveness. Often they are not. When the ATO (Australian Taxation Office) had to deal with its mass-marketed tax avoidance scheme debacle in the late 1990s, it worked through the above three responses in turn, first ignoring the burgeoning tax avoidance investment market (Braithwaite, J. 2005), then engaging in highly punitive action, and ultimately withdrawing all the negative sanctions, even going so far as to offer concessions to those owing taxes (Murphy 2003a, 2003b, 2004). While this spectacle of dysfunction brought to public attention a proportion of dismissively defiant taxpayers, most were also resistantly defiant (Murphy 2005). The tax authority rightly feared dismissiveness, but greatly exaggerated its presence, and overlooked resistance (Braithwaite, V. et al. 2007). It took them some time to recognize that the promoters of the schemes and their devotees should have been their targets, not the first-time investors who were captured by an offer that they later realized was too good to be true. In this case, the ATO would have benefited by having at the outset a strategy for dealing with resistance dialogically and constructively, while escalating regulatory attention in relation to dismissiveness.

This two-tier approach to defiance is derived from the basic difference between resistance and dismissiveness. The critical element in settling differences with those showing resistance is respect. The same gesture of respect is much less meaningful with dismissiveness. It is not that respect is not appropriate in these circumstances, just that it misses the mark in signalling an appreciation for why dismissive defiance is occurring. Indeed, offers of respect without an understanding of the basis of dismissiveness can be counterproductive. Those who are dismissively defiant will use gestures of respect from the authority to strengthen their own hand (Braithwaite, J. 2005; Braithwaite, V. et al. 2007). This is possibly why we see authorities jump so quickly from an avoidance to a crush response. Their reasonableness is short lived when they feel that they are losing control and played 'for a fool'. To avoid this knee-jerk response, authority should become far more knowledgeable about defiance.

HEARING DEFIANCE THROUGH DECENTRED GOVERNANCE

In order for defiance to be constructive, authorities must give the bearers of defiance time to understand and explain their dissatisfaction, and then adopt democratically fair principles for airing and acting on the issues raised. Most importantly, the emotionality that so often is attached to defiance must be allowed to work its way to reason. Reasons can be contested and debated, less so emotions. The process of reasoning that needs to accompany defiance addresses the following questions: what is the problem; how might it be corrected, what is the evidence that taking action would serve the community well; is this a priority for the community? Those who are defiant need a safe space for this process to occur (Mansbridge 1996). Opening up space for expression and discussion of defiance applies to dismissiveness as much as to resistance, even though dismissiveness is considered a greater threat to democratic governance. The basis for this position is that dismissiveness often gains a foot-hold by being closeted away from public scrutiny. When it is made public, it becomes social. Once dismissiveness is social, many other competing selves come to the fore to contest its validity.

A model of decentred governance draws our attention to the way in which nodes serve as sites for these much-needed deliberative processes over defiance. They provide a space for conversations about feelings that accompany resistance and dismissiveness. Views can be expressed openly outside the reach of the state and analysed with the intent of producing an account of defiance digestible for authority. The processes by which the account develops will admittedly be haphazard, with variation occurring across nodes and issues. For instance, the opportunities for conversation may be restricted to people who are similarly defiant or they may be inclusive of many different voices wanting to test their ideas against those of others. At some nodes, exclusivity of participation may greatly influence the message that is taken to authority. At other nodes, exclusivity may apply not so much to who is present, but to the ideas canvassed. The scope of deliberations may be narrow and 'silo-like' or it may be broad-ranging and outward-looking, with tolerance of peripheral issues.

When defiance is 'deconstructed' by nodal centres of governance, there will be neither consensus nor necessarily well-informed debate. The hope is a more basic one: defiance will be heard and if it is ostracized by one node, it will be given a sympathetic hearing by another. How defiance is engaged at different nodes is beyond control of any person or entity. That said, there is no reason why rules of engagement that promote the importance of respect and fairness cannot be promoted across the community. Furthermore, nodes that adopt practices that give people a fair and respectful hearing can be recognized as best practice and rewarded for their efforts.

The state may and should be interested in knowing and understanding the issues that create nodal discussion. This does not mean that the state needs to interfere and prematurely close down debates. To do so is to reignite emotional outrage and give the defiant a one-way ticket to alternative authorities over whom legitimate authorities have even less control. By not seeking to control nodes, even when they provide the first glimpse of defiance, the state demonstrates respect for the psychology of individuals and for the social processes that provide them with a sounding board for their thoughts. Everyone needs a safe space for testing out their ideas before being locked into positions from which they cannot withdraw without loss of face.

Arguably the media is guiltier than government of exploiting people whose feelings are driving their actions and who have not had time to think through their situation. Even so, the meddling of government carries with it more fear for consequences than the meddling of the media. The position of governments in times when media attention inflames emotions rather than reason becomes one of delicately balancing individual rights to expression with collective responsibility to be fair, reasonable and respectful. Perhaps in such times the role of government is to lead through example, finding ways to affirm the strengths of nodal deliberation while disapproving of premature airings of defiance. Nodes that provide space free of government interference may not always be resource rich for helping turn defiance into a well-argued case. But they are mixtures of economic, cultural, social and symbolic capital that can contribute to a process of unpacking defiance and understanding the reasons behind it.

While nodes offer potential for turning defiance into something that authorities are equipped to deal with reasonably, they can become dysfunctional, in spite of the huge investment that communities make in them. Nodes need to be connected within socially responsible webs that provide direction and support if they are to serve their communities well. In looking at the demise of the Australian tobacco-growing industry, Cartwright (2009) has recounted the way in which the tobacco-growers' cooperative failed a rural community that had pinned its hopes on it for the future. In the view of the defiant growers, the cooperative's senior management cultivated relationships with the tobacco manufacturers and the Australian government, while robbing growers of their forum for safely and privately sharing grievance and developing a collective voice. Cartwright's account of this cooperative's failure is a reminder that to be strong and effective, nodes need not only be resource rich but also be enmeshed in broader webs of influence. If they are not, they are at risk of being crushed before they have opportunity to work through their defiance. According to Cartwright, the profit-oriented agenda of the multinationals and the neglect of the state disempowered growers, incited participation in the illegal tobacco market (chop-chop) and shamed a community that had built its identity around 'the golden leaf'.

The above account provides insight into how government might play a proactive role in empowering nodes with responsibility for hearing and interpreting defiance. Enabling deliberation, defending principles of quality deliberation and listening to the outcomes provide government with a well-defined role in engaging constructively with defiance.

In summary, if nodes can capture voices of dissent and keep other powerful nodes at bay, they can be places where conversations of discovery are converted into a coherent presentation of a defiant position for the outside world – be it resistance or dismissiveness or both. In this way, nodes are translators of defiance, articulating what government authorities have done or not done to create dissatisfaction and what they are expected to do. It is to be expected that the argument for defiance developed at or communicated via nodes will not always be informed or socially responsible. There is no assumption that the node will develop a balanced perspective on the problem. But nodes can move defiance from the level of emotion to the level of reason.

TWO TIERS OF DEFIANCE DIPLOMACY

Once defiance is articulated in terms of problem, cause, consequence and desired remedial action, contestation of ideas can take place with the inclusion of government. John Braithwaite (2008) has presented a picture of regulatory capitalism in which deliberative denizenship takes place among interested parties all over the world, as a bottom-up enterprise outside the control of the state. Deliberative denizenship does not claim to be representative in any way of the public's thinking; it is more a way of canvassing widely for options and offerings of how things might work better. Issues of representation come into play with the idea of contestatory citizenship. The state exercises control as options are debated and contested to ensure observation of democratic processes.

Applying these ideas to defiance suggests a time for the state to be hands-off and a time to be hands-on. The state can be non-interfering in the process of allowing defiant individuals to express themselves through nodes of governance, but should re-enter at the point of contesting arguments and positions. Those who are resistantly defiant are looking for opportunities for deliberation with the state to make things work better; for this type of defiant reaction, engagement by the state is a mark of respect. The dismissively defiant, on the other hand, want to be left alone by the state. Yet the state needs to engage with dismissiveness, not because dismissiveness is necessarily harmful, but because it takes no account of how the agenda sits alongside bigger issues that affect other people. The state needs to engage with dismissiveness to help ensure that an acceptable balance of competing interests is preserved.

When the state is in hands-on mode, different approaches are required for resistance and dismissiveness. For resistance, deliberation is likely to prove productive. Whenever resistance is high, the role of government is to establish a respectful and responsive relationship. A deliberative process of listening, understanding, empathizing, problem solving, explaining options and taking action connects with the democratic collective self. When decisions are made, providing the process is fair, transparent and responsive, the outcome will more than likely be accepted: the moral self will carry the day, as articulated so well by one of our survey participants from Chapter 7 – '[my job is] to obey the law, even if an imbecile is in charge' (Maguire et al. 2007).

Prospects of such an outcome increase when relevant nodes of governance are more cooperative with the government. Resistance will dissipate more readily –unfortunately it may even be stifled in the presence of more cooperative players. It is to an authority's discredit to take advantage of this situation and sweep resistance to one side. High integrity by an authority would point to a different course of action. High integrity in time will win praise from those displaying resistant defiance, even when there does not appear to be a cooperative face in sight. That said, resistance does not go away; nor should it in a vibrant democracy. Resistance can be constructive when given a voice in the kinds of deliberative proceedings so strongly advocated in the participative democracy literature.

This is far more difficult to achieve in special circumstances where dismissiveness is high, but resistance is low. An authority's efforts to communicate are likely to be met with deep cynicism about motives and capacity. Yet the dismissively defiant have a right to a fair hearing. Third parties or nodes that are prepared to broker a peace between the dismissively defiant and the state may prove most effective in situations where authority needs to hear the voice of dimissiveness and both sides need another chance to arrive at a mutually satisfactory arrangement. A good outcome in third-party dialogue would bring resistance to the fore, while cynicism was placed temporarily on the back burner.

Even so, engagement with resistance and dismissiveness is not easy for authorities. If dismissiveness prevails, there is inevitably a tussle for power. The responsibility of government in this situation is complex – being responsive to public opinion but also ensuring stability and security for the democracy. Ultimately, a crisis of dismissiveness may only be handled by taking contested issues and renegotiating the power relationship, one issue at a time. There is little point in waiting for extensive dialogue to overcome the crisis of legitimacy; in the short term that battle has been lost. Immediate partnering enables the state and the defiant parties to function independently without further damage to either. In the long term, successful partnering may build trust and a new kind of legitimacy for the authority.

The special feature of dismissiveness that became so apparent in Chapter 6 is that it is unlikely to be satisfied by the 'soft' partnering we see in so much decentred governance. Commonly, the state takes its steering responsibilities very seriously, particularly when it passes money to a partnering agency (Grabosky 1995b). In such contexts, officials document carefully and manage risk cautiously to prove themselves reliable and trustworthy, with regard to both expenditure of public funds and adherence to the government's agenda. This is not the kind of partnering that will sit comfortably with the dismissively defiant, who are likely to resent the tightness of the control that government exercises. More than likely the difference will be unbridgeable through deliberation. Dismissiveness can only be dealt with by bringing leaders together to decide on a way forward. Having brought the dismissive to the table with government, the task is to keep them at the table until a binding and enforceable power-sharing agreement is in place. In some of the most intractable conflicts of the world, such as Northern Ireland, this has been the outcome. Partnering as power sharing is also illustrated in Canada with its First Nations Government, a governance arrangement that gives Indian communities far greater control over how they are governed.

The alternative to power sharing is complete domination, always a possible course of action for the dominant power. But domination is expensive, requiring never-ending surveillance and erasing social capital. The collateral damage to the social order that occurs when states dominate populations is unpredictable. Part of the explanation for this unpredictability lies in the permeable boundary that separates resistance and dismissiveness. Dismissiveness is unlikely to spread throughout a population – it is too bold; but resistance does, nagging away and wearing down the 'easy option' of capitulation. Dismissiveness and resistance can be very readily intertwined when social injustice prevails and hope for peaceful resolution of differences fades. Then the distinctiveness of the two forms of defiance is not readily discernible to outsiders. Distinguishing civilian populations (presumed to be predominantly resistant) from military populations (presumed to be predominantly dismissive) is just one instance of how the two forms of defiance cling together under conditions of domination and extreme threat. Practically differentiating the two in Timor Leste, West Papua and Aceh, where the Indonesian military have sought domination, or in Iraq, where the Coalition of the Willing has sought domination, is near impossible. In all these cases, local populations become enmeshed in webs of resistance and dismissiveness, and become increasingly socially distant from the dominating authority with its downward-spiralling integrity and legitimacy.

CONCLUSION

Dealing with defiance will always involve processes that are chaotic and unpredictable. Defiance, after all, is spirited rejection of imposed order. The idea that defiance has avenues of expression through the deliberative process jars with those who think that institutions are supposed to provide order and structure and weed out anyone or anything that might disrupt the flow of events. They presume that orderliness and cautious risk management are our best protection against threats to security and progress.

Others argue differently. Security and progress are regarded as most achievable if we come to terms with decentred governance and acquire a more sophisticated understanding of how various nodes work and are connected to each other in webs of influence. Security and progress are to be found through the 'regulatory craft' of knowing which threads of the web to pull to improve prospects for as many people as possible (Grabosky 1995b; Braithwaite, J. and Drahos 2000; Sparrow 2000; Wood and Shearing 2007).

This book seeks to complement the second perspective by explaining why a political solution of top-down control is bound to be counterproductive, given what we know about human motivation. The thesis starts from a humanistic premise. Individuals have a right to lead lives that enable them to grow and develop their skills, and to increase their understanding and experience of the world without denying others the same opportunities. But with the best of intentions, regulatory activities can squeeze the life out of populations, engendering fear, cutting off options in the name of managing risk, curtailing freedom, and removing hope. We do this to each other. Not surprisingly, governments do it too.

Through the concept of motivational posturing, we see how authorities are able to iron out the creases and wrinkles that make up our individual human psyches. We can be made to present ourselves compliantly, at times embracing orthodoxy, at other times keeping a safe distance, offering no more than we have to, and ritualistically following protocols that have no meaning for us. But we can also have moments when we display resistance, disengagement and game playing, expressed more confidently when authority offends our sense of justice or our rights, and more openly when others agree with us. Government can try to enrol our talents and capacities with monetary rewards and social recognition, but there comes a time when nothing makes up for the lost integrity of our authorities, save their acknowledging their failings and mending their ways.

Such a concession from authorities is necessary before they are able to come to terms with the proposition that they should deal with defiance respectfully, not with contempt or indifference. In the meantime, we shall continue to posture our defiance, through resistance and through the more dismissive postures of disengagement and game playing. We do it to allay our own insecurities, not the least of which is the belief that government has failed to meet its responsibilities to the community. Our defiance takes the form of grievance for ourselves and the collective (resistance); or we move on, seeking some kind of 'specialness' to satisfy our sense of worth as individuals (dismissiveness). Whichever way we practise our defiance, the path is not so easy going. Moral obligation tries to rein in our defiance. For some, morality may feel remote and inconsequential. That is rarely the case when brought to account before the law. Whether we like particular laws or not, legal institutions with their emphasis on the rule of law connect with our moral self.

As these forces of grievance, status seeking and moral constraint clash, it is not surprising that defiance has an emotional dimension. For this reason, defiance needs to be expressed, heard by others, engaged and interpreted. This does not necessarily mean that defiant views are endorsed or that they are legitimated, just that we accept that they are genuinely held and that underlying them there is tension. The most constructive and respectful process for individuals is to channel their defiance towards deliberation with others who are sympathetic, yet hold different views. Deliberation allows a disaggregation of issues, a shifting of sands and of alliances, and ultimately understanding and insights into how things could work better. This process is ideally suited to resistance. It is less obviously appropriate for unadulterated dismissiveness where authority is not trusted and has lost its moral sway. Resistance and dismissiveness need to be handled differently. Crises of resistance require a deliberative, responsive whole-of-government approach; but crises of dismissiveness require a targeted, nodal decision-making solution. To re-engage a dismissive Irish Republican Army, first, IRA nodes of second-track diplomacy needed to be given space; second, power sharing needed to be countenanced as an alternative to capitulation.

Managing crises of defiance is important, but the main purpose of this book is to argue that conversations should happen and action taken before a crisis point is reached. In part, crises develop because too little is understood about the complexities of human motivation and action, particularly in relation to how we navigate our way through institutional constraints and manage the expectations of authorities. Motivational posturing has been developed as a concept that fills this gap. The face we show cannot be thought of as superficial, as some cardboard cut-out that can be trifled with and manipulated by authority. Strategy we certainly have, but strategy is never completely disconnected from self-worth. Motivational postures capture the nexus of strategy, how we want to be seen and our sense of who we are.

Our postures are communication devices that are formulated around deeply held beliefs and highly valued identities that are both personal and social. We have a flexible array of postures that allow us to be highly adaptive, able to protect ourselves and also able to put our best self forward for others. Authorities need to appreciate these skills for their humanness, not discard them for their institutional inconvenience. When authorities are ready to commit to this step, it is but a short distance to embrace a regulatory spirit that brings the more socially productive postures to the fore and veers away from practices that unnecessarily generate the most divisive, intractable forms of defiance.

Appendices

APPENDIX A: STATISTICS FOR CHAPTER 5 SEM ANALYSES

Table A.1 Indicators of fit for model predicting Resistance *(Figure 5.4)*

Chi-square (χ^2) = 2.114, $df = 1$, $p = 0.146$
Goodness-of-fit index (GFI) = 0.999
Adjusted goodness-of-fit index (AGFI) = 0.994
Root mean-square error of approximation (RMSEA) = 0.025

Table A.2 Squared multiple correlations for the latent variables in model predicting Resistance *(Figure 5.4)*

	Estimate
Thinking morally	0.123
Feeling oppressed	0.009
Resistance	0.779

Table A.3 Indicators of fit for model predicting Dismissiveness *(Figure 5.5)*

Chi-square (χ^2) = 0.051, $df = 1$, $p = 0.820$
Goodness-of-fit index (GFI) = 1.000
Adjusted goodness-of-fit index (AGFI) = 0.1000
Root mean-square error of approximation (RMSEA) = 0.000

Table A.4 Squared multiple correlations for the latent variables in model predicting Dismissiveness *(Figure 5.5)*

	Estimate
Thinking morally	0.114
Feeling oppressed	0.012
Taking control	0.033
Dismissiveness	0.449

APPENDIX B: STATISTICS FOR CHAPTER 6 SEM ANALYSES

Table B.1 Indicators of fit for model predicting Resistance *(Figure 6.1)*

Chi-square (χ^2) = 0, df = 0 *
Goodness-of-fit index (GFI) = 1.00

* This model is 'just identified'; therefore the probability level cannot be computed.

Table B.2 Squared multiple correlations for the latent variables in model predicting Resistance *(Figure 6.1)*

	Estimate
Trust	0.306
Resistance	0.573

Table B.3 Indicators of fit for model predicting Dismissiveness *(Figure 6.2)*

Chi-square (χ^2) = 0.695, df = 1, p = 0.405
Goodness-of-fit index (GFI) = 0.999
Adjusted goodness-of-fit index (AGFI) = 0.995
Root mean-square error of approximation (RMSEA) = 0.000

Table B.4 Squared multiple correlations for the latent variables in model predicting Dismissiveness *(Figure 6.2)*

	Estimate
Trust	0.305
Dismissiveness	0.078

APPENDIX C: STATISTICS FOR CHAPTER 7 SEM ANALYSES

Table C.1 Indicators of fit for model predicting Resistance *(Figure 7.1)*

Chi-square (χ^2) = 13.723, df = 12, p = 0.319
Goodness-of-fit index (GFI) = 0.993
Adjusted goodness-of-fit index (AGFI) = 0.980
Root mean-square error of approximation (RMSEA) = 0.017

Table C.2 Squared multiple correlations for the latent variables in model predicting Resistance *(Figure 7.1)*

	Estimate
Winning	0.463
Legal cynicism	0.069
Aggressive adviser	0.191
Honest, no-risk adviser	0.164
Resistance	0.241

Table C.3 Indicators of fit for model predicting Dismissiveness *(Figure 7.2)*

Chi-square (χ^2) = 5.402, df = 9, p = 0.798
Goodness-of-fit index (GFI) = 0.997
Adjusted goodness-of-fit index (AGFI) = 0.990
Root mean-square error of approximation (RMSEA) = 0.000

Table C.4 Squared multiple correlations for the latent variables in model predicting Dismissiveness *(Figure 7.2)*

	Estimate
Legal cynicism	0.073
Winning	0.462
Aggressive adviser	0.195
Honest, no-risk adviser	0.181
Dismissiveness	0.527

APPENDIX D: STATISTICS FOR CHAPTER 8 SEM ANALYSES

Table D.1 Indicators of fit for model predicting Resistance *(Figure 8.1)*

Chi-square (χ^2) = 6.164, df = 5, p = 0.291
Goodness-of-fit index (GFI) = 0.997
Adjusted goodness-of-fit index (AGFI) = 0.981
Root mean-square error of approximation (RMSEA) = 0.021

Table D.2 Squared multiple correlations for the latent variables in the SEM model predicting Resistance *(Figure 8.1)*

	Estimate
Thinking morally	0.123
Feeling oppressed	0.306
Integrity	0.613
Honest, no-risk adviser	0.096
Resistance	0.576

Table D.3 Indicators of fit for model predicting Dismissiveness *(Figure 8.3)*

Chi-square (χ^2) = 12.220, df = 10, p = 0.271
Goodness-of-fit index (GFI) = 0.994
Adjusted goodness-of-fit index (AGFI) = 0.978
Root mean-square error of approximation (RMSEA) = 0.021

Table D.4 Squared multiple correlations for the latent variables in model predicting Dismissiveness *(Figure 8.3)*

	Estimate
Thinking morally	0.123
Feeling oppressed	0.412
Aggressive adviser	0.274
Honest, no-risk adviser	0.065
Dismissiveness	0.503

References

ABC Local Radio (31 May 2000), 'Unchain My Name to the GST Sales Melody: Cocker', http://www.abc.net.au/am/stories/s132891.htm.

ABC Radio National (8 November 2005), 'Abu Bakr Denied Terrorist Activity', reporter Nick McKenzie.

ABC Television (24 July 2005), '500 Targeted in Tax Evasion Crackdown', http://www.abc.net.au/insidebusiness/content/2005/s1421028.htm.

ABC Television (10 November 2005), 'Cleric Horrified by Terrorism Revelations', http://www.abc.net.au/lateline/content/2005/s1503116.htm.

Adler, P.S. and B. Borys (1996), 'Two types of bureaucracy: enabling and coercive', *Administrative Science Quarterly*, **41**(1), 61–89.

The Age (15 October 2002), 'Let's Not Allow Politicians to Undercut Democracy', reporter Greg Barns.

The Age (16 August 2005), 'Tax Office Puts the Heat on Contractors', reporter Stan Beer.

The Age (7 December 2005), 'Anti-Terror Laws Rammed through – Minus Debate', reporter Jewel Topsfield.

Ahmed, Eliza (2001), 'Shame management: regulating bullying', in Eliza Ahmed, Nathan Harris, John Braithwaite and Valerie Braithwaite (eds), *Shame Management through Reintegration*, Cambridge: Cambridge University Press, pp. 211–311.

Ahmed, Eliza (2005), 'Preliminary findings from the Graduates' Hopes, Visions and Actions (GHVA) Survey', Centre for Tax System Integrity Working Paper 66, Australian National University, http://ctsi/publications/WP/66.pdf.

Ahmed, E. and V. Braithwaite (2004), 'When tax collectors become collectors of child support and student loans: jeopardizing the revenue base', *Kyklos*, **57**(3), 303–26.

Ahmed, E. and V. Braithwaite (2005), 'A need for emotionally intelligent policy: linking tax evasion with higher education funding', *Legal and Criminological Psychology*, **10**(2), 1–19.

Ahmed, E. and V. Braithwaite (2007), 'Higher education loans and tax evasion: a response to perceived unfairness', *Law and Policy*, **29**(1), 121–36.

Ahmed, Eliza, Nathan Harris, John Braithwaite and Valerie Braithwaite

(2001), *Shame Management through Reintegration*, Cambridge: Cambridge University Press.

Ajzen, I. (1985), 'From intentions to actions: a theory of planned behavior', in J. Kuhl and J. Beckmann (eds), *Action Control: From Cognition to Behavior*, Heidelberg: Springer-Verlag, pp. 11–39.

Ajzen, Icek and Martin Fishbein (1980), *Understanding Attitudes and Predicting Social Behaviour*, Englewood Cliffs, NJ: Prentice Hall.

Akers, Ronald L. (1998), *Social Learning and Social Structure: A General Theory of Crime and Deviance*, Boston, MA: Northeastern University Press.

Allport, G.W. (1943), 'The ego in contemporary psychology', *Psychological Review*, **50**(5), 451–78.

Alm, J., I. Sanchez and A. deJuan (1995), 'Economic and noneconomic factors in tax compliance', *Kyklos*, **48**(1), 3–18.

Andreoni, J., B. Erard and J. Feinstein (1998), 'Tax compliance', *Journal of Economic Literature*, **XXXVI**, 818–60.

Antonovsky, A. (1972), 'Breakdown: a needed fourth step in the conceptual armamentarium of modern medicine', *Social Science and Medicine*, **6**(5), 537–44.

Antonovsky, A. (1990), 'A somewhat personal odyssey in studying the stress process', *Stress Medicine*, **6**(2), 71–80.

Arbuckle, James (2005), *Amos 6.0 User's Guide*, Chicago, IL: SPSS.

Arendt, Hannah (1964), *Eichmann in Jerusalem: A Report on the Banality of Evil*, New York: Viking Press.

Argyris, C. (1985), *Strategy, Change and Defensive Routines*, Boston: MA: Pitman Publishing.

Argyris, C. and D.A. Schön (1988), 'Reciprocal integrity: creating conditions that encourage personal and organizational integrity', in Suresh Srivastva (ed.), *Executive Integrity: The Search for High Human Values in Organizational Life*, San Francisco, CA: Jossey-Bass Publishers, pp. 197–222.

Article 19 (2006), *The Impact of UK Anti-Terror Laws on Freedom of Expression: Submission to ICJ Panel of Eminent Jurists on Terrorism, Counter-Terrorism and Human Rights*, London, http://www.article19.org.

Aryee, S., P.S. Budhwar and Z.X. Chen (2002), 'Trust as a mediator of the relationship between organizational justice and work outcomes: test of a social exchange model', *Journal of Organizational Behaviour*, **23**(3), 267–85.

Asian Economic News (3 July 2000), 'Australia Prepares for 10% Consumption Tax'.

Australian and New Zealand Banking Group (2004), 'ATO crackdown nets property tax cheats', *Home Essentials*, Issue 16, November/

December, http://www.anz.com/aus/promo/Homeessentials016/Eco1.asp, 12 January 2008.

Australian Financial Review (11 November 2005), 'Big Boots to Fill at Tax Office', Editorial.

Australian Taxation Office (2002a), *Compliance Program 2002–03*, Canberra: Australian Taxation Office.

Australian Taxation Office (2002b), *Taxation Statistics: A Summary of Taxation, Superannuation and Industry Benchmark Statistics 1999–2000 and 2000–01*, Canberra: Australian Taxation Office.

Australian Taxation Office (2002c), '87% of Mass Marketed Scheme Investors Accept Tax Office Settlement Offer', Canberra: Media Release 2002/55.

Australian Taxation Office (2003a), *Compliance Program 2003–04*, Canberra: Australian Taxation Office.

Australian Taxation Office (2003b), *Taxpayers' Charter – in Detail*, Canberra: Australian Taxation Office.

Australian Taxation Office (2003c), *Making It Easier to Comply*, Canberra: Australian Taxation Office.

Australian Taxation Office (2004a), *Making It Easier to Comply: The Easier, Cheaper and More Personalised Program*, Canberra: Australian Taxation Office.

Australian Taxation Office (2004b), *Compliance Program 2004–05*, Canberra: Australian Taxation Office.

Australian Taxation Office (2005), *Compliance Program 2005–06*, Canberra: Australian Taxation Office.

Australian Taxation Office (2007), *Taxpayers' Charter – What You Need to Know*, Canberra: Australian Taxation Office.

Avery Jones, J. (1996), 'Tax law: rules or principles', *Fiscal Studies*, **17**(3), 63–89.

Avi-Yonah, R.S. (2000), 'Globalization, tax competition, and the fiscal crisis of the welfare state', *Harvard Law Review*, **113**(7), 1575–676.

Ayres, Ian and John Braithwaite (1992), *Responsive Regulation: Transcending the Deregulation Debate*, New York: Oxford University Press.

Babbitt, Susan E. (1996), *Impossible Dreams: Rationality, Integrity and Moral Imagination*, Boulder, CO: Westview Press.

Bandura, Albert (1977), *Social Learning Theory*, Englewood Cliffs, NJ: Prentice-Hall.

Bandura, Albert (1986), *Social Foundations of Thought and Action: A Social Cognitive Theory*, Englewood Cliffs, NJ: Prentice-Hall.

Bandura, A. (1989), 'Human agency in social cognitive theory', *American Psychologist*, **44**(9), 1175–84.

Bandura, A. (1999), 'Moral disengagement in the preparation of inhumanities', *Personality and Social Psychology Review*, **3**(3), 193–209.

Bandura, A., C. Barbaranelli, G. Caprara and C. Pastorelli (1996), 'Mechanisms of moral disengagement in the exercise of moral agency', *Journal of Personality and Social Psychology*, **71**(2), 364–74.

Bardach, Eugene and Robert A. Kagan (1982), *Going by the Book: The Problem of Regulatory Unreasonableness*, Philadelphia, PA: Temple University Press.

Barling, J. and M. Phillips (1993), 'Interactional, formal, and distributive justice in the workplace: an exploratory study', *Journal of Psychology*, **127**(6), 649.

Barry, Paul (1993), *The Rise and Rise of Kerry Packer*, New York: Bantam.

BBC News (25 May 2007), 'Chinese Challenge One-Child Policy', reporter James Reynolds.

BBC News (1 November 2007), 'Does New Zealand Face a Terror Threat?', reporter Colin Peacock.

Beams, J., R. Brown and L. Killough (2003), 'An experiment testing the determinants of non-compliance with insider trading laws', *Journal of Business Ethics*, **45**(4), 309–23.

Beck, Ulrich (1999), *World Risk Society*, Cambridge: Polity Press.

Benjamin, M. (1990), *Splitting the Difference: Compromise and Integrity in Ethics and Politics*, Lawrence, KS: University Press of Kansas.

Benson, M.L. (1990), 'Emotions and adjudication: status degradation among white-collar criminals', *Justice Quarterly*, **7**(3), 515–28.

Bentham, Jeremy (1995 [1787]), *The Panopticon Writings*, London: Verso.

Bentley, D. (2003), 'Influence from the shadows: the OECD, the shape of domestic tax policy and lessons for federal systems', *Revenue Law Journal*, **13**(1), 128–46.

Bentley, Duncan (2007), *Taxpayers' Rights: Theory, Origin and Implementation*, Alphen aan den Rijn: Kluwer Law International.

Berman, E.M. (1997), 'Dealing with cynical citizens', *Public Administration Review*, **57**(2), 105–12.

Bernstein, Marver H. (1955), *Regulating Business by Independent Commission*, Princeton, NJ: Princeton University Press.

Bevir, M. (2006), 'Democratic governance: systems and radical perspectives', *Public Administration Review*, **66**(3), 426–36.

Bies, R.J. and J.F. Moag (1986), 'International justice communication criteria of fairness', in R.J. Lewicki, B.H. Sheppard and M.H. Bazerman (eds), *Research on Negotiations in Organizations*, Greenwich, CT: JAI Press, pp. 43–55.

Bikhchandani, S. and S. Sharma (2000), 'Herd behavior in financial markets – a review', IMF Working Papers 00/48, International Monetary Fund.
Black, Donald (1976), *The Behavior of Law*, New York: Academic Press.
Black, J. (1998), 'Talking about regulation', *Public Law,* Spring, 77–105.
Black, J. (2002), 'Regulatory conversations', *Journal of Law and Society*, **29**(1), 166–96.
Blamey, R. and V. Braithwaite (1997), 'The validity of the security–harmony social values model in the general population', *Australian Journal of Psychology*, **49**(2), 71–7.
Blodgett, J.G., D.J. Hill and S.S. Tax (1997), 'The effects of distributive, procedural, and interactional justice on postcomplaint behaviour', *Journal of Retailing*, **73**(2), 185–210.
Bloomfield, D., K. Collins, C. Fry and R. Munton (2001), 'Deliberation and inclusion: Vehicles for increasing trust in UK public governance?', *Environment and Planning C: Government and Policy*, **19**(4), 501–13.
Body, J. (2008), 'Design in the Australian Taxation Office', *Design Issues*, **24**(1), 55–67.
Bogardus, Emory S. (1928), *Immigration and Race Attitudes*, Boston, MA: D.C. Heath & Co.
Bourdieu, Pierre (1984), *Distinction: A Social Critique of the Judgement of Taste*, Cambridge, MA: Harvard University Press.
Bourdieu, Pierre (1986), 'The forms of social capital', in John G. Richardson (ed.), *Handbook of Theory and Research for the Sociology of Education*, New York: Greenwood Press, pp. 241–58.
Bourdieu, Pierre and Jean-Claude Passeron (1990), *Reproduction in Education, Society and Culture*, London: Sage.
Braithwaite, John (1985), *To Punish or Persuade: Enforcement of Coal Mine Safety*, Albany, NY: State University of New York Press.
Braithwaite, John (1989), *Crime, Shame and Reintegration*, Cambridge: Cambridge University Press.
Braithwaite, John (2002), *Restorative Justice and Responsive Regulation*, New York: Oxford University Press.
Braithwaite, John (2003), 'Through the eyes of the advisers: a fresh look at high wealth individuals', in Valerie Braithwaite (ed.), *Taxing Democracy: Understanding Tax Avoidance and Evasion*, Aldershot: Ashgate, pp. 245–70.
Braithwaite, John (2005), *Markets in Vice, Markets in Virtue*, Sydney: The Federation Press.
Braithwaite, John (2008), *Regulatory Capitalism: How It Works, Ideas for Making it Work Better*, Cheltenham, UK and Northampton, MA, USA: Edward Elgar.

Braithwaite, John and Peter Drahos (2000), *Global Business Regulation*, Cambridge: Cambridge University Press.

Braithwaite, J. and T. Makkai (1991), 'Testing an expected utility model of corporate deterrence', *Law and Society Review*, **25**(1), 7–39.

Braithwaite, J. and T. Makkai (1994), 'Trust and compliance', *Policing and Society*, **4**(1), 1–12.

Braithwaite, John and Philip Pettit (1990), *Not Just Deserts : A Republican Theory of Criminal Justice*, Oxford: Clarendon Press.

Braithwaite, John, Judith Healy and Kathryn Dwan (2005), *The Governance of Health Safety and Quality: A Discussion Paper*, Canberra: Commonwealth of Australia.

Braithwaite, John, Toni Makkai and Valerie Braithwaite (2007), *Regulating Aged Care: Ritualism and the New Pyramid*, Cheltenham, UK and Northampton, MA, USA: Edward Elgar.

Braithwaite, V. (1982), 'The structure of social values: validation of Rokeach's two-value model', *British Journal of Social Psychology*, **21**, 203–11.

Braithwaite, V. (1987), 'The development of a new measure of neuroticism based on the EASI-III temperament survey', *Psychological Medicine*, **17**, 217–25.

Braithwaite, Valerie (1992), *First Steps: Business Reactions to Implementing the Affirmative Action Act. A Report to the Affirmative Action Agency*, Canberra: Research School of the Social Sciences, Australian National University.

Braithwaite, V. (1993), 'The Australian government's affirmative action legislation: achieving social change through human resource management', *Law and Policy*, **15**(4), 327–54.

Braithwaite, V. (1994), 'Beyond Rokeach's equality–freedom model: two dimensional values in a one dimensional world', *Journal of Social Issues*, **50**(4), 67–94.

Braithwaite, V. (1995), 'Games of engagement: postures within the regulatory community', *Law and Policy*, **17**(3), 225–55.

Braithwaite, V. (1997), 'Harmony and security value orientations in political evaluation', *Personality and Social Psychology Bulletin*, **23**(4), 401–14.

Braithwaite, Valerie (1998a), 'Designing the process of workplace change through the Affirmative Action Act', in Moira Gatens and Alison Mackinnon (eds), *Gender and Institutions*, Cambridge: Cambridge University Press, pp. 107–28.

Braithwaite, V. (1998b), 'The value balance model of political evaluations', *British Journal of Psychology*, **89**(2), 223–47.

Braithwaite, V. (1998c), 'The value orientations underlying liberalism–conservatism', *Personality and Individual Differences*, **25**(3), 575–89.

Braithwaite, Valerie (1998d), 'Communal and exchange trust norms: their value base and relevance to institutional trust', in Valerie Braithwaite and Margaret Levi (eds), *Trust and Governance*, New York: Russell Sage Foundation, pp. 46–74.

Braithwaite, Valerie (2001), 'The Community Hopes, Fears and Actions Survey: goals and measures', Centre for Tax System Integrity Working Paper 2, Australian National University, http://ctsi/publications/WP/2.pdf.

Braithwaite, Valerie (2003a), 'Dancing with tax authorities: motivational postures and non-compliant actions', in Valerie Braithwaite (ed.), *Taxing Democracy: Understanding Tax Avoidance and Evasion*, Aldershot, UK: Ashgate, pp. 15–40.

Braithwaite, Valerie (2003b), 'Tax system integrity and compliance: the democratic management of the tax system', in Valerie Braithwaite (ed.), *Taxing Democracy: Understanding Tax Avoidance and Evasion*, Aldershot: Ashgate, pp. 271–90.

Braithwaite, V. (2003c), 'Perceptions of who's not paying their fair share', *Australian Journal of Social Issues*, **38**(3), 335–62.

Braithwaite, V. (2007), 'Responsive regulation and taxation: introduction', *Law and Policy*, **29**(1), 3–10.

Braithwaite, V. and R. Blamey (1998), 'Consensus, stability and meaning in abstract social values', *Australian Journal of Political Science*, **33**(3), 373–90.

Braithwaite, V. and J. Braithwaite (2006), 'Democratic sentiment and cyclical markets in vice', *British Journal of Criminology*, **46**, 1110–27.

Braithwaite, V. and H.G. Law (1985), 'The structure of human values: testing the adequacy of the Rokeach value survey', *Journal of Personality and Social Psychology*, **49**(1), 250–63.

Braithwaite, Valerie and Monika Reinhart (2005a), 'Preliminary findings and codebook for the Australian Tax System – Fair or Not Survey', Centre for Tax System Integrity Working Paper 79, Australian National University, http://ctsi.anu.edu.au/publications/WP/WPlist.html.

Braithwaite, Valerie and Monika Reinhart (2005b), 'Preliminary findings and codebook for the How Fair, How Effective Survey: The Collection and Use of Taxation in Australia', Centre for Tax System Integrity Working Paper 84, Australian National University, http://ctsi.anu.edu.au/publications/WP/WPlist.html.

Braithwaite, Valerie and Michael Wenzel (2008), 'Integrating explanations of tax evasion and avoidance', in Alan Lewis (ed.), *Psychology and Economic Behaviour*, Cambridge: Cambridge University Press, pp. 304–31.

Braithwaite, V., J. Braithwaite, D. Gibson and T. Makkai (1994),

'Regulatory styles, motivational postures and nursing home compliance', *Law and Policy*, **16**(4), 363–94.
Braithwaite, Valerie, Monika Reinhart, Malcolm Mearns and Rochelle Graham (2001), 'Preliminary findings from the Community Hopes, Fears, and Actions Survey', Centre for Tax System Integrity Working Paper No 3, Australian National University, http://ctsi/publications/WP/3.pdf.
Braithwaite, Valerie, Eliza Ahmed, Brenda Morrison and Monika Reinhart (2003), 'Researching prospects for restorative justice practice in schools: The Life at School Survey 1996–1999', in Lode Walgrove (ed.), *Repositioning Restorative Justice: Restorative Justice, Criminal Justice and Social Context*, Cullompton, UK: Willan Publishing, pp. 165–85.
Braithwaite, Valerie, Tony Hodges and Beth Lyons (2006), *Trust, Hope and Democracy Project, Progress Report No. 1*, Australian National University, http://demgov/publications/reports/ProgressReportNo1Dec2006VersionForWeb01.5.07.pdf.
Braithwaite, V., K. Murphy and M. Reinhart (2007), 'Taxation threat, motivational postures, and responsive regulation', *Law and Policy*, **29**(1), 137–58.
Brand, P. (1996), 'Compliance: a 21st century approach', *National Tax Journal*, **49**(3), 413–19.
Brehm, Sharon S. and Jack W. Brehm (1981), *Psychological Reactance: A Theory of Freedom and Control*, New York: Academic Press.
Brooks, Neil (1998), 'The challenge of tax compliance: globalization, information technology and mobility', in Chris Evans and Abe Greenbaum (eds), *Tax Administration: Facing the Challenge of the Future*, St Leonards, NSW: Prospect Media Pty Ltd, pp. 7–33.
Burgess, R.L. and R.L. Akers (1966), 'A differential association-reinforcement theory of criminal behavior', *Social Problems*, **14**(2), 128–47.
Burgess, R. and N. Stern (1993), 'Taxation and development', *Journal of Economic Literature*, **31**(2), 762–830.
Burton, Mark (2007), 'Chaos, rhetoric and the legitimation of "democratic" government – a critical review of Australia's tax legislative process', paper presented at the RegNet Seminar Series, Regulatory Institutions Network, Australian National University, 10 April.
Byrne, Barbara M. (2001), *Structural Equation Modelling with Amos: Basic Concepts, Applications, and Programming*, Mahwah, NJ: Lawrence Erlbaum.
Calhoun, C. (1995), 'Standing for something', *The Journal of Philosophy*, **92**(5), 235–60.
Canada Revenue Agency (2003a), *Our Fairness Edge*, http://www.cra-arc.gc.ca/agency/fairness/pledge-e.html.

Canada Revenue Agency (2003b), *Fairness and Client Rights: An Overview*, http://www.cra-arc.gc.ca/agency/fairness/menu-e.html.

Cartwright, Sophie (2009), *Policy, Obligation and Justice in Australia's Tobacco Growing Industry*, PhD Thesis, Regulatory Institutions Network, Canberra: Australian National University (forthcoming).

Carver, Charles S. and Michael F. Scheier (1998), *On the Self-Regulation of Behavior*, Cambridge: Cambridge University Press.

Carver, C.S., M.F. Scheier and J.K. Weintraub (1989), 'Assessing coping strategies: a theoretically based approach', *Journal of Personality and Social Psychology*, **56**(2), 267–83.

Cash Economy Task Force (1998), *Improving Tax Compliance in the Cash Economy*, Canberra: Australian Taxation Office.

Centre for Tax Policy and Administration (2001), *Principles for Good Tax Administration, Practice Note GAP001*, OECD Tax Guidance Series, Paris: Organisation for Economic Co-operation and Development, http://www.oecd.org/dataoecd/34/39/1907918.pdf.

Centre for Tax Policy and Administration (2003), *Taxpayers' Rights and Obligations*, *Practice Note GAP002*, OECD Tax Guidance Series, Paris: Organisation for Economic Cooperation and Development, http://www.oecd.org/dataoecd/24/52/17851176.pdf.

Centre for Tax Policy and Administration (2006), *Fundamental Reform of Personal Income Tax*, OECD Tax Policy Studies No. 13, Paris: Organisation for Economic Co-operation and Development, http://titania.sourceoecd.org.

China Daily (14 February 2006), 'China: Drug Bid to Beat Child Ban'.

Chong, A. (2006), 'Anti-terror laws and the Muslim community: where does terror end and security begin?', *Borderlands*, **5**(1).

Clegg, Stuart (1975), *Power, Rule and Domination: A Critical and Empirical Understanding of Power in Sociological Theory and Organizational Life*, New York: Routledge.

www.cnn.com (16 September 2001), 'Bush Vows to Rid the World of "Evil-Doers"', reporter Manuel Perez-Rivas.

Cohen, Albert K. (1955), *Delinquent Boys: The Culture of the Gang*, Glencoe, IL: Free Press.

Cohen, A.K. (1965), 'The sociology of the deviant act: anomie theory and beyond', *American Sociological Review*, **30**(1), 5–14.

Cohen, Albert K. (1966), *Deviance and Control*, Englewood Cliffs, NJ: Prentice-Hall.

Cohen, D. and R.E. Nisbett (1997), 'Field experiments examining the culture of honour: the role of institutions in perpetuating norms about violence', *Personality and Social Psychology Bulletin*, **23**(11), 1188–99.

Cohen, Stanley (2001), *States of Denial: Knowing About Atrocities and Suffering*, Cambridge: Polity.

Cohen-Charash, Y. and P.E. Spector (2001), 'The role of justice in organizations: a meta-analysis', *Organizational Behaviour and Human Decision Processes*, **86**(2), 278–321.

Coleman, C. and L. Freeman (1997), 'Cultural foundations of taxpayer attitudes to voluntary compliance', *Australian Tax Forum*, **13**(3), 311–36.

Coleman, J. (1987), 'Toward an integrated theory of white-collar crime', *American Journal of Sociology*, **93**(2), 406–39.

The Commission on Taxation and Citizenship (2000), *Paying for Progress: A New Politics of Tax for Public Spending*, London: The Fabian Society.

Commissioner of Taxation (2001), *Annual Report 2000–01*, Canberra: Australian Taxation Office.

Commissioner of Taxation (2002), 'Listening to the community: easier, cheaper, more personalised', paper presented at the Address to the American Chamber of Commerce, 14 March.

Commissioner of Taxation (2003), *Annual Report 2002–2003*, Canberra: Australian Taxation Office.

Commissioner of Taxation (2006), 'The Australian approach to GST', paper presented at the Twenty Years of GST: The Best Path Forward, Wellington, New Zealand, 16–18 November.

Commissioner of Taxation (2007), 'Compliance program 2007–08: meeting the challenges of a changing environment', speech presented in Sydney, 16 August 2007, http://www.ato.gov.au.

Committee of Fiscal Affairs (1990), *Taxpayer Rights and Obligations – A Survey of the Legal Situation in OECD Countries*, Paris: Organisation for Economic Cooperation and Development.

Comstock, Amy (2001), 'Maintaining government integrity: the perspective of the U.S. Office of Government Ethics', paper presented at the Global Forum II Law Enforcement Workshop, The Hague, Netherlands, 29 May.

Conference Board of Canada (1998), *At the Heart of Fairness: Achieving Revenue Canada's Commitment to Fairness through Service*, Canada: The Conference Board of Canada.

Cooley, Charles H. (1902), *Human Nature and the Social Order*, New York: Scribner's.

Cressey, Donald R. (1953), *Other People's Money: A Study in the Social Psychology of Embezzlement*, Glencoe, IL: The Free Press.

Crockenberg, S. and C. Litman (1990), 'Autonomy as competence in 2-year-olds: maternal correlates of child defiance, compliance, and self-assertion', *Developmental Psychology*, **26**(6), 961–71.

Cropanzano, R., C.A. Prehar and P.Y. Chen (2002), 'Using social exchange theory to distinguish procedural from interactional justice', *Group and Organizational Management*, **27**(3), 324–51.

Cross, S. and H. Markus (1991), 'Possible selves across the life span', *Human Development*, **34**(4), 230–55.

Crush, J. (1985), 'Colonial coercion and the Swazi tax revolt of 1903–1907', *Political Geography Quarterly*, **4**(3), 179–90.

Culbert, S.A. and J.J. McDonough (1988), 'Organizational alignments, schisms, and high-integrity managerial behavior', in Suresh Srivastva (ed.), *Executive Integrity: The Search for High Human Values in Organizational Life*, San Francisco, CA: Jossey-Bass Publishers, pp. 223–42.

Cullis, J.G. and A. Lewis (1997), 'Why people pay taxes: from a conventional economic model to a model of social convention', *Journal of Economic Psychology*, **18**(2/3), 305–21.

Cummings, L.L. and P. Bromiley (1996), 'The Organizational Trust Inventory (OTI): development and validation', in R.M. Kramer and T.R. Tyler (eds), *Trust in Organizations: Frontiers of Theory and Research*, Thousand Oaks, CA: Sage, pp. 302–30.

Dahl, Robert A. (1990), *Democracy and Its Critics*, New Haven, CT: Yale University Press.

Davion, V. (1991), 'Integrity and radical change', in Claudia Card (ed.), *Feminist Ethics*, Lawrence, KS: University of Kansas Press, pp. 180–92.

Day, Carla L. (2006), *The Role of Values in Employee Decision Making in the Australian Department of Defence,* PhD thesis, Regulatory Institutions Network, Canberra: Australian National University.

Dean, P., T. Keenan and F. Kenney (1980), 'Taxpayers' attitudes to income tax evasion: an empirical study', *British Tax Review*, **28**, 28–44.

Deutsch, Morton (1973), *The Resolution of Conflict*, New Haven, CT: Yale University Press.

DiMaggio, P.J. and W.W. Powell (1983), 'The iron cage revisited: institutional isomorphism and collective rationality in organizational fields', *American Sociological Review*, **48**(2), 147–60.

Douglas, Mary (1986), *How Institutions Think*, Syracuse, NY: Syracuse University Press.

Dryzek, J.S. (1983), 'Don't toss coins in garbage cans: a prologue to policy design', *Journal of Public Policy*, **3**(4), 345–68.

Dryzek, John S. (1990), *Discursive Democracy: Politics, Policy, and Political Science*, Cambridge: Cambridge University Press.

Dryzek, J. (1994), 'Australian discourses of democracy', *Australian Journal of Political Science*, **29**(2), 221–39.

Dryzek, J.S. and J. Berejikian (1993), 'Reconstructive democratic theory', *American Political Science Review*, **87**(1), 48–60.

Dryzek, J.S. and V.A. Braithwaite (2000), 'On the prospects for democratic deliberation: values analysis applied to Australian politics', *Political Psychology*, **21**(2), 241–66.

Durkheim, Emile (1952), *Suicide: A Study in Sociology*, London: Routledge & Kegan Paul.

Edelman, L.B., S. Petterson, E. Chambliss and H.S. Erlanger (1991), 'Legal ambiguity and the politics of compliance: affirmative action officer's dilemma', *Law and Policy*, **13**(1), 73–97.

Eisenstein, Hester (1996), *Inside Agitators: Australian Femocrats and the State*, Philadelphia, PA: Temple University Press.

Elias, Norbert (1978), *The History of Manners: The Civilizing Process: Volume I*, New York: Pantheon Books.

English, H.B. and A.C. English (1958), *A Comprehensive Dictionary of Psychological and Psychoanalytical Terms*, London: Longmans.

Epstein, S. (1973), 'The self-concept revisited: or a theory of a theory', *American Psychologist*, **28**(5), 404–16.

Erard, B. (1993), 'Taxation with representation: an analysis of the role of tax practitioners in tax compliance', *Journal of Public Economics*, **52**(2), 163–97.

Evans, C. (2005), 'Avoiding the issue: countering the termites in the Australian tax system', *Australian Review of Public Affairs*, 12 September, http://www.australianreview.net/digest/2005/09/evans.html.

Feld, Lars P. and Bruno S. Frey (2005), *Tax Compliance as the Result of a Psychological Contract: The Role of Incentives and Responsive Regulation*, Centre for Tax System Integrity Working Paper 76, Canberra: Australian National University.

Feld, L.P. and B.S. Frey (2007), 'Tax compliance as the result of a psychological tax contract: the role of incentives and responsive regulation', *Law and Policy*, **29**(1), 102–20.

Fishbein, Martin and Icek Ajzen (1975), *Belief, Attitude, Intention, and Behavior*, Reading, MA: Addison-Wesley.

Forsyth, N.H.M. (1981), 'Tax avoidance and the responsibility of the professional legal adviser', *The Australian Law Journal*, **55**(8), 582–9.

Foucault, Michel (1977), *Discipline and Punish: The Birth of the Prison*, London: Allen Lane.

Frederickson, George, H. and Richard K. Ghere (2005), *Ethics in Public Management*, Armonk, NY: M.E. Sharpe.

Freedman, J. (2004), 'Defining taxpayer responsibility: in support of a general anti-avoidance principle', *British Tax Review*, **2004**(4), 332–57.

Freeman, J. (2002), 'Tax, crime and human rights', *British Tax Review*, **2002**(6), 445.

Freiberg, A. (1988), 'Ripples from the bottom of the harbour: some social ramifications of taxation fraud', *Criminal Law Journal*, **12**, 136–92.

Freiberg, A. (1990), 'Reconceptualizing tax sanctions', *Australian Tax Forum*, **7**(1), 1–24.

Frey, Bruno S. (1997), *Not Just for the Money: An Economic Theory of Personal Motivation*, Cheltenham, UK and Lyme, USA: Edward Elgar.

Frey, Bruno S. (2003), 'The role of deterrence and tax morale in taxation in the European Union', paper presented at the Jelle Zijlstra Lecture, Netherlands Institute for Advanced Study in the Humanities and Social Sciences (NIAS), 29 November 2002, http://www.nias.knaw.nl/en/new_3/new_1/new_12.

Frey, Bruno S. and Lars P. Feld (2001), 'The tax authority and the taxpayer: an exploratory analysis', paper presented at the Second International Conference on Taxation, Centre for Tax System Integrity, Australian National University, Canberra, 10–11 December.

Fromm, Erich (1947), *Man for Himself: An Inquiry into the Psychology of Ethics*, New York: Rinehart & Co.

Fromm, Erich (2005), *The Art of Listening*, New York: Continuum International Publishing Group.

Fung, A. (2004), 'Deliberation's darker side: six questions for Iris Marion Young and Jane Mansbridge', *National Civic Review*, **93**(4), 47–54.

Galanter, M. (1974), 'Why the "haves" come out ahead: speculations on the limits of legal change', *Law and Society Review*, **9**(1), 95–160.

Gamson, William A. (1968), *Power and Discontent*, Homewood, IL.: The Dorsey Press.

Geertz, Clifford (1973), *The Interpretation of Cultures*, New York: Basic Books.

Geis, Gilbert (1967), 'The heavy electrical equipment antitrust cases of 1961', in Marshall B. Clinard and Richard Quinney (eds), *Criminal Behavior Systems: A Typology*, New York: Holt, Rinehart & Winston, pp. 139–50.

Geis, Gilbert and Ivan Bunn (1997), *A Trial of Witches: A Seventeenth-Century Witchcraft Prosecution*, New York: Routledge.

Gibson, J.L. (1991), 'Institutional legitimacy, procedural justice, and compliance with supreme court decisions: a question of causality', *Law and Society Review*, **25**(3), 631–6.

Giddens, Anthony (1984), *The Constitution of Society*, Cambridge: Polity Press.

Giddens, Anthony (1998), 'Risk society: the context of British politics', in Jane Franklin (ed.), *The Politics of Risk Society*, Cambridge: Polity Press, pp. 23–34.

Gladwell, Malcolm (2000), *The Tipping Point*, Boston, MA: Little Brown.

Glaser, Daniel (1978), *Crime in Our Changing Society*, New York: Holt, Rinehart, & Winston.
Gobert, James and Maurice Punch (2007), 'Because they can: motivations and intent of white-collar criminals', in Henry N. Pontell and Gilbert Geis (eds), *International Handbook of White-Collar and Corporate Crime*, New York: Springer, pp. 98–122.
Goffman, E. (1956), 'Embarrassment and social organization', *The American Journal of Sociology*, **62**(3), 264–71.
Goffman, Erving (1963), *Stigma: Notes on the Management of Spoiled Identity*, Englewwood Cliffs, NJ: Prentice-Hall.
Goffman, Erving (1969), *Where the Action Is: Three Essays*, London: Allen Lane.
Goffman, E. (1983), 'The interaction order: American Sociological Association, 1982 Presidential Address', *American Sociological Review*, **48**(1), 1–17.
Goleman, Daniel (1995), *Emotional Intelligence*, New York: Bantam Books.
Goodin, Robert E. (1996), 'Institutions and their design', in Robert E. Goodin (ed.), *The Theory of Institutional Design*, Cambridge: Cambridge University Press, pp. 1–53.
Gordon, Ray D. (2007), *Power, Knowledge and Domination*, Frederiksberg, Denmark: Copenhagen Business School Press.
Gorsuch, R.L. and J. Ortberg (1983), 'Moral obligation and attitudes: their relation to behavioral intentions', *Journal of Personality and Social Psychology*, **44**(5), 1025–28.
Gottfredson, Michael and Travis Hirschi (1990), *A General Theory of Crime*, Stanford: Stanford University Press.
Grabosky, P. (1995a), 'Counterproductive regulation', *International Journal of the Sociology of Law*, **23**(4), 347–69.
Grabosky, P.N. (1995b), 'Using non-governmental resources to foster regulatory compliance', *Governance*, **8**(4), 527–50.
Grabosky, P.N. (1997), 'Inside the pyramid: towards a conceptual framework for the analysis of regulatory systems', *International Journal of the Sociology of Law*, **25**(3), 195–201.
Grabosky, Peter (2007), *Electronic Crime*, Upper Saddle River, NJ: Pearson-Prentice Hall.
Grabosky, Peter and John Braithwaite (1986), *Of Manners Gentle: Enforcement Strategies of Australian Business Regulatory Agencies*, Melbourne, Australia: Oxford University Press.
Gramsci, Antonio (1973), *Letters from Prison*, New York: Harper and Row.
Grasmick, H.G. and R.J. Bursik Jr (1990), 'Conscience, significant others, and rational choice: extending the deterrence model', *Law and Society Review*, **24**(3), 837–61.

Grasmick, H.G. and W.J. Scott (1982), 'Tax evasion and mechanisms of social control: a comparison with grand and petty theft', *Journal of Economic Psychology*, **2**(3), 213–30.

Grbich, Y. (1976), 'Posing critical questions about tax avoidance', *University of New South Wales Law Journal*, **1**(3/4), 211–40.

Greenbaum, Abe (1998), 'United States Taxpayer Bill of Rights 1, 2 and 3: A Path to the Future or Old Whine in New Bottles', in Duncan Bentley (ed.), *Taxpayers' Rights: An International Perspective*, Bond University: Revenue Law Journal, pp. 347–79.

Greenwald, A.G. (1980), 'The totalitarian ego: fabrication and revision of personal history', *American Psychologist*, **35**(7), 603–18.

The Guardian (31 October 2007), 'I Should Pay More Tax, Says US Billionaire Warren Buffett', reporter Andrew Clark.

Gump, B.B. and J.A. Kulik (1997), 'Stress, affiliation, and emotional contagion', *Journal of Personality and Social Psychology*, **75**(2), 305–19.

Gunningham, Neil (1993), 'Thinking about regulatory mix: regulating occupational health and safety, futures markets and environmental law', in Peter Grabosky and John Braithwaite (eds), *Business Regulation and Australia's Future*, Canberra, Australia: Australian Institute of Criminology, pp. 133–49.

Gunningham, Neil (2007), *Mine Safety: Law, Regulation and Policy*, Sydney: Federation Press.

Gunningham, Neil and Peter Grabosky (1998), *Smart Regulation: Designing Environmental Policy*, New York: Oxford University Press.

Gunningham, Neil and Darren Sinclair (2002), *Leaders and Laggards: Next Generation Environmental Regulation*, Sheffield: Greenleaf Publishing.

Gunningham, Neil, Robert A. Kagan and Dorothy Thornton (2003), *Shades of Green: Business, Regulation, and Environment*, Stanford, CA: Stanford University Press.

Habermas, Jürgen (1987), *The Theory of Communicative Action II: Lifeworld and System*, Boston, MA: Beacon.

Habermas, Jürgen (1996), *Between Facts and Norms: Contributions to a Discourse Theory of Law and Democracy*, Cambridge: Polity Press.

Hagan, J. (1997), 'Defiance and despair: subcultural and structural linkages between delinquency and despair in the life course', *Social Forces*, **76**(1), 119–34.

Hagan, J., G. Hefler, G. Classen, K. Boehnke and H. Merkens (1998), 'Subterranean sources of subcultural delinquency beyond the American dream', *Criminology*, **36**(2), 309–42.

Halfon, Mark S. (1989), *Integrity: A Philosophical Inquiry*, Philadelphia, PA: Temple University Press.

Hamilton, Clive (2007), *Scorcher: The Dirty Politics of Climate Change*, Melbourne: Black Inc.

Hamilton, S. (2003), 'Putting the client first: the emerging Copernican revolution of tax administration', *Tax Notes International*, **29**(6), 569–76.

Harris, Nathan (2001), 'Shaming and shame: regulating drink driving', in Eliza Ahmed, Nathan Harris, John Braithwaite and Valerie Braithwaite (eds), *Shame Management through Reintegration*, Cambridge: Cambridge University Press, pp. 73–207.

Harris, N. (2007), 'Shame, ethical identity and conformity: lessons from research on the psychology of social influence', Regulatory Institutions Network Occasional Paper 12, Australian National University, http://ctsi.anu.edu.au/publications/OccPaper12.pdf.

Harris, N. and J. McCrae (2005), 'Perceptions of tax and participation in the cash economy: examining the role of motivational postures in small businesses', Regulatory Institutions Network Working Paper 80, Australian National University, http://ctsi.anu.edu.au/publications/WP/WPlist.html.

Harrison, R. (1988), 'Quality of service: a new frontier for integrity in organizations', in Suresh Srivastva (ed.), *Executive Integrity: The Search for High Human Values in Organizational Life*, San Franscisco, CA: Jossey-Bass Publishers, pp. 45–67.

Hasseldine, J. and Z. Li (1999), 'More tax evasion research required in new millennium', *Crime, Law and Social Change*, **31**(2), 91–104.

Hawkins, Keith (1984), *Environment and Enforcement: Regulation and the Social Definition of Pollution*, Oxford: Clarendon Press.

Hawkins, Keith (2002), *Law as Last Resort: Prosecution Decision-Making in a Regulatory Agency*, Oxford: Oxford University Press.

Heimer, Carol A. (1998), 'The routinization of responsiveness: regulatory compliance and the construction of organizational routines', paper presented at the Law and Society Annual Meeting, Aspen, Colorado, 4–7 June.

Heimer, C.A. (2008), 'Thinking about how to avoid thought: deep norms, shallow rules, and the structure of attention', *Regulation and Governance*, **2**(1), 30–47.

Hessing, D.J., H. Elffers, H.S.J. Robben and P. Webley (1992), 'Does deterrence deter? Measuring the effect of deterrence on tax compliance in field studies and experimental studies', in Joel Slemrod (ed.), *Why People Pay Taxes: Tax Compliance and Enforcement*, Ann Arbor, MI: University of Michigan Press, pp. 291–305.

Hite, P. (1997), 'Identifying and mitigating taxpayer non-compliance', *Australian Tax Forum*, **13**(2), 155–76.

Hite, P.A. and G.A. McGill (1992), 'An examination of taxpayer preference for aggressive tax advice', *National Tax Journal*, **45**(4), 389–403.

Hite, Peggy A., John Hasseldine, Abeer Al-Khoury, Simon James, Steve Toms and Marika Toumi (2003), 'Tax practitioners and tax compliance', in Andrew Lymer and David Salter (eds), *Contemporary Issues in Taxation Research*, Aldershot: Ashgate, pp. 17–44.

Hobbes, Thomas (1968 [1651]), *Leviathan*, Aylesbury, UK: Penguin.

Hobson, K. (2002), '"Say no to the ATO": the cultural politics of protest against the Australian Taxation Office', Centre for Tax System Integrity Working Paper No. 37, Australian National University, http://ctsi/publications/WP/37.pdf.

Hobson, Kersty (2003), 'Championing the compliance model: from common sense to common action?', in Valerie Braithwaite (ed.), *Taxing Democracy: Understanding Tax Avoidance and Evasion*, Aldershot, UK: Ashgate, pp. 131–58.

Hoffman, Martin (2000), *Empathy and Moral Development: Implications for Caring and Justice*, New York: Cambridge University Press.

Hogg, Michael A. and Dominic Abrams (1988), *Social Identifications: A Social Psychology of Intergroup Relations and Group Processes*, London: Routledge.

Hood, C. (1991), 'A public management for all seasons', *Public Administration Review*, **69**(1), 3–19.

Hood, Christopher, Colin Scott, Oliver James, George Jones and Tony Travers (1999), *Regulation inside Government: Waste-Watchers, Quality Police, and Sleaze-Busters*, Oxford: Oxford University Press.

Hornsey, M.J., L. Majkut, D.J. Terry and B.M. McKimmie (2003), 'On being loud and proud: non-conformity and counter-conformity to group norms', *The British Journal of Social Psychology,* **42**, 319–35.

Hutter, Bridget (1997), *Compliance: Regulation and Environment*, Oxford: Clarendon Press.

Inglehart, Ronald (1977), *The Silent Revolution: Changing Values and Political Styles among Western Publics*, Princeton, NJ: Princeton University Press.

Inglehart, Ronald (1990), *Culture Shift in Advanced Industrial Society*, Princeton, NJ: Princeton University Press.

Inglehart, Ronald (1997), *Modernization and Postmodernization: Cultural, Economic, and Political Change in 43 Societies*, Princeton, NJ: Princeton University Press.

Inglehart, Ronald and Christian Welzel (2005), *Modernization, Cultural Change, and Democracy: The Human Development Sequence*, Cambridge: Cambridge University Press.

IRS Customer Service Task Force (1997), *Report on the IRS: Reinvention, Recourse, Rights, Reform*, Washington, DC: IRS Customer Service Task Force.

Irvin, R.A. and J. Stansbury (2004), 'Citizen participation in decision making: is it worth the effort?' *Public Administration Review*, **64**(1), 55–65.

Jackson, B.R. and V.C. Milliron (1986), 'Tax compliance research: findings, problems, and prospects', *Journal of Accounting Literature*, **5**, 125–65.

James, S. and C. Alley (1999), 'Tax compliance, self-assessment, and tax administration in New Zealand – is the carrot or the stick more appropriate to encourage compliance?', *New Zealand Journal of Taxation Law and Policy*, **5**(1), 3–14.

James, S., K. Murphy and M. Reinhart (2004), 'The Taxpayers' Charter: a case study in tax administration', *Journal of Australian Taxation*, **7**(2), 336–56.

James, William (1915), *Psychology: The Briefer Course*, New York: Holt.

Joannou, Maroula and June Purvis (1998), *The Women's Suffragette Movement: New Feminist Perspectives*, Manchester and New York: Manchester University Press.

Job, J. (2002), 'Preliminary findings from the "Community Participation and Citizenship" survey about trust and social capital', Centre for Tax System Integrity, Australian National University, http://ctsi.anu.edu.au/research/trustcodebook.pdf.

Job, J. (2005), 'How is trust in government created?: it begins at home, but ends in the parliament', *Australian Review of Public Affairs*, **6**(1), 1–23.

Job, Jenny and David Honaker (2003), 'Short-term experience with responsive regulation in the Australian Tax Office', in Valerie Braithwaite (ed.), *Taxing Democracy: Understanding Tax Avoidance and Evasion*, Aldershot, UK: Ashgate, pp. 111–30.

Job, J. and M. Reinhart (2003), 'Trusting the tax office', *Australian Journal of Social Issues*, **38**(3), 307–34.

Job, J., A. Stout and R. Smith (2007), 'Culture change in three taxation administrations: from command-and-control to responsive regulation', *Law and Policy*, **29**(1), 84–101.

Johnston, Les and Clifford Shearing (2003), *Governing Security: Explorations in Policing and Justice*, London: Routledge.

Joint Committee of Public Accounts (1993), *An Assessment of Tax: A Report on an Enquiry into the Australian Taxation Office*, Canberra: Australian Government Publishing Service.

Jost, J.T. and O. Hunyady (2002), 'The psychology of system justification and the palliative function of ideology', *European Review of Social Psychology*, **13**, 111–53.

Judd, Charles Hubbard (1926), *The Psychology of Social Institutions*, New York: The Macmillan Company.

Kagan, Robert A. (1978), *Regulatory Justice: Implementing a Wage Freeze Policy*, New York: Russell Sage Foundation.

Kagan, R.A. (1989), 'Editor's introduction: understanding regulatory enforcement', *Law and Policy*, **11**(2), 89–120.

Kagan, Robert A. and John T. Scholz (1984), 'The "criminology of the corporation" and regulatory enforcement strategies', in Keith Hawkins and John M. Thomas (eds), *Enforcing Regulation*, The Hague: Kluwer–Nijhoff Publishing, pp. 67–95.

Kalb, L.M. and R. Loeber (2003), 'Child disobedience and noncompliance: a review', *Pediatrics*, **111**(3), 641–52.

Karlinsky, Stewart and Joseph Bankman (2002), 'Developing a theory of cash businesses tax evasion behavior and the role of their cash preparers', paper presented at the Fifth International Conference on Tax Administration, Australian Taxation Studies Program (ATAX), University of New South Wales, 4–5 April.

Karstedt, S. (2006), 'Democracy, values, and violence: paradoxes, tensions, and comparative advantages of liberal inclusion', *Annals of the American Academy of Political and Social Science*, **605**, 50–81.

Karstedt, S. and G. LaFree (2006), 'Democracy, crime and justice', *Annals of the American Academy of Political and Social Science*, **605**, 6–23.

Kelman, H.C. (1958), 'Compliance, identification, and internalization: three processes of attitude change', *Journal of Conflict Resolution*, **2**(1), 51–60.

Kelman, H.C. (1961), 'Processes of opinion change', *Public Opinion Quarterly*, **25**(1), 57–78.

Kelman, Herbert C. and V. Lee Hamilton (1989), *Crimes of Obedience*, New Haven, CT: Yale University Press.

Kettl, D.F. (2000), 'The transformation of governance: globalization, devolution, and the role of government', *Public Administration Review*, **60**(6), 488–97.

King, Roger (2007), *The Regulatory State in an Age of Governance: Soft Words and Big Sticks*, Basingstoke, New York: Palgrave Macmillan.

Kinsey, K.A. and H.G. Grasmick (1993), 'Did the tax reform act of 1986 improve compliance? Three studies of pre- and post-TRA compliance attitudes', *Law and Policy*, **15**(4), 293–325.

Kirchler, E. (1999), 'Reactance to taxation: employers' attitudes towards taxes', *Journal of Socio-Economics*, **28**(2), 131–8.

Kirchler, Erich (2007), *The Economic Psychology of Tax Behaviour*, Cambridge: Cambridge University Press.

Klein, Naomi (2000), *No Logo*, London: Flamingo.

Klepper, S. and D. Nagin (1989), 'The role of tax preparers in tax compliance', *Policy Sciences*, **22**(2), 167–94.

Klepper, S., M. Mazur and D. Nagin (1991), 'Expert intermediaries and legal compliance: the case of tax preparers', *Journal of Law and Economics*, **34**(1), 205–29.

Knight, J. and J. Johnson (1994), 'Aggregation and deliberation: on the possibility of democratic legitimacy', *Political Theory*, **22**(2), 277–96.

Kornberg, A. and H.A. Clarke (1994), 'Beliefs about democracy and satisfaction with democratic government: the Canadian case', *Political Research Quarterly*, **47**(3), 537–63.

La Piere, R. (1934), 'Attitudes vs actions', *Social Forces*, **13**(2), 230–37.

LaFree, Gary (1998), *Losing Legitimacy: Street Crime and the Decline of Social Institutions in America*, Boulder, CO: Westview Press.

Lareau, A. (2002), 'Invisible inequality: social class and child rearing in black families and white families', *American Sociological Review*, **67**(5), 747–76.

Larsen, Arthur J. (1934), *Crusader and Feminist: Letters of Jane Grey Swisshelm 1858–1865*, St Paul, MN: Minnesota Historical Society.

Lazarus, Richard S. and Susan Folkman (1984), *Stress, Appraisal and Coping*, New York: Springer.

Lazarus, R.S., A. DeLongis, S. Folkman and R. Gruen (1985), 'Stress and adaptational outcomes: the problem of confounded measures', *American Psychologist*, **40**(7), 770–79.

Levi, Margaret and Valerie Braithwaite (1998), 'Introduction', in Valerie Braithwaite and Margaret Levi (eds), *Trust and Governance*, New York: Russell Sage Foundation, pp. 1–5.

Lewin, Kurt (1951), *Field Theory in Social Science: Selected Theoretical Papers*, New York: Harper & Row.

Lewis, Alan (1982), *The Psychology of Taxation*, Oxford: Martin Robertson.

Lewis, Helen B. (1971), *Shame and Guilt in Neurosis*, New York: International Universities Press.

Lind, E. Allan and Tom R. Tyler (1988), *The Social Psychology of Procedural Justice*, New York: Plenum Press.

Lipset, S.M. and W. Schneider (1987), 'The confidence gap during the Reagan years, 1981–1987', *Political Science Quarterly*, **102**(1), 1–23.

Littlewood, Michael (2001), 'Taxation without representation: the history of Hong Kong's troublingly successful tax system', paper presented at the Joint meetings of the Law and Society Association and Research Committee on Sociology of Law of the International Sociological Association, Budapest, Hungary, 4–7 July.

Long, Susan B. and Judyth A. Swingen (1988), 'The role of legal complexity in shaping taxpayer compliance', in Peter J. van Koppen (ed.), *Lawyers on Psychology and Psychologists on Law. Series on Law and Psychology, No. 1,* Lisse, Netherlands: Swets & Zeitlinger, pp. 127–46.

Los Angeles Times (12 May 2002), 'Political Comedian Will Durst Chronicles Life on the Road as He Tries to Amuse a Post-Sept. 11 Nation'.

Lowndes, V., L. Pratchett and G. Stoker (2006), 'Diagnosing and remedying the failings of official participation schemes: the CLEAR framework', *Social Policy and Society*, **5**(2), 281–91.

Maguire, Peter, Monika Reinhart, Malcolm Mearns and Valerie Braithwaite (2007), *Trust, Hope and Democracy Project, Progress Report No. 2*, Canberra: Regulatory Institutions Network, Australian National University.

Major, Brenda and Toni Schmader (2001), 'Legitimacy and the construal of social disadvantage', in John T. Jost and Brenda Major (eds), *The Psychology of Legitimacy: Emerging Perspectives on Ideology, Justice and Intergroup Relations*, Cambridge: Cambridge University Press, pp. 176–204.

Makkai, T. and J. Braithwaite (1993), 'Praise, pride and corporate compliance', *International Journal of the Sociology of Law*, **21**(1), 73–92.

Makkai, T. and J. Braithwaite (1994a), 'Reintegrative shaming and compliance with regulatory standards', *Criminology*, **32**(3), 361–83.

Makkai, T. and J. Braithwaite (1994b), 'The dialectics of corporate deterrence', *Journal of Research in Crime and Delinquency*, **31**(4), 347–73.

Mansbridge, Jane (1996), 'Using power/fighting power: the polity', in Seyla Benhabib (ed.), *Democracy and Difference: Contesting the Boundaries of the Political*, Princeton, NJ: Princeton University Press, pp. 46–66.

Maranville, D. (2004), 'Unemployment insurance meets globalization and the modern workforce', *Santa Clara Law Review*, **44**(4), 1129–58.

Markus, H. and P. Nurius (1986), 'Possible selves', *American Psychologist*, **41**(9), 954–69.

Maruna, Shadd (2001), *Making Good: How Ex-Convicts Reform and Rebuild Their Lives*, Washington, DC: American Psychological Association.

Maruna, Shadd and Heith Copes (2004), 'Excuses, excuses: what have we learned from five decades of neutralization research?', in Michael Tonry (ed.), *Crime and Justice, Vol. 32: A Review of Research*, Chicago, IL: University of Chicago Press, pp. 221–320.

Maruna, S. and R.E. Mann (2006), 'A fundamental attribution error? rethinking cognitive distortions', *Legal and Criminal Psychology*, **11**(2), 155–77.
Maslow, Abraham (1968), *Toward a Psychology of Being* (2nd edn), Princeton, NJ: Van Nostrand Reinhold.
Mason, R. and L.D. Calvin (1978), 'A study of admitted income tax evasion', *Law and Society*, **13**(1), 73–89.
Massey, D.S. (2002), 'A brief history of human society: the origin and role of emotion in social life: 2001 Presidential Address', *American Sociological Review*, **67**(1), 1–29.
Mathiesen, Thomas (2004), *Silently Silenced: Essays on the Creation of Acquiescence in Modern Society*, Winchester, UK: Waterside Press.
Matza, David (1964), *Becoming Deviant*, Englewood Cliffs, NJ: Prentice-Hall.
Mayo, Elton (1949), *The Social Problems of an Industrial Civilization*, London: Routledge & Kegan Paul.
McAdams, D.P. (1985), *Power, Intimacy and the Life Story: Personological Inquiries into Identity*, New York: Guilford Press.
McAdams, D.P. (1993), *The Stories We Live By: Personal Myths and the Making of the Self*, New York: William Morrow.
McAdams, R.H. (2000), 'A focal point theory of expressive law', *Virginia Law Review*, **86**(8), 1649–730.
McAdams, R.H. and J. Nadler (2005), 'Testing the focal point theory of legal compliance: the effect of third-party expression in an experimental hawk/dove game', *Journal of Empirical Legal Studies*, **2**(1), 87–123.
McAllister, I. (2005), 'The Australian federal election, October 2004', *Electoral Studies*, **24**(3), 545–51.
McAllister, I. and C. Bean (2000), 'The electoral politics of economic reform in Australia: the 1998 election', *Australian Journal of Political Science*, **35**(3), 383–99.
McBarnet, D. (1988), 'Law, policy and legal avoidance: can law effectively implement egalitarian policies?', *Journal of Law and Society*, **15**(1), 113–21.
McBarnet, D. (1991), 'Whiter than white collar crime: tax, fraud insurance and the management of stigma', *British Journal of Sociology*, **42**(3), 323–44.
McBarnet, D. (1992), 'Legitimate rackets: tax evasion, tax avoidance, and the boundaries of the law', *The Journal of Human Justice*, **3**(2), 56–74.
McBarnet, D. (2001), 'When compliance is not the solution but the problem: from changes in law to changes in attitude', Centre for Tax

System Integrity Working Paper 18, Australian National University, http://ctsi.anu.edu.au/publications/WP/18.pdf.
McBarnet, Doreen (2003), 'When compliance is not the solution but the problem: from changes in the law to changes in attitude', in Valerie Braithwaite (ed.), *Taxing Democracy: Understanding Tax Avoidance and Evasion*, Aldershot: Ashgate, pp. 229–44.
McBarnet, Doreen and Christopher Whelan (1999), *Creative Accounting and the Cross-Eyed Javelin Thrower*, Chichester, UK: John Wiley.
McCracken, S.K. (2002), 'Going, going, gone . . . global: a Canadian perspective on international tax administration issues in the "exchange-of-information age"', *Canadian Tax Journal*, **50**(6), 1869–912.
McDougall, William (1926), *An Introduction to Social Psychology*, Boston, MA: John W. Luce.
McFall, L. (1987), 'Integrity', *Ethics*, **98**(1), 5–20.
McFarland, D. (2001), 'Student resistance: how the formal and informal organization of classroms facilitate everyday forms of student defiance', *American Journal of Sociology*, **107**(3), 612–78.
McGeer, V. (2004), 'The art of good hope', *Annals of the American Academy of Political and Social Science*, **592**, 100–27.
McGraw, K.M. and J.T. Scholz (1991), 'Appeals to civic virtue versus attention to self-interest: effects on tax compliance', *Law and Society Review*, **25**(3), 471–98.
Mead, George Herbert (1934), *Mind, Self, and Society*, Chicago, IL: University of Chicago Press.
Mearns, Malcolm and Valerie Braithwaite (2001), 'The Community Hopes, Fears and Actions survey: survey method, sample representativeness and data quality', Centre for Tax System Integrity Working Paper No. 4, Australian National University, http://ctsi/publications/WP/4.pdf.
Meidinger, E. (1987a), 'Regulatory culture: a theoretical outline', *Law and Policy*, **9**(4), 355–86.
Meidinger, E. (1987b), 'Regulatory culture and democratic theory', Baldy Center for Law and Social Policy Working Paper, State University of New York, Buffalo.
Menzel, Donald C. (2007), *Ethics Management for Public Administrations: Building Organizations of Integrity*, Armonk, NY: M.E. Sharpe.
Merton, Robert K. (1968), *Social Theory and Social Structure*, New York: Free Press.
Milgram, S. (1963), 'Behavioral study of obedience', *Journal of Abnormal and Social Psychology*, **67**(4), 371–8.
Milgram, Stanley (1974), *Obedience to Authority: An Experimental View*, New York: Harper & Row.

Miller, D.T. (2001), 'Disrespect and the experience of injustice', *Annual Review of Psychology*, **52**, 527–53.

Mills, C.W. (1940), 'Situated actions and vocabularies of motive', *American Sociological Review*, **5**(6), 904–13.

Mitchell, Ronald B. (1994), *Intentional Oil Pollution at Sea: Environmental Policy and Treaty Compliance*, Cambridge, MA: The MIT Press.

Modigliani, A. and F. Rochat (1995), 'The role of interaction sequences and the timing of resistance in shaping obedience and defiance to authority', *Journal of Social Issues*, **51**(3), 107–23.

Moore Tax News (May 2005), 'Income tax exempt entities – ATO crack-down imminent'.

Morales, Alfonso (1998), 'Income tax compliance and alternative views of ethics and human nature', *Journal of Accounting, Ethics and Public Policy*, **1**(3), 380–400.

Morgan, Bronwen and Karen Yeung (2007), *An Introduction to Law and Regulation*, Cambridge: Cambridge University Press.

Moscovici, Serge (1976), *Social Influence and Social Change*, London: Academic Press.

Moscovici, Serge and Willem Doise (1994), *Conflict and Consensus: A General Theory of Collective Decisions*, London: Sage Publications.

Mumford, Ann (2002), *Taxing Culture: Towards a Theory of Tax Collection Law*, Burlington, VT and Aldershot, UK: Ashgate.

Murphy, K. (2003a), 'An examination of taxpayers' attitudes towards the Australian tax system: findings from a survey of tax scheme investors', *Australian Tax Forum*, **18**(2), 209–424.

Murphy, K. (2003b), 'Procedural justice and tax compliance', *Australian Journal of Social Issues*, **38**(3), 379–408.

Murphy, K. (2004), 'The role of trust in nurturing compliance: a study of accused tax avoiders', *Law and Human Behavior*, **28**(2), 187–209.

Murphy, K. (2005), 'Regulating more effectively: the relationship between procedural justice, legitimacy and tax non-compliance', *Journal of Law and Society*, **32**(4), 562–89.

Murphy, Katrina and Yuka Sakurai (2001), 'Aggressive tax planning: differentiating those playing the game from those who don't', Centre for Tax System Integrity Working Paper No 25, Australian National University, http://ctsi/publications/WP/25.pdf.

Nadler, J. (2005), 'Flouting the law', *Texas Law Review*, **83**(5), 1399–441.

Nagin, D.S. (1990), 'Policy options for combatting tax noncompliance', *Journal of Policy Analysis and Management*, **9**(1), 7–22.

National Commission on Restructuring the Internal Revenue Service (1997), *A Vision for a New IRS*, Washington, DC: National Commission on Restructuring the Internal Revenue Service.

Neal, Cathy, Pascale Quester and Del I. Hawkins (2004), *Consumer Behaviour: Implications for Marketing Strategy*, North Ryde, NSW: McGraw-Hill.

New York Times (23 November 2003), 'F.B.I. Scrutinizes Antiwar Rallies', reporter Eric Lichtblau.

Nielsen, Vibeke L. and Christine Parker (2005), *The ACCC Enforcement and Compliance Survey: Report of Preliminary Findings*, Canberra: Centre for Competition and Consumer Policy, Regulatory Institutions Network, Australian National University.

Nye, Joseph S., Philip D. Zelikow and David C. King (1997), *Why People Don't Trust Government*, Cambridge, MA: Harvard University Press.

Office of Public Affairs (2002), Treasury Releases First in Series of Tax Simplification Proposals (Single Definition of Child). PO-2088, Washington, DC: The Department of the Treasury.

Oliver, C. (1991), 'Strategic responses to institutional processes', *The Academy of Management Review*, **16**(1), 145–79.

Olson, James M. and Carolyn L. Hafer (2001), 'Tolerance of personal deprivation', in John T. Jost and Brenda Major (eds), *The Psychology of Legitimacy: Emerging Perspectives on Ideology, Justice and Intergroup Relations*, Cambridge: Cambridge University Press, pp. 157–75.

Organisation for Economic Co-operation and Development (2006), *Assessment by the Global Forum on Taxation*, Paris: OECD.

Organisation for Economic Co-operation and Development (2007), *Assessment by the Global Forum on Taxation*, Paris: OECD.

Orviska, M. and J. Hudson (2002), 'Tax evasion, civic duty and the law abiding citizen', *European Journal of Political Economy*, **19**(1), 83–102.

Owens, J. (2006), 'Tax in a borderless world', *OECD Observer*, **257**(October).

Oyserman, D. and H. Markus (1990), 'Possible selves and delinquency', *Journal of Personality and Social Psychology*, **59**(1), 112–25.

Papadakis, E. (1999), 'Constituents of confidence and mistrust in Australian institutions', *Australian Journal of Political Science*, **34**(1), 75–93.

Parker Follett, Mary (1965), *The New State*, Gloucester, MA: Peter Smith.

Parker, Christine and John Braithwaite (2003), 'Regulation', in Peter Cane and Mark Tushnet (eds), *The Oxford Handbook of Legal Studies*, Oxford: Oxford University Press, pp. 119–45.

Paulhus, D.L. and O.P. John (1998), 'Egoistic and moralistic biases in self-perception: the interplay of self-deceptive styles with basic traits and motives', *Journal of Personality*, **66**(6), 1025–60.

Pearlin, L.I. and C. Schooler (1978), 'The structure of coping', *Journal of Health and Social Behavior*, **19**(1), 2–21.

Perrow, Charles (1984), *Normal Accidents: Living with High-Risk Technologies*, New York: Basic Books.
Petrick, J. and J. Quinn (2000), 'The integrity capacity construct and moral progress in business', *Journal of Business Ethics*, **23**(1), 3–18.
Pettit, Philip (1997), *Republicanism: A Theory of Freedom and Government*, Oxford: Oxford University Press.
Pharr, Susan J. and Robert D. Putnam (eds) (2000), *Disaffected Democracies: What's Troubling the Trilateral Countries*, Princeton, NJ: Princeton University Press.
Phillips, Anne (1991), *Engendering Democracy*, Cambridge: Polity Press.
Phillips, Anne (1999), *Which Equalities Matter?*, Cambridge: Polity Press.
Picciotto, Sol (1992), *International Business Taxation: A Study in the Internationalization of Business Regulation*, London: Weidenfeld & Nicolson.
Picciotto, Sol (1999), 'Offshore: the state as legal fiction', in Mark Hampton and Jason Abbott (eds), *Offshore Finance Centres and Tax Havens: The Rise of Global Capital*, Basingstoke: Macmillan, pp. 43–79.
Picciotto, S. (2007), 'Constructing compliance: game playing, tax law and the regulatory state', *Law and Policy*, **29**(1), 11–30.
Piller, Charles (1991), *The Fail-Safe Society: Community Defiance and the End of American Technological Optimism*, New York: Basic Books.
Pope, J., R. Fayle and D.L. Chen (1993), *The Compliance Costs of Employment-Related Taxation in Australia*, Sydney: Australian Tax Research Foundation.
Porcano, T.M. and C.E. Price (1993), 'The effects of social stigmatization on tax evasion', *Advances in Taxation*, **5**, 197–217.
Prabhu, R.K. and U.R. Rao (1969), *The Mind of Mahatma Gandhi* (3rd edn), Ahmedabad: Navajivan.
Pruitt, Dean G. and Peter J. Carnevale (1993), *Negotiation in Social Conflict*, Pacific Grove, CA: Brooks/Cole.
Purvis, J. (1995), 'The prison experiences of suffragettes in Edwardian Britain', *Women's History Review*, **4**(1), 103–33.
Pusey, Michael (2003), *The Experience of Middle Australia: The Dark Side of Economic Reform*, Cambridge: Cambridge University Press.
Putnam, Robert D. (2000), *Bowling Alone: The Collapse and Revival of American Community*, New York: Simon & Schuster.
Putnam, Robert D., Robert Leonardi and Raffaella Y. Nanetti (1993), *Making Democracy Work: Civic Traditions in Modern Italy*, Princeton, NJ: Princeton University Press.
Rai, S.M. (1995), 'Women negotiating boundaries: gender, law and the Indian state', *Social and Legal Studies*, **4**(3), 391–410.

Ramsay, Hayden (1997), *Beyond Virtue*, London: Macmillan.

Rawlings, G. (2003), 'Cultural narratives of taxation and citizenship: fairness, groups and globalisation', *Australian Journal of Social Issues*, **38**(3), 269–306.

Rawlings, G. (2004), 'Laws, liquidity and Eurobonds: the making of the Vanuatu tax haven', *Journal of Pacific History*, **39**(3), 325–41.

Rawlings, G. (2005), 'Mobile people, mobile capital and tax neutrality: sustaining a market for offshore finance centres', *Accounting Forum*, **29**(3), 289–310.

Rawlings, G. and V. Braithwaite (2003), 'Voices for change: Australian perspectives on tax administration', *Australian Journal of Social Issues*, **38**(3), 263–8.

Rees, Joseph V. (1994), *Hostages of Each Other: The Transformation of Nuclear Safety since Three Mile Island*, Chicago, IL and London: University of Chicago Press.

Retzinger, Suzanne M. (1991), *Violent Emotions: Shame and Rage in Marital Quarrels*, Newbury Park, CA: Sage Publications.

Reus-Smit, C. (2007), 'International crises of legitimacy', *International Politics*, **44**(2/3), 157–74.

Review of Business Taxation (1999), *A Tax System Redesigned: More Certain, Equitable and Durable*, Canberra: The Treasury, Australian Government.

Richardson, G. (2006), 'Determinants of tax evasion: a cross-country investigation', *Journal of International Accounting, Auditing and Taxation*, **15**, 150–69.

Roche, D. (2006), 'Firm and fair regulatory enforcement?', RegNet Occasional Paper No. 9, Australian National University, http://ctsi/publications/rop9_roche.pdf.

Rokeach, Milton (1968), *Beliefs, Attitudes and Values: A Theory of Organization and Change*, San Francisco, CA: Jossey-Bass.

Rokeach, Milton (1973), *The Nature of Human Values*, New York: Free Press.

Rossotti, Charles O. (2002), *Report to the IRS Oversight Board: Assessment of the IRS and the Tax System*, Washington, DC: Internal Revenue Service.

Rothengatter, M. (2005), '"Sticks, carrots or sermons?" Improving voluntary tax-compliance among migrant small-business entrepreneurs of a multi-cultural nation', Centre for Tax System Integrity Working Paper 82, Australian National University, http://ctsi.anu.edu.au/publications/WP/82.pdf.

Rotter, Julian B. (1954), *Social Learning and Clinical Psychology*, New York: Prentice-Hall.

Rude, George (1995), *Ideology and Popular Protest*, Chapel Hill, NC: University of North Carolina Press.

Sakurai, Y. and V. Braithwaite (2003), 'Taxpayers' perceptions of practitioners: finding one who is effective and does the right thing?', *Journal of Business Ethics*, **46**(4), 375–87.

Sampson, R.J. and D.J. Bartusch (1998), 'Legal cynicism and (subcultural?) tolerance of deviance: the neighbourhood context of racial differences', *Law and Society Review*, **32**(4), 777–804.

San Francisco Chronicle (10 April 2005), 'How the Rich Get Richer: All the Rest Pay More', reporter David C. Johnston.

Sartori, Giovanni (1987), *The Theory of Democracy Revisited*, Chatham, NJ: Chatham House.

Satterfield, J., J. Swanson, A. Schell and F. Lee (1994), 'Prediction of antisocial behavior in attention-deficit hyperactivity disorder boys from aggression/defiance scores', *Journal of the American Academy of Child and Adolescent Psychiatry*, **33**(2), 185–90.

Sawer, Marion (1990), *Sisters in Suits: Women and Public Policy in Australia*, Sydney: Allen & Unwin.

Schachar, R., S. Sandberg and M. Rutter (1986), 'Agreement between teachers' ratings and observations of hyperactivity, inattentiveness, and defiance', *Journal of Abnormal Child Psychology*, **14**(2), 331–45.

Schacter, Stanley (1959), *The Psychology of Affiliation: Experimental Studies of the Sources of Gregariousness*, Stanford, CA: Stanford University Press.

Scheff, Thomas J. (1990), *Microsociology: Discourse, Emotion and Social Structures*, Chicago, IL: University of Chicago Press.

Scheff, Thomas J. and Suzanne M. Retzinger (1991), *Emotions and Violence: Shame and Rage in Destructive Conflicts*, Lexington, MA: Lexington Books.

Schmölders, G. (1970), 'Survey research in public finance – a behavioural approach to fiscal theory', *Public Finance*, **25**, 300–306.

Scholz, J. (2003), 'Contractual compliance and the federal income tax system', *Washington University Journal of Law and Policy*, **13**, 139–203.

Scholz, J.T. and M. Lubell (1998a), 'Trust and taxpaying: testing the heuristic approach to collective action', *American Journal of Political Science*, **42**(2), 398–417.

Scholz, J.T. and M. Lubell (1998b), 'Adaptive political attitudes: duty, trust, and fear as monitors of tax policy', *American Journal of Political Science*, **42**(3), 903–20.

Scholz, J.T. and N. Pinney (1995), 'Duty, fear and tax compliance – the heuristic basis of citizenship behaviour', *American Journal of Political Science*, **39**(2), 490–512.

Schwartz, R. and S. Orleans (1967), 'On legal sanctions', *University of Chicago Law Review*, **34**(2), 274–300.
Scott, Richard (2001), *Institutions and Organizations*, Thousand Oaks, CA: Sage.
Scott, William A. (1965), *Values and Organizations: A Study of Fraternities and Sororities*, Chicago: Rand McNally.
Scott, William A. (1968), 'Attitude measurement', in Gardner Lindzey and Elliot Aronson (eds), *The Handbook of Social Psychology*, Reading, MA: Addison-Wesley, pp. 204–73.
Scott, W. Richard (1992), *Organizations: Rational, National and Open Systems*, Englewood Cliffs, NJ: Prentice Hall.
Seligman, Martin E.P. (2002), *Authentic Happiness: Using the New Positive Psychology to Realize Your Potential for Lasting Fulfillment*, New York: Free Press.
Selznick, Philip (1992), *The Moral Commonwealth: Social Theory and the Promise of Community*, Berkeley, CA: University of California Press.
Senate Economics References Committee (2002), *Inquiry into Mass Marketed Tax Effective Schemes and Investor Protection: Final Report*, Canberra: Parliament of the Commonwealth of Australia.
Shearing, Clifford and Phillip C. Stenning (1984), 'From the Panopticon to Disney World: the development of discipline', in Anthony N. Doob and Edward L. Greenspan QC (eds), *Perspectives in Criminal Law: Essays in Honour of John L.J. Edwards*, Aurora, Ontario: Canada Law Book Inc., pp. 335–49.
Shearing, C. and J. Wood (2003), 'Nodal governance, democracy, and the new "denizens"', *Journal of Law and Society*, **30**(3), 400–419.
Sherman, L.W. (1993), 'Defiance, deterrence, and irrelevance: a theory of the criminal sanction', *Journal of Research in Crime and Delinquency*, **30**(4), 445–73.
Sherman, Lawrence W. (2002), 'Reinventing justice: theory, innovation, and research for an emotionally intelligent system', paper presented at the Presidential address to the 54th Annual Meeting of the American Society of Criminology, Chicago, IL, 15 November.
Sherman, L.W. (2003), 'Reason for emotion: reinventing justice with theories, innovations, and research – the American Society of Criminology 2002 presidential address', *Criminology*, **41**(1), 1–37.
Shover, Neal (2007), 'Generative worlds of white-collar crime', in Henry N. Pontell and Gilbert Geis (eds), *International Handbook of White-Collar and Corporate Crime*, New York: Springer, pp. 81–97.
Shover, Neal, Jenny Job and Anne Carroll (2003), 'The ATO compliance model in action: a case study of building and construction', in Valerie

Braithwaite (ed.), *Taxing Democracy: Understanding Tax Avoidance and Evasion*, Aldershot, UK: Ashgate, pp. 159–76.

Simpson, S.S. and N.L. Piquero (2002), 'Low self-control, organizational theory, and corporate crime', *Law and Society*, **36**(3), 509–48.

Skinner, B.F. (1971), *Beyond Freedom and Dignity*, Harmondsworth, UK: Penguin.

Skinner, E.A., K. Edge, J. Altman and H. Sherwood (2003), 'Searching for the structure of coping: a review and critique of category systems for classifying ways of coping', *Psychological Bulletin*, **129**(2), 216–69.

Slemrod, J. (1992), 'Why people pay taxes: introduction', in *Why People Pay Taxes: Tax Compliance and Enforcement*, Ann Arbor, MI: University of Michigan Press, pp. 1–8.

Smith, Julie P. (1993), *Taxing Popularity: The Story of Taxation in Australia*, Canberra, Australia: Federalism Research Centre, Australian National University.

Smith, K.W. (1992), 'Reciprocity and fairness: positive incentives for tax compliance', in Joel Slemrod (ed.), *Why People Pay Taxes: Tax Compliance and Enforcement*, Ann Arbor, MI: University of Michigan Press, pp. 223–50.

Smith, K.W. and K.A. Kinsey (1987), 'Understanding taxpayer behavior: a conceptual framework with implications for research', *Law and Society Review*, **21**(4), 639–63.

Smith, K.W. and L.J. Stalans (1991), 'Encouraging tax compliance with positive incentives: a conceptual framework and research directions', *Law and Policy*, **13**(1), 35–53.

Sørensen, E. and J. Torfing (2005), 'The democratic anchorage of governance networks', *Scandinavian Political Studies*, **28**(3), 195–218.

Sparrow, Malcolm K. (2000), *The Regulatory Craft: Controlling Risks, Solving Problems, and Managing Compliance*, Washington, DC: Brookings Institution Press.

The Spectator (29 May 1999), 'In a Word, Defiance', reporter Julian Manyon.

Srivastva, Suresh (ed.) (1988), *Executive Integrity: The Search for High Human Values in Organizational Life*, San Francisco, CA: Jossey-Bass.

Srivastva, S. and D.L. Cooperrider (1988), 'Introduction: the urgency for executive integrity', in Suresh Srivastva (ed.), *Executive Integrity: The Search for High Human Values in Organizational Life*, San Francisco, CA: Jossey-Bass, pp. 1–28.

Steele, Claude M. (1988), 'The psychology of self-affirmation: sustaining the integrity of the self', in Leonard Berkowitz (ed.), *Advances in Experimental Social Psychology, Volume 21*, New York: Academic Press, pp. 261–302.

Stern, Paul C. and Harvey V. Fineberg (eds) (1996), *Understanding Risk: Informing Decisions in a Democratic Society*, Washington, DC: National Academy Press.

Stoker, G. (2005), 'Public value management: a new narrative for networked governance?', *American Review of Public Administration*, **36**(1), 41–57.

Strazdins, Lyndall (2000), *Emotional Work: A Psychological Perspective*, PhD thesis, Psychology Department, Canberra: Australian National University.

Suchman, M.C. (1995), 'Managing legitimacy: strategic and institutional approaches', *Academy of Management Review*, **20**(3), 571–610.

Suedfeld, P. (1992), 'Cognitive managers and their critics', *Political Psychology*, **13**(3), 435–53.

Sutherland, Edwin H. (1937), *The Professional Thief*, Chicago, IL: University of Chicago Press.

Sutherland, Edwin H. (1947), *Principles of Criminology* (4th edn), Philadelphia, PA: Lippencott.

Sutton, T. (1997), *Child Support Questionnaire: National Telephone Survey April–May 1997*, Child Support Agency, Canberra: Commonwealth of Australia.

Sydney Morning Herald (7 June 2001), 'Lawyer Had a Few Drinks to Blot Out His $1m Tax Debt', reporter Ellen Connolly.

Sydney Morning Herald (8 October 2005), 'Sellers Beware – the Tax Man Wants a Share', reporter Matt Wade.

Sykes, G.M. and D. Matza (1957), 'Techniques of neutralization: a theory of delinquency', *American Sociological Review*, **22**(6), 664–70.

Tajfel, Henri (1972), 'La categorisation sociale', in Serge Moscovici (ed.), *Introduction a la Psychologie Sociale*, Paris: Larousse, pp. 272–302.

Tajfel, Henri (ed.) (1978), *Differentiation between Social Groups: Studies in the Social Psychology of Intergroup Relations*, London: Academic Press.

Tan, L.M. (1999), 'Taxpayers' preference for type of advice from tax practitioner: a preliminary examination', *Journal of Economic Psychology*, **20**, 431–47.

Tangney, J.P., J. Stuewig and D.J. Mashek (2007), 'Moral emotions and moral behaviour', *Annual Review of Psychology*, **58**, 345–72.

Tanzi, Vito (2000), *Globalization, Technological Developments and the Work of Fiscal Termites*, Washington, DC: International Monetary Fund.

Tanzi, Vito (2001), 'Creating effective tax administrations: the experience of Russia and Georgia', in Janos Kornai, Stephen Haggard and Robert

R. Kaufman (eds), *Reforming the State: Fiscal and Welfare Reform in Post-Socialist Countries,* Cambridge: Cambridge University Press, pp. 53–74.

Tanzi, V. and P. Shome (1994), 'A primer on tax evasion', *International Bureau of Fiscal Documentation*, **48**, 328–37.

Taylor, G. (1981), 'Integrity', *Proceedings of the Aristotelian Society*, Supplementary Volume, **55**, 143–59.

Taylor, Natalie (2001), 'Taxpayers who complain about paying tax: what differentiates those who complain from those who don't?', Centre for Tax System Integrity Working Paper No. 9, Australian National University, http://ctsi/publications/WP/9.pdf.

Taylor, N. (2003), 'Understanding taxpayer attitudes through understanding taxpayer identities', in Valerie Braithwaite (ed.), *Taxing Democracy: Understanding Tax Avoidance and Evasion*, Aldershot, UK: Ashgate, pp. 71–92.

Thurman, Q., C. St John and L. Riggs (1984), 'Neutralization and tax evasion: how effective would a moral appeal be in improving compliance to tax laws?', *Law and Policy*, **6**(3), 309–27.

Tittle, Charles R. (1980), *Sanctions and Social Deviance: The Question of Deterrence*, Westport, CT: Praeger Publishers.

Torgler, Benno (2003), *Tax Morale and Institutions*, CREMA Working Paper No. 2003-09, Basel.

Turk, Austin (1982), *Political Criminality: The Defiance and Defense of Authority*, Beverly Hills, CA: Sage Publications.

Turner, John C., Michael A. Hogg, Penelope J. Oakes, Stephen J. Reicher and Margaret S. Wetherell (1987), *Rediscovering the Social Group: A Self-Categorization Theory*, Oxford: Blackwell.

Tversky, A. and D. Kahneman (1974), 'Judgement under uncertainty: heuristics and biases', *Science*, **185**(4157), 1124–31.

Tyler, T.R. (1988), 'What is procedural justice?: criteria used by citizens to assess the fairness of legal procedures', *Law and Society Review*, **22**(1), 103–35.

Tyler, T.R. (1989), 'The psychology of procedural justice: a test of the group-value model', *Journal of Personality and Social Psychology*, **57**(5), 830–38.

Tyler, Tom R. (1990), *Why People Obey the Law*, New Haven, CT: Yale University Press.

Tyler, T.R. (1997), 'The psychology of legitimacy: a relational perspective on voluntary deference to authorities', *Personality and Social Psychology Review*, **1**(4), 323–45.

Tyler, T.R. (2001), 'Trust and law abidingness: a proactive model of social regulation', *Boston University Law Review*, **81**(2), 361–406.

Tyler, T.R. and R.J. Bies (1990), 'Beyond formal procedures: the interpersonal context of procedural justice', in J.S. Carroll (ed.), *Applied Social Psychology and Organizational Settings*, Hillsdale, NJ: Erlbaum, pp. 77–98.

Tyler, Tom R. and Steven L. Blader (2000), *Cooperation in Groups: Procedural Justice, Social Identity, and Behavioral Engagement*, Philadelphia, PA: Psychology Press.

Tyler, Tom R. and Robyn M. Dawes (1993), 'Fairness in groups: comparing the self-interest and social identity perspectives', in Jonathan Baron and Barbara Mellers (eds), *Psychological Perspectives on Justice: Theory and Application*, Cambridge: Cambridge University Press, pp. 87–108.

Tyler, Tom R. and E. Allan Lind (1992), 'A relational model of authority in groups', in M. Zanna (ed.), *Advances in Experimental Social Psychology*, New York: Academic Press, 25, pp. 115–91.

Tyler, T., P. Degoey and H. Smith (1996), 'Understanding why the justice of group procedures matters: a test of the psychological dynamics of the group-value model.' *Journal of Personality and Social Psychology*, **70**(5), 913–30.

Tyler, T., E.A. Lind, K.-I. Ohbuchi, I. Sugawara and Y.J. Huo (1998), 'Conflict with outsiders: disputing within and across cultural boundaries', *Personality and Social Psychology Bulletin*, **24**(2), 137–46.

Upfold, R. (1999), 'Attitudes to tax avoidance', *Australian Tax Review*, **28**(2), 95–103.

van Mill, D. (1996), 'The possibility of rational outcomes from democratic discourse and procedure', *Journal of Politics*, **58**(3), 734–52.

Vann, Richard (1996), *Tax Treaties: Linkages between OECD Member Countries and Dynamic Non-Member Economies*, Paris: OECD.

Vann, Richard (1997), *Taxing International Business: Emerging Trends in APEC and OECD Economies*, Paris: OECD.

Vaughan, Dianne (1996), *The Challenger Launch Decision: Risky Technology, Culture and Deviance at NASA*, Chicago, IL: Chicago University Press.

Waller, V. (2007), 'The challenge of institutional integrity in responsive regulation: field inspections by the Australian Taxation Office', *Law and Policy*, **29**(1), 67–83.

Wallschutzky, Ian G. (1985), *Taxpayer Attitudes to Tax Avoidance and Evasion, Research Study 1*, Sydney: Australian Tax Research Foundation.

Wallschutzky, Ian G. (1996), 'Issues in research methods: with reference to income tax research', unpublished manuscript, University of Newcastle, Newcastle, Australia.

Walzer, Michael (1970), *Obligations: Essays on Disobedience, War and Citizenship*, Cambridge, MA: Harvard University Press.

Washington Post (6 November 2007), 'Lawyers Take on Musharraf', p. A01, reporter Griff White.

Watts, M.M. (1999), 'Are there typical age curves in political behavior? The "age invariance" hypothesis and political socialization', *Political Psychology*, **20**(3), 477–99.

Webb, Bob (2006), 'The Tax Office Change Program: project management directions and learnings', paper presented at the ANZSOG Conference, Melbourne, August.

Webley, Paul, Caroline Adams and Henk Elffers (2002), 'VAT compliance in the United Kingdom', Centre for Tax System Integrity Working Paper 41, Australian National University, http://ctsi/publications/WP/41.pdf.

Weick, Karl (1979), *The Social Psychology of Organizing*, New York: McGraw-Hill.

Weigel, R.H., D.J. Hessing and H. Elffers (1987), 'Tax evasion research: a critical appraisal and theoretical model', *Journal of Economic Psychology*, **8**(2), 215–35.

Wenzel, M. (2002), 'The impact of outcome orientation and justice concerns on tax compliance: the role of taxpayers identity', *Journal of Applied Psychology*, **87**(4), 629–45.

Wenzel, Michael (2003), 'Tax compliance and the psychology of justice: mapping the field', in Valerie Braithwaite (ed.), *Taxing Democracy: Understanding Tax Avoidance and Evasion*, Aldershot, UK: Ashgate, pp. 41–69.

Wenzel, M. (2004a), 'The social side of sanctions: personal and social norms as moderators of deterrence', *Law and Human Behavior*, **28**(5), 547–67.

Wenzel, M. (2004b), 'Social identification as a determinant of concerns about individual-, group-, and inclusive-level justice', *Social Psychology Quarterly*, **67**(1), 70–87.

Wenzel, M. (2005), 'Motivation or rationalisation? Causal relations between ethics, norms and tax compliance', *Journal of Economic Psychology*, **26**(4), 491–508.

Wenzel, M. (2007), 'The multiplicity of taxpayer identities and their implications for tax ethics', *Law and Policy*, **29**(1), 31–50.

White, Michael and David Epston (1990), *Narrative Means to Therapeutic Ends*, New York: W.W. Norton & Co.

White, R.W. (1959), 'Motivation reconsidered: the concept of competence', *Psychological Review*, **66**(5), 297–333.

Wikström, Per-Olof H. (2002), *Adolescent Crime in Context*, Cambridge: University of Cambridge, Institute of Criminology.

Wikström, Per-Olof H. (2004), 'Crime as alternative: towards a cross-level situational action theory of crime causation', in J. McCord (ed.), *Beyond Empiricism*, New Brunswick, NJ: Transaction Publishers, pp. 1–37.

Williams, Bernard (1973), 'Integrity', in J.J.C. Smart and Bernard Williams (eds), *Utilitarianism: For and Against*, London: Cambridge University Press, pp. 108–17.

Williams, Bernard (1993), *Shame and Necessity*, Berkeley, CA: University of California Press.

Williams, D. (1998), 'United Kingdom tax collection: rights of and against taxpayers', in Duncan Bentley (ed.), *Taxpayers' Rights: An International Perspective*, Bond University: Revenue Law Journal, pp. 331–45.

Wilson, S. and T. Breusch (2003), 'Taxes and social spending: the shifting demands of the Australian public', *Australian Journal of Social Issues*, **38**(3), 39–56.

Winch, Peter (1972), 'Moral integrity', in P. Winch (ed.), *Ethics and Action*, London: Routledge & Kegan Paul, pp. 171–92.

Wolfe, Donald M. (1988), 'Is there integrity in the bottom line? Managing obstacles in executive integrity', in S. Srivastva (ed.), *Executive Integrity: The Search for High Human Values in Organizational Life*, San Francisco, CA: Jossey-Bass, pp. 140–71.

Wood, Jennifer and Clifford Shearing (2007), *Imagining Security*, Cullompton, UK: Willan.

Wrong, D. (1961), 'The oversocialized conception of man in modern sociology', *American Sociological Review*, **26**(2), 183–93.

Yaniv, G. (1992), 'Collaborated employee–employer tax evasion', *Public Finance*, **47**(2), 312–21.

Yeager, P.C. and G.E. Reed (1998), 'Of corporate persons and straw man: a reply to Herbert, Green, and Larragoite', *Criminology*, **36**(4), 885–97.

Yeung, Karen (2004), *Securing Compliance: A Principled Approach*, Oxford: Hart Publishing.

Young, Iris Marion (1990), *Justice and the Politics of Difference*, Princeton: Princeton University Press.

Young, Iris Marion (2000), *Inclusion and Democracy*, Oxford: Oxford University Press.

Zald, Mayer N. and Bert Useem (1987), 'Movement and countermovement interaction: mobilization, tactics, and state involvement', in Mayer N. Zald and John D. McCarthy (eds), *Social Movements in an Organizational Society: Collected Essays*, New Brunswick, NJ: Transaction Books, pp. 247–72.

Zelditch Jr, Morris (2001), 'Theories of legitimacy', in John Jost and Brenda Major (eds), *The Pyschology of Legitimacy*, Cambridge: Cambridge University Press, pp. 33–53.

Index

Abu Bakr 3
accountability 64, 65; *see also* responsibility
accountants 14, 193; *see also* tax professionals
adaptation 10–11, 44–5, 134, 181, 214
Adler, P.S. 182, 184–5
advertising 226, 228, 246, 300
agency 217
alienation 40, 41, 86, 90, 114
Allport, G.W. 71
alternative authorities 59, 217, 222, 250, 301
  tax advisers as 223–4, 236, 245
  tax authorities and 173, 212–13
  tax lawyers as 93–4
amorality, anomic 219
anomie 78, 219, 234
anti-terror laws 2, 3
Argyris, C. 180, 182, 190
art 10
Australia
  anti-terror laws 3
  democracy 126–9, 261
  goods-and-services tax 16, 68, 86, 115–17, 142, 191–2
  'New Tax System' 17, 86, 191–2, 207
  tax policy 68–69
  tax reform 16, 68, 277
  tax system 118–19, 142, 145, 178
'Australian Tax System: Fair or Not Survey' 105, 195
Australian Taxation Office 14, 52, 191, 255
  Cash Economy Task Force 192
  compliance model 88, 89, 192, 207
  Compliance Program 192, 207
  consultation 55, 196–7
  and defiance 34
  education and persuasion campaigns 16–17, 86, 192, 207
  effectiveness of 135, 189, 198
  and the GST 86, 115–17, 192, 207
  integrity of 178, 194, 199
  'Listening to the Community' project 192
  mass-marketed tax avoidance schemes 116, 191, 193, 194, 207, 215, 222, 305
  newspaper reporting of 230–31
  perceptions of 17, 52, 110
  reform program 271
  relationship building 178, 196
  respect for 226
  respect for the community 196–7, 208
  responsive regulation 192
  and tax avoidance 225, 227–8
    mass-marketed schemes 116, 191, 193, 194, 207, 215, 222, 305
  Taxpayers' Charter 88, 178, 211
    commitment to 179, 185, 191, 197–9
    and justice 192–5
  trust in 200–201, 208
  and used-car dealers 189–90
authenticity 23, 185–6, 207, 208
authorities
  control of social distance from 69–70
  credibility of 85, 90
  engagement with dismissiveness 305, 309–10
  feedback from the community 87, 98
  integrity of 297, 309
  legitimacy of 62–3, 148, 296, 303–4
  and the media 43
  public confidence in 43
  relationships with the regulated 16, 23
  responses to defiance 250, 305
  responsiveness of 51, 88, 295
  see also tax authorities

authority 97
  challenging through social distance 62–7
  compliance with 71
  and identity 153
  management of 62–74
  and motivational postures 62–74
autonomy 216
Ayres, Ian 51–2, 89, 186

Babbitt, Susan E. 181
Bandura, A. 5, 6, 216, 296
Bardach, Eugene 45, 49, 186
Bartusch, D.J. 237
Barwick, Chief Justice 94
beliefs 5, 219, 313
Benjamin, M. 180, 181
Bentham, Jeremy 8
Bentley, D. 176
Bernstein, Marver H. 97, 186–8
Bevir, M. 65
Bikhchandani, S. 222
Black, D. 39
Black, J. 186, 190
Bogardus, Emory S. 40, 67–8, 255, 296
Borys, B. 182, 184–5
Bourdieu, Pierre 12
Braithwaite, John 39, 51–2, 82, 89, 135, 186, 293, 309
Braithwaite, Valerie 121
Brehm, Jack W. 158
Brehm, Sharon S. 158
Bromiley, P. 201
Buffett, Warren 54
bureaucracy 184–5, 189

Canada 177, 260
  First Nations Government 310
capital 12
  social capital 233, 273, 290
capitulation 20, 78, 81, 91, 124, 158
Carnevale, Peter 67
Cartwright, Sophie 308
Centre for Tax Policy and Administration, OECD 55
Centre for Tax System Integrity, ANU 104
certainty 221; *see also* uncertainty
change, models of 184; *see also* social change
China 19
citizen juries 48
citizenship 44, 63, 309
civil liberties 3, 233, 241
Clegg, Stuart 33
Cocker, Joe 86
cognitive reframing 141–2, 147–50, 165
coherence 106, 180, 188
collective identity 252
comedy 10
command-and-control regulation 44–5, 51–5, 84
commitment 20, 78, 91, 99
  coherence in responses to survey items representing 106
  and harmony values 122–3
  and relationship to regulators 81
Commonwealth Ombudsman 193
communication 43
'Community Hopes, Fears and Actions Survey' 104–5, 109, 111, 119, 142, 159, 195, 234
competition 219, 237–8, 241
competitive pathway 243, 267, 269
  and deterrence 267
  variables in 258–9
compliance 44, 45, 76, 157, 189, 298
  behavioural 53
  creative compliance 92
  and defiance 53, 84–7, 87–9
  determinants of 74
  emotions and 82
  enforcement of 42
  improving 172
  management of 98
  and motivational postures 79–80
  and performance outcomes 31–2
  as process 29, 30
  and regulatory pyramids 87–9
  and responsive relationships 50–51
  substantive 30
  typology of 30
conflict 18, 34, 84
consciousness 72–3
consensus building 46, 99
consistency, and integrity 190
consumerism 65
contagion 220, 222, 223
contestation 41, 47, 308–9
control, expectation of 21

cooperation 12, 21, 22, 34, 38, 85, 91, 178
and disengagement 81
and justice 80
relational accounts of 62
and values 125
willingness for 69, 186
coping styles 140–42, 263
cognitive reframing 141–2, 147–50, 165
and defiance 166–168, 169, 249
and deterrence 163–6, 166–8, 170
and dismissiveness 170
emotion-focused coping style 141, 143–5
feeling oppressed 143–145, 160, 161–2, 263
hypotheses about 159–71
measurement of 142–51, 162
narratives 150
problem-focused coping style 141, 145–7
and resistance 170
and self-regulation 171
and social distance 171
and social infrastructure 163–6
taking control coping style 145–7, 160, 161–2, 172, 258
testing the model 159–71
thinking morally coping style 147–50, 160, 161–2, 263
external support for 151–3
corporations
as amoral calculators 75, 76
culture of 219
organizational incompetence 75, 76
as political citizens 75, 76
creative compliance 92
Crick, Harold 187
criminology 70
crowding-out theory 87
Crush, J. 11
Cummings, L.L. 201
Cummins, John 95
cynicism 97, 185, 269, 275
legal 235, 256
and defiance 234, 239, 242, 247, 261
measurement of 237–8
Davion, V. 181
defensiveness 111–13, 182, 183, 190
deference 22, 216, 217, 255
defiance
and anxiety 294
approaches to understanding 249–50, 255–6, 296–7
behavioural 27, 53
boundaries of 27–9
categories of 60–61
cognitive elements of 293
and cognitive reframing 249
and compliance 84–7, 87–9
constraints on 8–9
constructive 306
and coping styles 166–8, 169, 249
definition of 27–32, 215–16
and democratic expectations 233–4
differentiating dismissive and resistant 2, 14, 160, 207, 247, 305–6
directed to authority 31
and disillusionment with democracy 244, 262, 263, 298
dismissive 1, 22, 25, 80, 166, 173, 254–5, 288, 299–304
definition of 254
management of 270
models of 169–170, 206–7, 243–4, 267–9, 298–9
pathways to 289, 296
emotions and 138, 293, 294, 306, 312
escalation from resistance to dismissiveness 3–4
expressions of 4–7
and governance 306, 309
and individualism 272–6, 292
and inspiration 294
and institutions 9–10, 246
and integrity 174, 175–213, 209, 247, 250, 251, 289
intentional component of 27
management of 23, 268, 311, 312
mapping elements of 27–32, 293–5
measurement of 101–36, 191–205
models of 48–91, 205–7, 249–69
as motivational posturing 32–42
narratives of 216, 276–87
and nodes of influence 10–12, 35, 56

perceived deterrence 169, 170, 172, 263, 264, 265–6, 267–8, 298
and performance outcomes 31
and personal preferences and values 248
rationality and 138, 292–313
and regulatory culture 34–6
and regulatory intervention 290
and regulatory pyramids 87–9
resistant 1, 22, 25, 166, 254–5, 288, 304
definition of 254
models of 168–9, 205–6, 241–3, 264–6, 298, 299–304
pathways to 288–9, 296
and taxation 7
responses to 8, 250, 251–2
and responsibility 287–8
and responsive relationships 26–59
and role models 239–44
and selves 300
signals of 58
and social distance 151, 303–4
and social modelling 214–47, 250
space for 306
and status, economic 262
and taxation 12–15, 38, 51–9, 91, 270–72, 297
and the thinking morally coping style 169
threat and coping model of 137–74, 249
and trust 175–213, 208, 247
value of 250
and values 239–44
verbal 27, 53
defiance diplomacy 308–11
deliberation 47, 64, 180, 214, 215, 217, 303
and defiance 23, 27, 252, 311
democratic 18
resistance and 309
space for 290, 304, 308
deliberative polls 48
democracy 52, 65, 95, 172, 217, 289
communicative 48
and defiance 233–4, 252
deliberative 49, 64
dimensions of 260
direct 48
and dismissiveness 249, 305
hypotheses about 126–9
and motivational postures 126–9
participative 303
and resistance 108
values and hopes for 130, 138
democratic collective self 249, 260–62, 273
and defiance 252, 255–6, 275–6, 288–9, 300, 302–3
deterrence 22, 82, 152, 158, 160, 163, 169–70, 256
and competitive pathway 267
and coping styles 163–6, 166–8, 170
effects of 170–71
and feeling oppressed 265
and the grievance pathway 265–6
and the moral pathway 265
perceived deterrence 169, 170, 172, 263, 264, 265–6, 26–8, 298
and shame 166–8
dialogue 91, 98, 182, 190, 214, 254, 304
and defiance 244–5, 304
regulatory authorities and 24, 87, 99, 214
differential association 70
disengagement 5, 20, 21, 39, 78, 109, 216
and cooperation 81
management of 80
and taxation 90
and trust 81
and values 125
disillusionment with democracy 261, 266, 275
and cynicism 234, 241
and defiance 239, 244, 262, 263, 297, 298
and the grievance pathway 264–5
measurement of 236–7
and the moral pathway 267
and motivational postures 128
dismissiveness 1, 21, 135, 212–13, 254–5, 270, 299–304
and coping styles 170
as cultural background 132
definition of 254
and democracy 249, 305
engagement with 309–10

and expectations of government 282–3
and governance 249, 290
high versus low 280–87
and integrity 204, 206, 210, 212
management of 206, 270
models of 169–70, 206–7, 243–4, 262–9, 298–9
pathways to 289, 296, 299
prediction of 132–4, 314–17
psychological drivers of 137
and resistance 22
and respect 275–6
and responsibility to fellow citizens 284, 286–7
and responsibility to government 284–6
as social distance from authority 132–3
and taking control 169–70
and tax evasion 24, 271–2, 305
and the thinking morally coping style 169–70
and trust 204
and values 133, 241
see also under defiance
Disney World 8
disobedience 29
disrespect, cultures of 272–6, 288, 303
dissent 29, 64, 65–6, 250
dissidence 4, 29, 48
Doise, Willem 46
domination 33, 51–9, 175, 218, 311
Dryzek, J.S. 48, 49
Durst, Will 10

Elias, Norbert 173
emotion-focused coping style 141, 143–5
emotional feedback 154
emotional intelligence 63, 186
emotional work 274, 275
emotions 81
and defiance 138, 293, 294, 306, 312
and taxation 68, 82
empathy 63
Epstein, S. 71
equal opportunity 233, 234, 241
ethical decision making 181, 184, 185
ethical identity 82, 154, 157–8, 209, 211, 256, 265
expectations 18, 84, 148

fairness 52, 83–4, 90, 173, 186, 207, 307; *see also* justice
feeling oppressed coping style 143–5, 263, 264
and dismissiveness 169–70
Feld, Lars P. 209, 267
financial planning 145, 146, 193, 220, 221, 228
Foucault, Michel 8
freedom 1, 33, 216, 217, 233, 234, 293–4
freedom of choice 95
loss of 139–40, 256
threats to 15
Frey, B.S. 86–7, 209, 267

Galanter, M. 39
game playing 20, 21, 39, 62, 99, 109, 216
costs of 96
and democratic governance 96–7
and security values 125
and taxation 91–2, 93–6
Gamson, William A. 50, 86, 89, 90
Geis, Gilbert 219
Gibson, J.L. 210
Giddens, Anthony 72–3
Gladwell, Malcolm 219
globalization 13, 57
goal displacement 189
Gobert, James 218
Goffman, E. 41, 296
goods-and-services tax 16, 68, 86, 142, 191, 277
advertising campaign around 86
implementation of 115–17
governance 16, 44, 212, 233, 236
attitudes towards 15
decentred 306–8, 311
and defiance 1, 7, 249, 290, 293, 304–8, 309
and game playing 96–7
ideal of 64
and integrity 210
networked 35
nodal 212, 217, 228, 293, 307, 308, 309

openness of 65
and politics of consent 37
principles for 129
sites of 217
social control model 50
government 44, 185
dissatisfaction with the performance of 287
expectations of 277, 280
relationship with citizens 269, 289
responsibilities of 310
responsibilities to 277, 280
values and beliefs about 129
government, small 97, 128, 259–60, 261, 269
governments, legitimacy of 185
Grabosky, Peter 39, 52, 135
Gramsci, Antonio 33
Grbich, Yuri 93–5, 96
Greenwald, A.G. 71
grievance pathway 261–2, 275, 312
and deterrence 265–6
and resistance 264, 289, 298
group identity theory 206
group-value model 83, 209, 211
Grumpy Old Men and *Grumpy Old Women* 21
guilt 154–7, 158, 171, 172, 174
Gunningham, Neil 30

Habermas, Jürgen 48
Hagan, J. 28, 218–19, 228, 237
Halfon, Mark S. 181
Hamilton, Clive 251–2
Hamilton, V. Lee 233, 234
Harris, Nathan 154, 154–5, 173, 256
Hawkins, Keith 37, 42, 186
Heimer, Carol A. 186, 189
Hood, C. 39
'How Fair? How Effective? Collection and Use of Taxation in Australia' survey 105–6, 195, 234, 276
human rights 56
human security 63

identity 5, 72–4, 85, 221, 224, 258, 313
and authority 153
collective identity 252
ethical identity 82, 154, 157–8, 209, 211, 256, 265
group identity 206
honest taxpaying identity 22, 148, 150
and integrity 180
multiple identities 50, 70, 151–2
national identity 300
shared 209, 300
social identities 19, 152, 255
ideology 95, 259–60, 269
inclusiveness 48, 88, 92, 253–4
individualism 253–4
and defiance 272–6, 292
development of 273–5
influence 19, 72, 212, 214, 268
nodes of 10–12
social influence 85
webs of 35
information asymmetry 184, 215
infrastructure
physical 33
psychological 15, 17, 33
social 61, 151–3, 191, 193, 273, 290, 300
and coping styles 160, 163–6
Inglehart, Ronald 216–17, 234
innovation 219
instability 33
institution building 248
institutional constraint, defiance and 1–25
institutions 33, 63
authority of 9–10
credibility of 173
and defiance 246
design of 109, 216
difficulty in changing 9, 12
ethical decision making in 181
integrity of 55–7, 179, 180, 186, 191, 207, 261, 262
legitimacy of 2, 21, 49, 54, 233
performance of 297
power of 13
psychological 60
public confidence in 97
regulatory 35–6, 48, 49, 254
regulatory culture 6
integrity 17, 19, 67, 179–91, 262, 309
and authenticity 23
and consistency 190
and defiance 175–213, 209, 247, 289

definition of 179–80
and dismissiveness 206, 210, 212
external face of 179
and governance 210
hypotheses about 194–5
and identity 180
and interactional justice 210–12
internal face of 179
limits of 212
measurement of 191–205
organizational 181–5
perceptions of lack of 58
personal integrity 180–81
philosophical views on 180–81
and resistance 209, 212
social face of 181
and trust 202, 209

James, S. 71
judgement 81
just-world theory 39–40
justice 39–40, 44, 191
distributive 80, 144, 211
interactional 210, 211
procedural 82–4, 90, 206, 209, 210, 211
and cooperation 19, 51, 80, 88
tax authorities and 176, 196, 197
and resistance 4
restorative 82–4, 172
social 252, 261
and taxation 67, 199–200, 204
in taxation 208
and the Taxpayer's charter 192–5

Kagan, Robert A. 30, 45, 49, 75, 77, 81, 186
Karstedt, S. 233, 234
Kelman, H.C. 64, 66–7, 78, 84–5, 89, 90, 120
Kettl, D.F. 54–55
knowledge 63, 95, 180, 184, 215

LaFree, G. 233, 234
law 12, 14, 39, 221
rule of law 139, 170, 218–19, 234, 241
tax law 179, 223, 269
Law, H.G. 121
lawyers, tax 93–5
learning theory 220
Lewin, Kurt 7
life space 7, 8, 32–3
Lind, E. Allan 83
listening 43, 45, 48
Lowndes, V. 303
Lubell, M. 210
Luhrmann, Baz 10

Maguire, Peter 269
Makkai, Toni 82
marketing 225, 226, 228, 246, 300
markets free 128, 261, 269
markets in vice and markets in virtue 173, 222
mass-marketed tax avoidance schemes 116, 191, 193, 194, 207, 215, 222, 305
Mathiesen, Thomas 21
Matza, D. 5
McAdams, R.H. 221
McBarnet, D. 92
McDougall, William 74
media 226, 307
Meidinger, E. 36
Merton, Robert K. 78, 84
Milgram, Stanley 28, 275
Mills, C. Wright 20, 134, 296
modelling, and rule following 221–2
Modigliani, A. 28
moral agency 5, 19
moral commonwealth 188–91
moral pathway 139–41, 257, 264, 265, 267, 298, 312
moral self 249, 256–8, 262, 272, 288, 300–301
Morales, Alfonso 11
Moscovici, Serge 46
motivational postures 19, 20, 25, 60–100, 101–36, 312, 313
authority and 62–74
capitulation 20, 38, 78
commitment 20, 38, 78
and compliance outcomes 79–80
concept of 129–30
consistency in 119, 129
Cooperation–Resistance factor 114–15, 134
and defiance 32–42, 295–6
and democracy 126–9

disengagement 20, 21, 39, 78
and disillusionment with the democracy 128
Dismissiveness factor 114–15, 134
dynamic nature of 79, 115, 118
empirical testing of the concept 20
expression of 60–100
game playing 20, 21, 39
hypotheses about 109–10, 111–13
measurement of 36, 101–36
reliability of the scales 115–18
surveys 104–6, 106–7
validity of the scales 107–9, 113–15
overlap among 107
preference for tax advisers and 111–13
psychological function of 60
qualities of 296
recognizing 106–7
in regulatory theory 81–2, 89–90
resistance 20, 21, 38, 78
and responsive regulation 44–5
role of 74–7
and social demographic groups 119–20, 130, 135
and social distance 39–42, 78, 109, 110, 111, 113–15, 120, 137
stability of 67–9, 116, 118, 129, 135
supra-postures 115, 134, 135
dismissiveness 132–4
resistance 130–32
and taxation 20–21, 22, 38, 57–9, 91–7, 126
theoretical framework for 74–91, 295–6
types of 77–9
used to reduce threat 98
and values 20, 121–6, 128–9
multinational corporations 54; *see also* corporations
Murphy, K. 193

Nadler, J. 12, 221
narratives 47–8, 61
and cognitive reframing 142
of defiance 4, 276–87
newspapers 226, 228
reporting of the ATO 227–8, 230–31
support for tax minimization 229

Nicholson, Peter 116–17
Nielsen, Vibeke L. 52
nodes of influence 10–12, 35, 56
non-compliance 24, 91, 293, 303–4
measurement of 271
motivation for 75
responses to 87
nursing home regulation 8, 19, 293
Nursing Home Regulation in Action Project 74–5, 76, 82

Oliver, C. 60–61, 68
Omran, Sheikh Mohammed 3–4, 295
openness to knowledge 180
oppression 9–10, 143; *see also* feeling oppressed coping style
Organisation for Economic Co-operation and Development (OECD) 56, 197
Centre for Tax Policy and Administration 55
organizational integrity 181–5

Packer, Kerry 143
Parker, Christine 52
Parker Follett, Mary 253–4, 272
participation 303
partnerships 45, 177–8, 310
Pascal, Ana 187, 205
pathways to defiance 288–9
competitive pathway 24, 243, 246, 258–9, 267, 269, 299, 301–2
grievance pathway 24, 261–2, 289, 298, 302
moral pathway 24, 243, 245, 256, 267, 298, 300–301
and resistance 288–9
Pearlin, L.I. 296
performance outcomes, and defiance 31
Perrow, C. 48–9
personal growth and inner harmony 24, 234–9
persuasion 87, 90, 99
Picciotto, Sol 269
Piller, Charles 27
Piquero, N.L. 219
politics of consent 37
politics of envy 292
postmaterialism 216–19, 234, 295
postmaterialist values 224, 234–9

power 52–3
culture and 33
differentials of 8
dispersion of 64
and hegemony 33
imbalance of 47
of institutions 13, 20, 21
legitimacy of 185
loss of 46
of regulators 48, 50
sharing of 293, 310
preferences, consistency in 73
problem-focused coping style 141, 145–7
procedural justice 82–4, 176, 209, 210, 211
and the ATO 196
and cooperation 19, 51, 88, 90
and integrity 206
and the Taxpayer's charter 197
professional groups 14, 62, 92
Pruitt, Dean J. 67
Punch, Maurice 218
Putnam, Robert D. 273

Ramsay, Heyden 180, 181, 188
rationality 49, 81, 99
reasonableness 52, 57, 91, 173, 186
Rees, Joseph V. 186
regulation 312
attitudes and perceptions of the regulatee 18, 37, 77
'by the book' 75–6
coercive strategies 87, 185
command-and-control regulation 44–5, 51–5, 184
communitarian 186
effectiveness of 172
fairness of 284
inclusive relationships 45
internal 154, 156, 157, 160, 163, 165, 166
and the media 43
outcomes of 84, 158
politics of 187
and procedures 47, 48
and reasonableness 45
regulatory relationships 26
republican 186
responsive 26–59, 42, 172, 186
self-regulation 5, 19, 159, 166, 171, 174, 301
social dimension of 52
strategies for 79
sustainability of 44, 91
regulators 15, 31, 37
bounded rationality of 49
capture of 45
and defiance 290
education and persuasion campaigns 99
integrity of 185–6
and motivational postures 82
power of 48, 50
public confidence in 43
relationships with the regulated 40, 41, 46, 90
resources of 99, 191, 200, 223
rewards and punishments 85
regulatory capitalism 216–19, 309
regulatory commissions 186–8
regulatory community 26, 46
regulatory conversations 186, 190
regulatory culture 6, 36
contestation in 41
defiance within 34–6
regulatory pyramids 51–2, 91, 186
and compliance 87–9
and defiance 87–9
and motivational postures 89–90, 99
shared understanding at the bottom of 92
regulatory theory, motivational postures in 81–2
renewable energy 251–2
resistance 1, 20, 21, 38, 78, 99, 135, 254–5, 299–304
and coping styles 170
cultural factors in 130–31, 132
definition of 254
deliberation and 309
and dismissiveness 3–4, 22
and expectations of government 277, 278–9
as feedback 108
and the grievance pathway 298
high versus low 277–80
hypotheses about 242–3
and integrity 209, 212
management of 80

models of 168–9, 241–3, 262–9, 298
pathways to 296, 288–9
prediction of 130–32, 314–17
psychological drivers of 137
and relational stress 81
and respect 275–6
and responsibility to fellow citizens 280, 281–2
and responsibility to government 277, 279–80
and security values 124
as social distance from authority 131–2
and taxation 90
and values 241
see also under defiance
respect 178, 191–2, 306, 307, 309
for authorities 49, 70, 289
communication of 274
culture of 18, 274
and dismissiveness 275–6
for individuals 61, 88, 194, 209
justice of 211
passive 196–7
and resistance 275–6
responsibility 5, 188
of citizenship 63
and defiance 287–8
to fellow citizens 281, 284, 286–7
to government 279–80, 284
and taxation 22
responsive regulation 26–59, 60, 67, 172, 186, 189, 207
and motivational postures 44–5
objective of 42
and relationship building 57
responsive relationships 45–6, 88, 92, 184, 207, 210, 295, 309
and compliance 50–51
and defiance 42–51
Reus-Smit, C. 188
rhetoric 47–8, 185
rights 56, 97, 176–7, 177–8, 260
risk assessment 49, 292
ritualism 78, 186, 212
Rochat, F. 28
Rokeach, Milton 73–4, 121, 139–40, 296
role models 215, 219, 224, 236, 256
and defiance 239–44
tax advisers as 223–4, 238–9
and values 224, 239–244
rule following, and modelling 221–2
rule of law 139, 170, 218–19, 234, 241
Rwanda 183

Sampson, R.J. 237
sanctions 52
effects of 151, 153, 158, 159, 171, 299
regulatory pyramids and 88, 90, 99
Schmölders, G. 176
Scholz, J.T. 210
Schön, D.A. 180, 182
Schooler, C. 296
Scott, William A. 74
security 222, 311
self 32–3, 71, 121, 180
self-interest 69, 71, 216–19, 228
self-legitimation 5
self-regulation 5, 19, 32–3, 159, 166, 174, 171, 301
shame–guilt and 154–7
self-worth 255, 256, 274
selves
actual 152
and defiance 300, 304
democratic collective self 249, 260–62, 273
and defiance 252, 255–6, 275–6, 288–9, 300, 302–3
ethical self 255
good self 159
moral self 249, 256–8, 262, 272, 288, 300, 300–301
multiple 151–2
possible 152–3
status-seeking self 249, 255, 258–60
and defiance 262, 273, 275, 288, 300, 301–2, 312
Selznick, Philip 188–91, 191, 210
shame 82, 154–7, 158, 171, 172, 174, 211
acknowledgement of 155–7, 163–6, 173
and deterrence 166–8
displacement of 155–7, 163–6, 167
management of 163–6
and self-regulation 166
shame management, and deterrence 163–6

Sharma, S. 222
Shearing, Clifford 8
Sherman, L.W. 294
Shover, Neal 218
Simpson, S.S. 219
Smith, Adam 179
Smith, K.W. 209
social and political protest 2, 13, 40
social capital 233, 273, 290
social change 44, 51, 57, 64, 221, 269
social distance 21, 58, 255, 296
  between authorities and citizens 61, 62–7, 158
  control of 69–70
  and coping styles 171
  and defiance 151, 303–4
  dynamic nature of 67–9
  management of 99
  and motivational postures 39–42, 78, 98, 110, 111, 113–15, 120, 137
  optimal amount of 66–7, 85, 90–91
  psychological drivers of 71–2
  and regulatory pyramids 88
  signals of 41, 134
  and tax authorities 129, 133
social engagement 9
social exchange model 209
social identity theory 152
social infrastructure 61, 151–3, 191, 193, 273, 290, 300
  and coping styles 160, 163–6
social interdependence 273
social learning 220
social modelling 214–47, 264, 296, 297, 298, 299, 301–2
  and defiance 219–20, 251–2
  paradigm of 220–21
  and rule following 221–2
social networking 99
social order 84, 311
social rationality 49
social responsibility 184, 308
social space 64, 70, 95
socialization 154, 173
spin 18, 64, 185, 266, 303
Srivastva, Suresh 184
Stalans, L.J. 209
states, sovereign 41, 52, 54–5
status, economic 98, 233, 234, 236, 241
  and defiance 262
  measurement of 234–9
  and social distance 125
  status-seeking self 249, 255, 258–60
    and defiance 262, 273, 275, 288, 300, 301–2, 312
Steele, Claude M. 71
Stenning, Phillip C., 8
Stranger than Fiction 187, 205
Strazdins, Lyndall 274
Strictly Ballroom 10
structural equation modelling 167–8, 203, 314–17
supra-postures 115, 134, 135, 137, 295
  dismissiveness 132–4, 295
  resistance 130–32
surveys 7, 102
  coping styles 142–51
  motivational postures 104–7
  national random surveys 104–6
  samples for 105
  statistical procedures 107
Sutherland, Edwin H. 70
Swaziland 11
Sykes, G.M. 5

Tajfel, Henri 154
taking control coping style 145–7, 172, 258
tax administration, domination, defiance and competition 51–9
tax advisers 23, 70, 146
  aggressive 229, 233, 235, 236, 238–9, 243, 245, 258
    demand for 222, 225
  as alternative authorities 223–4, 245, 298
  credibility of 228
  honest no-risk advisers 23, 95, 235, 238–9, 243–4, 245
  and motivational postures 111–13
  preferences for 23, 224, 242, 243, 245–7, 263, 267, 298
  as role models 223–4, 238–9
tax authorities
  and alternative authorities 59, 173
  attitudes towards 138, 188
  codes of practice 176
  command-and-control regulation 52
  communication 55, 177
  competitiveness 253–4

complaints mechanisms 176
consultation 196–7
control 253–4
deference to 111–13, 134
deterrence 269
effectiveness of 266
enforcement strategies 200
engagement with 118–19
evaluation of by survey respondents 109–10
integrity of 17, 67, 214
management of 176–8, 185–6
perception of 27, 58, 175, 194, 261, 263, 264
legitimacy of 53, 97, 188
nodes of influence for 56
opposition to 125
outreach methods 177–8
posturing with 91–2
relationships with the regulated 157, 216, 244, 298
resources of 99, 191, 200, 223
responses to defiance 252
service model 177
showing respect for the community 196–7
and social distance 62–72, 129, 130, 133
taxpayer charters 178
threat posed by 58
trust in 200–201, 208, 261
tax avoidance 7, 13, 92, 93, 96, 109, 173, 192, 199, 302
cyclical theory of contagion of 222–3
industry of 71, 94
mass-marketed schemes 116, 191, 193, 194, 207, 215, 222, 305
newspaper reporting of ATO efforts to contain 227–8
tax defiance, culture of 225–3
tax evasion 153, 192
and defiance 270–72
and dismissiveness 271–2, 305
measurement of 270–71
self-reported 270–71
tax laws 179, 223, 269
tax minimization 111, 143, 145, 220
media support for 229
newspaper reports of celebrities and high-profile citizens and 231–3
promotion of 225–6
tax ombudsmen 56, 176
tax planning culture 215, 217, 221, 225, 245, 298
tax professionals 14, 62, 92, 193
tax systems
attitudes towards 11, 110
command-and-control regulation 51–5, 57
complexity of 91
constraint versus defiance in 12–15
and defiance 51–9, 144
domination and 51–9
honest no-risk advisers 111
and institutional integrity 55–7
manipulation of 54
and motivational postures 20–21
opposition to 125
progressive 98
self-assessment 53, 93, 118, 148
sustainable 14
in Swaziland 11
taxpayer responsiveness to 56
taxation 179
alternative authorities 93
attitudes towards 69, 98, 199–200
as a benefit to the community 178, 191–2, 194, 195–6
complexity of 215
and coping styles 150–51, 161–3
emotion-focused coping style 143–5
feeling oppressed coping style 143–5
problem-focused coping style 145–7
credibility of 290
cultural dimension of 101
and defiance 6, 14, 297
and emotions 68
equity of 199–200
game playing and 91–7
and governance 16
and justice 143, 199–200, 208
and motivational postures 22
opportunity costs of 143
perceptions of 53
public interest 52

regulation of 57–9
relevance of 210
and respect 191–2
and responsibility 22
social dimension of 51, 122
taking control coping style 145–7
thinking morally coping style 147–50
threat of 15, 66, 140, 150, 158, 159–71
working the system 146
taxpayer responsiveness to the tax system 56
Taxpayers' Charter 88, 178, 179, 185, 187–9, 211
commitment to 191, 194, 197–9
and justice 192–5, 197
taxpayers' rights 176–7, 177–8
taxpaying, culture of 66, 70, 178, 209, 226
Taylor, N. 300
thinking morally coping style 147–50, 153–4, 156, 157, 160, 263, 264, 268
and defiance 169
and dismissiveness 169–70
failure of 157–159
social infrastructure for 151–3
threat and coping model 137–94, 249, 296
threats 137–94
and coping styles 141–51, 161–3
definition of 139
model of 159–71
responses to 139–41
transparency 64, 65, 191
trust 49, 87, 297
and cooperation 178, 186
and defiance 175–213, 208, 247
and disengagement 81
and integrity 202, 203–4, 209
loss of 233
measurement of 191–205, 202
in tax authorities 65, 189, 200–201, 208, 216, 261
'trust heuristic' 210
trust norms 177
Tyler, Tom 51, 61, 83–4, 88, 209

uncertainty 33, 46, 68, 73, 222–3, 223–4
United Kingdom 177
United Nations 183
Upfold, Robert 94
United States, regulatory commissions 186–8
US Internal Revenue Service 43, 176

value–attitude–belief systems 5, 15, 17, 121, 221, 255
consistency in 19, 73–4
and motivational postures 20, 67, 296
values 74, 181, 221
and defiance 239–44, 243, 248
and democracy 130
and dismissiveness 133, 241
harmony values 122, 123–4
individual 235–6
individualistic 138
instrumental 121
and motivational postures 121–6
personal growth and inner harmony 24, 234–9
postmaterialist 224, 234–9, 245
and resistance 241
and role models 239–44
security values 122, 123–4
social values 137, 155
status values 225–33, 241, 258, 263
success values 246
terminal 121
Vaughan, Dianne 219

Waller, V. 189–90
Walzer, Michael 41
Warren G 63
webs of influence 12, 13, 35, 56, 308
Wenzel, M. 158, 224, 300
white-collar criminality 218
Williams, Bernard 154, 173
winning 235, 237–8, 260
Wolfe, Donald M. 182, 183, 184

Young, Iris Marion 47, 91